THE ST. MARTIN'S SOURCEBOOK FOR WRITING TUTORS

THIRD EDITION

Christina Murphy
MARSHALL UNIVERSITY

Steve Sherwood
TEXAS CHRISTIAN UNIVERSITY

BEDFORD / ST. MARTIN'S

BOSTON ♦ NEW YORK

For Bedford/St. Martin's

Developmental Editor: Nathan Odell
Production Editor: Blake Royer
Production Supervisor: Andrew Ensor
Marketing Manager: John Swanson
Art Director: Lucy Krikorian
Composition: Stratford/TexTech
Printing and Binding: Haddon Craftsmen, Inc., an R.R. Donnelley & Sons Company

President: Joan E. Feinberg
Editorial Director: Denise B. Wydra
Editor in Chief: Karen B. Henry
Director of Development: Erica T. Appel
Director of Marketing: Karen Melton Soeltz
Director of Editing, Design, and Production: Marcia Cohen
Managing Editor: Shuli Traub

Library of Congress Control Number: 2007922533

For information, write: Bedford/St. Martin's, 75 Arlington Street, Boston, MA 02116   (617-399-4000)

ISBN-10: 0-312-44226-2
ISBN-13: 978-0-312-44226-2

Acknowledgments

Anis Bawarshi and Stephanie Pelkowski. "Postcolonialism and the Idea of a Writing Center." *Writing Center Journal*, Volume 19, Number 2, Spring/Summer 1999. Copyright © 1999. Reprinted with permission.

Elizabeth H. Boquet. "Intellectual Tug-of-War: Snapshots of Life in the Center." From *Stories from the Center: Connecting Narrative and Theory in the Writing Center*, edited by Lynn Craigue Briggs and Meg Wollbright. Copyright © 2000 by the National Council of Teachers of English. Reprinted with permission.

Jeff Brooks. "Minimalist Tutoring: Making the Student Do All the Work." *Writing Lab Newsletter*, Volume 15, Number 6 1991. Copyright © 2003 Purdue University. All Rights and Title reserved unless permission is granted by Purdue University. Material will not be reproduced in any form without written express permission.

David A. Carlson and Eileen Apperson-Williams. "The Anxieties of Distance: Online Tutors Reflect." *Taking Flight with OWLs: Examining Electronic Writing Center Work* by James A. Inman and Donna N. Sewell. Copyright © 2000. Reprinted by permission of Lawrence Erlbaum Associates, Inc.

Acknowledgments and copyrights are continued at the back of the book on page 326, which constitutes an extension of the copyright page.

PREFACE

The third edition of *The St. Martin's Sourcebook for Writing Tutors*, like its predecessors, considers what knowledge would be most valuable to writing tutors in assisting the learning processes of others. Many concepts have remained as constants in the three years since the publication of the second edition — chief among them our belief that an understanding of theory enriches practice. For this reason, we retained in this edition essays that we consider key to comprehending the relationship of major theories to the daily practice of tutoring. We have also added new essays to reflect key changes occurring in tutoring: (1) ever more sophisticated approaches to tutoring students whose cultural backgrounds affect their understanding of college life, course demands, and approaches to writing; (2) significant increases in the variety of work tutors do in high-technology environments; and (3) the continued growth of writing associates and writing fellows programs in which peer tutors work with professors and students in the writing-intensive classroom.

Increasingly, the writing center is becoming the multiliteracy center. Tutors must know how to approach tutoring in an environment reliant on communication technologies. In this edition of *The St. Martin's Sourcebook for Writing Tutors,* we focus on new theories that highlight how technology has altered the way tutors help students obtain information, advance their knowledge, and hone their skills. Similarly, we focus on concepts of tutoring drawn from activity theory, in which language, literacy, and learning are defined by social practices and social communities as much as by the talent of individual minds. Since the construction of texts occurs within intellectual contexts largely defined by cultures and cultural knowledge, we also augment our section on "Affirming Diversity" to take into account the broad range of participants involved. "Diversity" has taken on many meanings over the last two decades; for us as writing tutors, "diversity" recognizes and honors the multiple backgrounds, personal experiences, interpretive frames, and values that individual writers and tutors share in the course of learning to write.

We believe the changes to the third edition of *The St. Martin's Sourcebook for Writing Tutors* enrich its usefulness for beginning and experienced tutors alike. We invite each tutor to see tutoring as an individualized practice informed by experience, conceptual understanding, and interpersonal skills. Toward that end, we envision *The St. Martin's Sourcebook for Writing Tutors* as both a source of insight and a guide, and we are proud that the third edition of the *Sourcebook*, like its predecessors, continues to complement the work of tutors within the community of practice.

We have come to this third edition with the help of many people. We thank our editors at Bedford/St. Martin's, Nathan Odell, Ester Bloom, and Katherine Paarlberg, for their guidance and insight as we developed this manuscript and, most especially, for the personal investment in our work that they continually showed. Special thanks go to the reviewers for this edition: Scott Berg from George Mason University; Valerie Balester from Texas A&M University; Caroline L. Eisner from the University of Michigan; Michele Eodice from the University of Kansas; Greg Wahl from Montgomery College, Takoma Park–Silver Spring Campus. Steve Sherwood dedicates this book to Jill, Evan, Scott, Jordan, and Kasey. Christina Murphy thanks Marshall University for the pleasure of working in an exceptionally supportive and empathetic academic environment that values the best in the human spirit.

Christina Murphy
Steve Sherwood

CONTENTS

I

The Tutoring Process:
Exploring Paradigms and Practices

We begin *The St. Martin's Sourcebook for Writing Tutors* with the principal ideas that will guide our discussion of the tutoring process and the tutor's role in writing instruction:

- *Tutoring is contextual.* Tutoring takes place within a number of sociocultural and interpersonal contexts that lend richness and complexity to the tutor's role. An understanding of these contexts extends the tutor's technical skill.
- *Tutoring is collaborative.* Tutoring is grounded in interpersonal transactions; it is, fundamentally, a *relationship* more than a body of techniques or even a body of knowledge. In the tutoring session, two people work together toward a common goal; they collaborate. The purpose of the collaboration is to assist writers in their own development. The dialogue between tutor and student — a conversation with a definite purpose — is the basis upon which tutors and students build a supportive working relationship. Thus, tutoring offers a conceptual and interpersonal framework for the sharing of ideas.
- *Tutoring is interpersonal.* Tutors must draw upon extensive interpersonal skills to work effectively with students who bring a range of educational and cultural backgrounds and a variety of learning styles to their tutoring sessions. Tutors need effective interpersonal skills because the purpose of tutoring is to meet the needs of individual writers.
- *Tutoring is individualized.* If there is any one truth about tutoring, it is that no single method of tutoring, no one approach, will work effectively with every student in every situation. Each tutor develops a style of tutoring primarily from experience, and experience is always a dynamic process of change. Tutoring sessions are as unique and individual as the students who come to be tutored.

With tutoring's complex philosophical background and its rich interpersonal dynamic, you might wonder, "Can I be an effective tutor?" The answer is "yes" — because you are already engaged in the essence of tutoring, which is conversation. With your teachers and fellow students, you have had numerous discussions of the writing process and of how writers learn to improve their work. Now, as a writing center tutor, you will build on these discussions with new thoughts and ideas from conversations with your fellow peer tutors and your writing center mentors. You will also have this sourcebook to enhance your understanding of the tutoring process.

The St. Martin's Sourcebook for Writing Tutors is not a philosophical treatise that separates theory from practice. Nor is it a how-to book of procedures and tactics. Such a simple technique-driven approach would be inadequate for operating in the fluid, unpredictable, give-and-take atmosphere of the tutorial. While tutoring is generally logical, it is seldom tactical; that is, it is not possible to learn a single method and apply it in all instances. Such a scenario fails to describe the complexity and richness of the encounters between tutor and writer.

Rather than a single scenario, then, we have chosen to present multiple views of tutorials and multiple commentaries on the learning experiences those tutorials embody. The essays here represent a valuable body of knowledge for both the novice and the experienced tutor. In them, we hear many voices commenting on the practice of tutoring — the hows, whys, why nots, shoulds, and should nots — together with the lines of reasoning and the personal experiences that support these viewpoints. We hear of success and failure and starting over again — of the continual rediscovery that tutoring represents as both a learning and a teaching experience. We hear the voices of theorists who are accomplished professionals in the field, as well as those of beginning tutors who are new to the field. We hear the voices of students who have come to tutors seeking knowledge, assistance, and reassurance. Above all, we hear the essence of tutoring: conversation. And we begin to realize that there is a broad, interdisciplinary, and theoretical conversation surrounding the practice of tutoring — a conversation this sourcebook invites you to join.

TUTORING AND THE PARADIGMS OF WRITING INSTRUCTION

As a method for teaching writing, tutoring has been influenced by the paradigms that have shaped writing instruction during the past several decades. Tutoring has also been instrumental in shaping those paradigms, largely because writing center tutorials provide practical opportunities to test theoretical assumptions about how students develop as writers.

Basic Theories in Writing Instruction

Since writing centers first appeared on the U.S. educational scene in the 1930s, three paradigms have predominated as models of how writing should be taught: current traditional rhetoric, expressivism (also sometimes called expressionism), and social constructionism. During the past decade, cultural studies, postcolonial, postmodern, and post-process theories of composition have also had an increasing influence on writing center tutorials.

Current traditional rhetoric focuses almost exclusively on the writer's text and its formal dimensions of grammatical correctness. Writing center tutors who adopt this approach would concern themselves with isolating errors and formal weaknesses in a student's text and providing information on how to correct those problems.

Because writing centers emerged at a time when current traditional rhetoric was the dominant paradigm, they often tended to take on the role of providing this kind of remedial help to students. As a consequence, writing centers became known, early on, as grammar "fix-it shops," as Stephen M. North puts it in "The Idea of a Writing Center" (on p. 32). In his essay, North opposes limiting writing center instruction to issues of grammatical correctness. Instead, he favors giving more attention to the writer than to the text — especially to how the writer can learn to become more fluent in expressing ideas. In his essay, he describes a model for such a perspective, one based on the philosophy of expressivism.

Expressivism, represented by the works of Peter Elbow, Donald Murray, and Ken Macrorie, dominated writing instruction from the 1970s to the mid-1980s. In this paradigm, writing is viewed as a means of self-discovery. By exploring language as a mode of self-expression, students come to know themselves and to develop an "authentic voice" in their writing. Expressivists tend to value the individual writer as a solitary creator who communicates ideas through personal explorations of language, experience, and individual identity.

An expressivist tutor explores the student's understanding of the writing process, particularly the stages of invention and drafting, in which the writer generates ideas and seeks an authentic voice. Expressivist tutors often employ "the Socratic dialogue," asking *heuristic,* or exploratory, questions as a way of getting the student to discover and think about ideas and how they can best be communicated.

North's essay and Jeff Brooks's "Minimalist Tutoring: Making the Student Do All the Work" (on p. 168) discuss in detail the philosophy of expressivist tutoring and the tutor's role within a Socratic dialogue. However, as you will discover in Andrea Lunsford's "Collaboration, Control, and the Idea of a Writing Center" (on p. 47), not all theorists view expressivism as a genuinely liberating form of writing instruction. Lunsford, for example, argues that the Socratic dialogue of the expressivist tutor can *seem* to be a freely structured exploration of ideas when, in fact, the tutor's so-called heuristic questions are actually leading questions — ones that lead the student toward conclusions already known and valued by the tutor. Lunsford also contends that expressivism places too much emphasis on the individual writer while minimizing or ignoring the social dimensions of language, knowledge, and writing. As a consequence, she argues against the limited scope of expressivism in favor of the philosophy of social constructionism.

While current traditional rhetoric emphasizes the writer's text and expressivism emphasizes the writer's creative processes, *social constructionism* focuses on the sociocultural and historical settings in which writers develop their understanding of language and knowledge. Social constructionism began to affect writing instruction in the mid-1980s and has since become one of the dominant paradigms. The most noted advocates of social constructionism are Kenneth A. Bruffee, Marilyn M. Cooper, James Berlin, and Patricia Bizzell.

As Lunsford's essay indicates, social constructionists do not believe in the romantic image of the writer as a solitary genius who only has to look inward to find the truth of self-expression. They maintain that knowledge, rather than being "found" uniquely through self-discovery, is "made" by agreement, or consensus, within discourse communities. For example, we as tutors come to have similar ways of talking (and thinking) about our work; other groups form other discourse communities.

The writing center practice advocated by social constructionists involves extensive use of peer group critiquing to reflect the workings of discourse communities and to downplay the role of the tutor as an authority figure or the single source of knowledge. Thus, collaboration and collaborative learning play an important role in social constructionist writing instruction. The tutor's voice is only one of many the writer will hear, and the tutor and writer are colearners who collaborate to negotiate meanings and construct knowledge.

Recent Innovations in Composition Theory

Cultural studies pedagogies, influenced by the ideas of Paulo Freire, Ira Shor, and Mikhail Bakhtin, take social constructionism a step further, asking writers and writing tutors to acknowledge the public and political nature of their work. Cultural studies proponents argue that writing center tutors often act as unthinking agents of acculturation for the dominant culture, as represented in the discursive practices of the academy. As Nancy Grimm argues in "The Regulatory Role of the Writing Center: Coming to Terms with a Loss of Innocence," tutors who see themselves as neutral helpers in reality "reinforce the status quo, to support the teacher and the institution" (11) and promote a "fixed notion of literacy, a singular standard," which not only "closes down meaning" (22) but supports a disguised "racist and classist agenda" (19). Marilyn M. Cooper makes a similar argument in "Really Useful Knowledge: A Cultural Studies Agenda for Writing Centers" (on p. 53). Cooper calls on tutors to adopt a subject position from which they can critique (and seek to reform) not only the dominant social order but also their own practices. In this view, the goal of writing tutorials should not be the simple improvement of student writing. Instead, the goal is to give student writers a heightened awareness of the social injustice perpetrated by the dominant culture's racist and classist agenda and to empower these writers to resist this agenda. In short, the goal of such tutoring is to make better citizens of both tutors and student writers.

In a similar vein, proponents of *postmodern, postcolonial,* and *post-process* theories of composition call for approaches to tutoring that emphasize plural perspectives, identities, and processes. In *Good Intentions: Writing Center Work for Postmodern Times,* Nancy Grimm argues that contemporary universities operate within a modernist framework that privileges essential truths and a stable notion of reality. Writing center tutors are positioned to challenge modernist notions, Grimm says, because "in the postmodern encounters of a writing center, essential truths come under questioning, 'reality' changes with a shift in perspective, one's identity shifts in response to different situations, and the coherence of an essay comes at the expense of complexity" (2). In *Noise from the Writing Center,* Elizabeth H. Boquet discusses the potential of noise (or feedback distortion) and chaos for generating ideas and more closely reflecting the complex composing processes of writers in the midst of their work. Rather than embracing a model of writing center practice rooted in the relative neatness of process theory, Boquet says, "I much prefer thinking of the work of the writing center as random chaos, or maybe controlled chaos, instead" (83). She invokes comparisons between musical improvisation, or jazz, and the work tutors do. In general, postmodern approaches, such as those of Grimm and Boquet, tend to value and support writers' plural identities and processes.

Postcolonial views of the writing center derive from both the cultural studies and postmodern movements. As Anis Bawarshi and Stephanie Pelkowski explain in "Postcolonialism and the Idea of a Writing Center" (on p. 79), most writing centers — especially those with a current traditional or expressivist orientation — are in the business of acculturating students, not fostering multiple perspectives on writing. Bawarshi and Pelkowski argue that whether such centers

> are involved in changing textual features ("old" writing centers) or changing writers ("new" writing centers), the idea is the same: the change is meant to transform the student and his or her texts into the acceptable standard of the university. The writing center has traditionally been and continues to be generally unconcerned with critiquing academic standards, only with facilitating students' participation within them.

Bawarshi and Pelkowski contend that nontraditional students, upon receiving their first exposure to academic writing, often feel as if they are losing something in the transformation — giving up a level of complexity and an awareness of alternative perspectives in order to fit their ideas into frameworks acceptable to the university. "Thus, academic discourses appear as stagnant, artificial, and arbitrary formulas to student writers, especially those for whom such discourses are not very accessible. . . ." To avoid this situation, and help students resist acculturation, Bawarshi and Pelkowski propose "a writing center strategy in which under-prepared students, especially those marginalized by race, class, and ethnicity, are encouraged to adopt critical consciousness as a means of functioning within the university and its discourses." The aim of this critical consciousness is to help students succeed in the university without surrendering their sense of who they are. This important aim is also endorsed by Meg Woolbright in "The Politics of Tutoring: Feminism within the Patriarchy" (on p. 67). Woolbright contends that tutorials often reflect hidden or overt agendas of political and social power that favor patriarchal values. This focus on imposing one set of values upon the tutoring session and its outcomes can undermine a student's sense of self. To avoid this destructive consequence, Woolbright urges a self-reflective practice for tutors that engages them in examining the power dynamics involved in their tutorials so that their practice can become more egalitarian.

A number of theorists, clustered under the heading of the *post-process* school, share with the postmodernists similar assumptions about the fragmented, highly contextual, and contingent nature of human perspectives on reality and therefore on writing. Because each piece of writing is situated in a specific rhetorical context, these theorists claim, the composition processes a writer uses will vary widely from one act of writing to the next. After the fact, a writer may be able to trace a series of steps he or she took in arriving at the finished piece, but this process may have no application to the writing of another piece. Therefore, post-process theorists object to the "one size fits all" approach they claim is at the heart of process theory. As Thomas Kent says, "Post-process theorists hold — for all sorts of different reasons — that writing is a practice that cannot be captured by a generalized process or Big Theory" (1). Gary A. Olson agrees with Kent in saying that "writing — indeed all communication — is radically contingent, radically situational. Consequently, efforts to pin down some version of 'the writing process' are misguided, unproductive, and misleading" (8–9). In view of these insights, post-process theorists are, David Foster says, "deeply skeptical of a writing pedagogy that assumes regularity and transferability in writing behavior. . . ." (152). Post-process theorists agree that the composition classroom is not an effective or appropriate site for learning how to write. Instead, what universities need are approaches to writing instruction that make allowances for changing circumstances, purposes, and needs. While post-process theorists make no specific recommendations for reforming composition programs, most prefer an approach based on experiential learning in highly specific settings — such as writing in the disciplines or apprenticeship on the job.

Writing center practices, as they have evolved during the past decade, match up well with postmodern, postcolonial, and post-process theories. By working with student writers from multiple disciplines and cultures, tutors generally develop a sensitivity to the contingent, contextual nature of writing, which requires them to respond to each writer's needs and sensibilities. Tutors realize that each piece of writing has a different audience, purpose, and set of rhetorical expectations — and quite possibly multiple processes through which the writer could succeed. Working with multiple disciplines and genres, and adopting multiple perspectives each day, tutors cultivate an unusual and valuable "mental agility" (Grimm, *Good Intentions* 2). As Grimm says:

> Writing centers are often places where people develop what scholars call *postmodern skills*: the ability to simultaneously maintain multiple viewpoints, to make quick shifts in discourse orientation, to handle rapid changes in information technology, to work elbow to elbow with people differently positioned in the university hierarchy, to negotiate cultural and social differences, to handle the inevitable blurring of authorial boundaries, and to regularly renegotiate issues of knowledge, power, and ownership. This ability to work the border between tradition and change, to simultaneously entertain multiple — often conflicting — perspectives is a valuable survival skill for the turn of the century. (2, emphasis in original)

As a tutor, you will discover that tutorials are rarely, if ever, exclusively the product of any one paradigm. Instead, they are often a creative, and highly individual, mix of approaches, as the needs of the student dictate. This philosophical complexity adds richness and challenge to the tutor's role and provides ongoing learning experiences in which to refine and personalize a tutoring style.

THE TUTOR'S ROLE: DEVELOPING AN INFORMED PRACTICE

We believe in the idea of an informed tutoring practice, and we hope this book will serve as a source of information and insight. A tutor who develops a sufficiently broad interpretive frame for understanding his or her own work can apply this knowledge to new situations. In the absence of such a perspective, the tutor has only hit-or-miss, trial-and-error experimentation to rely on — often at the student's expense. On the other hand, tutors who draw on an experience informed by insight and an evolving personal philosophy can bring to the tutoring session the technical skill and creativity needed to teach writing successfully.

This approach suggests a reflective practice, one in which the tutor views rules as guidelines and guidelines as avenues to further refinement of aptitude or "know-how." The "know-how" of good tutors comes from a willingness to reflect on their efforts and to keep learning. Such tutors are eager both to confirm what they do well and to question any practices that impede productive interactions with students. Ultimately, successful tutors are willing to modify their views and procedures as new insights emerge.

The capacity for reconceptualizing is also one of the most significant means for improving writing skills that we as tutors can offer a student. To be a capable writer, a student needs to shift perspective from that of the writer who generated the text to that of an objective reader able to assess his or her own text and its methods of communicating to an audience. Many of the students we work with, though, will have had little experience with reconceptualizing their own writing in this way.

Often students cannot think about their writing in meaningful and productive ways because they are unpracticed at extensive revision. They may see revision as tedious and frustrating. After all, expressing their ideas in writing was probably difficult enough the first time; doing it again in a revised form can seem overwhelming. Knowing how to guide such students through drafting and revising can be of enormous help. By modeling the act of revision, we are demonstrating the process of reflecting on their ideas and written work. We will also be providing the "moral support" that can help sustain motivation. As Muriel Harris, one of the most respected and influential figures in writing center theory and the author of *Teaching One-to-One: The Writing Conference,* says:

> Writers also need another kind of help when revising — some support and encouragement — because the messiness of working and reworking a paper can lead to surprise and dismay as a topic falls apart or changes direction during writing. Novice writers need to learn how to persist, and they need some encouragement to do so. (8)

In emphasizing the interpersonal dimensions of the working relationship between tutor and student, Harris shows how tutoring functions as an assistive process. Tutors have been described as mentors, teachers, therapists, editors, midwives, coaches, grammarmeisters, nurturers, diagnosticians, guides, facilitators, rescuers, advisors, consultants, and allies. Perhaps we are all of these. But primarily, tutors are collaborators: we assist writers in achieving their goals. Among the many traits effective tutors share are good intentions, strong writing and editing skills, flexibility, an eagerness to help, an analytical yet creative mind, a dedication to excellence, good listening skills, an ability to be supportive yet honest, a willingness to work hard, a sense of humor, sensitivity to others, careful judgment, patience, and a dedication to collaborative learning. We need all these traits because solving problems and motivating others are key interpersonal activities in the tutoring process.

THE STAGES OF THE TUTORIAL

While no tutorial is ever exactly like another, most tend to share common patterns. Generally, tutor and student must first establish a working relationship, or mutual understanding, as a basis for collaboration on improving the student's text. Together they set goals for future tutorials and for the direction of the student's independent learning. We have chosen to call these shared activities the pretextual, textual, and posttextual stages of the tutorial.

The Pretextual Stage

In the pretextual stage, tutor and student begin the process of developing the interpersonal relationship that will guide their collaborations. Educational theorists tell us that interpersonal relationships are exceptionally important because they provide a context for interactive learning. In the past, theorists did not place much emphasis on context because they viewed the mind of the learner as an "object" to be filled with information. The method of presenting that information was important, but not the context in which it occurred. But now the mind of the learner is viewed as a process of meaning-making activities. This process is highly influenced by contexts — especially interpersonal ones. As psychologist and learning theorist Richard G. Tiberius writes:

> Effective teachers form relationships that are trustful, open and secure, that involve a minimum of control, are cooperative, and are conducted in a reciprocal, interactive manner. They share control with students and encourage interactions that are determined by mutual agreement. Within such relationships learners are willing to disclose their lack of understanding, rather than hide it from their teachers; learners are more attentive, ask more questions, are more actively engaged. Thus, the better the relationship, the better the interaction; the better the interaction, the better the learning. (1–2)

Most writing center theorists tend to agree with Tiberius in stressing the quality of the interpersonal relationship between tutor and student. For example, in "Freud in the Writing Center: The Psychoanalytics of Tutoring Well" (on p. 95), Christina Murphy maintains that the mutual trust and rapport between tutor and student determine how successful the tutorial as a whole will be. To achieve this level of reciprocal learning, Murphy contends, tutors often need to break through psychological barriers that might otherwise impede collaboration.

In establishing an interpersonal relationship, the tutor must respond to various personality and learning styles and be sensitive to differences in gender, age, ethnicity, cultural and educational backgrounds, and attitudes toward writing. The ways in which individuals process information must always be taken into account, too, since people tend to interpret, understand, and evaluate ideas in diverse ways. Consequently, tutors need to engage in what Harris calls "perception checking" or "guessing the student's basic message and asking for affirmation of that guess" (57). In a similar vein, Emily Meyer and Louise Z. Smith claim that tutors "must listen carefully to distinguish underlying meanings in writers' comments" (9) and work diligently to ascertain that those meanings are understood. Tutors should strive to understand, not judge, the student and to recognize the importance of the student's problems and feelings. Students vary in levels of autonomy, sensitivity to criticism, ego strength, personal maturity, motivation, and perseverance. Relating to the student as an individual and empathizing with his or her particular personality and character traits will go a long way toward forming a special trust, one that provides the motivation, energy, and direction for the tutorial itself.

When individuals choose to work together, their transactions should be based on a shared dialogue. Too often collaborations that seem democratic may actually be autocratic and controlling, as Andrea Lunsford indicates in her essay. Sometimes in a tutorial we need to overcome an assumed hierarchy of power, with the tutor in command and the student acting as a subservient petitioner. A good question for tutors to ask ourselves is, "Who has the power in the collaboration and how is that power used?" Are we, for example, truly interested in what the student has to say, or are we too quick to announce our opinions? Are we acting as collaborators or as authority figures? Do our comments invite responses and show respect for the student's ideas, or do they foreclose further interaction and leave the student feeling intimidated? Carol Severino points out that tutors can analyze the collaboration rhetorically by considering how the agenda for the conference is decided, the length of each person's contributions to the discussions, and the rhetorical functions of verbal exchanges and of body language (56). As Elizabeth H. Boquet says in "Intellectual Tug-of-War: Snapshots of Life in the Center" (on p. 116), tutorials involving difficult interpersonal conflicts — with students or fellow tutors — can sometimes leave a tutor feeling "simply at a loss" and call into question his or her sense of "progress toward becoming the 'ideal' writing center tutor." Boquet suggests that such questioning is an important part of peer tutors' development since it can lead them to become "dynamic forces within their workplaces," reflecting on and possibly changing for the better aspects of their practice or work environment.

Clearly, one component of a tutor's reflective practice is responsiveness to the ethical issues that often emerge in tutoring sessions. Students often express ideas and opinions on social, political, and moral issues that run counter to the tutor's own views. Knowing how to handle such conflicts wisely for the benefit of the tutor and the student alike is a challenging aspect of tutoring practice. Advocates of nondirective tutoring might urge a largely objective, if not distant, role for the tutor in dealing with such students and situations. Others, like Stacey Freed in "Subjectivity in the Tutorial Session: How Far Can We Go?" (on p. 137) and Steve Sherwood in "Censoring Students, Censoring Ourselves: Constraining Conversations in the Writing Center" (on p. 129), challenge the nondirective principle common to tutoring practice in which tutors are urged to remain neutral on social and political issues. Freed says that tutors have not only a right but an obligation to challenge students' ill-conceived and sometimes morally questionable ideas. She claims that "we would be doing the students a disservice by not voicing our own opinions" and thus not forcing them to scrutinize their work. To do so, "we must make students aware of other points of view that may be 'disturbing' to them and may 'distress' them; and we should, if we believe an individual case warrants it, overstep the boundaries and be subjective — without being judgmental — in expressing these views." Steve Sherwood claims the idea that the tutor can remain ethically neutral in all tutoring sessions is naïve. He contends that the "ostensibly objective devil's advocate role" tutors are expected to play while responding to a student's text has to be balanced against broader concerns for the student's best interests that may require the tutor to adopt an interventionist strategy.

All of these dimensions of tutoring are available for your investigation during tutorials. Self-reflection can assist you in assessing your interpersonal transactions and in responding to students' needs. In "'Whispers of Coming and Going': Lessons from Fannie" (on p. 100), Anne DiPardo discusses another dimension of interpersonal sensitivity — an appreciation of diversity. The students you tutor will come from different backgrounds, often different cultures. Their ways of looking at the world and interpreting experience may be strikingly different from yours, though equally valid. As DiPardo notes, we can serve students best by avoiding stereotypical and preconceived ideas and by being curious about how their ways of thinking differ from ours. Appreciating the multiplicity of perspectives encountered among students will add to our skill as tutors. As examples of this diversity, consider the following scenarios based on actual writing center interactions.

Darren and Yaroslav Darren worked with Yaroslav, a Russian student, on an assignment for his composition class to write a letter to the editor to argue against changes in governmental policies. From their initial conversations, Darren saw that Yaroslav was a bright, articulate, and highly motivated student. Yet there seemed to be a problem. Yaroslav was reluctant to discuss the requirements of the assignment and to work with Darren toward a rudimentary outline or draft.

Darren was patient and continued to ask Yaroslav questions related to the assignment. Did he understand the requirements of a paper that asked for a writer to take a stand on an issue? Had he ever written a similar paper before? With that question, Yaroslav suddenly became very animated. "In my country," he said, "you do not write letters to the editor to complain about the government."

Thus, Darren discovered that the issues that had made the tutorial difficult to that point did not result from Yaroslav's weaknesses as a writer or from a lack of motivation to complete his assignment. Rather, they arose from a cultural difference that had to do with the freedom of an individual to be politically active in one society versus another.

Had Darren not patiently addressed the resistance he sensed in Yaroslav, he might have merely assumed that Yaroslav was scattered, disorganized, or not ready to begin and sent him off to work on his own for awhile. As it turned out, his sensitivity created a supportive atmosphere in which Yaroslav was able to talk through his fears and realize that what would be an unimaginable and terrifying act in his culture was an everyday, safe occurrence in Darren's culture. Darren encouraged Yaroslav to shift perspectives and imagine the political freedom to express negative opinions about governmental policies. What would this be like? What actions would Yaroslav want to take? What would he most want to change politically? Eventually, because Darren had made his discussions with Yaroslav nonjudgmental and nonthreatening, Yaroslav began the process of drafting his essay. The understanding Darren and Yaroslav had achieved made the tutorial successful.

Patrick and Sabah   Patrick worked with Sabah, a graduate student from Singapore, for several tutoring sessions on a paper Sabah was assigned on an event or experience in her life of which she was most proud. Sabah had difficulty choosing a topic, and Patrick had talked with her about her life and work experiences. He learned that Sabah had been a teacher for three years in her home country, working with elementary school children. Patrick asked Sabah about these experiences and was delighted to discover how quickly Sabah brightened with enthusiasm and fondness as she discussed her students and how she had enjoyed teaching them.

"So you were a good teacher?" Patrick inquired.

Sabah hesitated, and her mood became less effusive. Patrick was puzzled. He asked again, taking a different approach.

"I would think, from what you say, that you were an excellent teacher and one who had a great influence on the children's lives."

Again Sabah seemed to hesitate, and then she became quite embarrassed. Patrick was now even more confused and also worried that he had offended her in some way. Then it occurred to him to ask Sabah about what she was feeling and what might be troubling her.

"Is this awkward for you?" he asked. "Were there problems with your teaching?" Sabah was relieved and grateful for the chance to unburden her feelings.

"No," Sabah said. "There were no problems. It's just that in my country it is considered inappropriate and too prideful to brag on oneself. It is very difficult for me to say that I was an excellent teacher — even though . . ."

Sabah paused, and Patrick saw a good opening for reducing the tension of the conversation.

"Even though you were," he said, smiling.

Sabah, too, smiled and laughed. "Yes," she said, "even though I was."

What Patrick learned from this tutoring session was a greater appreciation for cultural differences. As an American, Patrick could boast of an accomplishment, or even take a justifiable pride in his achievements, but the same was not true for Sabah as a native of Singapore. Instead, her culture advocated restraint in discussing one's achievements and held that one should not claim excellence, but rather let the listener deduce one's qualities and talents from the conversation itself. Prior to his interaction with Sabah, it had never occurred to Patrick that cultural norms might make it difficult for a student to accept a compliment or to take pride in an achievement. He learned from this encounter to broaden his understanding of cultural attitudes and expectations. He also learned that he might strengthen his tutoring style by not starting with assumptions — as in his statement, "So you were a good teacher?" — but by letting the conversation itself provide him with contextual clues so that the speaker could help shape the direction or "flow" of the discussion. In essence, he learned not to think "just like an American," with no other sense of audience than an American one, and he also learned to be a more empathic and skilled listener and speaker. Because it became clear to him that telling Sabah how she should feel about her experiences was not a productive way to proceed with the tutorial, he adopted the strategy of getting Sabah herself to talk about her work as a teacher and to place the events she described into a narrative structure. His role was to locate the most important, vivid, moving, and persuasive details in the stories Sabah was telling about her teaching and then help her develop a framework that would highlight those experiences and enable them to lead inductively to an overall insightful experience for the reader. Patrick experienced, as a tutor, a shift in his frame of reference. His role was not to tell Sabah what type of teacher she was but, instead, to help her tell her own stories about being a teacher in a way that would convey the nature and the "feel" of the events in a meaningful way to Sabah's readers.

Laura and Ted Laura worked with Ted in a number of tutorials before he confided in her that he had a learning disability. He showed her his letter of accommodation from the coordinator for academic services and talked about how he usually could do well on tests if given a little extra time. Laura was surprised to discover that Ted had a learning disability. At that moment, in thinking about Ted in a new light, she realized that she had held a stereotypical view of students with learning disabilities as "slower" than "normal" students. Yet here was Ted, who was so hard-working and was zipping through his computer science courses with high grades. He didn't seem "slow" at all. In fact, he seemed bright and talented.

"I can't read," Ted said, laughing. "At least not the way you do. I have dyslexia. Letters kind of tumble around on the page — you know, upside down, backwards, the whole bit. But if I take my time and work with my colors, I can manage pretty well."

When Ted mentioned his colors, a lot became clear to Laura. She remembered the way Ted marked up his drafts in highlighter colors of green, yellow, pink, and orange. When they talked, Ted always took notes and then highlighted sections of the notes in the various colors.

Laura didn't think much about it at the time. She assumed that Ted had his own way of organizing his work. Now, as Ted explained his system, she realized that he was using his enormous visual memory to compensate for his difficulties in processing symbols. Ted could literally "see" his paper in his mind once he had the paper coded to show its organization and to emphasize certain stylistic techniques.

"It's all about neurological processing," he said. "Some of us do it differently."

At that moment, Laura felt embarrassed. She remembered that on her campus students with learning disabilities were not referred to as "disabled" but as "differently abled." She realized that she had never really understood that term as more than a slogan. Now Ted had made it real for her. He was exceptionally "abled," and he went about his learning and information processing in a different way. She admired his motivation and drive. Ted had to work many times harder and longer than the "normal" student, yet he persevered and actually became quite creative in finding new ways to learn and to succeed.

"You know, I was kind of hesitant to tell you I had a learning disability," Ted said. "Sometimes people can't handle it. They freak out and start treating you differently, or they assume you're a basket case and start doing everything for you. Or worse yet, they start distancing themselves from you, like you're some kind of freak they just can't cope with. It's no fun."

"I can imagine," Laura said.

"But I wanted to be honest," Ted said. "I wanted you to know me for who I am. And I wanted to thank you."

Laura was a bit surprised.

"You've always been very patient with me. When I needed something explained more than once, you always would. You went through your explanations step by step, and that helped me a lot. Like I said, I can usually do pretty well if I have a little extra time — and a little extra encouragement."

When Laura reviewed her tutorials with her peer tutoring coordinator, she told him she was dismayed to discover how unenlightened her attitude toward students with learning disabilities had been. "I just had a superficial knowledge," she said. "And lots of stereotypical thinking. I really learned a lot from Ted about encouraging people to speak openly about themselves and about not prejudging anybody."

Laura's tutorials with Ted confirm Julie Neff's views in "Learning Disabilities and the Writing Center" (on p. 237). Neff believes that students with learning disabilities may amass a wealth of specific knowledge about a discipline, but have trouble accessing that knowledge without assistance. Such students may need help brainstorming about topics, with the tutor asking probing questions and writing down the students' answers. Others may have difficulty at the strategic level. Because of the variety of learning disabilities, Neff suggests that tutors should remain open-minded and modify tutoring techniques to meet individual student writers' specific needs. Tutors can best work with students who have learning disabilities by discovering and encouraging each student's own way of processing information. Doing so allows the tutor to provide commentary relevant to the student's particular learning style.

Paul and Leonard Leonard had been the manager of a trucking company for over twenty years before being laid off. Now he was returning to the university to get a degree in engineering and pursue another career. Leonard was highly motivated, organized, and very sure of his abilities — except when it came to expressing himself in writing.

"I haven't had an English class in about thirty years," he said to Paul during their first tutorial. "Now I have to write a personal essay for my composition class, and I'm not even sure what a personal essay is. All I know is I have to write something about my experiences, and I can't seem to get started."

"Are you experiencing writer's block?" Paul asked.

"I guess I am."

"Are you kind of a perfectionist? I mean, do you expect to get everything right the first time?"

Leonard nodded. "When you're in the trucking business, you'd better get it right the first time."

"I'm sure that's true, but did it always work out that way?"

After some thought, Leonard conceded that the more complex the task, the greater the probability of error. As they talked, Paul sensed that Leonard liked his world to be clear-cut — simple, neat, and organized. Paul realized that his first priority was showing Leonard that the writing task could be more manageable than it seemed, but he also realized that Leonard would probably still experience setbacks along the way. He explained the drafting and revision stages. He also explained that most writers feel some measure of self-doubt, especially in the early stages of coming up with ideas and finding a way to express them. Paul said, "It seems to me that, since you were in the trucking business, you should have a lot of material for writing a personal essay."

Leonard's face brightened. "You mean I could write about my old job?"

"Sure. Why not? That's personal, isn't it?"

"Yeah, very." Leonard thought for a moment. "Oh I see," he said. "Personal — like from my life."

Paul asked Leonard, "If you were going to write about your old job, what would you want a reader to know?"

"The first thing I'd want to tell them is that you can work for a company for twenty years, do your best and put your life's blood into the business, but, when times get tough, you get the ax anyway."

"Could we set this up as a scene? You know, like a story — a narrative — so that people could experience this from your point of view?"

As the two discussed options for the essay, Paul suggested the idea of beginning the narrative with strong visual imagery and perhaps some dialogue. This idea appealed to Leonard because his last conversation with his ex-boss was still fresh in his mind. As he told Paul, it was raining and bitterly cold the night he lost his job. He had driven to the dispatch office and brought his thermos of coffee in from the car. He still remembered how cold the metal thermos had felt, even after he had stepped into the warm office. Then he saw his boss's pained expression. Even though Leonard suspected what was coming, he still couldn't believe it when it happened.

"What you've just told me is very vivid," Paul said. "I can feel the coldness of the thermos, too. Why don't we begin with that scene and perhaps the conversation you and your boss had that night?"

Leonard liked this approach and began brainstorming with Paul to come up with more details he could include. In a short while, the two had begun work on a preliminary outline, and the idea of a personal essay no longer seemed so mysterious or intimidating to Leonard.

Paul helped build Leonard's confidence as a writer by making him aware of competencies he already had. He pointed out to Leonard how visual his descriptions were and how he could use this talent to his advantage in a personal essay. He also helped Leonard see that his past experiences were relevant now.

Paul's work with Leonard affirms that tutoring nontraditional students often involves, as Cynthia Haynes-Burton says in "'Thirty-something' Students: Concerning Transitions in the Writing Center" (on p. 269), "showing them how to channel the confidence they possess in other areas of their life and apply it to writing problems." Richard G. Tiberius echoes this same idea in stating that "the best we can do to help students learn is to connect what we say to their previous experience and knowledge" (1).

Each of these tutorials demonstrates the power of the interpersonal relationship to accommodate diversity, foster communication, and allow the student to take positive action. In this supportive environment,

- The tutor can help reduce the student's anxieties, self-doubts, and insecurities that can lead to writer's block, a sense of failure, and poor self-esteem.
- The tutor can help the student break a writing project of intimidating size and scope into smaller pieces (or stages) that the student can more easily manage.
- The student can get his or her ideas out in the open where they can be reacted to, examined, discussed, clarified, tested, and, if necessary, revised.
- The student has an opportunity to practice collaborative problem solving with an experienced writer who has the student's best interest in mind.
- The student can observe, reflect upon, and perhaps internalize the invention processes of the tutor.

Ultimately, a positive interpersonal relationship built in the pretextual stage allows for a fluid transition to a consideration of the student's text.

The Textual Stage

Students bring to the writing center the type of textual problems faced by writers at all levels of ability. They suffer from writer's block or from not knowing when to stop writing; they have something they want to say but can't quite put into words; or their most beloved passages are incomprehensible to their readers. In addition, they often have problems with grammar, style, syntax, logic, organization, tone, diction, and focus. To find solutions that remain true to a student's writing style and intent, a tutor must learn to address the student's needs while also creating a collaborative space within which confidence and skills can flourish.

The goal of most tutors is to assist students in making long-term improvements in their writing. In "Provocative Revision" (on p. 156), Toby Fulwiler argues that teaching writers how to improve involves teaching them how to revise. He adds that "revision is the primary way that both thinking and writing evolve, mature, and improve." Many students, though, identify tutoring with proofreading, or simple error detection and correction. They may be primarily interested in making sure their papers are grammatically and mechanically correct and only secondarily interested in your assessment of the quality of their ideas and the effectiveness of their organization. This attitude can put tutor and student at cross-purposes, creating a central dilemma for the tutor about how much to intervene in the student's overall writing processes. In essence, should we serve as editors of basic errors or as commentators on larger concerns when critiquing a student's writing and offering assistance?

This dilemma arises in nearly all tutoring situations. As you will see in Brooks's essay (on p. 168), some tutors attempt to resolve this dilemma by taking a hands-off, or *minimalist,* approach to the text. They focus on global issues such as thesis, structure, diction, tone, and the logical development of ideas. Students read their texts aloud; the tutor comments. As commentators, minimalist tutors assist students in solving their own problems. They ask heuristic questions — questions that encourage students to analyze their work and seek solutions to the difficulties the writing presents. Questions such as "Are you aware of the many simple sentences you use throughout your essay and the monotonous effect this can produce for a reader?" or "Have you thought about reorganizing your ideas along another line?" might prove more beneficial to a student's growth as a writer than simply correcting errors and sending the student off to reproduce a clean, error-free copy to hand in to the teacher. Minimalist tutors believe that proofreading and editing must be understood within the broader context of the writing process. Basic grammatical or mechanical errors may be symptomatic of deeper problems with text development, and just correcting those errors for the student will not resolve the larger issues.

Minimalist tutoring can present its own set of difficulties, however. A tutor who listens to a student read a text aloud and does not look at the text might not be able to detect certain types of formal errors that may affect meaning. For example, the sentence "The auditors role is to evaluate financial statements and certify that the statements have been fairly presented without material error" sounds correct when read aloud. But when viewed as a written text, the sentence's apostrophe error becomes apparent.

The difference between spoken and written text is further demonstrated by the interaction between Steve, a tutor, and Shafik, an ESL student who came to the writing center with a paper on the Muslim religion. Shafik asked for help in expressing his ideas clearly. Steve had him read his paper aloud and listened to the most polished, well-organized essay he had come across in weeks. "Your ideas seem clear enough to me," Steve said.

"When I speak them, yes," Shafik said as he handed Steve the manuscript, "but I have a slight problem with English grammar."

It turned out that Shafik's essay was a single paragraph, ten pages long, punctuated haphazardly, with a comma roughly every fifty words and a period every hundred. What Shafik needed and wanted was a close editing of the grammatical errors in his text. This meant that Steve, as the tutor, had to decide whether to follow his training in nondirective tutoring or address Shafik's specific needs by proofreading his paper. Shafik's case points to at least one problem a strictly minimalist approach can lead to. It can fail to help students like Shafik, who come to a tutorial with expectations that differ from those of native writers. As Muriel Harris states in "Cultural Conflicts in the Writing Center: Expectations and Assumptions of ESL Students" (on p. 206):

> For ESL students, finding their own answers rather than being told what the answer is or what they must learn can be a new process. As tutors, we have to suppress any discomfort with ESL students who seem to want us to tell them how to fix their papers. There is a cross-cultural problem in the clash between ESL students who sit with pencil poised, waiting to write down what we tell them, and us, as we keep trying to return responsibility for revision to the writer. When the tutor asks, "What is the connection between these two sentences?" or "Is there a word missing there?" and the polite student waits for the tutor to answer the question, the two parties are acting out assumptions and expectations from very different worlds.

Like Harris, Sharon A. Myers casts doubt on the value of minimalist, or nondirective, tutoring for ESL students. In fact, Myers argues that a tutor should feel free to work on so-called "sentence-level" errors with ESL students since these errors often point to problems with creating and processing meaning. By helping ESL students correct these errors, the tutor can guide students toward deeper knowledge of English syntax — an important step in their becoming better readers and writers of the language. As she says, "The central insight in foreign language pedagogy in the last thirty years is that, in fact, language acquisition emerges from learners wrestling with meaning in acts of communicating or trying to communicate. That is exactly what ESL students are doing in writing centers, person to person." Such learning often takes a long time — "years, not months" — and may not become immediately apparent to either the student or the tutor. By refusing to work with ESL students' grammar and style errors, she suggests, tutors may unwittingly slow the students' progress toward second language acquisition.

Not all tutors, of course, object to editing a student's text. Some consider modeling this part of the revision process for the student a significant aid to comprehension. Linda K. Shamoon and Deborah H. Burns (on p. 173), for example, challenge nondirective tutoring orthodoxy, or "pure tutoring," and call for a reexamination of writing center ideology to permit direct intervention in students' writing when necessary. As they point out, in disciplines such as music, master artists work with various levels of students in a highly directive manner. "The tutorial typically begins with one student's performance; then the master teacher works over a section of the piece with the student, suggesting different ways to play a passage. . . . On occasion, the master teacher will play the passage herself and ask the student to play it with her or immediately after her." In what amounts to a direct, hierarchical handing down of technique, the master demonstrates and the student imitates — and neither questions the ethics of this transaction. As Shamoon and Burns say, "Rather than assuming that this imitation will prevent authentic self-expression, the tutor and the student assume that imitation will lead to improved technique, which will enable freedom of expression." While they do not make an unqualified endorsement of directive tutoring, Shamoon and Burns argue that it is an appropriate response to a number of tutoring situations, especially in helping novices learn writing skills related to specific disciplines. They point out the weaknesses of expressivist and social constructionist viewpoints and suggest that writing center scholars reexamine mentorship and directive tutoring, accommodating such practices if they make knowledge and achievement more accessible to students.

For many tutors, the dilemma of how much help to give can be personally troubling. This dilemma intensifies as the definition of "help" shifts within the many contexts of tutoring and within the full range of the tutor's responsibilities. The natural tendency to be helpful and supportive may conflict with a sense that doing too much of the student's work will not produce the desired result of improving his or her writing abilities and critical-thinking skills. A related issue is the question of how candid to be in critiquing a student's work. Some students are mature enough to deal with having their work critiqued. Other students are far more fragile. As Peter Elbow says in *Writing with Power,* "Some people are terrified no matter how friendly the audience is, while others are not intimidated even by sharks" (184–85). With the complex of problems, needs, ego strengths, and personality styles students bring to the tutoring situation, what courses of action should the tutor pursue to be effective? The following ideas might prove helpful:

- *Give a candid opinion of the strengths and weaknesses of the work in progress; in the process, be sensitive to the student's reactions.* Such candor can be difficult, but honesty about the problems you detect with the reasoning, structure, or content of an essay is essential for improvement. This is not to say that criticism doesn't hurt. It sometimes does. But anything short of a truthful — but also sensitive — appraisal is a betrayal of the student's trust.
- *Suggest ways to enhance the strengths and minimize the weaknesses in the student's writing.* A tutorial that focuses exclusively, or even primarily, on

weaknesses can leave a student feeling demoralized. Noting strengths and achievements in the writing can build a student's confidence and set the tone for comments and suggestions that follow.

- *Recognize that every text and every writer is a work in progress.* Writers progress at different rates, but they do progress — in part because they acquire greater intellectual maturity, and in part because writing is an ongoing learning experience. Writers learn to be better writers by striving to improve. The issue is not whether they will make mistakes — because they will; the issue is whether they will learn from those mistakes or be defeated by them. Here the tutor can be instrumental. As a supportive ally and a candid critic, a tutor can encourage progress by fostering potential.

The Posttextual Stage

The posttextual stage has two major functions: it provides a sense of closure for the tutorial and it offers a *template,* or model, for future learning experiences. The most helpful tutorials do not simply "end"; they are brought to a satisfactory conclusion. Tutor and student seek an overview that brings the strategic insights of the tutorial into focus and clarifies what work still remains to be done. Ultimately, this perspective contributes to the student's ease in working with a tutor and makes future tutoring sessions seem natural extensions of an ongoing learning process.

This concluding stage also contributes to students' feelings of empowerment, providing them with the confidence they need to take the insights they have gained and apply them in new writing situations. In this regard, the concluding stage requires that you encourage self-motivated and independent learning styles for the student as a way of preventing the student from becoming overly dependent on your help. You can accomplish this objective in several ways: first, by leaving the student with a clear sense of where to go from here; second, by letting the student know that revision is well within the limits of his or her abilities; third, by providing a perceptive audience for the student's future work; and fourth, by refusing to be satisfied with anything less than the student's best effort. Not all students will respond to your demands for their best work. Those who do will grow as a result of learning to push themselves rather than settling for the easy solution. Eventually, if they internalize these expectations, they can become their own best audience.

As an example of a tutorial that was successful in encouraging independent learning, consider Barbara, a student who came to the writing center with a paper about William Faulkner's *Sanctuary.* During the initial "reading" of the student to establish a working relationship, Steve, the tutor, interviewed Barbara to learn a number of key pieces of information. For instance, Barbara told Steve that her professor had refused to grade her essay, saying that she needed help at all stages of her writing. Steve also learned that Barbara was a mother of three who had quit college as a sophomore nine years earlier and was now trying to pick up where she had left off. Barbara admitted she was feeling discouraged, saying, "It's been ten years since I've taken a writing course, and I've lost the knack. Anyway, my professor has a problem with the way I write. I'm worried about this paper," she said, "but I'm more worried about what's going to happen next year if I don't improve my writing."

Barbara moved the tutorial into the textual stage by showing Steve a heavily marked-up manuscript. "My teacher says I need to make a point and that I have problems with sentence structure," she said. She read her essay aloud, and Steve primarily noted rough transitions and a general lack of organization. In the essay, Barbara tended to repeat herself, to think in circles rather than systematically developing her main idea. Even so, Steve told Barbara that, circular or not, her ideas were good, that she had something interesting to say on Faulkner's motives for writing about particular characters. Together, they worked out a tentative essay structure. Since Barbara's main stylistic and mechanical errors were short, choppy sentences, errors of diction, and sentence fragments, Steve also went over individual sentences, asking Barbara to add the necessary elements.

Toward the end of the tutorial, Steve reviewed what they had accomplished, gave Barbara some words of encouragement, and then sent her away to write. Three days later, Barbara returned. Her paper had taken a new direction, and, though the paper occasionally wandered off the point, Steve felt it might work with some adjustments. He encouraged Barbara to rewrite along the lines they had discussed.

Steve did not see Barbara for over a week; then she returned to say she had received a B+ on the essay. "The best thing is, I did most of the work on my own," she said proudly. She was feeling independent and ready to face the challenges of future assignments. Through discussion, questioning, and being open both to small corrections and major changes in thinking, Barbara had gained at least an initial sense of her composing process.

Stimulating independent learning is an important aspect of the tutoring process and is the primary objective of the posttextual stage. When the posttextual stage is successful, students work to develop their own strengths separately from those of the tutor, taking what they can from the more experienced member of the relationship and adding this knowledge to an already existing repertoire of technique and understanding. In so doing, they build a knowledge indebted to, but independent of, their tutor's. As Wallace Stegner, a noted author and creative writing teacher, says, "Something unpredictable has happened in your head or on your typewriter, and no teacher did it — though a teacher may have helped it along" (19).

As a tutor, you can help foster independent learning and writing by

- letting students do what they can for themselves
- reminding students of any challenges they have conquered on their own or with minimal help

- recognizing and praising any steps they take toward independence in their writing
- refusing to let students credit you with their successes
- letting them know that, while you value their increasing independence, you will gladly help them cope with future challenges they might feel unable to face alone

As Christina Murphy states, "a good tutor function[s] to awaken individuals to their potentials and to channel their creative energies toward self-enhancing ends."

TUTORING ONLINE

Many of the principles of good tutoring apply to all tutorials, whether face-to-face or online, although online tutorials present tutors with fresh challenges.

For example, online tutorials take place primarily at the textual stage. When a tutorial is asynchronous, with a long delay between submission and response, and when it involves a writer and tutor who have never met, the tutor may find it hard to establish a personal relationship with the writer. The interaction consists of exchanges of e-mail text messages — disembodied language — with the accompanying danger of misinterpretation. Consider the following opening sentences from an OWL tutorial, for example. The tutor begins the session by saying, "Although your paper presented a plethora of perspectives pertaining to computer/technology issues, I was puzzled as to what particular position you were promoting. That is, I was unclear what the focus of your paper was, and what exact argument you were making." One obvious problem with the first sentence is the phrasing, which is not only elevated but also makes extensive use of alliteration, as if the tutor is attempting to sound clever, poetic, and overly academic. The dangers of using such phrasing include confusing and even angering a student writer. Another problem is the sentences' lack of warmth, which immediately gets in the way of establishing a rapport with the writer.

A disadvantage of asynchronous tutorials, beyond confusion and misinterpretation, is the inability to ask a student writer for immediate clarification of purpose, audience, and meaning of particular passages. As Michael Spooner argues in "A Dialogue on OWLing in the Writing Lab: Some Thoughts About Online Writing Labs," such essential aspects of the writing conference as facial expressions, tone of voice, gestures, and pauses for thought are lost in online tutorials (6–8). In making judgments about what advice to give a writer, the tutor must depend on the implied rhetorical context surrounding the piece of writing, the implied personality of the writer embodied in the "voice" of the piece, and any information a writer volunteers. Tutors who enjoy the interpersonal aspects of face-to-face tutoring are sometimes reluctant, at first, to engage in online tutorials. In "The Anxieties of Distance: Online Tutors Reflect" (on p. 285), David A. Carlson and Eileen Apperson-Williams observe, "For us, the face-to-face relationship is one of the joys, as well as a reason for success in a tutoring session. With online tutoring, this relationship is severed. The tutoring table is replaced with a computer screen: cold, sterile, and, to many, uninviting."

Despite such drawbacks, tutoring via e-mail has some definite advantages. As Carlson and Apperson-Williams suggest, e-mail tutorials do away with some of the personal anxieties that accompany face-to-face meetings and "foreground students' texts instead of the mediated relationships between tutors and students." Similarly, David Coogan argues that the anonymity of e-mail tutoring allows the tutor to speak more frankly about what he or she sees in a writer's text. In "E-mail Tutoring: A New Way to Do New Work," he says, "E-mail enabled me to perform close readings of student work — or more precisely, of the student — without the old fear of 'how will the student react?' What seems like a disadvantage (not seeing the student) can at times be an advantage" (176). Coogan concludes that focusing on e-mail text puts the emphasis of tutoring where it belongs — back on the writing itself.

Of course, such a focus raises ethical concerns about whether an online tutor, unable to engage in a timely dialogue, might simply revise student writers' papers, making the OWL a drop-off editing service. For this reason, a number of experienced online tutors recommend limiting commentary to general issues, such as structure, development of ideas, and overall impressions, rather than specific issues, such as punctuation and sentence errors — limitations that may run counter to student writers' needs. Other experienced tutors suggest using the "comment" function of their word processor to give student writers feedback without changing the text itself. Such feedback can range from remarks about structure and content to instructions on how to correct simple errors in punctuation, and tutors often find themselves in the same dilemmas they confront in face-to-face tutorials — forced to decide to what extent they should be directive or nondirective. In "Protocols and Process in Online Tutoring" (on p. 309), George Cooper, Kara Bui, and Linda Riker advise tutors to set a friendly, informal tone at the start of the tutorial, thus beginning the process of building an interpersonal relationship with the writer. They also suggest that tutors make frequent use of questions to encourage a dialogue with the writer — and to make it clear that much of the responsibility for the piece of writing rests with the writer. To help students improve grammar and style without resorting to proofreading, tutors should identify patterns of error in a piece of writing and make sample corrections that guide revision. Finally, to leave a student writer feeling confident in his or her ability to revise, they recommend closing online sessions by summarizing strengths and weaknesses in the student's text and restating plans for revision.

Synchronous tutoring through a virtual environment such as a MUD (multi-user dimension) or a MOO (multi-user dimension, object–oriented) may solve some of the problems inherent in asynchronous tutoring since a MUD or a MOO allows tutors and writers to interact in real time. If both tutor and writer are experienced computer users, accustomed to chatting online, such "emoticons" as wink or smile symbols can replace some of the interpersonal features of face-to-face tutorials. As Joanna Castner points out, synchronous online tutoring offers opportunities for dialogue between tutors and writers, allowing them to build a relationship, clarify misunderstandings, and collaboratively create knowledge (124–27).

Greater student access to technology and knowledge about building Web sites will likely mean that writing center tutors will soon not only be doing a significant portion of their work online, but also that this work may involve critiquing or assisting students with the composition of hypertext documents. As Michael A. Pemberton says in "Planning for Hypertexts in the Writing Center . . . Or Not" (on p. 294), writing center tutors should begin to prepare themselves to cope with "the emerging world of multimedia, hyperlinked, digital documents." As part of this preparation, he suggests that administrators and tutors consider what aspects of their knowledge about linear, hierarchically organized print texts might apply to nonlinear hypertexts and in what areas they should seek training in and greater knowledge about new media. Pemberton observes that writing centers have a history of adapting to new technology and will no doubt find ways to accommodate writers working in hypertext. The extent to which a writer benefits from online tutoring or from tutoring involving hypertext documents will depend, of course, not only on his or her attitude and energy, but also on the training, insight, and enthusiasm the tutor brings to the tutorial.

ON BECOMING AN EFFECTIVE TUTOR

We hope that investigating the tutoring process from a number of perspectives has revealed to you its philosophical complexity, interpersonal richness, and educational significance. We also hope that it has intensified both your desire to be a tutor and your willingness to continue learning how to improve your craft. Actually, tutoring is more than a craft; it is also an art form — one that will continue to evolve as you acquire more experience and wisdom. Everyone who has ever tutored has stood where you stand now — at the beginning of the journey into tutoring or a little bit further down the road. We assume you have started on that journey because you believe in the value of your work as a tutor. That value is often hard to measure in a quantitative sense, but it is exceptionally easy to experience as personal satisfaction when the work you do is helpful to another. We believe that assisting others is best achieved in an informed practice that blends experience, theory, and reflection. We hope this sourcebook will assist you in developing a philosophy and style of your own and, ultimately, in achieving your full potential as a tutor.

Works Cited

Boquet, Elizabeth H. *Noise from the Writing Center.* Logan, UT: Utah State UP, 2002.

Castner, Joanna. "The Asynchronous, Online Writing Session: A Two-Way Stab in the Dark?" *Taking Flight with OWLs: Examining Writing Center Work.* Ed. James A. Inman and Donna N. Sewell. Mahwah: Lawrence Erlbaum, 2000. 119–28.

Coogan, David. "E-mail Tutoring: A New Way to Do New Work." *Computers and Composition* 12 (1995): 171–81.

Elbow, Peter. *Writing with Power: Techniques for Mastering the Writing Process.* New York: Oxford UP, 1981.

Foster, David. "The Challenge of Contingency: Process and the Turn to the Social in Composition." *Post-Process Theory: Beyond the Writing-Process Paradigm.* Ed. Thomas Kent. Carbondale: Southern Illinois UP, 1999. 149–62.

Grimm, Nancy. *Good Intentions: Writing Center Work for Postmodern Times.* Portsmouth: Heinemann, 1999.

———. "The Regulatory Role of the Writing Center: Coming to Terms with a Loss of Innocence." *Writing Center Journal* 17.1 (1996): 5–29.

Harris, Muriel. *Teaching One-to-One: The Writing Conference.* Urbana: NCTE, 1986.

Kent, Thomas, ed. *Post-Process Theory: Beyond the Writing-Process Paradigm.* Carbondale: Southern Illinois UP, 1999.

Meyer, Emily, and Louise Z. Smith. *The Practical Tutor.* New York: Oxford UP, 1987.

Olson, Gary A. "Toward a Post-Process Composition: Abandoning the Rhetoric of Assertion." *Post-Process Theory: Beyond the Writing-Process Paradigm.* Ed. Thomas Kent. Carbondale: Southern Illinois UP, 1999. 7–15.

Severino, Carol. "Rhetorically Analyzing Collaboration(s)." *The Writing Center Journal* 13.1 (1992): 53–64.

Spooner, Michael. "A Dialogue on OWLing in the Writing Lab: Some Thoughts About Online Writing Labs." *Writing Lab Newsletter* 18.6 (1994): 6–8.

Stegner, Wallace. *On the Teaching of Creative Writing.* Hanover: UP of New England, 1988.

Tiberius, Richard G. "The Why of Teacher/Student Relationships." *Teaching Effectiveness: Toward the Best in the Academy* 6.1 (1994–95): 1–2.

II

Readings:
Entering the Professional Conversation

This group of essays introduces you to many of the ideas and issues currently defining the practice of tutoring. In a sense, it provides a body of knowledge about the function of tutoring within the broader context of educational theory.

The theorists and practitioners whose work is presented here examine the role of the tutor, speculate on the types of instructional and ethical transactions that occur in tutorials, consider tutoring in relation to current ideas about composition instruction, discuss tutoring's significance to multicultural issues, and review the benefits and pitfalls of tutoring in virtual environments. Their essays have been grouped according to the following common concerns: (1) theoretical constructs that underlie instruction in the writing center; (2) interpersonal dynamics of tutoring; (3) ethical aspects of tutoring; (4) techniques for critiquing students' texts; (5) affirming diversity; and (6) tutoring online.

Stephen M. North's "The Idea of a Writing Center" and Andrea Lunsford's "Collaboration, Control, and the Idea of a Writing Center" examine the paradigms, or models, of composition instruction that have shaped writing center tutorials. As discussed in the previous section, such paradigms include current traditional rhetoric, expressivism, and social constructionism. In responding to the constraints of current traditional rhetoric, North rejects the stereotypical image of the writing center as a "fix-it shop" and "skills center" for remediation. Instead, he validates the principles of expressivism in viewing the writing center as an instructional site in which "the object is to make sure that writers, and not necessarily their texts, are what get changed by instruction." As tutors, "our job is to produce better writers, not better writing," North claims, moving the focus of writing center instruction from the text to the writer. Lunsford provides an overview of how writing centers have progressed from the "storehouses" of current traditional rhetoric, to the "garrets" of expressivism, to the "Burkean parlors" of social constructionism. Like North, she finds limited value in the emphases of current traditional rhetoric, but she also challenges expressivism's belief in the interiority of knowledge and its romantic view of the writer as a solitary creator.

Marilyn Cooper, Meg Woolbright, Anis Bawarshi, and Stephanie Pelkowski offer insights into postmodern theories that influence writing center practice. In "Really Useful Knowledge: A Cultural Studies Agenda for Writing Centers," Cooper discusses the tutor's role in helping students understand how social and cultural traditions affect their writing. A writing center that takes a cultural studies approach can, she argues, teach student writers to find within professors' restrictive writing assignments autonomous spaces from which to address their own experiences and beliefs. Woolbright, in "The Politics of Tutoring: Feminism within the Patriarchy," compares writing center and feminist pedagogies and finds similarities in their egalitarian agendas, interactive teaching methods, emphasis on the personal, and critiques of patriarchal distributions of socioeconomic power. Since tutors, too, often reflect the hidden patriarchal agenda within academic power structures, she urges tutors to adopt a feminist perspective by examining the cultural assumptions that underlie their own thinking and tutoring practices. In "Postcolonialism and the Idea of a Writing Center," Anis Bawarshi and Stephanie Pelkowski extend the cultural studies model by questioning the writing center's role as "mainly a place of acculturation." Acculturation, they argue, is a totalizing mode in which the writing center smooths out cultural and economic differences among the populations it serves and replaces difference and diversity with homogeneity. Rather than have tutors function as agents of "affiliation" in which the dominant culture continues to reproduce and maintain its values, they argue for a "critical consciousness" in writing center practice that will enable tutors to help students through their writing "become more effective participants in the communities to which they belong."

While the modern and postmodern theorists in the "Theoretical Constructs" section consider the epistemological, or knowledge-related, issues that define the philosophical boundaries of writing center tutorials, Christina Murphy in "Freud in the Writing Center: The Psychoanalytics of Tutoring Well," Anne DiPardo in "'Whispers of Coming and Going': Lessons from Fannie," and Elizabeth H. Boquet in "Intellectual Tug-of-War: Snapshots of Life in the Center" examine the interpersonal dynamics involved in the tutor's role. Murphy explores the quality and importance of the interpersonal relationships tutors build with students by comparing such relationships to those psychoanalysts develop with their clients; according to Murphy, "a good psychoanalyst and a good tutor both function to awaken individuals to their potential and to channel their creative energies toward self-enhancing ends." Reinforcing the emphasis Murphy places on the bond between tutor and student, DiPardo discusses the tutor-student relationship in terms of multicultural sensitivity, emphasizing how tutors can facilitate successful interactions with students from diverse cultural backgrounds. She tells of Fannie, a Native American student, and of the dialogues through which Fannie and her tutor negotiated a working relationship sensitive to the "hidden corners" of a student's cultural heritage. As DiPardo states, "Often placed on the front lines of efforts to provide respectful, insightful attention to these students' diverse struggles with academic discourse, writing tutors likewise occupy multiple roles, remaining learners even while emerging as teachers, perennially searching for a suitable social stance. . . ." Boquet examines the complexities of the writing center as an institutional construct and thus the roles that tutors must undertake in seeking to serve both the goals of the institution and the needs of individual writers. She states that tutors must be engaged in a type of "systematic thinking" that can be "institutionally pervasive" and that often includes "production" as its goal. She contends that, while tutors may not be able to change that aspect of institutions, tutors can control *what* they "re(produce)" and thus can function more humanely, sensitively, and individualistically in how they teach others to write.

Analyzing the psychodynamics and hidden agendas within tutorials is also the main focus of the authors who examine ethics and tutoring. Steve Sherwood, in "Censoring Students, Censoring Ourselves: Constraining Conversations in the Writing Center," discusses the ethical issues of free speech, censorship, and self-censorship within tutorials and explores the options tutors have for responding to papers they may find ethically or morally repugnant. Stacey Freed critiques nondirective concepts of tutoring in "Subjectivity in the Tutorial Session: How Far Can We Go?" and argues against a tutoring style in which tutors must remain objectively removed and distant from their students. Instead, she advocates a wise use of subjectivity through which tutors challenge students' views and make them aware of other points of view that may be "disturbing to them" and "may distress them." Otherwise, she argues, we would be doing our students a "disservice" by not engaging them in the process of critiquing their own work. Jay Jacoby offers us a model drawn from the practice of medicine to investigate the extent to which a tutor can intervene in the student's writing processes. In "'The Use of Force': Medical Ethics and Center Practice," he explores the ethics of such intrusiveness and suggests that the concept of informed consent in medical ethics may function well as an exemplary practice for tutors.

Toby Fulwiler in "Provocative Revision," Jeff Brooks in "Minimalist Tutoring: Making the Student Do All the Work," and Linda K. Shamoon and Deborah H. Burns in "A Critique of Pure Tutoring" describe the tutor's assistive role in augmenting the student's understanding of the writing process. Fulwiler emphasizes revision, pointing out that "teaching writing is teaching rewriting." He provides a model for teaching the revision process so that tutors can help writers understand that "re-seeing writing in a different form is . . . generative, liberating, and fun." Fulwiler's view is that teaching and modeling revision are major components of tutoring as an assistive process. Brooks, on the other hand, argues against a tutor's intervening directly by editing the student's text; instead, he advocates "minimalist" tutoring, in which the tutor is a commentator rather than an editor. By discussing the areas of the student's writing that need improvement and by examining the student's options for revision, the tutor fulfills an important and highly individualized instructional role. As Brooks indicates, "Fixing flawed papers is easy; showing the students how to fix their papers is complex and difficult." Shamoon and Burns find value in both approaches and argue that tutors should be encouraged to explore both directive and nondirective practices in their tutoring in order to be the most effective instructors for their students. They state that the result of such a synthesis "would be an enrichment of tutoring repertoires, stronger connections between the writing center and writers in other disciplines, and increased attention to the cognitive, social, and rhetorical needs of writers at all stages of development." Joan Mullin, Neil Reid, Doug Enders, and Jason Baldridge in "Constructing Each Other: Collaborating Across Disciplines and Roles" discuss tutoring within writing across the curriculum and explore the complexities involved in examining disciplines as modes of inquiry and as rhetorical constructs. Their essay is constructed from the institutional role of each author — from writing center director, to writing tutor linked to a writing intensive class, to geography professor, to student in the geography class — and from the extensive range of conversations and philosophical explorations the authors go through in collaborating to create an effective and meaningful approach to tutoring across disciplines.

Muriel Harris in "Cultural Conflicts in the Writing Center: Expectations and Assumptions of ESL Students," Sharon A. Myers in "Reassessing the 'Proofreading Trap': ESL Tutoring and Writing Instruction," Julie Neff in "Learning Disabilities and the Writing Center," Beatrice Mendez Newman in "Centering in the Borderlands: Lessons from Hispanic Student Writers," Cynthia Haynes-Burton in "'Thirty-something' Students: Concerning Transitions in the Writing Center," and Margaret E. Weaver in "Transcending 'Conversing': A Deaf Student in the Writing Center" explore through case histories and narrative examples the value of tutoring as a one-to-one, individual process. These writers also focus on the educational and sociocultural backgrounds of multicultural and nontraditional students, examining how these dimensions influence tutorials. Harris encourages tutors to become "more sensitive to cross-cultural differences that may impede ESL students' ability to profit from writing tutorials." As Harris states, "without shared assumptions about what will happen, the tutor and ESL student can proceed on opposite tracks and spend their tutorial time trying to get the other person to move in their direction." Clearly, both Myers and Newman share Harris's view of sensitivity to cultural differences and an awareness of the role cultures play in defining writers and tutors. Myers challenges the common practice of focusing tutoring sessions for ESL writers on proofreading for surface-level errors while overlooking ways to enhance the intellectual development of ESL students as writers, and Newman focuses her essay on the ways that "the very component that disrupts institutional norms — the writing center — is what helps borderlands Hispanic students center themselves in the institution." Cynthia

Haynes-Burton develops a perspective similar to Harris's views of shared assumptions versus working at cross-purposes in her essay on the needs of nontraditional students. She questions whether commonly accepted models of the tutoring process have as great a relevance for nontraditional students whose life experiences and capabilities tend to differ from those of traditional students. Both Neff and Weaver present narratives that affirm the value of shared assumptions when working with students who are differently abled.

Most writing centers now offer tutoring in virtual environments, and with this relatively new service have come some challenges and concerns. One challenge facing online tutors is how to build interpersonal relationships with student writers they do not meet face-to-face. In "The Anxieties of Distance: Online Tutors Reflect," David A. Carlson and Eileen Apperson-Williams explore the pros and cons of replacing face-to-face tutoring "with a computer screen: cold, sterile, and, to many, uninviting." Since tutors sometimes find it hard to make the transition to a virtual environment, where a sensitive writer could find their commentary tactless and coldhearted, Carlson and Apperson-Williams emphasize the important role of dialogue in closing the social distance between tutor and writer. Michael Pemberton in "Planning for Hypertexts in the Writing Center . . . Or Not" questions "whether writing centers should continue to dwell exclusively in the linear, non-linked world of the printed page or whether they should plan to redefine themselves — and retrain themselves — to take residence in the emerging world of multimedia, hyperlinked, digital documents." George Cooper, Kara Bui, and Linda Riker give good, practical advice for tutors in their article "Protocols and Process in Online Tutoring." Among other suggestions, they advise tutors to begin an online tutorial with a friendly greeting, to encourage student participation by asking open-ended questions, to address larger composition issues rather than focusing on mechanics, and to end the session by helping to establish clear, realistic goals for the writer. They also caution that online tutors should remain flexible in their approaches to student writers, adapting their techniques as the situation demands.

Because all the authors included in this sourcebook discuss the tutoring process and explore the central issues concerning writing center practices in clear and helpful terms, their essays can provide an initiation into the field for novice tutors while also reminding experienced tutors of the complexity and richness of their work. Reading essays like these can help tutors avoid what DiPardo calls "a vision of 'collaboration' that casts it as a set of techniques rather than a new way to think about teaching and learning . . . a fossilized creed, a shield against more fundamental concerns." Instead, as informed tutors, aware of the ongoing professional conversation that contributes to defining writing center practice, we can set about developing our own philosophies of tutoring.

THEORETICAL CONSTRUCTS

The Idea of a Writing Center

Stephen M. North _____

STATE UNIVERSITY OF NEW YORK AT ALBANY

Stephen M. North contends that many students, writing instructors, and faculty in other disciplines do not understand the role of the writing center. They tend to view the writing center as a "skills center" or "fix-it shop" for grammar correction and writer remediation rather than as a place of active learning and student enrichment. North directs tutors toward examining a student's text as an indicator of the processes that produced it, rather than as a product that must be reworked to meet accepted standards of form and correctness. In this fashion, and in his assertion that tutoring should be "student-centered" rather than text-oriented, he endorses the primary tenets of expressivism in writing center pedagogy. A classic essay, frequently quoted and cited in writing center scholarship, "The Idea of a Writing Center" is important for tutors in contrasting two models of writing center instruction — one that stresses "the correction of textual problems" and another that focuses on the writer's intellectual and personal involvement in the creation of texts. North's essay is also important for its examination of the tutor's role within a "student-centered" pedagogy in which the writing center's "primary responsibility" and "only reason for being" is "to talk to writers." This essay originally appeared in 1984 in College English.

This is an essay that began out of frustration. Despite the reference to writing centers in the title, it is not addressed to a writing center audience but to what is, for my purposes, just the opposite: those not involved with writing centers. Do not exclude yourself from this group just because you know that writing centers (or labs or clinics or places or however you think of them) exist; "involved" here means having directed such a place, having worked there for a minimum of 100 hours, or, at the very least, having talked about writing of your own there for five or more hours. The source of my frustration? Ignorance: the members of my profession, my colleagues, people I might see at MLA or CCCC or read in the pages of *College English,* do not understand what I do. They do not understand what does happen, what can happen, in a writing center.

Let me be clear here. Misunderstanding is something one expects — and almost gets used to — in the writing center business. The new faculty member in our writing-across-the-curriculum program, for example, who sends his students to get their papers "cleaned up" in the writing center before they hand them in; the occasional student who tosses her paper on our reception desk, announcing that she'll "pick it up in an hour"; even the well-intentioned administrators who are so happy that we deal with "skills" or "fundamentals" or, to use the word that seems to subsume all others, "grammar" (or usually "GRAMMAR") — these are fairly predictable. But from people in English departments, people well trained in the complex relationship between writer and text, so painfully aware, if only from the composing of dissertations and theses, how lonely and difficult writing can be, I expect more. And I am generally disappointed.

What makes the situation particularly frustrating is that so many such people will vehemently claim that they do, *really,* understand the idea of a writing center. The non-English faculty, the students, the administrators — they may not understand what a writing center is or does, but they have no investment in their ignorance, and can often be educated. But in English departments this second layer of ignorance, this false sense of knowing, makes it doubly hard to get a message through. Indeed, even as you read now, you may be dismissing my argument as the ritual plaint of a "remedial" teacher begging for respectability, the product of a kind of professional paranoia. But while I might admit that there are elements of such a plaint involved — no one likes not to be understood — there is a good deal more at stake. For in coming to terms with this ignorance, I have discovered that it is only a symptom of a much deeper, more serious problem. As a profession I think we are holding on tightly to attitudes and beliefs about the teaching and learning of writing that we thought we had left behind. In fact, my central contention — in the first half of this essay, anyway — is that the failure or inability of the bulk of the English teaching profession, including even those most ardent spokespersons of the so-called "revolution" in the teaching of writing, to perceive the idea of a writing center suggests that, for all our noise and bother about composition, we have fundamentally changed very little.

Let me begin by citing a couple of typical manifestations of this ignorance from close to home. Our writing center has been open for seven years. During that time we have changed our philosophy a little bit as a result of lessons learned from experience, but for the most part we have always been open to anybody in the university community, worked with writers at any time during the composing of a given piece of writing, and dealt with whole pieces of discourse, and not exercises on what might be construed as "subskills" (spelling, punctuation, etc.) outside of the context of the writer's work.

We have delivered the message about what we do to the university generally, and the English department in particular, in a number of ways: letters, flyers, posters, class presentations, information booths, and so on. And, as long as there has been a writing committee, advisory to the director of the writing program, we have sent at least one representative. So it is all the more surprising, and disheartening, that the text for our writing program flyer, composed and approved by that committee, should read as follows:

> The University houses the Center for Writing, founded in 1978 to sponsor the interdisciplinary study of writing. Among its projects are a series of summer institutes for area teachers of writing, a resource center for writers and teachers of writing, *and a tutorial facility for those with special problems in composition.* (My emphasis)

I don't know, quite frankly, how that copy got past me. What are these "special problems"? What would constitute a regular problem, and why wouldn't we talk to the owner of one? Is this hint of pathology, in some mysterious way, a good marketing ploy?

But that's only the beginning. Let me cite another, in many ways more common and painful instance. As a member, recently, of a doctoral examination committee, I conducted an oral in composition theory and practice. One of the candidate's areas of concentration was writing centers, so as part of the exam I gave her a piece of student writing and asked her to play tutor to my student. The session went well enough, but afterward, as we evaluated the entire exam, one of my fellow examiners — a longtime colleague and friend — said that, while the candidate handled the tutoring nicely, he was surprised that the student who had written the paper would have bothered with the writing center in the first place. He would not recommend a student to the center, he said, "unless there were something like twenty-five errors per page."

People make similar remarks all the time, stopping me or members of my staff in the halls, or calling us into offices, to discuss — in hushed tones, frequently — their current "impossible" or difficult students. There was a time, I will confess, when I let my frustration get the better of me. I would be more or less combative, confrontational, challenging the instructor's often well-intentioned but not very useful "diagnosis." We no longer bother with such confrontations; they never worked very well, and they risk undermining the genuine compassion our teachers have for the students they single out. Nevertheless, their behavior makes it clear that for them, a writing center is to illiteracy what a cross between Lourdes and a hospice would be to serious illness: one goes there hoping for miracles, but ready to face the inevitable. In their minds, clearly, writers fall into three fairly distinct groups: the talented, the average, and the others; and the writing center's only logical *raison d'être* must be to handle those others — those, as the flyer proclaims, with "special problems."

Mine is not, of course, the only English department in which such misconceptions are rife. One comes away from any large meeting of writing center people laden with similar horror stories. And in at least one case, a member of such a department — Malcolm Hayward of the Indiana University of Pennsylvania — decided formally to explore and document his faculty's perceptions of the center, and to compare them with the views the center's staff held.[1] His aim, in a two-part survey of both groups, was to determine, first, which goals each group deemed most important in the teaching of writing; and, second, what role they thought the writing center ought to play in that teaching, which goals it ought to concern itself with.

Happily, the writing center faculty and the center staff agreed on what the primary goals in teaching writing should be (in the terms offered by Hayward's questionnaire): the development of general patterns of thinking and writing. Unhappily, the two groups disagreed rather sharply about the reasons for referring students to the center. For faculty members the two primary criteria were grammar and punctuation. Tutors, on the other hand, ranked organization "as by far the single most important factor for referral," followed rather distantly by paragraphing, grammar, and style. In short, Hayward's survey reveals the same kind of misunderstanding on his campus that I find so frustrating on my own: the idea that a writing center can only be some sort of skills center, a fix-it shop.

Now if this were just a matter of local misunderstanding, if Hayward and I could straighten it out with a few workshops or lectures, maybe I wouldn't need to write this essay for a public forum. But that is not the case. For whatever reasons, writing centers have gotten mostly this kind of press, have been represented — or misrepresented — more often as fix-it shops than in any other way, and in some fairly influential places. Consider, for example, this passage from Barbara E. Fassler Walvoord's *Helping Students Write Well: A Guide for Teachers in All Disciplines* (New York: Modern Language Association, 1981). What makes it particularly odd, at least in terms of my argument, is that Professor Walvoord's book, in many other ways, offers to faculty the kind of perspective on writing (writing as a complex process, writing as a way of learning) that I might offer myself. Yet here she is on writing centers:

> If you are very short of time, if you think you are not skilled enough to deal with mechanical problems, or if you have a number of students with serious difficulties, you may wish to let the skills center carry the ball for mechanics and spend your time on other kinds of writing and learning problems. (p. 63)

Don't be misled by Professor Walvoord's use of the "skills center" label; in her index the entry for "Writing centers" reads "See skills centers" — precisely the kind of interchangeable terminology I find so abhorrent. On the other hand, to do Professor Walvoord justice, she does recommend that teachers become "at least generally aware of how your skills center works with students, what its basic philosophy is, and what goals it sets for the students in your class," but it seems to me that she has already restricted the possible scope of such a philosophy pretty severely: "deal with mechanical problems"? "carry the ball for mechanics"?

Still, as puzzling and troubling as it is to see Professor Walvoord publishing misinformation about writing centers, it is even more painful, downright maddening, to read one's own professional obituary; to find, in the pages of a reputable professional journal, that what you do has been judged a failure, written off. Maxine Hairston's "The Winds of Change: Thomas Kuhn and the Revolution in the Teaching of Writing" (*College Composition and Communication*, 33, [1982], 76–88) is an attempt to apply the notion of a "paradigm shift" to the field of composition teaching. In the course of doing so Professor Hairston catalogues, under the subheading "Signs of Change," what she calls "ad hoc" remedies to the writing "crisis":

> Following the pattern that Kuhn describes in his book, our first response to crisis has been to improvise ad hoc measures to try to patch the cracks and keep the system running. Among the first responses were the writing labs that sprang up about ten years ago to give first aid to students who seemed unable to function within the traditional paradigm. Those labs are still with us, but they're still only giving first aid and treating symptoms. They have not solved the problem. (p. 82)

What first struck me about this assessment — what probably strikes most people in the writing center business — is the mistaken history, the notion that writing labs "sprang up about ten years ago." The fact is, writing "labs," as Professor Hairston chooses to call them, have been around in one form or another since at least the 1930s when Carrie Stanley was already working with writers at the University of Iowa. Moreover, this limited conception of what such places can do — the fix-it shop image — has been around far longer than ten years, too. Robert Moore, in a 1950 *College English* article, "The Writing Clinic and the Writing Laboratory" (7 [1950], 388–393), writes that "writing clinics and writing laboratories are becoming increasingly popular among American universities and colleges as remedial agencies for removing students' deficiencies in composition" (p. 388).

Still, you might think that I ought to be happier with Professor Hairston's position than with, say, Professor Walvoord's. And to some extent I am: even if she mistakenly assumes that the skill and drill model represents all writing centers equally well, she at least recognizes its essential futility. Nevertheless — and this is what bothers me most about her position — her dismissal fails to lay the blame for these worst versions of writing centers on the right heads. According to her "sprang up" historical sketch, these places simply appeared — like so many mushrooms? — to do battle with illiteracy. "They" are still with "us," but "they" haven't solved the problem. What is missing here is a doer, an agent, a creator — someone to take responsibility. The implication is that "they" done it — "they" being, apparently, the places themselves.

But that won't wash. "They," to borrow from Walt Kelly, is *us*: members of English departments, teachers of writing. Consider, as evidence, the pattern of writing center origins as revealed in back issues of *The Writing Lab Newsletter*: the castoff, windowless classroom (or in some cases, literally, closet), the battered desks, the old textbooks, a phone (maybe), no budget, and, almost inevitably, a director with limited status — an untenured or non–tenure track faculty member, a teaching assistant, an undergraduate, a "paraprofessional," etc. Now who do you suppose has determined what is to happen in that center? Not the director, surely; not the staff, if there is one. The mandate is clearly from the sponsoring body, usually an English department. And lest you think that things are better where space and money are not such serious problems, I urge you to visit a center where a good bit of what is usually grant money has been spent in the first year or two of the center's operation. Almost always, the money will have been used on materials: drills, texts, machines, tapes, carrels, headphones — the works. And then the director, hired on "soft" money, without political clout, is locked into an approach because she or he has to justify the expense by using the materials.

Clearly, then, where there is or has been misplaced emphasis on so-called basics or drill, where centers have been prohibited from dealing with the writing that students do for their classes — where, in short, writing centers have been of the kind that Professor Hairston is quite correctly prepared to write off — it is because the agency that created the center in the first place, too often an English department, has made it so. The grammar and drill center, the fix-it shop, the first aid station — these are neither the vestiges of some paradigm left behind nor pedagogical aberrations that have been overlooked in the confusion of the "revolution" in the teaching of writing, but that will soon enough be set on the right path, or done away with. They are instead, the vital and authentic reflection of a way of thinking about writing and the teaching of writing that is alive and well and living in English departments everywhere.

But if my claims are correct — if this is not what writing centers are or, if it is what they are, it is not what they should be — then what are, what *should* they be? What is the idea of a writing center? By way of answer, let me return briefly to the family of metaphors by which my sources have characterized their idea of a writing center: Robert Moore's "removing students' deficiencies," Hairston's "first aid" and "treating symptoms," my colleague's "twenty-five errors per page," Hayward's punctuation and grammar referrers, and Walvoord's "carrying the ball for mechanics" (where, at least, writing centers are athletic and not surgical). All these imply essentially the same thing: that writing centers define their province in terms of a given curriculum, taking over those portions of it that "regular" teachers are willing to cede or, presumably, unable to handle. Over the past six years or so I have visited more than fifty centers, and read descriptions of hundreds of others, and I can assure you that there are indeed centers of this kind, centers that can trace their conceptual lineage back at least as far as Moore. But the "new" writing center has a somewhat shorter history. It is the result of a documentable resurgence, a renaissance if you will, that began in the early 1970s. In fact, the flurry of activity that caught Professor Hairston's attention, and which she mistook for the beginnings of the "old" center, marked instead the genesis of a center which defined its province in a radically different way. Though I have some serious reservations about Hairston's use of Kuhn's paradigm model to describe what happens in composition teaching, I will for the moment put things in her terms: the new writing center, far from marking the end of an era, is the embodiment, the epitome, of a new one. It represents the marriage of what are arguably the two most powerful contemporary perspectives on teaching writing: first, that writing is most usefully viewed as a process; and second, that writing curricula need to be student-centered. This new writing center, then, defines its province not in terms of some curriculum, but in terms of the writers it serves.

To say that writing centers are based on a view of writing as a process is, original good intentions notwithstanding, not to say very much anymore. The slogan — and I daresay that is what it has become — has been devalued, losing most of its impact and explanatory power. Let me use it, then, to make the one distinction of which it still seems capable: in a writing center the object is to make sure that writers, and not necessarily their texts, are what get changed by instruction. In axiom form it goes like this: our job is to produce better writers, not better writing. Any given project — a class assignment, a law school application letter, an encyclopedia entry, a dissertation proposal — is for the writer the prime, often the exclusive concern. That particular text, its success or failure, is what brings them to talk to us in the first place. In the center, though, we look beyond or through that particular project, that particular text, and see it as an occasion for addressing *our* primary concern, the process by which it is produced.

At this point, however, the writing-as-a-process slogan tends to lose its usefulness. That "process," after all, has been characterized as everything from the reception of divine inspiration to a set of nearly algorithmic rules for producing the five paragraph theme. In between are the more widely accepted and, for the moment, more respectable descriptions derived from composing aloud protocols, interviews, videotaping, and so on. None of those, in any case, represent the composing process we seek in a writing center. The version we want can only be found, in as yet unarticulated form, in the writer we are working with. I think probably the best way to describe a writing center tutor's relationship to composing is to say that a tutor is a holist devoted to a participant-observer methodology. This may seem, at first glance, too passive — or, perhaps, too glamorous, legitimate, or trendy — a role in which to cast tutors. But consider this passage from Paul Diesing's *Patterns of Discovery in the Social Sciences* (Hawthorne, N.Y.: Aldine, 1971):

> Holism is not, in the participant-observer method, an a priori belief that everything is related to everything else. It is rather the methodological necessity of pushing on to new aspects and new kinds of evidence in order to make sense of what one has already observed and to test the validity of one's interpretations. A belief in the organic unity of living systems may also be present, but this belief by itself would not be sufficient to force a continual expansion of one's observations. It is rather one's inability to develop an intelligible and validated partial model that drives one on. (p. 167)

How does this definition relate to tutors and composing? Think of the writer writing as a kind of host setting. What we want to do in a writing center is fit into — observe and participate in — this ordinarily solo ritual of writing. To do this, we need to do what any participant-observer must do: see what happens during this "ritual," try to make sense of it, observe some more, revise our model, and so on indefinitely, all the time behaving in a way the host finds acceptable. For validation and correction of our model, we quite naturally rely on the writer, who is, in turn, a willing collaborator in — and, usually, beneficiary of — the entire process. This process precludes, obviously, a reliance on or a clinging to any predetermined models of "the" composing process, except as crude topographical guides to what the "territory" of composing processes might look like. The only composing process that matters in a writing center is "a" composing process, and it "belongs" to, is acted out by, only one given writer.

It follows quite naturally, then, that any curriculum — any plan of action the tutor follows — is going to be student-centered in the strictest sense of that term. That is, it will not derive from a generalized model of composing, or be based on where the student ought to be because she is a freshman or sophomore, but will begin from where the student is, and move where the student moves — an approach possible only if, as James Moffett suggests in *Teaching the Universe Of Discourse* (Boston: Houghton Mifflin, 1968), the teacher (or tutor in this case) "shifts his gaze from the subject to the learner, for the subject is in the learner" (p. 67). The result is what might be called a pedagogy of direct intervention. Whereas in the "old" center instruction tends to take place after or apart from writing, and tends to focus on the correction of textual problems, in the "new" center the teaching takes place as much as possible during writing, during the activity being learned, and tends to focus on the activity itself.

I do not want to push the participant-observer analogy too far. Tutors are not, finally, researchers: they must measure their success not in terms of the constantly changing model they create, but in terms of changes in the writer. Rather than being fearful of disturbing the "ritual" of composing, they observe it and are charged to change it: to interfere, to get in the way, to participate in ways that will leave the "ritual" itself forever altered. The whole enterprise seems to me most natural. Nearly everyone who writes likes — and needs — to talk about his or her writing, preferably to someone who will really listen, who knows how to listen, and knows how to talk about writing too. Maybe in a perfect world, all writers would have their own ready auditor — a teacher, a classmate, a roommate, an editor — who would not only listen but draw them out, ask them questions they would not think to ask themselves. A writing center is an institutional response to this need. Clearly writing centers can never hope to satisfy this need themselves; on my campus alone, the student-to-tutor ratio would be about a thousand to one. Writing centers are simply one manifestation — polished and highly visible — of a dialogue about writing that is central to higher education.

As is clear from my citations in the first half of this essay, however, what seems perfectly natural to me is not so natural for everyone else. One part of the difficulty, it seems to me now, is not theoretical at all, but practical, a question of coordination or division of labor. It usually comes in the form of a question like this: "If I'm doing process-centered teaching in my class, why do I need a writing center? How can I use it?" For a long time I tried to soft-pedal my answers to this question. For instance, in my dissertation ("Writing Centers: A Sourcebook," Diss. SUNY at Albany, 1978) I talked about complementing or intensifying classroom instruction. Or, again, in our center we tried using, early on, what is a fairly common device among writing centers, a referral form; at one point it even had a sort of diagnostic taxonomy, a checklist, by which teachers could communicate to us their concerns about the writers they sent us.

But I have come with experience to take a harder, less conciliatory position. The answer to the question in all cases is that teachers, as teachers, do not need, and cannot use, a writing center: only writers need it, only writers can use it. You cannot parcel out some portion of a given student for us to deal with ("You take care of editing, I'll deal with invention"). Nor should you require that all of your students drop by with an early draft of a research paper to get a reading from a fresh audience. You should not scrawl, at the bottom of a failing paper, "Go to the writing center." Even those of you who, out of genuine concern, bring students to a writing center, almost by the hand, to make sure they know that we won't hurt them — even you are essentially out of line. Occasionally we manage to convert such writers from people who have to see us to people who want to, but most often they either come as if for a kind of detention, or they drift away. (It would be nice if in writing, as in so many things, people would do what we tell them because it's good for them, but they don't. If and when *they* are ready, we will be here.)

In short, we are not here to serve, supplement, back up, complement, reinforce, or otherwise be defined by any external curriculum. We are here to talk to writers. If they happen to come from your classes, you might take it as a compliment to your assignments, in that your writers are engaged in them enough to want to talk about their work. On the other hand, we do a fair amount of trade in people working on ambiguous or poorly designed assignments, and far too much work with writers whose writing has received caustic, hostile, or otherwise unconstructive commentary.

I suppose this declaration of independence sounds more like a declaration of war, and that is obviously not what I intend, especially since the primary casualties would be the students and writers we all aim to serve. And I see no reason that writing centers and classroom teachers cannot cooperate as well as coexist. For example, the first rule in our writing center is that we are professionals at what we do. While that does, as I have argued, give us the freedom of self-definition, it also carries with it a responsibility to respect our fellow professionals. Hence we never play student-advocates in teacher-student relationships. The guidelines are very clear. In all instances the student must understand that we support the teacher's position completely. (Or, to put it in less loaded terms — for we are not teacher advocates either — the instructor is simply part of the rhetorical context in which the writer is trying to operate. We cannot change that context: all we can do is help the writer learn how to operate in it and other contexts like it.) In practice, this rule means that we never evaluate or second-guess any teacher's syllabus, assignments, comments, or grades. If students are unclear about any of those, we send them back to the teacher to get clear. Even in those instances I mentioned above — where writers come in confused by what seem to be poorly designed assignments, or crushed by what appear to be unwarrantedly hostile comments — we pass no judgment, at least as far as the student is concerned. We simply try, every way we can, to help the writer make constructive sense of the situation.

In return, of course, we expect equal professional courtesy. We need, first of all, instructors' trust that our work with writers-in-progress on academic assignments is not plagiarism, any more than a conference with the teacher would be — that, to put it the way I most often hear it, we will not write students' papers for them. Second, instructors must grant us the same respect we grant them — that is, they must neither evaluate nor second-guess our work with writers. We are, of course, most willing to talk about that work. But we do not take kindly to the perverse kind of thinking represented in remarks like, "Well, I had a student hand in a paper that he took to the writing center, and it was *still* full of errors." The axiom, if you will recall, is that we aim to make better writers, not necessarily — or immediately — better texts.

Finally, we can always use classroom teachers' cooperation in helping us explain to students what we do. As a first step, of course, I am asking that they revise their thinking about what a writing center can do. Beyond that, in our center we find it best to go directly to the students ourselves. That is, rather than sending out a memo or announcement for the teachers to read in their classes, we simply send our staff, upon invitation, into classes to talk with students or, better yet, to do live tutorials. The standard presentation, a ten-minute affair, gives students a person, a name, and a face to remember the center by. The live tutorials take longer, but we think they are worth it. We ask the instructor to help us find a writer willing to have a draft (or a set of notes or even just the assignment) reproduced for the whole class. Then the writing center person does, with the participation of the entire class, what we do in the center: talk about writing with the writer. In our experience the instructors learn as much about the center from these sessions as the students.

To argue that writing centers are not here to serve writing class curricula is not to say, however, that they are here to replace them. In our center, anyway, nearly every member of the full-time staff is or has been a classroom teacher of writing. Even our undergraduate tutors work part of their time in an introductory writing course. We all recognize and value the power of classroom teaching, and we take pride in ourselves as professionals in that setting too.

But working in both situations makes us acutely aware of crucial differences between talking about writing in the context of a class, and talking about it in the context of the center. When we hold student conferences in our classes, we are the teacher, in the writers' minds especially, the assigner and evaluator of the writing in question. And for the most part we are pretty busy people, with conference appointments scheduled on the half hour, and a line forming outside the office. For efficiency the papers-in-progress are in some assigned form — an outline, a first draft, a statement of purpose with bibliography and note cards; and while the conference may lead to further composing, there is rarely the time or the atmosphere for composing to happen during the conference itself. Last but not least, the conference is likely to be a command performance, our idea, not the writer's.

When we are writing center tutors all of that changes. First of all, conferences are the writer's idea; he or she seeks us out. While we have an appointment book that offers half-hour appointment slots, our typical session is fifty minutes, and we average between three and four per writer; we can afford to give a writer plenty of time. The work-in-progress is in whatever form the writer has managed to put it in, which may make tutoring less efficient, but which clearly makes it more student-centered, allowing us to begin where the writers are, not where we told them to be. This also means that in most cases the writers come prepared, even anxious to get on with their work, to begin or to keep on composing. Whereas going to keep a conference with a teacher is, almost by definition, a kind of goal or deadline — a stopping place — going to talk in the writing center is a means of getting started, or a way to keep going. And finally — in a way subsuming all the rest — we are not the teacher. We did not assign the writing, and we will not grade it. However little that distinction might mean in our behaviors, it seems to mean plenty to the writers.

What these differences boil down to, in general pedagogical terms, are timing and motivation. The fact is, not everyone's interest in writing, their need or desire to write or learn to write, coincides with the fifteen or thirty weeks they spend in writing courses — especially when, as is currently the case at so many institutions, those weeks are required. When writing does become important, a writing center can be there in a way that our regular classes cannot. Charles Cooper, in an unpublished paper called "What College Writers Need to Know" (1979), puts it this way:

> The first thing college writers need to know is that they can improve as writers and the second is that they will never reach a point where they cannot improve further. One writing course, two courses, three courses may not be enough. If they're on a campus which takes writing seriously, they will be able to find the courses they need to feel reasonably confident they can fulfill the requests which will be made of them in their academic work. . . . Throughout their college years they should also be able to find on a drop-in, no-fee basis expert tutorial help with any writing problem they encounter in a paper. (p. 1)

A writing center's advantage in motivation is a function of the same phenomenon. Writers come looking for us because, more often than not, they are genuinely, deeply engaged with their material, anxious to wrestle it into the best form they can: they are motivated to write. If we agree that the biggest obstacle to overcome in teaching anything, writing included, is getting learners to decide that they want to learn, then what a writing center does is cash in on motivation that the writer provides. This teaching at the conjunction of timing and motivation is most strikingly evident when we work with writers doing "real world" tasks: application essays for law, medical, and graduate schools, newspaper and magazine articles, or poems and stories. Law school application writers are suddenly willing — sometimes overwhelmingly so — to concern themselves with audience, purpose, and persona, and to revise over and over again. But we see the same excitement in writers working on literature or history or philosophy papers, or preparing dissertation proposals, or getting ready to tackle comprehensive exams. Their primary concern is with their material, with some existential context where new ideas must merge with old, and suddenly writing is a vehicle, a means to an end, and not an end in itself. These opportunities to talk with excited writers at the height of their engagement with their work are the lifeblood of a writing center.

The essence of the writing center method, then, is this talking. If we conceive of writing as a relatively rhythmic and repeatable kind of behavior, then for a writer to improve that behavior, that rhythm, has to change — preferably, though not necessarily, under the writer's control. Such changes can be fostered, of course, by work outside of the act of composing itself — hence the success of the classical discipline of imitation, or more recent ones like sentence combining or the tagmemic heuristic, all of which, with practice, "merge" with and affect composing. And, indeed, depending on the writer, none of these tactics would be ruled out in a writing center. By and large, however, we find that the best breaker of old rhythms, the best creator of new ones, is our style of live intervention, our talk in all its forms.

The kind of writing does not substantially change the approach. We always want the writer to tell us about the rhetorical context — what the purpose of the writing is, who its audience is, how the writer hopes to present herself. We want to know about other constraints — deadlines, earlier experiences with the same audience or genre, research completed or not completed, and so on. In other ways, though, the variations on the kind of talk are endless. We can question, praise, cajole, criticize, acknowledge, badger, plead — even cry. We can read: silently, aloud, together, separately. We can play with options. We can both write — as, for example, in response to sample essay exam questions — and compare opening strategies. We can poke around in resources — comparing, perhaps, the manuscript conventions of the Modern Language Association with those of the American Psychological Association. We can ask writers to compose aloud while we listen, or we can compose aloud, and the writer can watch and listen.

In this essay, however, I will say no more about the nature of this talk. One reason is that most of what can be said, for the moment, has been said in print already. There is, for example, my own "Training Tutors to Talk About Writing" (*CCC*, 33, [1982], 434–41), or Muriel Harris' "Modeling: A Process Method of Teaching" (*College English*, 45, [1983], 74–84). And there are several other sources, including a couple of essay collections, that provide some insights into the hows and whys of tutorial talk.[2]

A second reason, though, seems to me more substantive, and symptomatic of the kinds of misunderstanding I have tried to dispel here. We don't know very much, in other than a practitioner's anecdotal way, about the dynamics of the tutorial. The same can be said, of course, with regard to talk about writing in any setting — the classroom, the peer group, the workshop, the teacher-student conference, and so on. But while ignorance of the nature of talk in those settings does not threaten their existence, it may do precisely that in writing centers. That is, given the idea of the writing center I have set forth here, talk is everything. If the writing center is ever to prove its worth in other than quantitative terms — numbers of students seen, for example, or hours of tutorials provided — it will have to do so by describing this talk: what characterizes it, what effects it has, how it can be enhanced.

Unfortunately, the same "proofreading-shop-in-the-basement" mentality that undermines the pedagogical efforts of the writing center hampers research as well. So far most of the people hired to run such places have neither the time, the training, nor the status to undertake any serious research. Moreover, the few of us lucky enough to even consider the possibility of research have found that there are other difficulties. One is that writing center work is often not considered fundable — that is, relevant to a wide enough audience — even though there are about a thousand such facilities in the country, a figure which suggests that there must be at least ten to fifteen thousand tutorials every school day, and even though research into any kind of talk about writing is relevant for the widest possible audience. Second, we have discovered that focusing our scholarly efforts on writing centers may be a professional liability. Even if we can publish our work (and that is by no means easy), there is no guarantee that it will be viewed favorably by tenure and promotion review committees. Composition itself is suspect enough; writing centers, a kind of obscure backwater, seem no place for a scholar.

These conditions may be changing. Manuscripts for *The Writing Center Journal,* for example, suggest that writing center folk generally are becoming more research-oriented; there were sessions scheduled at this year's meetings of the MLA and NCTE on research in or relevant to writing centers. In an even more tangible signal of change, the State University of New York has made funds available for our Albany center to develop an appropriate case study methodology for writing center tutorials. Whether this trend continues or not, my point remains the same. Writing centers, like any other portion of a college writing curriculum, need time and space for appropriate research and reflec- tion if they are to more clearly understand what they do, and figure out how to do it better. The great danger is that the very misapprehensions that put them in basements to begin with may conspire to keep them there.

It is possible that I have presented here, at least by implication, too dismal a portrait of the current state of writing centers. One could, as a matter of fact, mount a pretty strong argument that things have never been better. There are, for example, several regional writing center associations that have annual meetings, and the number of such associations increases every year. Both *The Writing Lab Newsletter* and *The Writing Center Journal,* the two publications in the field, have solid circulations. This year at NCTE, for the first time, writing center people met as a recognized National Assembly, a major step up from their previous Special Interest Session status.

And on individual campuses all over the country, writing centers have begun to expand their institutional roles. So, for instance, some centers have established resource libraries for writing teachers. They sponsor readings or reading series by poets and fiction writers, and annual festivals to celebrate writing of all kinds. They serve as clearinghouses for information on where to publish, on writing programs, competitions, scholarships, and so on; and they sponsor such competitions themselves, even putting out their own publica- tions. They design and conduct workshops for groups with special needs — essay exam takers, for example, or job application writers. They are involved with, or have even taken over entirely, the task of training new teaching assistants. They have played central roles in the creation of writing-across-the- curriculum programs. And centers have extended themselves beyond their own institutions, sending tutors to other schools (often high schools), or help- ing other institutions set up their own facilities. In some cases, they have made themselves available to the wider community, often opening a "Grammar Hot- line" or "Grammaphone" — a service so popular at one institution, in fact, that a major publishing company provided funding to keep it open over the summer.

Finally, writing centers have gotten into the business of offering academic credit. As a starting point they have trained their tutors in formal courses or, in some instances, "paid" their tutors in credits rather than money. They have set up independent study arrangements to sponsor both academic and nonaca- demic writing experiences. They have offered credit-bearing courses of their own; in our center, for example, we are piloting an introductory writing course that uses writing center staff members as small group leaders.

I would very much like to say that all this activity is a sure sign that the idea of a writing center is here to stay, that the widespread misunderstandings I described in this essay, especially those held so strongly in English depart- ments, are dissolving. But in good conscience I cannot. Consider the activities we are talking about. Some of them, of course, are either completely or mostly public relations: a way of making people aware that a writing center exists, and that (grammar hotlines aside) it deals in more than usage and punctuation. Others — like the resource library, the clearinghouse, or the training of new teaching assistants — are more substantive, and may well belong in a writing center, but most of them end up there in the first place because nobody else wants to do them. As for the credit generating, that is simply pragmatic. The bottom line in academic budget making is calculated in student credit hours; when budgets are tight, as they will be for the foreseeable future, facilities that generate no credits are the first to be cut. Writing centers — even really good writing centers — have proved no exception.

None of these efforts to promote writing centers suggest that there is any changed understanding of the idea of a writing center. Indeed it is as though what writing centers do that really matters — talking to writers — were not enough. That being the case, enterprising directors stake out as large a claim as they can in more visible or acceptable territory. All of these efforts — and, I assure you, my center does its share — have about them an air of shrewdness, or desperation, the trace of a survival instinct at work. I am not such a purist as to suggest that these things are all bad. At the very least they can be good for staff morale. Beyond that I think they may eventually help make writing centers the centers of consciousness about writing on campuses, a kind of physical locus for the ideas and ideals of college or university or high school commitment to writing — a status to which they might well aspire and which, judging by results on a few campuses already, they can achieve.

But not this way, not via the back door, not — like some marginal ballplayer — by doing whatever it takes to stay on the team. If writing centers are going to finally be accepted, surely they must be accepted on their own terms, as places whose primary responsibility, whose only reason for being, is to talk to writers. That is their heritage, and it stretches back farther than the late 1960s or the early 1970s, or to Iowa in the 1930s — back, in fact, to Athens, where in a busy marketplace a tutor called Socrates set up the same kind of shop: open to all comers, no fees charged, offering, on whatever subject a visitor might propose, a continuous dialectic that is, finally, its own end.

Notes

[1] "Assessing Attitudes Toward the Writing Center," *The Writing Center Journal*, 3, No. 2 (1983), 1–11.

[2] See, for example, *Tutoring Writing: A Sourcebook for Writing Labs*, ed. Muriel Harris (Glenview, Ill.: Scott-Foresman, 1982); and *New Directions for College Learning Assistance: Improving Writing Skills*, ed. Phyllis Brooks and Thom Hawkins (San Francisco: Jossey-Bass, 1981).

Collaboration, Control, and the Idea of a Writing Center

Andrea Lunsford ⎯⎯⎯⎯⎯⎯⎯⎯⎯⎯⎯⎯⎯⎯⎯⎯⎯⎯⎯⎯

STANFORD UNIVERSITY

Andrea Lunsford has helped define for writing instructors the significance of collaborative learning and the social construction of knowledge. In this essay, Lunsford extends her discussion to writing center pedagogy. As she shows us, collaborative writing centers pose "a threat as well as a challenge to the status quo in higher education" by challenging the firmly held notion of authorship as a solitary activity and knowledge as "individually derived, individually held." Lunsford argues that writing centers are excellent sites for undertaking the difficult task of "creating a collaborative environment" that "promotes excellence" and "encourages active learning." Her essay, which originally appeared in 1991 in The Writing Center Journal, *is especially helpful for tutors in providing an overview of social constructionism and its impact on writing center philosophies. In essence, the essay establishes a theoretical context for the work tutors do by contrasting the collaborative writing center with earlier writing center models, shaped by expressivism and current traditional rhetoric.*

The triple focus of my title reflects some problems I've been concentrating on as I thought about and prepared for the opportunity to speak last week at the Midwest Writing Centers Association meeting in St. Cloud, and here at the Pacific Coast/Inland Northwest Writing Centers meeting in Le Grande. I'll try as I go along to illuminate — or at least to complicate — each of these foci, and I'll conclude by sketching in what I see as a particularly compelling idea of a writing center, one informed by collaboration and, I hope, attuned to diversity.

As some of you may know, I've recently written a book on collaboration, in collaboration with my dearest friend and coauthor, Lisa Ede. *Singular Texts/Plural Authors: Perspectives on Collaborative Writing* was six years in the research and writing, so I would naturally gravitate to principles of collaboration in this or any other address.

Yet it's interesting to me to note that when Lisa and I began our research (see "Why Write . . . Together?"), we didn't even use the term "collaboration"; we identified our subjects as "co- and group-writing." And when we presented our first paper on the subject at the 1985 CCCC meeting, ours was the only such paper at the conference, ours the only presentation with "collaboration" in the title. Now, as you know, the word is everywhere, in every journal, every conference program, on the tip of every scholarly tongue. So — collaboration, yes. But why control? Because as the latest pedagogical bandwagon, collaboration often masquerades as democracy when it in fact practices the same old authoritarian control. It thus stands open to abuse and can, in fact, lead to poor teaching and poor learning. And it can lead — as many of you know — to disastrous results in the writing center. So amidst the rush to embrace collaboration, I see a need for careful interrogation and some caution.

We might begin by asking where the collaboration bandwagon got rolling. Why has it gathered such steam? Because, I believe, collaboration both in theory and practice reflects a broad-based epistemological shift, a shift in the way we view knowledge. The shift involves a move from viewing knowledge and reality as things exterior to or outside of us, as immediately accessible, individually knowable, measurable, and shareable — to viewing knowledge and reality as mediated by or constructed through language in social use, as socially constructed, contextualized, as, in short, the product of *collaboration*.

I'd like to suggest that collaboration as an embodiment of this theory of knowledge poses a distinct threat to one particular idea of a writing center. This idea of a writing center, what I'll call "The Center as Storehouse," holds to the earlier view of knowledge just described — knowledge as exterior to us and as directly accessible. The Center as Storehouse operates as [an] information station or storehouse, prescribing and handing out skills and strategies to individual learners. They often use "modules" or other kinds of individualized learning materials. They tend to view knowledge as individually derived and held, and they are not particularly amenable to collaboration, sometimes actively hostile to it. I visit lots of Storehouse Centers, and in fact I set up such a center myself, shortly after I had finished an M.A. degree and a thesis on William Faulkner.

Since Storehouse Centers do a lot of good work and since I worked very hard to set up one of them, I was loath to complicate or critique such a center. Even after Lisa and I started studying collaboration in earnest, and in spite of the avalanche of data we gathered in support of the premise that collaboration is the norm in most professions (American Consulting Engineers Council, American Institute of Chemists, American Psychological Institute, Modern Language Association, Professional Services Management Association, International City Management Association, Society for Technical Communication), I was still a very reluctant convert.

Why? Because, I believe, collaboration posed another threat to my way of teaching, a way that informs another idea of a writing center, which I'll call "The Center as Garret." Garret Centers are informed by a deep-seated belief in individual "genius," in the Romantic sense of the term. (I need hardly point out that this belief also informs much of the humanities and, in particular, English studies.) These Centers are also informed by a deep-seated attachment to the American brand of individualism, a term coined by Alexis de Tocqueville as he sought to describe the defining characteristics of this Republic.

Unlike Storehouse Centers, Garret Centers don't view knowledge as exterior, as information to be sought out or passed on mechanically. Rather they see knowledge as interior, as inside the student, and the writing center's job as helping students get in touch with this knowledge, as a way to find their unique voices, their individual and unique powers. This idea has been articulated by many, including Ken Macrorie, Peter Elbow, and Don Murray, and the idea usually gets acted out in Murray-like conferences, those in which the tutor or teacher listens, voices encouragement, and essentially serves as a validation of the students' "I-search." Obviously, collaboration problematizes Garret Centers as well, for they also view knowledge as interiorized, solitary, individually derived, individually held.

As I've indicated, I held on pretty fiercely to this idea as well as to the first one. I was still resistant to collaboration. So I took the natural path for an academic faced with this dilemma: I decided to do more research. I did a *lot* of it. And, to my chagrin, I found more and more evidence to challenge my ideas, to challenge both the idea of Centers as Storehouses or as Garrets. Not incidentally, the data I amassed mirrored what my students had been telling me for years: not the research they carried out, not their dogged writing of essays, not *me* even, but their work in groups, their *collaboration,* was the most important and helpful part of their school experience. Briefly, the data I found all support the following claims:

1. Collaboration aids in problem finding as well as problem solving.
2. Collaboration aids in learning abstractions.
3. Collaboration aids in transfer and assimilation; it fosters interdisciplinary thinking.
4. Collaboration leads not only to sharper, more critical thinking (students must explain, defend, adapt), but to deeper understanding of *others.*
5. Collaboration leads to higher achievement in general. I might mention here the Johnson and Johnson analysis of 122 studies from 1924– 1981, which included every North American study that considered achievement or performance data in competitive, cooperative/collaborative, or individualistic classrooms. Some 60% showed that collaboration promoted higher achievement, while only 6% showed the reverse. Among studies comparing the effects of collaboration and independent work, the results are even more strongly in favor of collaboration. Moreover, the superiority of collaboration held for all subject areas and all age groups. See "How to Succeed Without Even Vying," *Psychology Today,* September 1986.
6. Collaboration promotes excellence. In this regard, I am fond of quoting Hannah Arendt: "For excellence, the presence of others is always required."
7. Collaboration engages the whole student and encourages active learning; it combines reading, talking, writing, thinking; it provides practice in both synthetic and analytic skills.

Given these research findings, why am I still urging caution in using collaboration as our key term, in using collaboration as the idea of the kind of writing center I now advocate?

First, because creating a collaborative environment and truly collaborative tasks is damnably difficult. Collaborative environments and tasks must *demand* collaboration. Students, tutors, teachers must really need one another to carry out common goals. As an aside, let me note that studies of collaboration in the workplace identify three kinds of tasks that seem to call consistently for collaboration: high-order problem defining and solving; division of labor tasks, in which the job is simply too big for any one person; and division of expertise tasks. Such tasks are often difficult to come by in writing centers, particularly those based on the Storehouse or Garret models.

A collaborative environment must also be one in which goals are clearly defined and in which the jobs at hand engage everyone fairly equally, from the student clients to work-study students to peer tutors and professional staff. In other words, such an environment rejects traditional hierarchies. In addition, the kind of collaborative environment I want to encourage calls for careful and ongoing monitoring and evaluating of the collaboration or group process, again on the part of all involved. In practice, such monitoring calls on each person involved in the collaboration to build a *theory* of collaboration, a theory of group dynamics.

Building such a collaborative environment is also hard because getting groups of any kind going is hard. The students', tutors', and teachers' prior experiences may work against it (they probably held or still hold to Storehouse or Garret ideas); the school day and term work against it; and the drop-in nature of many centers, including my own, works against it. Against these odds, we have to figure out how to constitute groups in our centers; how to allow for evaluation and monitoring; how to teach, model, and learn about careful listening, leadership, goal setting, and negotiation — all of which are necessary to effective collaboration.

We must also recognize that collaboration is hardly a monolith. Instead, it comes in a dizzying variety of modes about which we know almost nothing. In our books, Lisa and I identify and describe two such modes, the hierarchical and the dialogic, both of which our centers need to be well versed at using. But it stands to reason that these two modes perch only at the tip of the collaborative iceberg.

As I argued earlier, I think we must be cautious in rushing to embrace collaboration because collaboration can also be used to reproduce the status quo; the rigid hierarchy of teacher-centered classrooms is replicated in the tutor-centered writing center in which the tutor is still the seat of all authority but is simply pretending it isn't so. Such a pretense of democracy sends badly mixed messages. It can also lead to the kind of homogeneity that squelches diversity, that waters down ideas to the lowest common denominator, that erases rather than values difference. This tendency is particularly troubling given our growing awareness of the roles gender and ethnicity play in all learning. So regression toward the mean is not a goal I seek in an idea of a writing center based on collaboration.

The issue of control surfaces most powerfully in this concern over a collaborative center. In the writing center ideas I put forward earlier, where is that focus of control? In Storehouse Centers, it seems to me control resides in the tutor or center staff, the possessors of information, the currency of the Academy. Garret Centers, on the other hand, seem to invest power and control in the individual student knower, though I would argue that such control is often appropriated by the tutor/teacher, as I have often seen happen during Murray or Elbow style conferences. Any center based on collaboration will need to address the issue of control explicitly, and doing so will not be easy.

It won't be easy because what I think of as successful collaboration (which I'll call Burkean Parlor Centers), collaboration that is attuned to diversity, goes deeply against the grain of education in America. To illustrate, I need offer only a few representative examples:

1. Mina Shaughnessy, welcoming a supervisor to her classroom in which students were busily collaborating, was told, "Oh . . . I'll come back when you're teaching."
2. A prominent and very distinguished feminist scholar has been refused an endowed chair because most of her work had been written collaboratively.
3. A prestigious college poetry prize was withdrawn after the winning poem turned out to be written by three student collaborators.
4. A faculty member working in a writing center was threatened with dismissal for "encouraging" group-produced documents.

I have a number of such examples, all of which suggest that — used unreflectively or *un*cautiously — collaboration may harm professionally those who seek to use it and may as a result further reify a model of education as the top-down transfer of information (back to The Storehouse) or a private search for Truth (back to The Garret). As I also hope I've suggested, collaboration can easily degenerate into busy work or what Jim Corder calls "fading into the tribe."

So I am very, very serious about the cautions I've been raising, about our need to examine carefully what we mean by collaboration and to explore how those definitions locate control. And yet I still advocate — with growing and deepening conviction — the move to collaboration in both classrooms and centers. In short, I am advocating a third, alternative idea of a writing center, one I know many of you have already brought into being. In spite of the very real risks involved, we need to embrace the idea of writing centers as Burkean Parlors, as centers for collaboration. Only in doing so can we, I believe, enable a student body and citizenry to meet the demands of the twenty-first century. A recent Labor Department report tells us, for instance, that by the mid-1990s workers will need to read at the 11th grade level for even low-paying jobs; that workers will need to be able not so much to solve prepackaged problems but to identify problems amidst a welter of information or data; that they will need to reason from complex symbol systems rather than from simple observations; most of all that they will need to be able to work with others who are different from them and to learn to negotiate power and control (Heath).

The idea of a center I want to advocate speaks directly to these needs, for its theory of knowledge is based not on positivistic principles (that's The Storehouse again), not on Platonic or absolutist ideals (that's The Garret), but on the notion of knowledge as always contextually bound, as always socially constructed. Such a center might well have as its motto Arendt's statement: "For excellence, the presence of others is always required." Such a center would place control, power, and authority not in the tutor or staff, not in the individual student, but in the negotiating group. It would engage students not only in solving problems set by teachers but in identifying problems for themselves; not only in working as a group but in monitoring, evaluating, and building a theory of how groups work; not only in understanding and valuing collaboration but in confronting squarely the issues of control that successful collaboration inevitably raises; not only in reaching consensus but in valuing dissensus and diversity.

The idea of a center informed by a theory of knowledge as socially constructed, of power and control as constantly negotiated and shared, and of collaboration as its first principle presents quite a challenge. It challenges our ways of organizing our centers, of training our staff and tutors, of working with teachers. It even challenges our sense of where we "fit" in this idea. More importantly, however, such a center presents a challenge to the institution of higher education, an institution that insists on rigidly controlled individual performance, on evaluation as punishment, on isolation, on the kinds of values that took that poetry prize away from three young people or that accused Mina Shaughnessy of "not teaching."

This alternative, this third idea of a writing center, poses a threat as well as a challenge to the status quo in higher education. This threat is one powerful and largely invisible reason, I would argue, for the way in which many writing centers have been consistently marginalized, consistently silenced. But organizations like this one are gaining a voice, are finding ways to imagine into being centers as Burkean Parlors for collaboration, writing centers, I believe, which can lead the way in changing the face of higher education.

So, as if you didn't already know it, you're a subversive group, and I'm delighted to have been invited to participate in this collaboration. But I've been talking far too long by myself now, so I'd like to close by giving the floor to two of my student collaborators. The first — like I was — was a reluctant convert to the kind of collaboration I've been describing tonight. But here's what she wrote to me some time ago:

> Dr. Lunsford: I don't know exactly what to say here, but I want to say something. So here goes. When this Writing Center class first began, I didn't know what in the hell you meant by collaboration. I thought — hey! yo! — you're the teacher and you know a lot of stuff. And you better tell it to me. Then I can

tell it to the other guys. Now I know that you know even more than I thought. I even found out I know a lot. But that's not important. What's important is knowing that knowing doesn't just happen all by itself, like the cartoons show with a little light bulb going off in a bubble over a character's head. Knowing happens with other people, figuring things out, trying to explain, talking through things. What I know is that we are all making and remaking our knowing and ourselves with each other every day — you just as much as me and the other guys, Dr. Lunsford. We're all — all of us together — collaborative re-creations in process. So — well — just wish me luck.

And here's a note I received just as I got on the plane, from another student/ collaborator:

I had believed that Ohio State had nothing more to offer me in the way of improving my writing. Happily, I was mistaken. I have great expectations for our Writing Center Seminar class. I look forward to every one of our classes and to every session with my 110W students [2 groups of 3 undergraduates he is tutoring]. I sometimes feel that they have more to offer me than I to them. They say the same thing, though, so I guess we're about even, all learning together. (P.S. This class and the Center have made me certain I want to attend graduate school.)

These students embody the kind of center I'm advocating, and I'm honored to join them in conversation about it, conversation we can continue together now.

Works Cited

Corder, Jim W. "Hunting for Ethos Where They Say It Can't Be Found." *Rhetoric Review* 7 (1989): 299–316.

Ede, Lisa S., and Andrea A. Lunsford. "Why Write . . . Together?" *Rhetoric Review* 1 (1983): 150–58.

———. *Singular Texts/Plural Authors: Perspectives on Collaborative Writing*. Carbondale: Southern Illinois UP, 1990.

Heath, Shirley Brice. "The Fourth Vision: Literate Language at Work." *The Right to Literacy*. Ed. Andrea A. Lunsford, Helen Moglen, and James Slevin. New York: Modern Language Association, 1990.

Khon, Alfie. "How to Succeed Without Even Vying." *Psychology Today* Sept. 1986: 22–28.

Really Useful Knowledge:
A Cultural Studies Agenda for Writing Centers

Marilyn M. Cooper _____

MICHIGAN TECHNOLOGICAL UNIVERSITY

In this article, Marilyn Cooper discusses tutors' roles in helping students understand the cultural constraints that affect their writing. Instead of simply serving as unthinking purveyors of university traditions and rules, she says, tutors should become "organic intellectuals," who fuse theory and practice into a temporarily cohesive whole — a subject position from which they can critique, and seek to reform, not only the dominant social order but also their own pedagogy. She suggests that a writing center rooted in a cultural studies approach can help to empower student writers by teaching them to find within professors' restrictive writing assignments autonomous spaces from which to address their own experiences and beliefs. In comparison with earlier discussions of writing center theory and practice, which tend to portray tutors as neutral helpers, Cooper's article, which originally appeared in The Writing Center Journal *in 1994, complicates our view of writing center interactions. Perhaps most importantly, it introduces tutors to critical pedagogy, urging them to examine how their own culture and the politics of the university influence their work with student writers.*

People — not just my students — often tell me that as a writing teacher, I am "different" (if they're being polite) or "crazy" or "bizarre" (if they're being frank). I believe students should be intellectually challenged in their writing classes, that they need to be engaged in a struggle over complex ideas that matter to them. I give them hard books to read, I ask them hard questions, I ask them to make up their own assignments. I believe that college students are completely capable of reading hard books and writing in interesting ways. I also know that they often don't believe that, and that they have faced a variety of obstacles that have taught them that they are "bad" or "nonstandard" or (what is sometimes worse) "good" writers. Changing their attitude toward writing and their understanding of what it means to write well is a long and difficult task, not to be achieved in one or two classes or by a single teacher. So as a writing teacher I see writing centers as essential places where students can go to continue the conversations about ideas begun in class and in electronic conferences, to find people they can complain to, to work out solutions to the problems they face in their writing, to find a friend and a colleague and an advocate — all of those things I cannot really be for them. But because I have also worked with the writing center research group at MTU and am now directing dissertations by a number of graduate students who are doing research in the writing center, I also see writing centers as a site of a great deal of exciting research, a site where we can really begin to see what goes on with students' writing and what keeps them from writing.

The question I have already begun to answer — what is the function of writing centers? or, as it is alternatively framed, what is the role of the writing center tutor or coach or consultant in teaching writing? — is, I would venture to say, the central concern of recent discussions of writing centers. In fact, the ongoing discussion over what to call writing center tutors is a good demonstration of the centrality of this concern. I want to align myself with certain answers to this question: that writing centers are in a good position to serve as a site of critique of the institutionalized structure of writing instruction in college, and that, as a consequence of this, the role of the tutor should be to create useful knowledge about writing in college and to empower students as writers who also understand what writing involves and who act as agents in their writing — these two goals being closely intertwined. Since I know that writing centers vary a lot from site to site, I should say at the outset that I am thinking primarily about writing centers that are staffed by undergraduate students and that allow students to work over a period of time with a single tutor, although I believe that all types of writing centers and all kinds of tutors can have the function and role I describe. I should also say that my ideas about these questions have been most heavily influenced by Nancy Grimm, who directs the writing center at Michigan Tech and who has written very directly about a critical role for writing centers. Nancy says, "Writing centers are places where students struggle to connect their public and private lives, and where they learn that success in the academy depends on uncovering and understanding tacit differences in value systems and expectations" (5). In this struggle, students and their tutors come to know a lot about the real situation of college writing.

What I want to do here is to develop a rationale for thinking of writing centers as having the essential function of critiquing institutions and creating knowledge about writing, a rationale that will make clear the politics of such a belief and that will connect the goal of inquiry with the daily practice of writing center tutors. This rationale also will have clear implications for what tutors should know and how they should be trained. But I'd like to start by suggesting why it is useful to think of writing centers in this way by looking closely at some advice on tutoring offered by Jeff Brooks in his article on minimalist tutoring that came out in 1991 in the *Writing Lab Newsletter.*

I chose Brooks' article because it has been widely admired and because it enunciates very clearly some oft-heard advice for tutors. I also like a great deal of what he suggests, particularly his emphasis on tutors' responsiveness to students and on students as active writers. He argues that tutors should not be in the business of "fixing" student papers but rather should focus on students as writers, offering them strategies and support and encouraging them to fix their own papers; he says, "The student, not the tutor, should 'own' the paper and take full responsibility for it. The tutor should take on a secondary role, serving mainly to keep the student focused on his own writing" (2). He goes on to suggest how this principle can be implemented, pointing out that "The primary value of the writing center tutor to the student is as a living human body who is willing to sit patiently and help the student spend time with her paper" (2). He offers a list of "ways we can put theory into practice" (3) and concludes, "If, at the end of the session, a paper is improved, it should be because the student did all the work" (4).

Perhaps because I am "outside" the writing center culture, I did also find a couple of things odd in Brooks' suggestions. For one thing, almost all of his specific suggestions involve tactics designed to distance tutors from students' papers in order to "establish the student as sole owner of the paper and [the tutor] as merely an interested outsider" (4). I worry about the notion of students' owning papers, and this worry connects with the other thing I find odd in Brooks' suggestions: the focus on improving individual student papers. Brooks repeatedly asserts that in writing center sessions tutors are not to focus on papers but instead on students and on their writing. But students are still expected to focus on their papers, and thus their individual papers remain the focus of writing center sessions.

Now, of course, in some ways this is not odd: students overwhelmingly show up at writing centers to get help with particular papers and particular assignments, and it would be incredibly perverse for writing center tutors simply to refuse to respond to this very real need. At the same time, it is not obvious to me — even though classroom teachers often believe this — that helping students fix papers is or should be the central purpose of writing centers, and I expect many of you agree with me on this. But I also think that it is this assumption that writing center sessions must focus on improving individual papers that leads to the trap Brooks describes, the trap of tutors serving as editors of student papers, and that leads to his emphasizing negative tactics that help tutors to refuse that role.

When writing center sessions remain resolutely focused on how a student can fix a paper, it is difficult for tutors to focus instead on what students know and need to know about writing. In such sessions, tutors can find little to do other than directly fix papers, indirectly show students how to fix papers, or simply abdicate all responsibility for mistakes in papers. Though Brooks asserts that "we forget that students write to learn, not to make perfect papers," he remains fixated on the notion of perfection in student texts: "student writing . . . has no real goal beyond getting it on the page," he says, and, "Most students simply do not have the skill, experience, or talent to write the perfect paper" (3). Given these assumptions, it is not at all surprising that, as Brooks says, "writing papers is a dull and unrewarding activity for most students" (2). Nor do I think that, in this situation, simply insisting that students take responsibility for their papers and treat them as valuable will either change their attitude toward writing in college or help them learn much about writing.

In order to make my point, I've emphasized how Brooks' suggestions lead to a focus on fixing student papers. But clearly, other things besides editing for effectiveness and correctness go on in the kind of writing center sessions he is talking about. Tutors help students learn processes of writing by helping them figure out what an assignment asks them to do or by helping them brainstorm in response to assignments. By asking students, "What do you mean by this?" tutors help students learn that readers often need more information or explanation in order to understand what writers had in mind. By asking students, "What's your reason for putting Q before N?" and similar questions, tutors help students learn to think about the decisions they make in writing as reasonable rather than simply a matter of following rules. By asking students to read final drafts aloud in order to find mistakes, tutors help students learn that they can correct many of their own mistakes. As long as students understand that it is what they are learning about writing in these activities that is important, not that their papers are being improved, these are useful things to do.

This, of course, is the position advocated by Stephen North in the axiom which has become a writing center mantra: "Our job is to produce better writers, not better writing." North explains,

> Any given project — a class assignment, a law school application, an encyclopedia entry, a dissertation proposal — is for the writer the prime, often the exclusive concern. That particular text, its success or failure, is what brings them to talk to us in the first place. In the center, though, we look beyond or through that particular project, that particular text, and see it as an occasion for addressing *our* primary concern, the process by which it is produced. (438)

In other words, tutors can use the situation of students writing particular papers to focus on what students know and need to know about college writing. Brooks certainly has activities like this in mind when he suggests that tutors have better things to do with their time than to edit student papers, when he says that "we sit down with imperfect papers, but our job is to improve their writers" (2). But North's formulation of this position also makes clear how the goals of students and tutors can conflict: students come for help in making their document perfect (for very good reasons, like getting into law school, getting their dissertation proposal approved, passing the course and getting their degree) and are confronted with tutors who have their own primary concern, a concern with the process of writing. In this situation, I think that tutors must not only make clear what their concern in tutoring sessions is but also explain why they think this concern should be primary for students as well, and they must negotiate a common goal in their sessions, one that does not simply ignore the students' concerns. If tutors are not upfront about their concerns, they risk losing track of them as they strive to help students or frustrating and confusing students with their uncooperativeness — both of these reactions seem inevitable in the kind of minimalist tutoring Brooks describes.

At the same time, in spite of the problems I see in Brooks' suggestions for minimalist tutoring, I think he is reaching for a purpose for writing centers beyond that enunciated by North. Brooks wants students to get more from writing center session than just instruction in how to write well. In his insistence that "we need to make the student the primary agent in the writing center session" (2) and that "ideally the student should be the only active agent in improving the paper" (4), I hear the desire to empower students as agents that has characterized many recent calls for reforms in writing pedagogy. It is a desire I heartily endorse, but also one that has turned out to be decidedly difficult to enact. One of the difficulties in implementing this goal arises, as

Lester Faigley has pointed out, from the strong rationalist and expressivist traditions in composition studies that encourage us to see agency in writing as Brooks does in his article, in terms of owning or taking responsibility for a text. These are the same traditions Andrea Lunsford sees operating to produce the notions of the writing center as a storehouse of positivistic knowledge or as a garret where individual students get in touch with their genius.

As Lunsford points out, both traditions "tend to view knowledge as individually derived" (4), and, as Faigley points out, both traditions deny "the role of language in constructing selves" (128). For both rationalists and expressivists, knowledge and writing are dependent on a preexisting coherent and rational self. Given this assumption, agency in writing becomes a matter of subduing the text to the self by achieving personal control over it, either by creating it in a rational and coherent point of view on the topic addressed, a point of view that is dependent on the rational and coherent self of the writer, or by expressing one's personal vision or true self in it — often referred to as achieving an authentic voice. Unfortunately, as the modern world taught us that selves (or, as we learned to call them, subject positions) are constantly in the process of construction and that one of the activities that contributes most to the construction of subject positions is language use (including writing), we came to understand that writers cannot and do not achieve agency in writing by subduing language to their selves but rather by using language to construct subject positions. Agency in writing depends not on owning or taking responsibility for a text but on understanding how to construct subject positions in texts. From Brooks' point of view, it is ironic, then, that what this comes down to is that tutors can best help students become agents of their own writing by helping them understand how and the extent to which they are *not* owners of their texts and *not* responsible for the shape of their texts, by helping them understand, in short, how various institutional forces impinge on how and what they write and how they can negotiate a place for their own goals and needs when faced with these forces.

Students know that they don't own their texts only too well, and tutors know it too, but the overwhelming discourse in textbooks, classroom advice, training materials for teachers and tutors, and in much of the scholarship and research in composition studies on the importance of individual control in producing writing works to obscure this fact and to keep both students and tutors from realizing what they know. In her *Writing Center Journal* article, Nancy Welch observes,

> my work in the writing center at a large public university has also introduced me to students who arrive at the center already aware, sometimes painfully so, that their meanings are contested and that their words are populated with competing, contradictory voices. . . . Even alone, these students write with and against a cacophony of voices, collaborating not with another person but with the Otherness of their words. (4)

Students and tutors who are outside mainstream culture are usually more aware of the way language coerces them, but all students and tutors know how institutions coerce them in writing classes. They know that students in writing classes are offered and can exercise little or no control over such things as the topic or genre of their papers, and the style or register of language in their papers. Students know that in order to get a good grade they must carefully follow assignments that specify these things, and tutors are advised explicitly not to criticize or in any way try to subvert teachers' assignments. Students and tutors respond — quite rationally — by trying to make the papers match as perfectly as possible the specifications of assignments while at the same time — quite irrationally — trying to believe that in doing this students are asserting ownership over their texts and learning to write. Meg Woolbright says, "In thinking one thing and saying another, the tutor is subverting the conflict she feels" (23); she is not being honest, and thus she subverts her chances of establishing egalitarian conversations with her students and alienates both herself and them (28–29).

But if tutors need to help students — and themselves — realize that what they know about institutional constraints is true and important, they also need to help students understand that if they are to achieve agency in writing, they must learn how to challenge these constraints productively in the service of their own goals and needs. Agency in writing is not a matter of simply taking up the subject positions offered by assignments but of actively constructing subject positions that negotiate between institutional demands and individual needs. In his discussion of what cultural studies offers to teachers of writing, John Trimbur explains that "one of the central tasks that [cultural studies] sets for radical intellectuals is to point out the relatively autonomous areas of public and private life where human agency can mediate between the material conditions of the dominant order and the lived experience and aspirations of the popular masses" (9). Because writing assignments, no matter how tightly specified, require the active participation of human agents, they offer relatively autonomous spaces in which the institutional constraints on writing imposed by the dominant order can be made to respond to the lived experience and aspirations of students.

If tutors want to help students develop agency in writing, they need to cast themselves as radical intellectuals who help students find and negotiate these spaces. Such tutors cannot, as Stephen North advises them to do, simply help students operate within the existing context without trying to change it. And, yes, I *am* thinking about undergraduate tutors, whose cogent critiques of assignments often leak out in writing center sessions even when they don't make them explicit. Furthermore, in helping students become agents of their own writing, tutors also become agents of change in writing pedagogy, helping teachers create better assignments, letting teachers know what students are having trouble with. As intellectuals, tutors contribute both to the endeavor of helping students learn about writing and to the endeavor of creating useful knowledge about writing. Speaking of what tutors can learn and how they can affect writing pedagogy, Nancy Grimm says,

> Our excursions into students' heads, like our excursions into films and novels, change the way we see and the way we act and the way we think and the way we teach. Our promise to support the teachers' position completely prevents us from sharing these altered perspectives that can in turn change the rhetorical context of teaching. In a writing center, one discovers how smart students are and how arbitrary and limiting linguistic conventions and educational hierarchies can be. (6)

And, I want to argue, it is in a writing center that one discovers how the goal of empowering students as agents of their writing can actually be achieved, for writing center tutors, by virtue of their constant contact with institutional constraints *and* with students' lived experiences, are best positioned to serve as what Trimbur calls radical intellectuals, or what Gramsci calls organic intellectuals.

In order for you to better understand why I believe that the goal of empowering students can best be achieved in a writing center and why tutors are more likely to be organic intellectuals than are classroom teachers of writing, I now want to explain the rationale that underlies my argument. To do so, I will draw on some theories that are connected with work in cultural studies and especially on the ideas of a theorist who has arguably had the most influence on cultural studies, Antonio Gramsci. Gramsci's work has also heavily influenced Paulo Freire, and recently we have begun to see some direct influences of Gramsci in composition studies. As a member of the Communist Party in Italy, Gramsci was arrested by Mussolini in 1924. In his trial, the prosecutor claimed, "We must stop this brain working for twenty years!" But, during the eight years he spent in prison, Gramsci wrote 2,848 pages in thirty-two notebooks, working out his theories of how social groups gain legitimacy and power, how political change comes about, and, most importantly for us as writing teachers, what role intellectuals and education play in this process.

Gramsci argues that the function of education in a democratic society is to produce intellectuals, for "democracy, by definition, cannot mean merely that an unskilled worker can become skilled. It must mean that every 'citizen' can 'govern' and that society places him, even if only abstractly, in a general condition to achieve this" (40). According to Gramsci, everyone is on some level and potentially an intellectual:

> each man . . . carries on some form of intellectual activity, that is, he is a "philosopher," an artist, a man of taste, he participates in a particular conception of the world, has a conscious line of moral conduct, and therefore contributes to sustain a conception of the world or to modify it, that is, to bring into being new modes of thought. (9)

Thus, intellectuals are produced not by "introducing from scratch a scientific form of thought into everyone's individual life, but [by] renovating and making 'critical' an already existing activity" (330–31). According to Gramsci, intellectuals become intellectuals not by virtue of any inherent qualifications but by virtue of their efforts to elaborate critically and systematically the philosophy of their social group.

When a social group becomes well established and dominant, its intellectuals often come to see what they do as valuable in and of itself and see themselves as somehow specially qualified for intellectual activities; they lose sight of how their activities function primarily to further the goals of their particular social group. These intellectuals are what Gramsci calls traditional intellectuals, intellectuals who because of their tenure as the intellectuals of a successful and powerful social group come to see themselves as "autonomous and independent of the dominant social group" (7). A second characteristic of traditional intellectuals is that they are the apologists for a dominant group whose vision is failing, whose ideas are no longer productive in a changing society. In his recent article on Gramsci in Pre/Text, Victor Villanueva offers E. D. Hirsch as a good example of an American traditional intellectual, an apologist for the status quo whose recommendations for instilling cultural literacy in all students, though well intentioned, are neither disinterested nor progressive, but rather serve the interests of an established but increasingly discredited elite.

Traditional intellectuals are no longer agents of change in a society for these two reasons: they have lost contact with the purposes and goals of the group whose philosophy they represent, and they serve, although often unknowingly, the status quo. Organic intellectuals, in contrast, are those intellectuals who understand that their function as intellectuals derives from their involvement in the work and the purposes of their social group. Furthermore, they are the intellectuals of an emergent social group, one which is not yet dominant but whose vision is more directly responsive to the current historical conditions of the society than that of the dominant group, whose vision developed out of past historical conditions. Organic intellectuals exemplify the basic marxist postulate of the unity of theory and practice. Gramsci calls them "the whalebone in the corset," "*elites* . . . of a new type which arise directly out of the masses, but remain in contact with them" (340).

Organic intellectuals are agents of change because they develop through their fusion of theory and practice and through critique of the common sense of their group the philosophy of an emergent social group. Both contact with everyday practice and critique are important in this process. Contact with everyday practice ensures that the philosophy of the group more accurately represents the real historical situation; critique of the commonsense knowledge of the group frees it from the influence of the views and beliefs of the dominant social group, who have achieved power in large part because of their success in persuading all groups in a society that their world view is true and useful. Organic intellectuals must work to achieve critical understanding of the current situation of a society; they must sort through the various arguments and perspectives that are represented in the common sense of their group in order to produce what Richard Johnson has called really useful knowledge, knowledge that arises out of everyday practice and that is purified of contradictory beliefs left over from the world view of the dominant group. In Johnson's terms, critique is always an ongoing process that resists closure and is antithetical to the procedures of academic codification and disciplinarity, for critique offers "procedures by which other traditions are approached both for what they may yield and for what they inhibit" (38). Ongoing critique ensures that organic intellectuals do not turn into traditional intellectuals, that really useful knowledge is not turned into disciplinary knowledge, that knowledge is continually produced in the contact of theory and practice. Really useful knowledge, Johnson argues, demands that the priority always be "to become more 'popular' rather than more academic" (40).

To return now from the realms of theory to the situation of students writing in college, I want to argue that composition studies and its scholars and researchers and classroom teachers function for the most part as traditional intellectuals of the dominant social group, intellectuals who have lost sight of how their beliefs and practices are dependent on the world view of the white middle class of America and whose everyday experience is quite separate from and foreign to the life experiences of most students in college writing classes. Some scholars and teachers, it is true, struggle to remain in contact with the everyday experience of students in writing classes and struggle to define their problems and practices on the basis of this contact, but neither scholars nor classroom teachers of writing are favorably positioned to succeed in this effort. Whether scholars or teachers, whether regular faculty, part-time teachers, or graduate students, their position in the writing classroom is guaranteed by the institutional structures of the dominant social group: they are responsible to standards developed by this group in service to its purposes; they are subject to education and training that has developed within the perspective of the dominant group; they are in daily contact with the discourse of other traditional intellectuals; and, finally, they are usually expected to separate theory from practice. In the case of faculty and graduate students they are admonished that their own work should have priority over teaching, and, in the case of part-time teachers, they are subjected to work loads that preclude efforts at reflection and critique and theory building. It is thus not surprising that it is difficult for classroom writing teachers to empower students as agents of their own writing, for the main prerequisite of such an endeavor is, as Freire has long pointed out, having some idea of what students' purposes and experiences are.

In contrast, tutors in writing centers who are in close contact with students and their everyday writing concerns, who reflect on their practices as tutors, and who study and critique theories of writing and language in light of their practice are better positioned to be organic intellectuals, who, along with their students, develop really useful knowledge of writing practices and of ways of teaching writing that help students achieve agency. Because writing centers are marginalized in relation to the central institutional structures of writing pedagogy and because writing center tutors are not generally expected to perform the function of intellectuals, the pressure on them to promulgate beliefs and practices that serve the purposes of the dominant group is less organized and less direct, although it is certainly not absent. North details some of the informal attempts of faculty to bring writing center practice into line with the authorized knowledge about writing, and his widely followed stricture that tutors are to support the classroom teacher's position completely is clear evidence of how writing centers do not escape domination. Yet one of the benefits of being excluded from the dominant group is that in this position one has less to protect and less to lose. Undergraduate students who serve as tutors have little investment in disciplinary beliefs and practices, and they are thus less responsive to its standards and expectations than they are to the needs and experiences of their peers. And, even for classroom teachers and graduate students, the continuous contact with the needs and experiences of writing students moves tutors to critique, to observe both what the traditional practices of writing instruction yield and what they inhibit.

I could continue to argue in support of my contention that tutors should and can serve as agents of change who empower students and who produce really useful knowledge, but I suspect that I can win your agreement better in another way. I want to conclude by recounting examples of how this is already happening in writing centers across the country. Following are five examples of practices of tutors and writing center administrators that seem to me to exemplify how writing centers can serve as a site of critique and how tutors can function as organic intellectuals.

1. Alice Gillam draws on Bakhtin to suggest a dialogic approach to tutoring that encourages students to negotiate between the demands of an assignment and their own interests in writing. She asks "whether the univocal conventional wisdom about reading ought to organize [a particular student's] interpretation of her [reading] experience or whether [the student's] experiences ought to reorganize or complicate conventional wisdom" (6), and she suggests that

> opening or dialogizing this text through the play of oppositions might enable Mary to see ways of satisfying her teacher's demand for focus without sacrificing [her own] richness of voice and detail. . . . Rather than stripping her "story" to the bone in order to impose a focus, perhaps Mary needs to flesh out the contradictions embedded in the text and puzzle over the off-key shifts in voice as a way of discovering focus. . . . In short, a Bakhtinian perspective might have allowed [Mary's tutor] to help Mary see the dissonances in voice and narrative as opportunities to dialogize and clarify meaning rather than as the enemies of focus, as forces to be subdued and "normalized." (7)

2. Lucy Chang demonstrates how through conversation with a Chinese student she "came to understand the cultural reasoning" that dictated the

shape of the student's paper, which she describes as "a chaotic dance of ten letter words" (17). She found out that

> First, in China a scholar's intellectual power is measured by the number of Chinese characters he or she knows, not by how coherently words are arranged as this particular assignment demanded. Second, the words she knew in English translated into something else, a distant relative of her initial thought. She believed that with one English word she could express everything she was feeling as she could with one Chinese character. Third, she believed that good writing was the kind that is found in textbooks, language that is condensed and lacking in emotion. The confusion and conflict began here. Last, her deficiency in English grammar was a huge insecurity. As a result, she took no responsibility for her writing, as a means of protecting herself from the shame of her grammatical mistakes. (17–18)

Chang concludes, "From this collective understanding, I believe that I was better equipped to facilitate her writing process" (18). Chang's experience contrasts strikingly with the experience of the tutor described by Anne DiPardo, whose ignorance of her Native American student's culture and experiences with writing frustrated all her persistent and well-intentioned efforts to help the student succeed.

3. Kate Latterell, in exploring the actual practices of student-centered tutoring, discovers that, for the two tutors she interviewed,

> being student-centered . . . does not seem to mean being passive, for they both stressed the importance of developing personal relationships with students as being a big factor. . . . Suzanne . . . suggests that "the more effective teaching that I've seen happens in places like this . . . where there's personal interaction and personal factors that are helping out." And Dave seems to suggest the same thing, saying, "I really believe very strongly in the powerful influences of individual and personal relationships" in making learning meaningful. (10)

Dave also refers to the importance of active engagement between tutor and student when he tells Kate that his idea of what tutoring involves has changed "'from believing that this is totally undirected stuff' to thinking that his role is to provide a focus for the session by 'keying in on' what the student needs to talk about" (9).

4. Drawing on Julia Kristeva's notion of exile as the creation of a space in which writers can question received knowledge and social norms and in the process transform them, Nancy Welch elaborates a style of tutoring that enables both tutors and students to achieve critical distance. She recounts her work with Margie, who is engaged in writing about the experience of sexual harassment for a panel discussion during the university's annual Women's Week. Welch notes how, early in the process, she has "already constructed a template of what [Margie] should eventually write for her Women's Week panel" and is "disturbed by the gap between that 'Ideal Text' (to borrow

Knoblauch and Brannon's term) and the actual text [Margie] reads to" her and how, when she resists "the pressure of perfection," Margie "displaces that template text I had formed and encourages me to listen to her emerging text instead" (9–10). At the end of a prolonged series of sessions, when Margie is about to write a draft of the actual presentation, Welch offers her only one suggestion, that she remind herself to describe what happened to her. Welch recounts Margie's reaction: "Margie grins. 'Sure, I get it,' she replies. 'I still tend to avoid that. Yeah. The monster needs a description. *I* can do that. *I* know what the monster looks like'" (16).

5. Tom Fox describes the tutor training program at Chico in which tutors are asked "to reflect critically on how social and educational inequalities affect writing and learning" and how he explores with tutors "how the institution around us is shot through with actual hierarchies and habits of hierarchies and how we more easily fall into these habits than into a truly democratic writing center, no matter whether the tables are round or square" (21). His tutors read theory — "Paulo Friere on how all education is political, Dale Spender, Richard Ohmann, Geneva Smitherman-Donaldson, and John Ogbu on how gender, class, and race affect language use, and . . . Mike Rose on how institutional history and politics shape our conceptions of writing, especially remedial writing" (22–23) — and they reflect on their own practices and educational histories. Fox concludes,

> When tutors reflect on and define their own role in a multi-cultural writing center and explore the relationship between a progressive writing center and a conservative university, they gain a sense of control over the interpretation of their experience. This control can lead to action both within and without the writing center. (23)

In these practices I see the beginnings of a vision of a writing center as a site of inquiry and critique, where tutors not only are helping students learn how to improve their writing but also are developing better practices of teaching writing and really useful knowledge about the experiences of students writing in college and in our society. Rather than "always focusing on the paper at hand" (Brooks 2), tutors build personal relationships with their students and come to understand how their students' lives and experiences shape their writing practices. Rather than insisting that students are the only ones responsible for their texts, tutors help students understand how their words and their texts are inhabited by multiple and often alien voices that they must learn to deal with. Rather than "supporting the teacher's position completely" (North 441), tutors help students negotiate a place within the confines of writing assignments for interests and abilities that arise out of their experiences. Rather than lamenting the inability of students to produce perfect papers, tutors celebrate students' ability to develop new "templates" for texts. Rather than learning to sit across from the student and not write on their papers, tutors learn to critique the social and institutional setting of writing pedagogy and to reflect on their practices in light of theories of writing and language.

I think we can push this vision further. I would like, for example, to see writing center sessions sometimes focus on the critical reading of the syllabuses and assignments that students are given to work with so that tutors could help students see what subject positions are being offered to them in these texts and what spaces are left open in which they can construct different subject positions. Classroom teachers occasionally try to get their students to engage in such critical readings, but the teachers' investment in the subjectivities they have imagined for their students fairly regularly defeats their efforts. In critical reading sessions in writing centers, tutors could also help students figure out why their teachers' ideas of what they need to learn sometimes conflict with what they think they need to learn and how recognizing these conflicts can lead to change as well as to accommodation.

I would also like to see tutor training seminars begin to blend with research groups, so that faculty, writing center administrators, and/or graduate students work together with undergraduate tutors and with the students who come to writing centers to develop systematic inquiries into the nature of writing in college and the value of different methods of teaching writing. I know that this is happening in some writing centers, and I think that in such research we can begin to bridge the chasm that often separates writing center workers from classroom teachers and theorists of writing. Writing centers are and can be at the heart of our joint inquiry into the functions of literacy in our society. We need to make better use of these "border" spaces within our institutions, spaces where the lines of power blur and the demands of discipline and evaluation weaken in ways that allow us to create together better ways of writing and of teaching writing.

Works Cited

Brooks, Jeff. "Minimalist Tutoring: Making the Student Do All the Work." *Writing Lab Newsletter* 15.6 (1991): 1–4.

DiPardo, Anne. "'Whispers of Coming and Going': Lessons from Fannie." *The Writing Center Journal* 12.2 (Spring 1992): 125–44.

Faigley, Lester. *Fragments of Rationality: Postmodernity and the Subject of Composition.* Pittsburgh: U of Pittsburgh P, 1992.

Gillam, Alice M. "Writing Center Ecology: A Bakhtinian Perspective." *The Writing Center Journal* 12.2 (Spring/Summer 1992): 3–11.

Gramsci, Antonio. *Selections from the Prison Notebooks.* Ed. and tr. Quintin Hoare and Geoffrey Nowell Smith. New York: International, 1971.

Grimm, Nancy. "Contesting 'The Idea of a Writing Center': The Politics of Writing Center Research." *Writing Lab Newsletter* 17.1 (September 1992): 5–6.

Johnson, Richard. "What Is Cultural Studies Anyway?" *Social Text* 16 (1986/87): 38–80.

Latterell, Kate. "Revising Our Roles: Writing Center Coaches Talk about Their Roles." Paper delivered at the Midwest Writing Center Association, St. Louis, Missouri. 1 Oct. 1993.

Lunsford, Andrea. "Collaboration, Control, and the Idea of a Writing Center." *The Writing Center Journal* 12.1 (Fall 1991): 3–10.

North, Stephen M. "The Idea of a Writing Center." *College English* 46 (1984): 433–46.

Okawa, Gail Y., Thomas Fox, Lucy J. Y. Chang, Shana R. Windsor, Frank Bella Chavez, Jr., and LaGuan Hayes. "Multi-cultural Voices: Peer Tutoring and Critical Reflection in the Writing Center." *The Writing Center Journal* 12.1 (Fall 1991): 11–33.

Trimbur, John. "Cultural Studies and Teaching Writing." *Focuses* 1 (1988): 5–18. Villanueva, Victor, Jr. "Hegemony: From an Organically Grown Intellectual." *Pre/Text* 13 (1992): 18–34.

Welch, Nancy. "From Silence to Noise: The Writing Center as Critical Exile." *The Writing Center Journal* 14.1 (Fall 1993): 3–15.

Woolbright, Meg. "The Politics of Tutoring: Feminism within the Patriarchy." *The Writing Center Journal* 13.1 (Fall 1992): 16–30.

The Politics of Tutoring: Feminism within the Patriarchy

Meg Woolbright _____

SIENA COLLEGE

Meg Woolbright argues that a hidden curriculum privileges those who surrender to patriarchal values in the academy and urges writing center tutors to adopt a feminist perspective while working with student writers. She compares writing center and feminist pedagogies and finds similarities in their egalitarian agendas, interactive teaching methods, emphasis on the personal, and conflicts with the patriarchy over the distribution of power. At the same time, citing an example of an ostensibly feminist tutor who unintentionally dominates a student writer, she shows that the goal of helping a writer achieve academic success can overwhelm the feminist goals of sharing power and liberating the student's voice. Woolbright concludes that good tutoring requires tutors to openly acknowledge and confront the hidden agenda in their own practices. Her article, which originally appeared in The Writing Center Journal in 1992, serves as an important introduction to feminist tutoring and as a reminder to tutors to continually examine their own practices.

> *And why don't you write? Write! Writing is for you, you are for you. . . . I know why you haven't written . . . Because writing is at once too high, too great for you, it's reserved for the great — that is for "great men"; and it's "silly" . . . Write, let no one hold you back, let nothing stop you. . . . (246)*
> — Hélène Cixous

Feminist rhetoric has been described as very different from the traditional, patriarchal discourse of the academy. And although Hélène Cixous asserts in "The Laugh of the Medusa" that "it is impossible to define a feminine practice of writing," (253) for doing so would encode it, stifle it, in a masculinist framework, she does admit that we can "give form to its movement" (253) as we approximate its "near and distant byways" (253). The characteristics of this rhetoric have been variously described as its vibrancy, its personal voice, its sensuousness and open-endedness, set in striking contrast to the linear, objective, abstract, tightly argued prose of the academy. In "The Female and Male Modes of Rhetoric," Thomas J. Farrell describes the differences this way: "The female mode seems at times to obfuscate the boundary between the self of the author and the subject of the discourse, as well as between the self and the audience, whereas the male mode tends to accentuate such boundaries" (910). A dichotomy similar to that between feminist and patriarchal rhetoric can be seen in much current scholarship on feminist pedagogy.

In a recent volume of the *NWSA Journal,* Amy Shapiro describes a model for the feminist classroom, one based not on the traditional paradigm of knowledge as power, but on understanding as power. With this model, the classroom becomes not an arena of confrontation and debate focused on winners who "know" more than losers, but a place for conversation among equals. Students come to realize that they have authority, that they can learn from each other, and that through their conversations they can shape the knowledge of the discourse. Of the teacher's role in this conversation, Shapiro says that she "becomes a model in the sense that she must be the ultimate learner. Her role is to integrate and assist the students in articulating the texts to themselves and each other" (79). The goal of this pedagogy is "to liberate the tortured voice" (Juncker 428) imprisoned in what Verena Andermatt calls the "phallogocentric system of representation" (39). Our students, says Cixous, need to write themselves.

The difficulty with these simple constructs is, of course, that in being simple constructs they are, albeit tempting, by and large misleading. In constructing these categories, our aim is to blur differences, and to focus on commonalities, on what makes up the essence or foundation of feminism and the patriarchy. Attempting to use these constructs to describe a dynamic interaction is tricky stuff. Those of us who consider ourselves academic feminists — whether we are male or female — do not choose feminism *or* the patriarchy, so much as we do at all times situate our feminism *within* a deeply-seated patriarchal academy. When our feminist values of community and equality find some space within the power of the patriarchy, the result is not an Aristotelian either/or but a complex web of conflict. Nancy Sommers has recently said that "these either/or ways of seeing exclude life . . . by pushing us to safe positions, to what is known. They are safe positions that exclude each other and don't allow for any ambiguity, uncertainty" (29). She suggests that we look at the juncture of either *and* or.

For those of us who teach writing, whether in the classroom or in a writing center, the conflicts that result at the boundary between feminist rhetoric and pedagogy and the patriarchal values of the academy are manifested in our conversations with student writers. These conversations are dynamic, and as such are fraught with uncertainty and ambiguity. As Nancy Schniedewind asserts, in these conversations students learn at least as much from our practices, what she calls the "hidden curriculum" (170), as they do from our theories. In order to determine if our "hidden curriculum" suggests feminist values, Schniedewind suggests five process goals against which we can measure our interactions with students. These are the development of an atmosphere of mutual respect, trust, and community; shared leadership; a cooperative structure; the integration of cognitive and affective learning; and action. Because I recognize that the constructs of "feminist" and "patriarchal" are more points on a continuum than discrete categories, I believe these process goals can provide a useful framework for describing the multiple conflicts that result when one writing center tutor attempts to teach what she believes to be feminist pedagogy within the patriarchal system of the academy. I think these criteria are useful for two reasons: First, they are indicative of what I believe characterizes tutoring at its best. Feminist rhetoric and pedagogy and the "idea of a writing center" (North) have never been very far apart in my mind. Both feminist and writing center commentators advocate teaching methods that are non-hierarchical, cooperative, interactive ventures between students and tutors talking about issues grounded in the students' own experience. They are, above all, conversations between equals in which knowledge is constructed, not transmitted. The second — and most important — reason that I use these criteria is that they are synonymous with what this tutor thinks she is doing when teaching feminist values to her students.

The conference I am considering is one of eight conferences between the same tutor and student that I observed and audiotaped over the course of a semester. My reason for doing this, and for conducting post-conference interviews with the tutor, was not only to learn more about what it is we do when we talk to students about their writing, but also to see if what tutors think they do when they tutor bears any resemblance to my interpretation. The participants in this conference were a junior English major and a graduate student who has just passed the qualifying exams for her doctorate. The student is working on a revision of a paper on Hemingway's short story, "The Doctor and the Doctor's Wife." The student's teacher, who was also the tutor's doctoral examiner, has read and commented on the draft and is giving the student the opportunity to rewrite it. The student, the tutor, and the teacher are all women; both the tutor and the teacher identify themselves as feminists. In a post-conference interview with me, the tutor speaks of many layers of conflict in her interactions with this student. These can be identified broadly as conflicts between feminist and patriarchal pedagogy and rhetoric. On the level of rhetoric, the tutor says that a large part of what she tries to do with undergraduates involves teaching feminist values. She says that she encourages students to think and write clearly, in their own voices. She admits, however, the conflict that doing so causes her: Although she labels herself a feminist and says she believes in teaching according to feminist practice, she thinks that the student's success — which she equates with giving the teacher the traditional thesis-and-support format she wants — is her prime responsibility. For this tutor, there is a conflict between teaching feminist rhetoric and ensuring the student's academic success. Negotiating between these two is no easy task for her.

On the level of feminist pedagogy, the issue is one of power. Negotiating the uses of power is even more complex than the issue of rhetoric. bell hooks says that as feminist teachers one of the issues we need to contend with is that of using power without dominating and coercing our students (52). This is just the issue this tutor is struggling with. She says that one of her problems in teaching and tutoring in the past has been that she didn't "know how to have authority." She says, "I didn't know how to have control. I felt powerless." When she was able to convince herself that she had some authority, she says, "I felt better because then there wasn't any resistance from the students." She overcame these feelings of powerlessness not by confronting them, but by ignoring them.

These two levels of conflict are very real for this tutor: "I try to find out where the student is, and what they want. I ask, 'What do you like about it [the paper]?' I'm afraid however, that a lot of times I take over. If I see something that's disorganized or lacks connection, I want to do that for students. I pick out the problems. I guide it. The more problems I see, the more there's the danger of my taking over." The power of the patriarchy, the power of what the tutor perceives to be academic success, coupled with her tendency to subvert conflict, overwhelms her goals of feminist practice. As she tries to negotiate between the two, she chooses an uneasy alliance: In teaching the student what she considers to be the "correct" interpretation in the "correct" thesis-and-support format, her methodology is clearly that of the patriarchy; the interpretation, however, is a feminist reading of the text.

The result for the student is little more than confusion. Her situation in this patriarchal system results not in the liberation of an imprisoned voice, but in deafening silence and alienation. This student, far from learning to "write herself," learns instead just how far her self is from the discourse of the academy. Instead of seeing herself in relation to others, she is hurled headlong into the realization of her otherness. Toril Moi claims that no matter what it is we think or say we do, in our practices we find our politics (xiii). This is certainly true in this instance as the following excerpt illustrates.

Note on the text:
    S: Student
    T: Tutor
    . . . :   Words omitted
    . . . . : More than one line of text omitted
    < > :   Other person speaks but without taking a turn

    S: Did you pass?
    T: Yes, thank you very much.

S: Oh, congratulations!

T: You've been sending me all sorts of support during my exams. . . . So now what are you doing?

S: Ok, we read the short story "The Doctor and the Doctor's Wife." Our duty was to either describe the doctor . . . or the wife. <Uhhuh> And I chose to describe the doctor.

T: [Reads the paper and the teacher's comments.]

S: Oh, but I wish you wouldn't go by her [the teacher's] notes. I wish you'd go by your own.

T: I like this [She reads:] "Now as far as eye teeth is concerned, I don't know whether this combo really exists in American lingo or whether it was just said out of exasperation." [Both laugh] I just love that little, your kind of expressing your own exasperation. Ok . . . um, you have a real clear attitude toward this doctor, right? <Right> And where is it that you say that all together? Where have you, is there a place, any place in the paper, where you kind of summarize your feelings about the doctor?

S: I think right at the beginning. [She reads:] "He's a typical bourgeoise. The doctor seems to be conniving, selfish, a penny pincher, demanding respect from others, but facing up to no one, not even his wife."

T: Good. . . .

S: As I was reading the story, I got the sense that they are trying to uh, prove manhood . . . I'm not sure. I didn't have that problem.

T: This is interesting because you're suggesting that one of the issues in this story sounds like it's a test of manhood. . . . Oh, that's interesting. It sounds to me like you've landed on something that Hemingway's really trying to use to say something.

S: I couldn't figure out what it was though. It's like a puzzle. I don't know.

T: That sounds to me like an interesting thesis, especially given Hemingway's general themes . . . I mean, you're probably right . . . Um, Ok, do you think that you have in here any place . . . uh, the fact that what goes on between . . . Henry and Dick is a test of manhood?

S: I was going to do it . . . and I didn't do it because I thought, how am I going to prove that? Maybe I can just take a lot of quotes. I don't know.

T: Um, well, you already mentioned a couple of things. Um, how the doctor turns red . . . and how Dick walks out on him . . . Since you mentioned that, I think it's important to trust that it has something to do with this issue of manhood . . . Um, anything else that leads you to think that this is a test of manhood besides the confrontation between the two men? Um, up here you say his profession gives him status and makes him arrogant. . . . All right, I want to suggest to you that this is your thesis. . . . I want to hear some more things about why you think that this story is essentially a test of manhood. . . . So, if this is the thesis . . . what would your three main points be? . . . Ok, A) He's not intimidated and B) He knows what he's worth. What's the next thing you're going to do according to your thesis here?

S: [Silence]

T: What happens when I ask you these questions?

S: I'm trying to think of an answer — really hard!

T: Yeah, you go, "Ugh. I don't know." But . . . you know this stuff.

S: Yeah.

T: Somehow when I ask you questions, it freezes you, I think. Do you think that's possible?

S: I'm trying too hard for the answer or something. I don't know.

T: I think you have given me a whole lot of information around which I could organize your paper, given this thesis, and all I'm trying to help you do is see how you could take the information you have and all you need to do is trust your information enough to give your own explanation of how this point illustrates my main thesis. That's what I want you to be able to see.

S: I don't know. I'm really afraid of being wrong.

T: I agree. So at least in here, feel like I can risk it. Now, how does this point support the thesis?

At the beginning of the conference, the two participants exhibit signs of the sense of respect, trust, and community that Schniedewind has identified as characteristic of feminist pedagogy. The student knows that the tutor has just taken her qualifying examinations and starts the conference by asking the tutor if she has passed. When she learns that the tutor has passed, she seems genuinely happy. The tutor in turn acknowledges that the student has given her "all sorts of support" as she was taking her exams. These two have obviously shared personal information, an indication that they are operating out of a sense of mutual respect and trust. The relationship between the tutor and student is contrasted with the student's relationship with her teacher, evident when she tells the tutor not to pay any attention to the teacher's comments on her draft. She says, "I wish you wouldn't go by her notes. I wish you'd go by your own."

In the first substantive comment on the student's paper, the tutor praises her for what she sees as a particularly unique interpretation of a line from the story. She says, "I just love . . . your expressing your own exasperation there." At this, they both laugh. The first few minutes then, read like a promise of Schniedewind's first four process goals. They not only signal the sense of mutual respect, trust, and community that Schniedewind recommends, but are an explicit example of both her and Cixous' call for a new affective order, one that will "change the overly rational premises of male-dominated social relations and institutions" and will "incorporate priorities appreciative of human needs and feeling" while at the same time strengthening intellectual abilities, "so long suppressed by those same sexist norms and institutions" (Schniedewind 176). Further, the tutor's praise of the student's particular reading of the line suggests that perhaps the product of the conference will be characterized by the personal voice called for by feminist rhetoric. From the opening exchange, it seems that the leadership will be shared and the decision-making participatory in constructing a cooperative structure.

However, this does not happen. If we look at the tutor's post-conference remarks about the praise for the student, we see that it is not what it seems. When asked about the meaning of this line, the tutor says, "She [the student] didn't understand this very well. She's not using her sources well. She's using all sorts of references but not in a clear way. I wanted her to talk about the significance of the quote." The tutor goes on to say that she thought "the student was exasperated" because she didn't understand what she was saying. "Her intelligence," the tutor said, "is embedded in confusion." For Margo Adair and Sharon Howell, people dependent on those in power cannot afford to alienate them: "They end up thinking one thing and saying another" (221). Realizing the power of the student's teacher over both of them and uncomfortable with her own power over the student, "I just love . . . your expressing your own exasperation here," what she is thinking is "Boy, are you confused!" In thinking one thing and saying another, the tutor is subverting the conflict she feels. This initial subversion changes to confrontation in the next exchange.

According to Amy Shapiro, one of the ways that a sense of community is formed is through the types of questions that the teacher/tutor asks. Community breaks down when individuals ask "preset questions, questions that they already know the answers to, questions designed not to build trust and share understandings, but to challenge and exhibit power" (70). This is what the tutor does here. After taking a few minutes to read the paper, she asks her first substantive question about the text: "Um, you have a real clear attitude about this doctor, right? {Right} And where is it that you say all that together? Where have you, is there a place, any place in the paper where you kind of summarize your feelings about the doctor?" The tutor does not ask the student to articulate her attitude, but instead asks a simple yes/no question of where in the paper the student has this statement. Since the tutor has just finished reading the text, we can assume that it is a question she already knows the answer to.

This movement from personal conversation to subversion to confrontation is evidence of the conflict the tutor feels. It is fine to talk to students as equals, to share information and to build the sense of trust and respect called for with feminist pedagogy as long as the topic is a personal one; when the topic shifts to the work on the student's paper, the pedagogy shifts to an uneasy subversion and finally to the confrontation of the patriarchy. In this example, instead of talking as they have been and simply shifting topics, a strategy which might result in exploring the student's attitude toward the doctor, the tutor sees it as her responsibility to locate the thesis. In doing this, she is subverting the possibility of shared leadership and community, and reinforcing the patriarchal notion that meaning not only resides in the text, but is, in this instance, already there.

Although the tutor may want to create a conversation between equals, and although she may want to establish an atmosphere of trust, her keen sense of responsibility to teach students to write in the "correct" format overwhelms her feminist values. The tutor holds on to the responsibility — and the power. The conflict that doing so causes is apparent in the tutor's explanation of this line. She says, "I was trying to explain, to say more about it, so I could get her to put it together in one statement. But I was trying to get her to do it indirectly. I was afraid if I asked, 'What's the thesis?' she would shut up or back off."

When the student answers the tutor's question saying, "I think right in the beginning," and then goes on to read her summary description of the doctor, the tutor says, "Good," praising her for the correct answer. The atmosphere has changed from one of mutual respect, trust, and community to one of hierarchy. The tutor is saying one thing and meaning another; she is asking leading questions with the student trying to guess the answers. This exchange puts shared leadership, participatory decision-making, and cooperative structure very much in doubt.

As the conference progresses, this dynamic is intensified. A few minutes later the student mentions that in reading the story, she had the sense that it might have something to do with "proving manhood." As soon as the student mentions that she was considering this theme as a possibility, a possibility that she rejected when writing her first draft, the tutor begins trying to convince her that this is the right way to interpret the story: "This is interesting because you're suggesting that one of the issues in this story sounds like it's a test of manhood. . . . That's interesting. It sounds to me like you've landed on something that Hemingway's really trying to use to say something. . . ." The topic has shifted from what the tutor believes to be the "correct" format, to what she believes to be the "correct" interpretation. The student's uncertainty and alienation from this theme are not only evident when she says, "I'm not sure. I didn't have that problem" but in her response: "I couldn't figure out what it was though. It's like a puzzle. I, I don't know." To this, the tutor responds, "That sounds to me like an interesting thesis, especially given Hemingway's general themes. . . . Um, Ok, do you think that you have in here any place, the fact that what goes on between Henry and Dick is a test of manhood?" In her determination to teach this feminist interpretation, the tutor is, for the most part, leaving the student out of the interaction. Again, the form of the question — a yes/no location one instead of a problem one — reinforces the tutor's fervency and prevents any genuine sharing of power.

Instead of helping the student to interpret the story in a way she feels comfortable with, a way that has some connection to her own life and experience, the tutor increases the student's alienation by encouraging her to read the story through this lens. In doing this, she is not only not strengthening the student's intellectual abilities but she is preventing any sort of intellectual tension that could lead to cognitive growth. Further, instead of recognizing the power of the affective response the student has had to this reading, the tutor ignores it, telling her essentially that both her cognitive and affective reactions are wrong. In "Style as Politics: A Feminist Approach to the Teaching of Writing," Pamela Annas argues that we need to help our students overcome their alienation from language, their texts, their subjects, and themselves, and convince them that what they have to say is important and that they have an audience who will listen (361). This tutor, no matter how well meaning, is doing just the opposite.

In the student's response there is a conflict between her unwillingness to pursue this theme and her continuing trust and desire to please the tutor. It seems reasonable to expect that thoughts of a good grade also linger. She says, "I was going to do it . . . and I didn't do it because I thought, how am I going to prove that? Maybe I can just take a lot of quotes. I don't know." The tutor, firm in her resolve, suggests this theme once again: "Ok, well . . . I want to hear some more things about why you think that this story is essentially a test of manhood." Interestingly, the student has never said that she thinks the story is "essentially a test of manhood." This is what the tutor thinks, not the student. "Participatory decision-making" is taking a back seat to the "hierarchical authority" of the tutor. There is no evidence of shared leadership. The tutor is writing the paper based on what she considers to be the correct reading of the text and on what she thinks will get the student a good grade. She is not operating according to feminist pedagogy. In fact, she is simply further inculcating the masculinist values of the academy.

When asked about this exchange, the tutor comes to a realization. She says, "I just wrote the paper for her. I put it together. I didn't get her to put it together. And that's where things break down. She doesn't know what I'm talking about." The conflict between the tutor wanting to teach feminist values, wanting to encourage the student's own voice, wanting shared leadership and a cooperative goal structure — and wanting the student to succeed academically — remains in the realm of the tutor's subjectivity. The conflict is silenced. Because of this, it is not until the tutor hears herself on tape that she realizes what she is doing.

As the conference progresses, the movement away from an atmosphere of mutual trust and respect and toward one of hierarchy and domination becomes more evident both in the tutor's insistence on a thesis-support format for the paper and in the conversational patterns she uses to achieve that end. The tutor says: "So, if this [proving manhood] is the thesis . . . what would your three main points be?" She is teaching the student the traditional five-paragraph theme, with an emphasis on the objective, linear values of the patriarchy. The absence of shared leadership and participatory decision-making is evident when the tutor then answers her own question with two characteristics that will prove the thesis she is suggesting: "A) He's not intimidated; and B) He knows what he's worth." The tutor ends this exchange with a leading question, "All right, what's the next thing you're going to do according to your thesis here?" Twice more in the conference the tutor uses this conversational pattern of asking and answering her own questions. She says, "Do you have any place in here the fact that what goes on between Henry and Dick is a test of manhood?" When the student responds that, although she was thinking about that theme, she rejected it when she wrote the draft, the tutor answers the question for her. "Well," she says, "you already mentioned a couple of things. Um, how the doctor turns red . . . and how Dick walks out on him. . . ." Later on she says, "Ok, well, I want to hear some more things about why you think this story is essentially a test of manhood . . . Um, just off the top of your head, what are some of the other ways in which you think this is . . . a contest of manhood? You talk about Dick chewing the tobacco and spitting." Here she asks one question, does not wait for the student's response before rephrasing it and finally answers it herself. Later, she asks, "Um, anything else that leads you to think that this is . . . a test of manhood besides the confrontation between the two men? Um, up here you say . . . his profession gives him status and makes him arrogant."

In talking about this exchange, the tutor says, "I'm trying to show her how to develop it. I'm also doing all of the writing for her. The problem is I don't think she understands. What she's capable of isn't enough. I kept feeling that I wasn't reaching her, so I gave her more." What the tutor is doing is not authorizing the student's voice, but silencing it.

Faced with the conflict of trying to teach feminist values within a patriarchal system, and given the power that the patriarchy asserts over both her and the student, this tutor aligns herself with the patriarchy, the only concession to feminist practices being the interpretation of the text. In doing this, she assumes the role of the oppressor: her strategies do, for the most part, undermine any hope of establishing a cooperative goal structure for the conference, a structure that "an individual can complete . . . successfully if, and only if, all others with whom she is linked do otherwise" (174). In taking control of the text and the conversation, the tutor is essentially writing the paper and talking to and for herself. There is little indication that the student will be able to complete successfully what the tutor intends for her. Toward the end of the conference, the tutor says, "You have given me a whole lot of information around which *I* could organize your paper, given this thesis." Given the interaction thus far, this seems like a safe bet: The tutor could indeed write this paper. The problem is that the student cannot.

In the last minutes of the conference, the tutor finally notices that she has been engaged in a monologue for the better part of an hour. She has been so determined to write this paper according to her interpretation that she has hardly noticed the student's inactivity. When she asks the student a direct question of how a particular idea links to this thesis, the student's response is a full minute of silence. At this, the tutor moves into meta-conferencing, asking the student, "What happens when I ask you these questions?" The student responds, "I try to think of an answer — really hard." This response is not surprising given that the tutor has spent a good deal of time and energy teaching her that there is indeed a right answer — one the tutor knows and the student needs to guess. When the tutor continues, asking her why she "freezes," the student admits that she is "really afraid of being wrong." One of the things this tutor has achieved is to reinforce this fear. Perhaps the most ironic comment is when she says to the student, "I agree, but at least in here, feel like I can risk it." This after saying to the student, "Trust your information . . . of how this point illustrates *my* main thesis." I have to believe that the tutor is genuine in her wish that the student take risks. Unfortunately, the tutor is so dependent on the power of the academy that she cannot afford to risk alienation either for herself or for the student.

The writing conference seems the ideal location for Schniedewind's assertion that when individuals have "opportunities to come to know each other as people, speak honestly, take risks, and support each other . . . feminist values of community, communication, equality, and mutual nurturance are reinforced" (171). Throughout this conference, however, this does not happen. These two have the opportunity to come to know each other as people through a conversation about writing. But they do not. The tutor is caught between the conflict of wanting to teach feminist values but ever-mindful of the power structure in which she is working, doing so with the "correct" interpretation and in the "correct" form for the paper. In trying to persuade the student of these things, she is reinforcing the positivistic, partriarchal value that there is a "correct" reading, that she knows what that reading is, and that her job as a tutor is to teach this reading to this student. There is no evidence of "equality" between these conversants; there is no "mutual nurturance." Further, there is little evidence of participatory decision-making, shared leadership, or a cooperative goal structure. Indeed, there is little evidence that the student is considered at all. The tutor is clearly in control. She talks more than the student does and sets the agenda for what gets talked about, when, and for how long. In taking control of both the text and the conversation, she is stifling both the student's cognitive and affective capabilities. In insisting on a reading that the student has said she feels alienated from, she is reinforcing the values of the hierarchy and objectivity, while teaching the student to ignore her emotional responses. This is not only not good feminist pedagogy; this is not good tutoring.

The main reason that this interaction is neither good feminist practice nor good tutoring is that it is not honest. According to Schniedewind and others who write of feminist pedagogy, our interactions with students ought to be conversations with equals, based on the student's own experience, taking place in an atmosphere of trust, respect, nurturance. It seems to me that most of us who teach writing would agree with this. But none of this is possible if the tutor is not honest about the conflicts she feels.

So where does this leave us? It seems to me that the answer lies in Schniedewind's fifth criterion — action. About this, she says, "As long as we live in a sexist society, feminism inevitably implies taking action to transform institutions and values" (178). For Nancy Sommers, this action is "encouragement." She says that with "enough encouragement," our students will be "empowered to serve the academy and accommodate it, not to write in the persona of Everystudent, but rather to write essays that will change the academy" (30). I want to suggest that our action requires that the political circumstances in which we write and talk to our students be named. In naming, we create a space in which we can talk openly about the conflicts between feminism and the patriarchy. We can consider how and why different rhetorics and pedagogies come to be privileged and the implications of this privileging for how we both construct ourselves and are constructed by the institutions in which we work. With this naming, our students can be given power and the responsibility to negotiate between feminism and the patriarchy, between writing vibrantly, sensuously, in their own voices and writing the tightly argued prose of the academy.

In the conference I have considered, the student is never given the power or the responsibility to make this choice. The tutor is so dependent on the patriarchy that she cannot afford to risk this naming. And because the conflicts are not named, they remain solely within the realm of the subjective, in this case, the tutor's head. The result for both the tutor and the student is an alienation from themselves. For the tutor, the result is that she thinks one thing and says another: Her interaction with this student is directly opposite from what she perceives it to be. Far from transforming this student's values or the values of a sexist academy, in not articulating the conflicts and the power struggles at work here, this tutor is simply reinforcing institutional norms of silence and obedience. The fact that she does this through the guise of a feminist interpretation of the story makes it all the more harmful.

For the student, the result is that at the end of the conference, she is far more alienated from language and from herself than when the conference began. Ira Shor says that this alienation is the number one problem in education today, manifesting itself in our students' passivity and apathy. Whether we realize it or not, when we are silent about the conflicts we feel, we reinforce this apathy. No matter what we say, when our interactions with students are characterized by subversion and dominance, we are encouraging passivity and reinforcing alienation.

Hélène Cixous writes of the conflict between a world in which only "great men" write and a world in which all other writing is deemed "silly." Her call to "write, let no one hold you back, let nothing stop you" locates itself in the *and* between these two worlds. In negotiating between them, we need, above all, to be honest. We need to admit to ourselves and to our students the conflicts we feel when attempting to espouse feminist values within a patriarchal system, to admit the power inequities we live with, and to admit further that the dichotomization between feminist and patriarchal practices is a false one. Only if we confront these conflicts, only if we present our students with the options and the power to choose, will we be truly honest and will feminism — and good tutoring — have any chance at all.

Works Cited

Adair, Margo, and Sharon Howell. "The Subjective Side of Power." *Healing the Wounds: The Promise of Ecofeminism.* Ed. Judith Plant. Philadelphia: New Society Publishers, 1989.

Andermatt, Verena. "Hélène Cixous and the Uncovery of a Feminine Language." *Women and Literature* 7.1 (1979): 38–47.

Annas, Pamela J. "Style as Politics: A Feminist Approach to the Teaching of Writing." *College English* 47 (1985): 360–71.

Cixous, Hélène. "The Laugh of the Medusa." *New French Feminisms.* Ed. Elaine Marks and Isabelle de Coutrivron. New York: Shocken Books, 1980.

Farrell, Thomas J. "The Female and Male Modes of Rhetoric." *College English* 40 (1979): 922–27.

Freire, Paulo. *Pedagogy of the Oppressed.* New York: Continuum, 1988.

hooks, bell. "Toward a Revolutionary Feminist Pedagogy." *Talking Back: Thinking Feminist, Thinking Black.* Boston: South End Press, 1989.

Juncker, Clara. "Writing (with) Cixous." *College English* 50 (1988): 424–34.

Moi, Toril. *Sexual/Textual Politics: Feminist Literary Theory.* London: Methuen, 1985.

North, Stephen M. "The Idea of a Writing Center." *College English* 46 (1984): 433–46.

Rich, Adrienne. *On Lies, Secrets, & Silences.* New York: W. W. Norton & Co., 1979.

Rorty, Richard. *Philosophy and the Mirror of Nature.* Princeton: Princeton UP, 1979.

Schniedewind, Nancy. "Feminist Values: Guidelines for Teaching Methodology in Women's Studies." *Freire for the Classroom.* Ed. Ira Shor. Portsmouth NH: Heinemann Educational Books, Inc., 1987.

Shapiro, Amy. "Creating a Conversation: Teaching All Women in the Feminist Classroom." *NWSA Journal* 3 (Winter 1991): 70–80.

Shor, Ira. "Educating the Educators: A Freirean Approach to the Crisis in Teacher Education." *Freire for the Classroom.* Ed. Ira Shor. Portsmouth, NH: Heinemann Educational Books, Inc., 1987.

Sommers, Nancy. "Between the Drafts." *College Composition and Communication* 43 (1992): 23–31.

Postcolonialism and the Idea of a Writing Center

Anis Bawarshi and Stephanie Pelkowski _____

UNIVERSITY OF WASHINGTON AND UNIVERSITY OF KANSAS

In their article, Anis Bawarshi and Stephanie Pelkowski argue that writing centers with a current traditional or process orientation are in the business of acculturating student writers instead of fostering multiple perspectives on writing. Whether the tutors in such centers aim their efforts at transforming writers' texts (as in current traditional centers) or transforming writers (as in process centers), their goal is to help the text or the writer meet "the acceptable standard of the university." Bawarshi and Pelkowski argue that nontraditional students, upon receiving their first exposure to academic writing, often feel as if they are losing something in the exchange — giving up a level of complexity and an awareness of alternative perspectives in order to fit their ideas into the more rigid and acceptable modes permitted in academic discourse. Many also come to view the standards of academic writing as arbitrary and inaccessible. In order to help these students thrive in the academy without surrendering their unique identities, Bawarshi and Pelkowski propose the creation of "postcolonial" writing centers, which, in the postmodern tradition, would welcome and foster in writers multiple styles, processes, and perspectives. Tutors in such writing centers would adopt, and encourage student writers to adopt, a critical consciousness toward academic discourse. The article, which originally appeared in The Writing Center Journal *in 1999, is an important reminder for tutors to value the perspectives of students coming from multicultural backgrounds.*

We are mixed in with one another in ways that most national systems of education have not dreamed of. To match knowledge in the arts and sciences with these integrative realities is, I believe, the intellectual and cultural challenge of the moment.

–Edward Said

To teach writing is to argue for a version of reality.

–James Berlin

The terms "remediation" and "Basic Writing" emerged at critical moments in the history of American higher education. Used originally to describe students who suffered from neurological problems, "remediation" became a popular designation in education journals in the 1920s in response to an ever-increasing number of under-prepared lower class and immigrant students who began to enter the educational system at the turn of the century (Rose 343, 349). These students' reading and writing "disabilities" needed "remediation" before the students were prepared to enter the academic community. Similarly, "Basic Writing" instruction matured as a field in the 1970s, the era of the G.I. Bill and the open admission policy at CUNY. Open admissions prepared the way for thousands of non-traditional students "whose difficulties with the written language [Mina Shaughnessy tells us] seemed of a different order . . . as if they had come, you might say, from a different country" (2). These students, Shaughnessy explains, were indeed "strangers in academia, unacquainted with the rules and rituals of college life" (3). These racial and rural "strangers" whose "other" languages and dialects posed problems so great as to appear, in the words of their teachers, "irremediable" (Shaughnessy 3) had to be prepared for the university, and so Basic Writing became the shibboleth for the academically under-prepared.

Beginning in the 1920s and 1970s respectively, remediation and Basic Writing emerged as preemptive strikes, defensive moves as it were, at once to initiate under-prepared students into the ways of the university and to protect the university from the threat posed by the racial, rural, immigrant, under-privileged, under-prepared Other. Their purpose: to acculturate students who speak, read, and write Other dialects, Other languages, Other discourses, and initiate them into academic discourses. These remedial spaces — at once within and outside of the university (few, if any, provide credit hours toward graduation and many are located in peripheral and subterranean places such as basements) — accept, in the words of E. D. Hirsch, that "the acculturative responsibility of the schools is primary and fundamental" (19) and so serve that end.

Today, the writing center stands as the most accessible and visible place of remediation within the university. And true to the tradition of remediation it inherits dating back to the 1920s, the writing center is mainly a place of acculturation. Yet due to its physically and politically peripheral place — marginalized from and yet part of the university — we argue that the writing center is an ideal place in which to begin teaching and practicing a critical and self-reflective form of acculturation, what Edward Said calls "critical consciousness." Drawing from work in postcolonial theory, we posit that the writing center can become what Mary Louise Pratt has termed a "contact zone," a place in which different discourses grapple with each other and are negotiated.

Acculturation Versus the Goals of Critical Consciousness

Acculturation, as Min-zhan Lu and Victor Villanueva have argued, is driven by an essentialist and hegemonic pedagogical imperative that academic discourses are universal and empowering — that they are the discourses of inquiry, knowledge, and truth, suited to address issues fundamental to all humanity. As Lu has demonstrated, Geoffrey Wagner's *The End of Education* (1976), an apocalyptic book written in response to open admissions, posits just such a view of academic discourse. Wagner laments that "illiterate" students, whom he variously refers to as "dunces" (43), "misfits" (129), "hostile mental children" (247), and "the most sluggish of animals" (163) (he even describes one student as sitting "in a half-lotus pose in back of class with a transistor radio strapped to his Afro, and nodding off every two minutes" [134]), threaten to disrupt the rarefied air of the university. By introducing different dialects, different discourses, and different identities, these students threaten to introduce race, politics, class, gender, and other social and political realities into academic discourses, thus infecting them with an ideology that ostensibly was not there before.

Acculturation, therefore, becomes a means not only of precluding the Other, but also of validating the academic culture to itself, a process, Edward

Said writes, "by which superiority and power are lodged both in a rhetoric of belonging, or being 'at home,' so to speak, and in a rhetoric of administration: the two become interchangeable" (13). In short, acculturation becomes a means of administrating one's own power within one's own place. Said refers to such acculturation, academic or otherwise, as "affiliation." He claims that affiliative structures — the means by which knowledge, power, consciousness, and ideology are reproduced and maintained within a culture — are meant to appear as if they were representations of filial structures — the means by which human beings biologically reproduce, emotionally interact with, and construct personal relationships among one another (16–25). Said's point here is that hegemony succeeds when it convinces members of a culture that its affiliative structures — for example, the Eurocentric literary canon it privileges and teaches in the university at the expense of other, non-Eurocentric texts — are legitimate representations of natural, filial systems. Thus, affiliation becomes a form of representing on the cultural level the filiative processes supposedly to be found in nature — for instance, Matthew Arnold's notion of a "culture" as the best that has been thought and said. So dominant culture becomes legitimized when it is made to appear as if it were based on certain natural, commonsensical principles.

When we encounter texts or any other forms of cultural production, Said argues, we are affiliated into the dominant culture. Academic discourse is no exception. In order to attain what Said calls "critical consciousness" (critical affiliation), we need to become aware of how affiliation and filiation cooperate. That is, we need to "arrive at some acute sense of what political, social, and human values are entailed in the reading, production, and transmission of every text" (26). Thus critical consciousness is about both being critical of discursive formations and how they are in the service of reproducing certain power relationships (filiations), as well as critical of one's own subject positions and social relations within these formations.

In this paper, we propose a writing center strategy in which under-prepared students, especially those marginalized by race, class, and ethnicity, are encouraged to adopt critical consciousness as a means of functioning within the university and its discourses. David Bartholomae and Mina Shaughnessy have provided us with what are now classic examples of the struggles basic writers face as they invent or write their way into the university. But what has been overlooked, especially in the case of Shaughnessy, are the epistemological demands that such academic writing places on these students' ways of experiencing, ordering, and making sense of the world — in short, the subject positions and habits of mind that such academic discourses force them to adopt when they become acculturated into the cultures of the university. Such consequences are rarely if ever made explicit to students who find themselves labeled "basic" or, what amounts to the same thing, "Other." This is why we reject uncritical acculturation as both ethically and, as we explain later, pedagogically unsound, and propose instead a writing center–based pedagogy that allows basic and other marginalized students to become aware of how and why academic discourses situate them within certain power relationships and require of them particular subject positions. The goal of such pedagogy is *not* to subvert academic discourse or to suggest that students reject it, but rather to teach students how self-consciously to use and be used by it — how rhetorically and critically to choose and construct their subject positions within it. Ultimately, we agree with Said that "critical consciousness is a part of its actual social world and of the literal body that the consciousness inhabits, not by any means an escape from either one or the other" (16). Acculturation denies such consciousness, and, as we will demonstrate, also denies basic writing students, indeed all students, the opportunity to explore how discourse helps construct various subject positions and social practices. The critical consciousness we advocate invites students to consider how to "be in the world and self-aware simultaneously" (Said 29).

In "The Discourse on Language," Michel Foucault claims that it is on the margins of discourse — the margins of knowledge and knowing — that self-reflection is most acute because it is there that we can achieve what he calls "exteriority," a critical perspective that perceives discourse in relation to the various and often conflicting conditions of its existence. Because of its traditionally marginalized status, the writing center is a potentially rich site in which to achieve and practice this exteriority, a contact zone in which students and staff learn to negotiate multiple subject positions as they rhetorically negotiate multiple discourses within and outside of the academy.

The Traditional Writing Center

Those involved in writing center theory and practice are most likely familiar with Stephen North's landmark and now classic essay, "The Idea of a Writing Center" (1984). Suffice it to say, North helps legitimize the writing center by arguing that, instead of being merely a service branch of the composition classroom, the writing center can and must become its own place, providing a unique holistic "participant-observer methodology" unavailable in the traditional composition classroom:

> The result is what might be called a pedagogy of direct intervention. Whereas in the "old" center instruction tends to focus on the correction of textual problems, in the "new" center the teaching takes place as much as possible during writing, during the activity being learned, and tends to focus on the activity itself. (North 239)

In his "new" version of the writing center, the emphasis is on the process, not the product, on the writer, not the text: "in a writing center, the object is to make sure that *writers*, and not necessarily their texts, *are what get changed* by instruction" (North 237; emphasis added).

Stephen North's assumption is that such a change in the writer is a good thing. At the very least, he assumes, as many of us do, that an ability to effect such a change in the writer legitimatizes the writing center, placing it on a par with, if not above, the composition classroom in terms of writing instruction. Yet nowhere in the article does North actually critique such instruction.[1] Nowhere does he question the nature of academic discourse itself or what effect it has on the student writers who are "changed" by it. The basic assumption for North is that changed writers are improved writers because changed writers are writers who can better function within academic discourses and the university. Such transformation seems a natural and positive consequence of a "pedagogy of direct intervention."

But lack of critical consideration, as Said warns, often results in the kinds of affiliative social practices that assume a filial, natural foundation. Notice, for example, how North describes the tutor's role, a description echoed throughout the essay: [Tutors] must measure their success not in terms of the constantly changing model they create, but in terms of changes in the writer. Rather than being fearful of disturbing the "ritual" of composing, they observe it and are *charged to change it: to interfere,* to get in the way, to participate in ways that will leave the "ritual" itself forever altered. *The whole enterprise seems to me most natural.* (239; emphasis added)

The rhetoric in the above citation, even as we acknowledge North's well-meaning intentions, is unmistakably colonialist. The shift from a product- to a process-based pedagogy becomes an invitation to interfere with not just the body of the text but also the body of the writer — his or her "ritual" — in ways reminiscent of imperialist practices around the world. We do not wish to belabor the issue here. We simply want to suggest that the colonialist language with which North unwittingly rallies his tutors to interfere with and ultimately change students' writing rituals as if such interference was a "most natural" enterprise betrays the acculturative and, as we shall see shortly, hegemonic agendas of much basic writing pedagogy.

In so far as it does transform students who seem unable to function within standardized academic discourses, the writing center should indeed be acknowledged as a formidable place within the university. And in so far as it provides a context for learning independent of what North calls the university's "external curriculum" (240), the writing center does indeed "help students revise their attitudes towards themselves as writers and towards writing . . . [by restoring] to students the sense of their own authority and responsibility" (Warnock and Warnock 19).[2] But should such transformations and revisions be lauded uncritically? Is the change the writing center produces in writers and their "rituals," especially basic and other marginalized writers, a positive change? The answer cannot be an innocent "yes." And it should certainly not be treated as a "most natural" enterprise. As recent postmodern and postcolonial considerations of discourse, particularly academic discourses, suggest, we need to question essentialist notions of writing as somehow ideologically innocent or even empowering — a means of translating thought into language. Such considerations ask us to take a closer look at what it means to teach standard academic discourses, and what is at stake when we introduce students to a particular academic style or genre or ritual. As such, they make us aware of the role writing plays in the construction of master narratives, narratives that define students' values, goals, and epistemologies, and that perpetuate power relationships and subject positions. There are serious political consequences, thus, to the kind of student transformations the writing center promises and is so often successful in achieving, consequences that have only recently begun to receive critical attention.

Acculturation and Colonialism

Both the "old" current-traditional and "new" process-oriented versions of the writing center as described by Stephen North are ultimately in the business of acculturation. Whether they are involved in changing textual features ("old" writing centers) or changing writers ("new" writing centers), the idea is the same: the change is meant to transform the student and his or her texts into the acceptable standard of the university. The writing center has traditionally been and continues to be generally unconcerned with critiquing academic standards, only with facilitating students' participation within them.

And so acculturation continues. In her recent article, "From the Margins to the Mainstream: Reconceiving Remediation," Mary Soliday argues that mainstreaming Basic Writers offers a better alternative to remedial courses. One advantage of mainstreaming, she contends, is that it encourages "students to use the unfamiliar language of the academy to describe and analyze familiar aspects of everyday language use and cultural experience" (87). This is accomplished by giving the students an opportunity "to raise issues about social difference and to explore these using conventional academic ways of thinking such as description, analysis, and interpretation" (87). Regarding her case study, Derek, a mainstreamed African-American Basic Writer, Soliday triumphantly concludes: "More *successfully* than in his past essays, Derek uses a formal language here which subordinates one idea to another to approximate his version of college-level discourse" (94; emphasis added). What, however, does Soliday mean by "successfully"? And perhaps even more importantly, what has happened to Derek's ideas in the process of his learning to subordinate one idea to another? The research Soliday presents tells us, for example, that prior to his being exposed to the concept of subordination, Derek had resisted taking a position in his writing, opting instead not to resolve contradiction. In the process of learning how to resolve contradiction and subordinate his ideas, what has Derek unwittingly been asked to do? How has his home cultural identity been transformed? Has he been forced to accept uncritically a different epistemology, a different way of experiencing and making sense of the world? And if so, what are the pedagogical and political implications?

Linda Brodkey and Min-zhan Lu would say, yes, his ideas have been altered, his home discourse has been silenced. As Brodkey's work with the "literacy letters" demonstrates, the rhetorical context of the university, its academic discourses, is constituted by and in turn constitutes the social and political agenda of the dominant culture. Academic discourses not only reflect the university's social and political formations; they also reproduce these formations. In short, they are affiliative. And when Basic Writing students, so called because they have yet to be acculturated into these privileged discourses, are taught how to function within them by such institutions as the writing center, they are not innocently being introduced to a new set of discourses; they are being constituted by these discourses. Derek's learning how to subordinate ideas to one another is not simply an example of his acquiring a new discourse into which he can "put" his thoughts. The very academic discourse in which he has learned to reproduce his experiences reconstitutes his experiences. The process of subordination, a seemingly innocent rhetorical formation, alters the way Derek perceives his experiences — forcing him to order his experiences hierarchically (something he previously resisted doing), and determining to some extent what aspect of his experiences can fit into the subordination and what aspects cannot.

In the "Literacy Letters," Brodkey describes how discourses of power, in this case academic discourses, transform Basic Writers' experiences. She gives as one example a letter by an adult Basic Writer, a white working-class woman she calls Dora, written to a white middle-class male teacher she calls Don. In the letter, Dora, who up to this point had assumed the subject role of audience to Don's narrative, attempts to reverse this pattern. Here is a portion of Dora's letter as printed in Brodkey:

> I don't have must to siad this week a good frineds husband was kill satday at 3:15 the man who kill him is a good man he would give you the shirt off of his back it is really self-defense but anyway I see police academy three it was funny but not is good as the first two. (286)

Nowhere in the "Literacy Letters" is the struggle between marginalized narrative and the discourse of mastery more clear. Even as Dora attempts to introduce her own narrative — her home subject position — into the conversation, she cannot sustain her experience, her story, within the discursive practices of the academy. This is why as soon as she resists her academic subject position by telling her own version of reality, Dora quickly retreats into a subordinate discursive position and narrates her experiences in a way that Don has sanctioned as academically appropriate — she silences her own narrative about the murder (a real and complex event in her life) in order to write about what Don likes: movies. Commenting on this tension, Brodkey writes, "the abrupt shift from herself as narrator who reflects on the aftermath of violence to herself as the student who answers a teacher's questions . . . is, for me, one of those moments when the power of discourse seems the most absolute" (286). The way we use discourse constitutes our reality — what parts of our experiences we can narrate and conceptualize within the discourse and what parts we cannot.

Mainstreaming or acculturation appears to neglect that meaning is constituted, interpreted, and valued differently in different discourses. Soliday certainly assumes that Derek becomes a "better" writer when he learns to explore his experiences "using conventional academic ways of thinking" such as subordination (87). But at what cost? What does Derek have to give up in order to become a more successful writer? Soliday does not say. But we have learned from the work that Min-zhan Lu has done with basic writing instruction that the cost can be great. Not only can marginalized discourses be silenced by academic discourses as we saw in the case of Dora, but as Lu argues, "mastery of academic discourse is often accompanied by a change in one's point of view" (332). A change in style can thus suggest a change in thinking — "in the way one perceives the world around one and relates to it" (Lu 332). Such a change in style, often accompanied by a change in place (i.e., academic discourse/university), demands a change in subject position. This is quite common. But the university and its discourse become dangerously hegemonic when they refuse to make explicit this change in subject position. Instead, they force marginalized students like Derek and Dora to consent to the discursive practices of education by first reminding them that they are Other and in need of remediation, and then convincing them that being academically literate is the most prestigious, most civilized state of being — that, in fact, the university is a place that emancipates them from their familiar subject positions by teaching them a universal, objective discourse which provides them access to culture, knowledge, and truth. Thus, the university, too often with the help of the writing center, imposes on students one more subject position to which they "willingly" consent because they are not conscious of it as being a subject position, a particular, politically embedded, and discursive way of experiencing and articulating knowledge and reality.

Like the appropriately named basic writing course at Indiana University–Indianapolis, the writing center truthfully ought to be called the "Access Center," a kind of "scholarly quarantine" (to use Mike Rose's phrase), in which those marginalized as Basic Writers are cleansed and prepared for the rarefied air of the university. As Gail Stygall explains, "paradoxically, the Access Center restricts and regulates access to the university" (327). Clearly, for those students entering the university from the margins, the writing center serves as a place offering training in how to operate as productive academic citizens. North himself admits, "[the writing center] cannot change [the rhetorical context of the university]: all we can do is help the writer learn how to operate in it and other contexts like it" (240). This is certainly a laudable goal. But without adding the adjective "critically" to "operate," the writing center runs the risk of becoming not much different, as we will see shortly, from traditional colonialist practices.

As a way of precluding this risk, we suggest that the writing center should become a site in which marginalized students can become critically conscious of how and why academic discourses construct various subject positions so that students like Derek recognize and contend with the threat to their home subject positions — their racial, class-based, gendered points of view and experiences — resulting from their mastery of academic discourses. At the same time, they develop what Gloria Anzaldua refers to as border residency/consciousness — a consciousness resulting from occupying contradictory and ambivalent subject positions simultaneously, a "third element which is greater than the sum of its severed parts": "a mestiza consciousness" (79–80).

Toward a Postcolonial Writing Center

North's landmark essay began a rich conversation about ways to move beyond the old version of the writing center as a skills fix-it shop or quarantine. Many subsequent participants in this conversation have borrowed critical theories from areas traditionally outside of composition studies to continue forging a new direction for writing centers. Betty Garrison Shiffman makes use of one such popular critical approach, that of feminism. In her article "Writing Center Instruction: Fostering an Ethic of Caring," Shiffman advocates an "overt awareness and acknowledgment that various factors, particularly social ones such as gender, race, class, economic or educational background, play a considerable role in everyone's learning and teaching processes" (2). The study begins to build on Brodkey's findings in the "Literacy Letters," but the methods of change Shiffman prescribes are potentially damaging. Shiffman cites the work done in feminist education by Belenky, Clinchy, Goldberger, and Tarule to describe the ideal teacher "who would help [students] articulate and expand their latent knowledge" (2). This and other statements that rely on the birthing metaphor for nourishing the student's ideas into the world of writing are based on essentialist assumptions which assume that thought develops separately from writing. The goal of the writing center, in this case, is to provide a comfortable environment in which students can "give birth" to their ideas. What is so dangerous about these assumptions, as Lu's work has brought to the forefront, is the belief that writing cannot alter thought. Under this assumption, when we ask students to write in the form of academic discourse we are asking them only to write in a different form from that to which they are accustomed; a change in genre cannot change thought since writing and thought are separate. Although Shiffman's approach recognizes that social factors are tied to learning, it still fails to recognize the effect writing has on one's subject position.

It is here that the field of postcolonial theory makes us aware of the effect that sanctioned academic discourse has on basic writers. Like feminist theory, many strands of postcolonial theory are practice oriented: the two are equally focused on helping people identify and resist hegemonic constructs. As postcolonial theory looks critically at the once heralded ideals of bringing a proper education and technological growth to a country in exchange for assimilation, the writing center should look critically at the changes we are asking basic writers to accept. As colonial subjects usually had to learn to speak in a language different from their own, so basic writers are expected to speak an academic language foreign to them in many ways. The idea of the basic writer as a colonial subject certainly seems to be extreme, but when we speak of changing the student writer and his or her "ritual" in ways described earlier the university clearly becomes a site for an "exchange of services" in the spirit of economist Maurice Godelier. Godelier theorized that "no domination, even when born of violence, can last if it does not assume the form of an exchange of services" (151). In other words, the "exchange" is hegemonically constructed when dominance is called a service; in accepting the service (in this case, instruction in "good writing"), the oppressed consent to their own domination.

To examine just how this theory is put into practice, we can look to the work of Edward San Juan, who finds an appeal to this sort of "exchange" in the history of the United States' relationship to the Philippines. As San Juan points out, William Howard Taft's policy toward the Philippines stressed a sort of contractual agreement, in which Filipinos would speak and write in English in exchange for decent jobs and protection by the United States (74). Most contemporary historians continue to view U.S.–Philippine relations as a failed *collaboration,* rather than a dependency imposed by the U.S. (70). But the Filipino response to American education demanded by the U.S. requires more than a simple shift in language use. If language could indeed be separated from thought, as Shiffman assumes, then the Filipino's "fit[ting] himself . . . in English" would indeed mean nothing more than fitting oneself in a different set of clothing, as Taft's turn of phrase implies (qtd. in San Juan 73). Renato Constantino presents a different version of this "exchange" in his retelling of his miseducation. As he tells it, "In exchange for a smattering of English, we yielded our souls" (46). This sort of immaterial cultural domination is the primary means of domination in the Philippines, more powerful than any tangible monetary "aid."

Certainly, parallel effects of imposing academic discourse on marginalized writers and calling it a "service" have been documented by Brodkey and Lu, as seen above. The colonial (or neocolonial) situation of the marginalized writer, then, leads to the following question: when presented with the choice of acculturation or of a complete rejection of the "exchange," which should writers choose? Many writing teachers have the understandable fear that students will not survive or succeed if they completely reject the exchange. This fear usually leads teachers like Soliday to concern themselves with the lesser of two evils — acculturation — since the situation is thus presented as an either/or dilemma. However, as Anzaldua reminds us, there is a third option, a "mestiza consciousness." For this, we can look to those postcolonial writers who choose self-consciously to write in the language of the colonizing country. Derek Walcott is one such author from the Caribbean, who writes in the stylistic tradition of the English poets, but who does so consciously, which allows him to recreate the subject matter as he recreates his subject position. Speaking of himself and other poets who use the traditional Western form, he writes, "when these writers cunningly describe themselves as classicists and pretend an indifference to change, it is with an irony as true as the fury of the radical" (370). These "classicists" are clearly aware of the subject position they take on at any moment. The comparisons between the writers' detached irony and the radicals' aggression testifies to the power in this awareness. For Walcott, a complete rejection of the dominant/dominating genre and language is limiting. Nor does his choice of the "classical" form mean acculturation: it is instead an act of creation and of resistance: "it is this awe of the numinous, this elemental privilege of naming the new world which annihilates history in our great poets" (372). Walcott thus is able to appropriate as potentially uplifting and capable of redefining his experience a language that some see as synonymous with historical servitude. In this case, he uses the colonizer's discourse — a discourse used to impose on him a subject position — in order to redefine himself. To help writers far less experienced than Walcott achieve this mestiza consciousness — a consciousness marked by the ability to negotiate multiple, even contradictory, subject positions while rooted in dominant discourse — is the goal of the postcolonial writing center.

Mary Louise Pratt refers to mestiza or border sites as contact zones, that is, "social spaces where cultures meet, clash, and grapple with each other, often in contexts of highly asymmetrical relations of power, such as colonialism, slavery, or their aftermaths as they are lived out in many parts of the world today" (35). Within such contact zones, "subordinated subject[s]" learn how power relations get played out in culture and how they can use "the colonizer's language and verbal repertoire" to "single-handedly give [themselves] authority" to recreate their subject positions (Pratt 38).

We propose that the writing center become such a "contact zone" within the university. Rather than treating the writing center as a space in which marginalized students can "engage in the trial and error of putting their thoughts into writing," we suggest it be transformed into another kind of space, one in which students such as Derek can engage in the process of assessing what happens to their experiences — what happens to *them* — when they begin to master academic discourses. The writing center thus becomes not just a place in which students are introduced to academic discourses and taught how to function with them, but also how to "describe themselves in ways that engage with representations others have made of them" (Pratt 36). What we are suggesting, finally, is that the writing center, in addition to helping marginalized students function within academic discourses, should also make explicit how these discourses affect them — how these discourses rhetorically and socially function.

One way that the writing center can achieve this critical self-reflexivity is by making marginalized students aware of how the mastery of academic discourses affects their home discourses. To return to Soliday's example, Derek should be allowed the opportunity to examine how his learning to subordinate affects his point of view and experiences. This might mean that a tutor discusses with

Derek those contradictions he has been asked to rhetorically smooth over in his restructuring through subordination. In such a scenario, Derek and his tutor might compare the rhetorical strategies of his two texts — the one that resists subordination and the one that uses subordination to achieve cohesion — in order to reflect on the social and political effects such strategies create. This scenario presents a unique teachable moment in which Derek can consider *why* he wants to maintain contradiction — what is at stake, that is, for him to do so and what he might lose (and gain) by learning to subordinate. Subsequently, tutors might help Derek understand why the resulting closure is sometimes valued in particular academic discourses, and consider whether or not this is important to him and why. If Derek is not satisfied with the subject position he is working from in the revised essay, tutors might help find a revision strategy that would maintain the contradictions of his first draft, but be suitable to academic discourse. (A difficult task, no doubt, but possible — think, for example, of some of the academy's most prominent theorists.) This type of revision would reflect a move towards mestiza consciousness, in that contradictory (subject) positions are not simplified and erased, but held in relation to one another and examined critically in that state.

Above all, we should let those who are entering the university from the margins know what is at stake — not to discourage them from entering, but to make them aware of the extent to which discourse constructs reality and their place within it. The goal here is not to encourage marginalized students to resist academic discourses or to have them privilege one discourse over another. Rather, the goal of the writing center should be to teach its students how "to *reposition* themselves in relation to several continuous and conflicting discourses" (Harris 275) so that they become more aware of the power of discourse and what it means to "write." Occupying a space both within and at the same time on the margins of the university, the writing center is in a unique position to teach marginalized students how to negotiate diverse discourses, to encourage them towards what Joseph Harris refers to as "a kind of polyphony — an awareness of and pleasure in the various competing discourses that make up their own" (273). Aware of what subordination can do to his point of view, for example, Derek can learn how to perceive his experiences differently within different discourses, can learn, more specifically, how his version of reality is shaped and enabled by the discourse in which he tells it.

Such instruction can do more than solely teach marginalized students how to write "successfully." On the one hand, it teaches them that "success" in writing is contingent upon the kind of discourse they are writing, not some universal standard. That is, they learn that what a certain discourse community deems successful reveals much about its values, goals, and epistemologies, what knowledges it sanctions and why. On the other, it can teach them how writing does this and how they can manipulate writing in order to construct what Brodkey calls "multiple subject positions" (281). The point is not to discourage marginalized "Basic Writers" from functioning within academic discourses, but rather to teach them how to preserve their multiple, even conflicting social roles while doing so. As such, the writing center can, in a truly postmodern sense, become a structure within the university that examines and exposes its own structurality, a place that is continuously engaged in deconstructing its context at the same time as it functions within it.

As part of its postmodern position within the university, the writing center should encourage its students to examine the axioms upon which academic structures are formed — what assumptions lie behind the limits we impose on rhetorical conventions, and what social and power relations are served by such conventions. So, while the university, especially the English department, continues to perceive the writing center as a place in which students learn to reproduce particular features of academic discourses found lacking in their writing (with the help of an interactive, conversational, and process-oriented pedagogy, of course), a postmodern and postcolonial perspective allows us to reconceptualize the role of the writing center as a place in which students explicitly examine why and how certain features of academic discourse come to be features in the first place.

A primary goal of the postcolonial writing center, then, is to teach students how to retrace the formal and textual effects of academic discourses to their rhetorical and social sources, allowing them to look prior to and outside of these discourses in order to explore what it means to write. Marginalized students — actually students in general — are rarely if ever exposed to this kind of explicit instruction. Instead, they are told what the standards for academic writing are in composition classrooms (often in the form of a "grading criteria" handout, and more often in the margin comments of returned essays where teachers explain why the essay is *not* an academic essay) without really being told why the standards exist in the first place. In many cases, this act of withholding causes students to treat writing as a code they must somehow crack — a guessing game — instead of something that they must participate in creating. Thus, academic discourses appear as stagnant, artificial, and arbitrary formulas to student writers, especially those for whom such discourses are not very accessible, rather than dynamic discourses that respond to and reflect the rhetorical and social contexts that create them.

Perhaps this examining of discursive conventions and standards also means that we might do well to give back to grammar *some* of the prominence it enjoyed in the "fix-it shop"–writing center, as another way of discussing "surface" changes to a student's writing and how those affect the student's subjectivity as well as a springboard to discussing other types of academic standards. Maybe part of what we are after is a way of employing North's "old" writing center in critique of his "new" one — that is, a critical examination of the stylistic techniques of change to expose the "new" writing center (as well as the acculturative impulses of the university), interested in changing writers.

Not only, then, should the postcolonial writing center aim to demystify writing processes by giving marginalized students insight into why certain conventions exist for certain discourses; it should also aim to equip these students with the skills necessary for analyzing conventions so that they can translate their knowledge into successful writing practices beyond the university community. Knowing not only what writing does, but also why and where it does it, allows these student writers to make more informed choices. Writing becomes no longer a guessing game in which the student hopes eventually to "figure out" what the teacher wants. Rather, the student begins to recognize that the act of writing invests him or her into a community's social pattern of action, and that the discourse he or she writes is a rhetorical dramatization of that pattern. More importantly, by making marginalized students aware of how writing constitutes them into a discourse community's social pattern of action, the writing center can potentially preclude any threat to these students' home discourses. They will still learn how to subordinate their ideas to one another, because such a convention is an important feature of some academic discourses. But having learned what it means to subordinate ideas and why such a convention is important to certain parts of the academic community, Derek and marginalized students like him not only will be better prepared to reproduce such conventions, but also will be more aware of how these conventions constitute only one out of many different means of reproducing experience.

Such an approach to discourse enables the writing center to expand a student's understanding of what writing does and where it does it, the goal being that such critical literacy will teach students how to analyze the discourses of their culture, and how, through their writing, to become more effective participants in the communities to which they belong. Like Jacqueline Jones Royster, we too "see the critical importance of the role of negotiator, someone who can cross boundaries and serve as guide and translator for Others" (34). The postcolonial writing center can and should serve as such a guide and translator.

Notes

[1] Such critique is also absent in North's follow-up article, "Revisiting 'The Idea of a Writing Center'" (1994).

[2] When Warnock and Warnock laud the writing center as a liberatory place in which "faculty and textbooks are not the authorities: students are their own authors" (22), they seem to overlook the complexities of the notion of "authorship." Their notion of "self-authoring" is problematic because it suggests that students take on the responsibility of writing themselves into the academy. In this case, marginalized writers are given the "opportunity" to constitute themselves as willing subjects, to consent to their domination under the liberatory assumption that if they do it themselves, then they are free. Maurice Godelier, whom we cite later, refers to this "consent" as an "exchange of services," a hegemonic construct within which domination becomes renamed as a beneficial "service" rendered on behalf of the colonized.

Works Cited

Anzaldua, Gloria. *Borderlands/La Frontera: The New Mestiza.* San Francisco: spinsters/aunt lute, 1987.

Bartholomae, David. "Inventing the University." *When a Writer Can't Write*. Ed. Mike Rose. New York: Guilford, 1985. 134–65.

Berlin, James. "Contemporary Composition: The Major Pedagogical Theories." *College English* 44.8 (Dec. 1982): 765–77.

Brodkey, Linda. "On the Subject of Class and Gender in 'The Literacy Letters.'" *Rhetoric and Composition: A Sourcebook for Teachers and Writers*. Ed. Richard L. Graves. 3rd. ed. Portsmouth: Boynton Cook, 1990. 279–95.

Constantino, Renato. "The Miseducation of the Filipino." *The Philippines Reader*. Ed. Daniel Schirmer and Stephen Rosskamm Shalom. Boston: South End, 1987. 45–49.

Foucault, Michel. *The Archeology of Knowledge and the Discourse on Language*. Trans. A. M. Sheridan Smith. New York: Pantheon, 1972.

Godelier, Maurice. *The Mental and the Material: Thought, Economy, and Society*. Trans. Martin Thom. London, Verso, 1986.

Hairston, Maxine. "The Winds of Change: Thomas Kuhn and the Revolution in the Teaching of Writing." *College Composition and Communication* 33 (1982): 76–88.

Harris, Joseph. "The Idea of Community in the Study of Writing." *Rhetoric and Composition: A Sourcebook for Teachers and Writers*. Ed. Richard L. Graves. 3rd. ed. Portsmouth: Boynton Cook, 1990. 267–78.

Hawkins, Thom. "Introduction." *Writing Centers: Theory and Administration*. Ed. Gary Olson. Urbana: NCTE, 1984. xi–xiv.

Hirsch, E. D. *Cultural Literacy: What Every American Needs to Know*. Boston: Houghton Mifflin, 1987.

Lu, Min-zhan. "Redefining the Legacy of Mina Shaughnessy: A Critique of the Politics of Linguistic Innocence." *The Writing Teacher's Sourcebook*. Ed. Gary Tate, Edward P. J. Corbett, and Nancy Myers. 3rd ed. New York: Oxford UP, 1994. 327–37.

North, Stephen. "The Idea of a Writing Center." *Rhetoric and Composition: A Sourcebook for Teachers and Writers*. Ed. Richard L. Graves. 3rd ed. Portsmouth: Boynton Cook, 1990. 232–46.

Pratt, Mary Louise. "Arts of the Contact Zone." *Profession* 91 (1991): 33–40.

Rose, Mike. "The Language of Exclusion: Writing Instruction at the University." *College English* 47.4 (April 1985): 341–59.

Royster, Jacqueline Jones. "When the First Voice You Hear is Not Your Own." *College Composition and Communication* 47 (1996): 29–40.

Said, Edward. *The World, the Text, and the Critic*. Cambridge: Harvard UP, 1983.

San Juan, Jr., Edward. "Philippine Writing in English: Postcolonial Syncretism Versus a Textual Practice of National Liberation." *Ariel* 22 (1991): 69–88.

Shaughnessy, Mina. *Errors and Expectations: A Guide for the Teacher of Basic Writing*. New York: Oxford UP, 1977.

Shiffman, Betty Garrison. "Writing Center Instruction: Fostering an Ethic of Caring." *Writing Lab Newsletter* 19.10 (June 1995): 1–5.

Soliday, Mary. "From the Margins to the Mainstream: Reconceiving Remediation." *CCC* 47 (1996): 85–100.

Stygall, Gail. "Resisting Privilege: Basic Writing and Foucault's Author Function." *CCC* 45 (1994): 320–341.

Villanueva, Victor. *Bootstraps: From an American Academic of Color*. Urbana: NCTE, 1993.

Wagner, Geoffrey. *The End of Education*. New York: Barnes, 1976.

Walcott, Derek. "The Muse of History." *The Post-Colonial Studies Reader*. Ed. Bill Ashcroft, Gareth Griffiths, and Helen Tiffin. London: Routledge, 1995. 370–74.

Warnock, Tilly, and John Warnock. "Liberatory Writing Centers: Restoring Authority to Writers." *Writing Centers: Theory and Administration*. Ed. Gary Olson. Urbana: NCTE, 1984. 16–24.

INTERPERSONAL DYNAMICS

Freud in the Writing Center: The Psychoanalytics of Tutoring Well

Christina Murphy _____

MARSHALL UNIVERSITY

Christina Murphy explores the quality and importance of the interpersonal relationships that tutors build with students by comparing such relationships to those psychoanalysts develop with their clients. "A good psychoanalyst and a good tutor both function to awaken individuals to their potentials and to channel their creative energies toward self-enhancing ends," Murphy writes. To do so, tutors must form a bond of trust with students, who, in coming to the writing center for help, "make themselves vulnerable . . . to understanding or misunderstanding, judgment or acceptance, approval or disapproval." The relationship a student forms with a tutor differs from those formed with classroom teachers in that it is voluntary, more personal, and aimed at solving the student's problems. Because of this difference, the tutor-student bond "often is primarily supportive and affective, secondarily instructional, and always directed to each student as an individual in a unique, one-to-one interpersonal relationship." By introducing the psychoanalytic principles of personal empowerment through interaction, the essay, which originally appeared in The Writing Center Journal in 1989, also offers writing center tutors a theoretical bridge between the expressionist and social constructionist schools of thought.

"A Writing Teacher Is Like a Psychoanalyst, Only Less Well Paid," Jay Parini declares in a recent essay in *The Chronicle* of *Higher Education*. One part of Parini's equation is almost self-evident to writing teachers since they know that, of the degreed professionals, college professors are among the least well paid for their efforts. The second half of the equation, the ways in which teaching writing mirrors aspects of the psychoanalytic process, is perhaps less apparent and clear. I would like to suggest that this correlation is most apparent in the interaction between tutors in a writing center and those students who come to seek their services. Unlike students who enroll in courses for a spectrum of reasons from "the course is required" to "it fits into my schedule," students come to a writing center for one reason only — they want help with their writing.

The fact that students come to the writing center wanting help and assuming they will receive it places those students in a different type of relationship with the tutor than with the instructor in a traditional classroom setting. While the teacher's role is primarily informative and focused upon the method of presentation that will best convey instruction to the class as a whole, the tutor's role often is primarily supportive and affective, secondarily instructional, and always directed to each student as an individual in a unique, one-to-one interpersonal relationship.

As in psychoanalysis, the quality of that interpersonal relationship between therapist and client, tutor and student, determines how successful the interaction as a whole will be. L. D. Goodstein, in an essay titled "What Makes Behavior Change Possible," argues that the quality of a therapeutic relationship is "an essential ingredient of behavior change." And what are the qualities of a good relationship of supportive intervention like therapy or tutoring? Carl Rogers states that all good therapists or supportive interveners manifest a real concern for those in their charge. They direct to these individuals, in Rogers' terms, "unconditional positive regard" by demonstrating a basic interest, concern, and desire to help another human being. Empathetic understanding expressed as honesty or a genuine openness of character is the second quality. The more this quality is perceived or felt by clients or students, the more impact it has on them.

Rogers places such a high premium upon the nature of the interpersonal relationship between therapist and client because so many of the people who enter in therapy are "hurt" — they are suffering from negative feelings or emotions, interpersonal problems, and inadequate and unsatisfying behaviors. The same is often true of individuals who come to a writing center. They, too, are "hurt" in that they display insecurities about their abilities as writers or even as academic learners, express fear to the tutor that they will be treated in the same judgmental or abusive way that they have been treated by teachers or fellow students before, or exhibit behavior patterns of anxiety, self-doubt, negative cognition, and procrastination that only intensify an already difficult situation.

> "I know you're going to tear this paper to shreds," they say, "but here goes anyway."
>
> "I've never been able to write. This is hopeless."
>
> "I know you can't help me, but I thought I'd try the writing center anyway."
>
> Or maybe they are defensive: "This teacher gives dumb assignments. If he'd just give me something I could write about, I know I'd do better."
>
> Sometimes they are self-deceived: "I've always made A's in English in high school, so I know I should be making A's in college, too."
>
> Other times they are self-defeating: "Can you help me with this paper? It's due at 2:00."
>
> "Well, that only gives us thirty minutes."
>
> "I know, but maybe you could go over it and help me write an ending."

By and large, the students who come "hurt" to a writing center are those who suffer from writer's block or a high degree of inhibiting anxiety associated with the process of producing writing that will be evaluated by others. These students demonstrate the principle endorsed by Rogers and other humanistic educators that learning is not simply a cognitive process. These students do not have difficulty writing because of any inherent flaws or limitations in the type of instruction they have received from their teachers or because they necessarily lack abilities as writers. Instead, they represent individuals whose talents as writers and as academic learners can be realized only within a specific set of conditions and circumstances. C. H. Patterson, in *Theories of Counseling and Psychotherapy,* indicates that, for these types of individuals with inherent abilities but inhibiting fears, the psychoanalytic concept of information theory may provide the most productive conceptual understanding and approach. This theory "views the individual as actively attending to, selecting, operating on, organizing, and transforming the information provided by the environment and by internal sources. Thus, the individual defines stimuli and events and constructs his or her own world" (668).

For the tutor, "information-processing psychology is concerned with understanding the nature of internal events, and more particularly, processes occurring within the individual as he or she handles and organizes his or her experience" (Wexler and Rice 15–20). Achieving the goals and possibilities of this theory, or of any client-centered theory, requires an empathetic bond between tutor and student in the interventive process. When such a structure is established by the tutor, the relationship that develops is experienced by the student as "safe, secure, free from threat, and supporting but not supportive" (Patterson 498). Rogers describes this process as "one dealing with warm living people who are dealt with by warm living counselors" (Patterson 499).

Some might argue against or minimize the importance of the relationship that develops between tutor and student or claim that, even though this relationship is potent in itself, it really bears little resemblance to the relationships established in a psychoanalytic setting. Truax and Carkhuff, in *Toward Effective Counseling and Psychotherapy,* would contend, however, that fundamental and profound similarities exist amongst all the interventive processes, from therapy, to education, to the managerial interactions of employer and employee. They state "the person (whether a counselor, therapist, or teacher) who is better able to communicate warmth, genuineness, and accurate empathy is more effective in interpersonal relationships no matter what the goal of the interaction" (116–17).

Most of what goes on in a writing center is talking and the range of interpersonal interactions available through words. In coming to a writing center for assistance, students must explain to a tutor what they want and what they hope to achieve. In the course of this type of interaction, the students make themselves vulnerable in opening themselves up to understanding or misunderstanding, judgment or acceptance, approval or disapproval.

Jim W. Corder, in an interesting essay titled "A New Introduction to Psychoanalysis, Taken as a Version of Modern Rhetoric," describes psychoanalysis, from a rhetorical perspective, as "the talking cure." Thomas Szasz calls psychotherapy "iatrology," or "healing words" (29). Psychotherapy, like rhetoric, understands the power of words, especially "healing words." As psychotherapists or tutors, we function like the old medicine man in *Ceremony,* the novel by Leslie Silko, who says, "That was the responsibility that went with being human . . . the story behind each word must be told so that there could be no mistake in the meaning of what had been said" (35). As psychotherapists or tutors, we share with those in our charge the responsibility that goes with being human. And in our very human roles, we share the powers of language to express emotions, to inspire creative thought, and to change perceptions of the self and others. We share the power of language to transform thought and being.

It is to psychotherapy that we owe the clearest model of the types of transformative interactions and outcomes that can occur in a writing center setting. For psychotherapy to be successful, (1) two persons are in contact; (2) one person, the client, generally is in a state of incongruence, being vulnerable or anxious; (3) the other person, the therapist, is congruent in the relationship; (4) the therapist experiences unconditional positive regard toward the client; (5) the therapist experiences an empathetic understanding of the client's internal frame of reference; and (6) the client perceives, at least to a minimal degree, the therapist's empathetic understanding of the client's internal frame of reference. As a result of the process of psychotherapy, (1) the client is more congruent, more open to his or her experiences, less defensive; (2) as a result, the client is more realistic, objective, extensional in his or her perceptions; (3) the client is consequently more effective in problem-solving; (4) as a result of the increased congruence of self and experience, his or her vulnerability to threat is reduced; (5) as a result of the lowering of his or her vulnerability to threat or defeat, the client has an increased degree of self-regard; and (6) as a result of all of the above factors, the client's behavior is more creative, more uniquely adaptive, and more fully expressive of his or her own values (Patterson 486–87).

If we substitute *tutor* and *student* here for *therapist* and *client,* the model holds true for the learning strategies and experiential awarenesses that go on in a writing center environment. A good psychoanalyst and a good tutor both function to awaken individuals to their potentials and to channel their creative energies toward self-enhancing ends. Within the focus of the one-on-one tutorial, the student and tutor work to interpret the cognitive strategies the student has employed to be expressive, insightful, concise, and clear. To work with the student in deciphering and assessing creative processes, in suggesting new ways to interpret data, methods of inquiry, and philosophical perspectives, and in determining a philosophy of personal expression requires from the tutor a sensitivity to the affective and intellectual dimensions of the student's personality. At the core of tutoring and psychotherapy are the interactional dynamics of a search for insight that involves an intimate trans-ference of trust and vulnerability between two individuals intent upon and intimately involved in finding answers.

Jim W. Corder states that "human frailty sets immediate and overpowering limits":

> Every utterance belongs to, exists in, issues from, and reveals a rhetorical uni-verse. Every utterance comes from somewhere (its inventive origin), emerges as a structure, and manifests itself as a style. All of the features of utterance — invention, structure, and style — cycle, reciprocate, and occur simultaneously. Each of us is a gathering place for a host of rhetorical universes. Some of them we share with others, indeed with whole cultures; some of them we inhabit alone, and some of them we occupy without knowing that we do. Each of us is a busy corner where multiple rhetorical universes intersect. (141)

Part of the transformative power of a writing center is that it is a setting in which rhetorical universes are shared. In this way, the tutoring process, like the psychotherapeutic process, partakes in the power of language to reshape and empower consciousness. James Hillman in *Re-Visioning Psychology* calls words "independent carriers of soul between people" (9). Perhaps no better description of the interaction that goes on in tutoring and in therapy can be found. If it is true that words transform consciousness, and changes in con-sciousness transform the self, then language-based processes like therapy and tutoring provide a dynamic for self-awareness and self-actualization. To this extent, they are liberatory philosophies in the manner that Paulo Freire uses that term to describe how the power of words can empower the conscious-nesses of ourselves and others.

Perhaps, when all is said and done, the old medicine man of Leslie Silko's *Ceremony* is a Freudian, believing in the humanness of liberation and in the power of reintegrating consciousness through the language of one's tribe. Perhaps the old medicine man works daily in writing centers across America, responding to the questions of those who come, apprentice fashion, to learn.

"Can you help me with my writing?"

"Yes, I can, but first let us start with your words."

Works Cited

Corder, Jim W. "A New Introduction to Psychoanalysis, Taken as a Version of Modern Rhetoric." *PreText* 5.3–4 (1984): 137–69.

Goodstein, L. D. "What Makes Behavior Change Possible?" *Contemporary Psychology* 22 (1977): 578–79.

Hillman, James. *Re-Visioning Psychology.* New York: Harper and Row, 1975.

Parini, Jay. "A Writing Teacher is Like a Psychoanalyst, Only Less Well Paid." *The Chronicle of Higher Education* 2 Nov. 1988. B2.

Patterson, C. H. *Theories of Counseling and Psychotherapy.* 3rd ed. New York: Harper and Row, 1980.

Rogers, Carl R. "The Necessary and Sufficient Conditions of Therapeutic Personality Change." *Journal of Consulting Psychology* 21 (1957): 95–103.

Shor, Ira, and Paulo Freire. *A Pedagogy for Liberation: Dialogues on Transforming Education.* South Hadley: Bergin and Garvey, 1987.

Silko, Leslie Marmon. *Ceremony.* New York: Viking Penguin, 1977.

Szasz, Thomas. *The Myth of Psychotherapy: Mental Healing as Religion, Rhetoric, and Repression.* New York: Anchor Press/Doubleday, 1978.

Truax, C. B., and R. R. Carkhuff. *Toward Effective Training in Counseling and Psychotherapy.* Chicago: Aldine, 1967.

Wexler, D. A., and L. N. Rice, eds. *Innovations in Client-Centered Therapy.* New York: Wiley, 1984.

"Whispers of Coming and Going": Lessons from Fannie

Anne DiPardo

THE UNIVERSITY OF IOWA

Anne DiPardo's essay, a case study of her work with Fannie, a Native American student, was chosen the outstanding work of scholarship for 1993 by the National Writing Centers Association. DiPardo profiles Fannie's development over a number of writing center tutorials. Through details about Fannie's past and dialogue between Fannie and DiPardo, the reader comes to know Fannie well enough to care about her. The essay also explores the corresponding development of Morgan, a peer tutor, as she struggles with the collaborative techniques she attempts to incorporate in her work with Fannie. DiPardo's essay emphasizes multicultural sensitivity by encouraging tutors to question the assumptions they make about students and to seek clues to the "hidden corners" of a student's past, personality, and methods of learning. DiPardo supports the notion of reflective practice in tutoring by encouraging tutors to be "perennially inquisitive and self-critical" while learning from the students they attempt to teach. Perhaps the essay's greatest value is the insight it offers into an individual student and tutor as they negotiate a relationship. This essay first appeared in The Writing Center Journal *in 1992.*

> As a man with cut hair, he did not identify the rhythm of three strands, the whispers of coming and going, of twisting and tying and blending, of catching and of letting go, of braiding.
> —Michael Dorris, *A Yellow Raft in Blue Water*

We all negotiate among multiple identities, moving between public and private selves, living in a present shadowed by the past, encountering periods in which time and circumstance converge to realign or even restructure our images of who we are. As increasing numbers of non-Anglo students pass through the doors of our writing centers, such knowledge of our own shape-shifting can help us begin — if *only* begin — to understand the social and linguistic challenges which inform their struggles with writing. When moved to talk about the complexities of their new situation, they so often describe a more radically chameleonic process, of living in non-contiguous worlds, of navigating between competing identities, competing loyalties. "It's like I have two cultures in me," one such student remarked to me recently, "but I can't choose." Choice becomes a moot point as boundaries blur, as formerly distinct selves become organically enmeshed, indistinguishable threads in a dynamic whole (Bakhtin 275; Cintron 24; Fischer 196).

Often placed on the front lines of efforts to provide respectful, insightful attention to these students' diverse struggles with academic discourse, writing tutors likewise occupy multiple roles, remaining learners even while emerging as teachers, perennially searching for a suitable social stance (Hawkins) — a stance existing somewhere along a continuum of detached toughness and warm empathy, and, which like all things ideal, can only be approximated, never definitively located. Even the strictly linguistic dimension of their task is rendered problematic by the continuing paucity of research on the writing of nonmainstream students (see Valdés; "Identifying Priorities"; "Language Issues") — a knowledge gap which likewise complicates our own efforts to provide effective tutor training and support. Over a decade has passed since Mina Shaughnessy eloquently advised basic writing teachers to become students of their students, to consider what Glynda Hull and Mike Rose ("Rethinking," "Wooden Shack") have more recently called the "logic and history" of literacy events that seem at first glance inscrutable and strange. In this age of burgeoning diversity, we're still trying to meet that challenge, still struggling to encourage our tutors to appreciate its rich contours, to discover its hidden rigors, to wrestle with its endless vicissitudes.

This story is drawn from a semester-long study of a basic writing tutorial program at a west-coast university — a study which attempted to locate these tutor-led small groups within the larger contexts of a writing program and campus struggling to meet the instructional needs of non-Anglo students (see DiPardo, "Passport"). It is about one tutor and one student, both ethnic minorities at this overwhelmingly white, middle-class campus, both caught up in elusive dreams and uncertain beginnings. I tell their story not because it is either unusual or typical, but because it seems so richly revealing of the larger themes I noted again and again during my months of data collection — as unresolved tensions tugged continually at a fabric of institutional good intentions, and as tutors and students struggled, with ostensible good will and inexorable frustration, to make vital connections. I tell this story because I believe it has implications for all of us trying to be worthy students of our students, to make sense of our own responses to diversity, and to offer effective support to beginning educators entrusted to our mentorship.

"It, Like, Ruins Your Mind": Fannie's Educational History

Fannie was Navajo, and her dream was to one day teach in the reservation boarding schools she'd once so despised, to offer some of the intellectual, emotional, and linguistic support so sorely lacking in her own educational history. As a kindergartner, she had been sent to a school so far from her home that she could only visit family on weekends. Navajo was the only language spoken in her house, but at school all the teachers were Anglo, and only English was allowed. Fannie recalled that students had been punished for speaking their native language — adding with a wry smile that they'd spoken Navajo anyway, when the teachers weren't around. The elementary school curriculum had emphasized domestic skills — cooking, sewing, and, especially, personal hygiene. "Boarding school taught me to be a housemaid," Fannie observed in one of her essays, "I was hardly taught how to read and write." All her literacy instruction had been in English, and she'd never become literate in Navajo. Raised in a culture that valued peer collaboration (cf. Philips 391–93), Fannie had long ago grasped that Anglo classrooms were places where teachers assume center stage, where students are expected to perform individually: "No," her grade-school teachers had said when Fannie turned to classmates for help, "I want to hear *only* from *you.*"

Estranged from her family and deeply unhappy, during fifth grade Fannie had stayed for a time with an aunt and attended a nearby public school. The experience there was much better, she recalled, but there soon followed a series of personal and educational disruptions as she moved among various relatives' homes and repeatedly switched schools. By the time she began high school, Fannie was wondering if the many friends and family members who'd dropped out had perhaps made the wiser choice. By her sophomore year, her grades had sunk "from A's and B's to D's and F's," and she was "hanging out with the wrong crowd." By mid-year, the school wrote her parents a letter indicating that she had stopped coming to class. When her family drove up to get her, it was generally assumed that Fannie's educational career was over.

Against all odds, Fannie finished high school after all. At her maternal grandmother's insistence, arrangements were made for Fannie to live with an aunt who had moved to a faraway west-coast town where the educational system was said to be much stronger. Her aunt's community was almost entirely Anglo, however, and Fannie was initially self-conscious about her English: "I had an accent really bad," she recalled, "I just couldn't communicate." But gradually, although homesick and sorely underprepared, she found that she was holding her own. Eventually, lured by the efforts of affirmative action recruiters, she took the unexpected step of enrolling in the nearby university. "I never thought I would ever graduate from high school," Fannie wrote in one of her essays, adding proudly that "I'm now on my second semester in college as a freshman." Her grandmother had died before witnessing either event, but Fannie spoke often of how pleased she would have been.[1]

Fannie was one of a handful of Native Americans on the campus, and the only Navajo. As a second-semester first-year student, she was still struggling to find her way both academically and socially, still working to overcome the scars of her troubled educational history. As she explained after listening to an audiotape of a tutorial session, chief among these was a lingering reluctance to speak up in English, particularly in group settings:

> *Fannie:* When, when, I'm talking . . . I'm shy. Because I always think I always say something not right, with my English, you know. (Pauses, then speaks very softly.) It's hard, though. Like with my friends, I do that too. Because I'll be quiet — they'll say, "Fannie, you're quiet." Or if I meet someone, I, I don't do it, let them do it, I let that person do the talking.
>
> *A. D.:* Do you wish you were more talkative?
>
> *Fannie:* I wish! Well I am, when I go home. But when I come here, you know, I always think, English is my second language and I don't know that much, you know.
>
> *A. D.:* So back home you're not a shy person?
>
> *Fannie:* (laughing uproariously) No! (continues laughing).

I had a chance to glimpse Fannie's more audacious side later that semester, when she served as a campus tour guide to a group of students visiting from a distant Navajo high school. She was uncharacteristically feisty and vocal that week, a change strikingly evident on the tutorial audiotapes. Indeed, when I played back one of that week's sessions in a final interview, Fannie didn't recognize her own voice: "Who's that talking?" she asked at first. But even as she recalled her temporary elation, she described as well her gradual sense of loss:

> Sometimes I just feel so happy when someone's here, you know, I feel happy? I just get that way. And then (pauses, begins to speak very softly), and then it just wears off. And then they're leaving — I think, oh, they're leaving, you know.

While Fannie described their week together as "a great experience," she was disturbed to find that even among themselves, the Navajo students were speaking English: "That bothered me a lot," she admitted, surmising that "they're like embarrassed . . . to speak Navajo, because back home, speaking Navajo fluently all the time, that's like lower class." "If you don't know the language," Fannie wrote in one of her essays, "then you don't know who you are. . . . It's your identity . . . the language is very important." In striking contrast to these students who refused to learn the tribal language, Fannie's grandparents had never learned to speak English: "They were really into their culture, and tradition, and all of that," she explained, "but now we're not that way anymore, hardly, and it's like we're losing it, you know." Fannie hoped to attend a program at Navajo Community College where she could learn to read and write her native language, knowledge she could then pass on to her own students.

Fannie pointed to the high drop-out rate among young Navajos as the primary reason for her people's poverty, and spoke often of the need to encourage students to finish high school and go on to college. And yet, worried as she was about the growing loss of native language and tradition, Fannie also expressed concerns about the Anglicizing effects of schooling. Education is essential, she explained, but young Navajos must also understand its dangers:

> I mean like, sometimes if you get really educated, we don't really want that. Because then, it like ruins your mind, and you use it, to like betray your people, too . . . That's what's happening a lot now.

By her own example, Fannie hoped to one day show her students that it is possible to be both bilingual and bicultural, that one can benefit from exposure to mainstream ways without surrendering one's own identity:

> If you know the white culture over here, and then you know your own culture, you can make a good living with that . . . when I go home, you know, I know Navajo, and I know English too. They say you can get a good job with that.

Back home, Fannie's extended family was watching her progress with warm pride, happily anticipating the day when she would return to the reservation to teach. When Fannie went back for a visit over spring break, she was surprised to find that they'd already built her a house: "They sure give me a lot of attention, that's for sure," she remarked with a smile. Many hadn't seen Fannie for some time, and they were struck by the change:

> Everybody still, kind of picture me, still, um, the girl from the past. The one who quit school — and they didn't think of me going to college at all. And they were surprised, they were really surprised. And they were like proud of me too . . .'cause none of their family is going to college.

One delighted aunt, however, was the mother of a son who was also attending a west-coast college:

> She says, "I'm so happy! I can't wait to tell him, that you're going to college too! You stick in there, Fannie, now don't goof!" I'm like, "I'll try not to!"

"I Always Write Bad Essays": Fannie's Struggles with Writing

On the first day of class, Fannie's basic writing teacher handed out a questionnaire that probed students' perceptions of their strengths and weaknesses as writers. In response to the question, "What do you think is good about your writing?" Fannie wrote, "I still don't know what is good about my writing"; in response to "What do you think is bad about your writing?" she responded, "Everything."

Fannie acknowledged that her early literacy education had been neither respectful of her heritage nor sensitive to the kinds of challenges she would face in the educational mainstream. She explained in an interview that her first instruction in essay writing had come at the eleventh hour, during her senior year of high school: "I never got the technique, I guess, of writing good essays," she explained, "I always write bad essays." While she named her "sentence structure, grammar, and punctuation" as significant weaknesses, she also added that "I have a lot to say, but I can't put it on paper . . . it's like I can't find the vocabulary." Fannie described this enduring block in an in-class essay she wrote during the first week of class:

> From my experience in writing essays were not the greatest. There were times my mind would be blank on thinking what I should write about.
>
> In high school, I learned how to write an essay during my senior year. I learned a lot from my teacher but there was still something missing about my essays. I knew I was still having problems with my essay organization.
>
> Now, I'm attending a university and having the same problems in writing essays. The university put me in basic writing, which is for students who did not pass the placement test. Of course, I did not pass it. Taking basic writing has helped me a lot on writing essays. There were times I had problems on what to write about.
>
> There was one essay I had problems in writing because I could not express my feelings on a paper. My topic was on Mixed Emotions. I knew how I felt in my mind but I could not find the words or expressing my emotions.
>
> Writing essays from my mind on to the paper is difficult for me. From this experience, I need to learn to write what I think on to a paper and expand my essays.

"Yes," her instructor wrote at the bottom of the page, "even within this essay — which is good — you need to provide specific detail, not just general statements." But what did Fannie's teacher find "good" about this essay — or was this opening praise only intended to soften the criticism that followed? Fannie had noted in an interview that she panicked when asked to produce something within 45 minutes: "I just write anything," she'd observed, "but your mind goes blank, too." Still, while this assignment may not have been the most appropriate way to assess the ability of a student like Fannie, both she and her instructor felt it reflected her essential weakness — that is, an inability to develop her ideas in adequate detail.

At the end of the semester, her basic writing teacher confided that Fannie had just barely passed the course, and would no doubt face a considerable struggle in first-year composition. Although Fannie also worried about the next semester's challenge, she felt that her basic writing course had provided valuable opportunities. "I improved a lot," she said in a final interview, "I think I did — I know I — did. 'Cause now I can know what I'm trying to say, and in an afternoon, get down to that topic." One of her later essays, entitled "Home," bears witness to Fannie's assertion:

> The day is starting out a good day. The air smells fresh as if it just rained. The sky is full with clouds, forming to rain. From the triangle mountain, the land has such a great view. Below I see hills overlapping and I see six houses few feet from each other. One of them I live in. I can also see other houses miles apart.
>
> It is so peaceful and beautiful. I can hear birds perching and dogs barking echos from long distance. I can not tell from which direction. Towards north I see eight horses grazing and towards east I hear sheep crying for their young ones. There are so many things going on at the same time.
>
> It is beginning to get dark and breezy. It is about to rain. Small drops of rain are falling. It feels good, relieving the heat. The rain is increasing and thundering at the same time. Now I am soaked, I have the chills. The clouds is moving on and clearing the sky. It is close to late afternoon. The sun is shining and drying me off. The view of the land is more beautiful and looks greener. Like a refreshment.
>
> Across from the mountain I am sitting is a mountain but then a plateau that stretches with no ending. From the side looks like a mountain but it is a long plateau. There are stores and more houses on top of the plateau.
>
> My clothes are now dry and it is getting late. I hear my sister and my brother calling me that dinner is ready. It was a beautiful day. I miss home.

"Good description," her instructor wrote on this essay, "I can really 'see' this scene." But meanwhile, she remained concerned about Fannie's lack of sophistication: "Try to use longer, more complex sentences," she added, "avoid short, choppy ones." Overwhelmed by the demands of composing and lacking strategies for working on this perceived weakness, Fannie took little away from such feedback aside from the impression that her writing remained inadequate. Although Fannie was making important strides, she needed lots of patient, insightful support if she were to overcome her lack of experience with writing and formidable block. Only beginning to feel a bit more confident in writing about personal experience, she anticipated a struggle with the expository assignments that awaited her:

> She's having us write from our experience. It'll be different if it's like in English 101, you know how the teacher tells you to write like this and that, and I find that one very hard, 'cause I see my other friends' papers and it's hard. I don't know if I can handle that class.

Fannie was trying to forge a sense of connection to class assignments — she wrote, for instance, about her Native American heritage, her dream of becoming a teacher, and about how her cultural background had shaped her concern for the environment. But meanwhile, as her instructor assessed Fannie's progress in an end-of-term evaluation, the focus returned to lingering weaknesses: "needs to expand ideas w/examples/description/explanation," the comments read, not specifying how or why or to whom. Somehow, Fannie had to fill in the gaps in her teacher's advice — and for the more individualized support she so sorely needed, she looked to the tutorials.

"Are You Learnin' Anything from Me?": The Tutorials

Morgan, Fannie's African American tutor, would soon be student teaching in a local high school, and she approached her work with basic writers as a trial run, a valuable opportunity to practice the various instructional strategies she'd heard about in workshops and seminars. Having grown up in the predominantly Anglo, middle-class community that surrounded the campus, Morgan met the criticisms of more politically involved ethnic students with dogged insistence: "I'm first and foremost a member of the *human* race," she often said, going on to describe her firm determination to work with students of all ethnicities, to help them see that success in the mainstream need not be regarded as cultural betrayal. During the term that I followed her — her second semester of tutoring and the first time she'd worked with non-Anglo students — this enthusiasm would be sorely tested, this ambition tempered by encounters with unforeseen obstacles.

Morgan's work with Fannie was a case in point. Although she had initially welcomed the challenge of drawing Fannie out, of helping this shy young woman overcome her apparent lack of self-confidence, by semester's end Morgan's initial compassion had been nearly overwhelmed by a sense of frustration. In an end-of-term interview, she confessed that one impression remained uppermost: "I just remember her sitting there," Morgan recalled, "and talking to her, and it's like, 'well I don't know, I don't know' . . . Fannie just has so many doubts, and she's such a hesitant person, she's so withdrawn, and mellow, and quiet. . . . A lot of times, she'd just say, 'well I don't know what I'm supposed to write. . . . Well I don't like this, I don't like my writing.'"

Although Fannie seldom had much to say, her words were often rich in untapped meaning. Early in the term, for instance, when Morgan asked why she was in college, Fannie searched unsuccessfully for words that would convey her strong but somewhat conflicted feelings:

Fannie: Well . . . (long pause) . . . it's hard . . .
Morgan: You wanna teach like, preschool? Well, as a person who wants to teach, what do you want outta your students?
Fannie: To get around in America you have to have education . . . (unclear).
Morgan: And what about if a student chose not to be educated — would that be ok?
Fannie: If that's what he wants . . .

At this point Morgan gave up and turned to the next student, missing the vital subtext — how Fannie's goal of becoming a teacher was enmeshed in her strong sense of connection to her people, how her belief that one needs an education "to get around" in the mainstream was tempered by insight into why some choose a different path. To understand Fannie's stance towards schooling, Morgan needed to grasp that she felt both this commitment *and* this ambivalence; but as was so often the case, Fannie's meager hints went unheeded.

A few weeks into the semester, Morgan labored one morning to move Fannie past her apparent block on a descriptive essay. Fannie said only that she was going to try to describe her grandmother, and Morgan began by asking a series of questions — about her grandmother's voice, her presence, her laugh, whatever came to Fannie's mind. Her questions greeted by long silences, Morgan admitted her gathering frustration: "Are you learnin' anything from me?" she asked. Morgan's voice sounded cordial and even a bit playful, but she was clearly concerned that Fannie didn't seem to be meeting her halfway. In the weeks that followed, Morgan would repeatedly adjust her approach, continually searching for a way to break through, "to spark something," as she often put it.

The first change — to a tougher, more demanding stance — was clearly signaled as the group brainstormed ideas for their next essays. Instead of waiting for Fannie to jump into the discussion, Morgan called upon her: "Ok, your turn in the hot seat," she announced. When Fannie noted that her essay would be about her home in Arizona, Morgan demanded to know "why it would be of possible interest to us." The ensuing exchange shed little light on the subject:

> *Fannie:* Because it's my home!
> *Morgan:* That's not good enough . . . that's telling me nothing.
> *Fannie:* I was raised there.
> *Morgan:* What's so special about it?
> *Fannie:* (exasperated sigh) I don't know what's so special about it . . .
> *Morgan:* So why do you want to write about it, then?

Morgan's final question still unanswered, she eventually gave up and moved to another student. Again, a wealth of valuable information remained tacit; Morgan wouldn't learn for several weeks that Fannie had grown up on a reservation, and she'd understood nothing at all about her profound bond with this other world.

Two months into the semester, Morgan had an opportunity to attend the Conference on College Composition and Communication (CCCC), and it was there that some of her early training crystallized into a more definite plan of action, her early doubts subsumed by a new sense of authoritative expertise. Morgan thought a great deal about her work with Fannie as she attended numerous sessions on peer tutoring and a half-day workshop on collaborative learning. She returned to campus infused with a clear sense of direction: the solution, Morgan had concluded, was to assume an even more low-profile approach, speaking only to ask open-ended questions or to paraphrase Fannie's statements, steadfastly avoiding the temptation to fill silences with her own ideas and asides. As she anticipated her next encounter with Fannie, she couldn't wait to try out this more emphatic version of what had been called — in conference sessions and her earlier training — a "collaborative" or "nondirective" stance.

Still struggling to produce an already past-due essay on "values," Fannie arrived at their first post-CCCC tutorial hour with only preliminary ideas, and nothing in writing. Remembering the advice of Conference participants, Morgan began by trying to nudge her towards a focus, repeatedly denying that she knew more than Fannie about how to approach the piece:

Morgan: What would you say your basic theme is? And sometimes if you keep that in mind, then you can always, you know, keep that as a focus for what you're writing. And the reason I say that is 'cause when you say, "well living happily wasn't. . . ."

Fannie: (pause) . . . Well, America was a beautiful country, well, but it isn't beautiful anymore.

Morgan: Um hm. Not as beautiful.

Fannie: So I should just say, America was a beautiful country?

Morgan: Yeah. But I dunno — what do you think your overall theme is, that you're saying?

Fannie: (long pause). . . . I'm really, I'm just talking about America.

Morgan: America? So America as . . . ?

Fannie: (pause) . . . Um . . . (pause)

Morgan: Land of free, uh, land of natural resources? As, um, a place where there's a conflict, I mean, there, if you can narrow that, "America." What is it specifically, and think about what you've written, in the rest. Know what I mean?

Fannie: (pause) . . . The riches of America, or the country? I don't know . . .

Morgan: I think you do. I'm not saying there's any right answer, but I, I'm — for me, the reason I'm saying this, is I see this emerging as, you know, (pause) where you're really having a hard time with dealing with the exploitation that you see, of America, you know, you think that. And you're using two groups to really illustrate, specifically, how two different attitudes toward, um the richness and beauty of America, two different, um, ways people have to approach this land. Does that, does this make any sense? Or am I just putting words in your mouth? I don't want to do that. I mean that's what I see emerge in your paper. But I could be way off base.

Fannie: I think I know what you're trying to say. And I can kind of relate it at times to what I'm trying to say.

Morgan: You know, I mean, this is like the theme I'm picking up . . .
(pause) I think you know, you've got some real, you know, environmental issues here. I think you're a closet environmentalist
here. Which are real true, know what I mean? (pause) And when
you talk about pollution, and waste, and, um, those types of
things. So I mean, if you're looking at a theme of your paper,
what could you pick out, of something of your underlying
theme.

Fannie: (pause) . . . The resources, I guess?

Morgan: Well I mean, I don't want you to say, I want you to say, don't say
"I guess," is that what you're talkin' about?

Fannie: Yeah.

Morgan: "Yeah?" I mean, it's your paper.

Fannie: I know, I want to talk about the land . . .

Morgan: Ok. So you want to talk about the land, and the beauty of the
land . . .

Fannie: Um hm.

Morgan: . . . and then, um, and then also your topic for your, um, to
spark your paper . . . what values, and morals, right? That's
where you based off to write about America, and the land, you
know. Maybe you can write some of these things down, as we're
talking, as focusing things, you know. So you want to talk about
the land, and then it's like, what do you want to say about the
land?

What *did* Fannie "want to say about the land"? Whatever it was, one begins to
wonder if it was perhaps lost in her tutor's inadvertent appropriation of these
meanings — this despite Morgan's ostensible effort to simply elicit and reflect
Fannie's thoughts. While Fannie may well have been struggling to articulate
meanings which eluded clear expression in English, as Morgan worked to
move her towards greater specificity, it became apparent that she was assuming the paper would express commonplace environmental concerns:

Fannie: I'll say, the country was, um, (pause), more like, I can't say
perfect, I mean was, the tree was green, you know, I mean, um,
it was clean. (long pause) I can't find the words for it.

Morgan: In a natural state? Um, un-, polluted, um, untouched, um, let
me think, tryin' to get a . . .

Fannie: I mean everybody, I mean the Indians too, they didn't wear that
(pointing to Morgan's clothes), they only wore buffalo clothing,
you know for clothing, they didn't wear like . . . these, you
know, cotton, and all that, they were so . . .

Morgan: Naturalistic.

Fannie: Yeah. "Naturalistic," I don't know if I'm gonna use that
word . . . I wanna say, I wanna give a picture of the way the land
was, before, you know what I'm, what I'm tryin' to say?

The Navajos' connection to the land is legendary — a spiritual nexus, many
would maintain, that goes far beyond mainstream notions of what it means to
be concerned about the environment. However, later in this session, Morgan
observed that Fannie was writing about concerns that worry lots of people —
citing recent publicity about the greenhouse effect, the hole in the ozone layer,
and the growing interest in recycling. She then brought the session to a close
by paraphrasing what she saw as the meat of the discussion and asking, "Is
that something that you were tryin' to say, too?" Fannie replied, "Probably. I
mean, I can't find the words for it, but you're finding the words for me."
Morgan's rejoinder had been, "I'm just sparkin', I'm just sparkin' what you
already have there, what you're sayin'. I mean I'm tryin' to tell you what I hear
you sayin'."

Morgan laughed as, in an end-of-term interview, she listened again to
Fannie's final comment: "I didn't *want* to find the words for her," she mused;
"I wanted to show her how she could find 'em for herself." Still, she admitted,
the directive impulse had been hard to resist: "I wanted to just give her ideas,"
Morgan observed, adding that although Fannie had some good things to say,
"I wanted her to be able to articulate her ideas on a little higher level."

Although it was obvious to Morgan that the ideas in Fannie's paper were of
"deep-seated emotional concern," she also saw her as stuck in arid generalities: "'I don't know, it's just such a beautiful country,'" Morgan echoed as she
reviewed the audiotape. While Morgan emphasized that she "didn't wanna
write the paper for her," she allowed that "it's difficult — it's really hard to
want to take the bull by the horns and say, 'don't you see it this way?'" On the
one hand, Morgan noted that she'd often asked Fannie what she was getting
out of a session, "'cause sometimes I'll think I'm getting through and I'm
explaining something really good, and then they won't catch it"; on the other
hand, Morgan emphasized again and again that she didn't want to "give away"
her own thoughts.

Although Morgan often did an almost heroic job of waiting out Fannie's lingering silences and deflecting appeals to her authority, she never really surren-
dered control; somehow, the message always came across that Morgan knew
more than Fannie about the ideas at hand, and that if she could, she would
simply turn over pre-packaged understandings. While her frustration was certainly understandable, I often had the sense that Morgan was insufficiently
curious about Fannie's thoughts — insufficiently curious about how Fannie's
understandings might have differed from her own, about how they had been
shaped by Fannie's background and cultural orientation, or about what she
stood to learn from them.

When asked about Fannie's block, a weary Morgan wrote it off to her cultural background:

> You know, I would have to say it's cultural; I'd have to say it's her you know, Native American background and growing up on a reservation . . . maybe . . . she's more sensitive to male-female roles, and the female role being quiet.

On a number of occasions Morgan had speculated that Navajo women are taught to be subservient, a perception that contrasted rather strikingly with Fannie's assertion that she wasn't at all shy or quiet back home.[2] Hoping to challenge Morgan's accustomed view of Fannie as bashful and retiring, in a final interview I played back one of their sessions from the week that a group of Navajo students were visiting the campus. Fannie was uncharacteristically vocal and even aggressive that morning, talking in a loud voice, repeatedly seizing and holding the floor:

Fannie: You know what my essay's on? Different environments. Um, I'm talking, I'm not gonna talk about my relationship between my brothers, it's so boring, so I'm just gonna talk about both being raised, like my youngest brother being raised on the reservation, and the other being raised over here, and they both have very different, um, um, (Morgan starts to say something, but Fannie cuts her off and continues) characteristics or somethin' like that. You know, like their personalities, you know.

Morgan: Um. That's good. (Morgan starts to say something more, but Fannie keeps going.)

Fannie: It's funny, I'm cutting, I was totally mean to my brother here. (Morgan laughs.) Because, I called, I said that he's a wimp, you know, and my brother, my little brother's being raised on the reservation, is like, is like taught to be a man, he's brave and all that.

Luis: (a student in the group) That's being a man?!

Fannie: And . . .

Luis: That's not being a man, I don't find.

Fannie: (her voice raised) I'm sorry — but that's how I wrote, Ok?! That's your opinion, I mean, and it's . . .

Luis: I think a man is sensitive, caring, and lov —

Fannie: (cutting him off) No, no . . .

Luis: . . . and able to express his feelings. I don't think that if you can go kill someone, that makes you a man.

Fannie: I mean . . .

Luis: That's just my opinion (gets up and walks away for a moment).

Fannie: (watching Luis wander off) Dickhead.

Morgan listened with a widening smile to the rest of this session, obviously pleased with Fannie's sometimes combative manner and unflagging insistence that attention be directed back to her. "Ha! Fannie's so much more forceful," Morgan exclaimed, "and just more in control of what she wants, and what she needs." When asked what she thought might have accounted for this temporary change, Morgan sidestepped the influence of the visiting students:

> I would love to think I made her feel safe that way. And that I really um, showed her that she had, you know, by my interactions with her, that she really had every right to be strong-willed and forceful and have her opinions and you know, say what she felt that she needed to say, and that she didn't have to be quiet, you know. People always tell me that I influence people that way. You know? (laughs). "You've been hangin' around with Morgan too much!"

Hungry for feedback that she'd influenced Fannie in a positive way, Morgan grasped this possible evidence with obvious pleasure. Fannie was not a student who offered many positive signals, and it was perhaps essential to Morgan's professional self-esteem that she find them wherever she could. In this credit-taking there was, however, a larger irony: if only she'd been encouraged to push a little farther in her own thinking, perhaps she would have found herself assisting more often in such moments of blossoming.

Conclusion: Students as Teachers, Teachers as Students

When Morgan returned from the CCCC with a vision of "collaboration" that cast it as a set of techniques rather than a new way to think about teaching and learning, the insights of panelists and workshop leaders devolved into a fossilized creed, a shield against more fundamental concerns. Morgan had somehow missed the importance of continually adjusting her approach in the light of the understandings students make available, of allowing their feedback to shape her reflections upon her own role. At semester's end, she still didn't know that Fannie was a non-native speaker of English; she didn't know the dimensions of Fannie's inexperience with academic writing, nor did she know the reasons behind Fannie's formidable block.

Even as Morgan labored to promote "collaborative" moments — making an ostensible effort to "talk less," to "sit back more," to enact an instructional mode that would seem more culturally appropriate — Fannie remembered a lifetime of classroom misadventure, and hung back, reluctant. Morgan needed to know something about this history, but she also needed to understand that much else was fluid and alive, that a revised sense of self was emerging from the dynamic interaction of Fannie's past and present. Emboldened by a few treasured days in the company of fellow Navajos, Fannie had momentarily stepped into a new stance, one that departed markedly from her accustomed behavior on reservation and campus alike; but if her confidence recalled an earlier self, her playful combativeness was, as Fannie observed in listening to the tape, a new and still-strange manifestation of something also oddly familiar, something left over from long ago.

Rather than frequent urgings to "talk less," perhaps what Morgan most needed was advice to *listen more* — for the clues students like Fannie would provide, for those moments when she might best shed her teacherly persona and become once again a learner. More than specific instructional strategies, Morgan needed the conceptual grounding that would allow her to understand that authentically collaborative learning is predicated upon fine-grained insight into individual students — of the nature of their Vygotskian "zones of proximal development," and, by association, of the sorts of instructional "scaffolding" most appropriate to their changing needs (Bruner; Applebee and Langer). So, too, did Morgan need to be encouraged toward the yet-elusive understanding that such learning is never unilateral, inevitably entailing a reciprocal influence, reciprocal advances in understanding (Dyson). As she struggled to come to terms with her own ethnic ambivalence, to defend herself against a vociferous chorus proclaiming her "not black enough," Morgan had reason to take heart in Fannie's dramatic and rather trying process of transition. Had she thought to ask, Morgan would no doubt have been fascinated by Fannie's descriptions of this other cultural and linguistic context, with its very different perspectives on education in particular and the world in general (John; Locust). Most of all, perhaps, she would have been interested to know that Fannie was learning to inhabit both arenas, and in so doing, enacting a negotiation of admirable complexity — a negotiation different in degree, perhaps, but certainly not in kind, from Morgan's own.

Having tutored only one semester previously, Morgan was understandably eager to abandon her lingering doubts about her effectiveness, eager for a surefooted sense that she was providing something worthwhile. Her idealism and good intentions were everywhere apparent — in her lengthy meditations on her work, in her eager enthusiasm at the CCCC, in her persistent efforts to try out new approaches, and in the reassurance she extended to me when I confessed that I'd be writing some fairly negative things about her vexed attempts to reach Fannie. Morgan had been offered relatively little by way of preparation and support: beyond a sprinkling of workshops and an occasional alliance with more experienced tutors, she was left largely on her own — alone with the substantial challenges and opportunities that students like Fannie presented, alone to deal with her frustration and occasional feelings of failure as best she could. Like all beginning educators, Morgan needed abundant support, instruction, and modeling if she were to learn to reflect critically upon her work, to question her assumptions about students like Fannie, to allow herself, even at this fledgling stage in her career, to become a reflective and therefore vulnerable practitioner. That is not to suggest that Morgan should have pried into hidden corners of Fannie's past, insisting that she reveal information about her background before she felt ready to do so; only that Morgan be respectfully curious, ever attentive to whatever clues Fannie might have been willing to offer, ever poised to revise old understandings in the light of fresh evidence.

Those of us who work with linguistic minority students — and that's fast becoming us all — must appreciate the evolving dimensions of our task, realizing that we have to reach further than ever if we're to do our jobs well. Regardless of our crowded schedules and shrinking budgets, we must also think realistically about the sorts of guidance new tutors and teachers need if they are to confront these rigors effectively, guiding them towards practical strategies informed by understandings from theory and research, and offering compelling reminders of the need to monitor one's ethnocentric biases and faulty assumptions. Most of all, we must serve as models of reflective practice — perennially inquisitive and self-critical, even as we find occasion both to bless and curse the discovery that becoming students of students means becoming students of ourselves as well.

Notes

[1] "Fannie" was the actual name of this student's maternal grandmother. We decided to use it as her pseudonym to honor this lasting influence.

[2] Morgan's assumption is also contradicted by published accounts of life among the Navajo, which from early on have emphasized the prestige and power of female members of the tribe. Gladys Reichard, an anthropologist who lived among the Navajos in the 1920s, reported that "the Navajo woman enjoys great economic and social prestige as the head of the house and clan and as the manager of economic affairs, and she is not excluded from religious ritual or from attaining political honors" (55). Navajo women often own substantial property, and children retain the surname of the matrilineal clan; the status accorded women is further reflected in the depictions of female deities in Navajo myths (Terrell 57; 255).

Acknowledgments

Special thanks to Sarah Warshauer Freedman for encouragement and sage advice throughout this project. Thanks also to Don McQuade, Guadalupe Valdés, and the members of my fall 1991 writing research class at The University of Iowa. This work was supported by a grant from the NCTE Research Foundation.

Works Cited

Applebee, Arthur, and Judith Langer. "Reading and Writing Instruction: Toward a Theory of Teaching and Learning." *Review of Research in Education*. Vol. 13. Ed. E. Z. Rothkopf. Washington, DC: American Educational Research Association, 1986.

Bakhtin, Mikhail Mikhailovich. *The Dialogic Imagination: Four Essays by M. M. Bakhtin*. Ed. Michael Holquist, trans. Caryl Emerson and Michael Holquist. Austin: U of Texas P, 1981.

Bruner, Jerome. "The Role of Dialogue in Language Acquisition." *The Child's Conception of Language*. Ed. A. Sinclair. New York: Springer-Verlag, 1978.

Cintron, Ralph. "Reading and Writing Graffiti: A Reading." *The Quarterly Newsletter of the Laboratory of Comparative Human Cognition* 13 (1991): 21–24.

DiPardo, Anne. "Acquiring 'A Kind of Passport': The Teaching and Learning of Academic Discourse in Basic Writing Tutorials." Diss. UC Berkeley, 1991.

———. *'A Kind of Passport': A Basic Writing Adjunct Program and the Challenge of Student Diversity*. Urbana: NCTE, 1993.

Dorris, Michael. *A Yellow Raft in Blue Water.* New York: Holt, 1987.

Dyson, Anne. "Weaving Possibilities: Rethinking Metaphors for Early Literacy Development." *The Reading Teacher* 44 (1990): 202–13.

Fischer, Michael. "Ethnicity and the Postmodern Arts of Memory." *Writing Culture: The Poetics and Politics of Ethnography.* Ed. J. Clifford and G. E. Marcus. Berkeley: U of California P, 1986.

Hawkins, Thom. "Intimacy and Audience: The Relationship Between Revision and the Social Dimension of Peer Tutoring." *College English* 42 (1980): 64–68.

Hull, Glynda, and Mike Rose. "Rethinking Remediation: Toward a Social-Cognitive Understanding of Problematic Reading and Writing." *Written Communication* 6 (1989): 139–54.

———. "This Wooden Shack: The Logic of an Unconventional Reading." *College Composition and Communication* 41 (1990): 287–98.

John, Vera P. "Styles of Learning — Styles of Teaching: Reflections on the Education of Navajo Children." *Functions of Language in the Classroom.* Ed. Courtney B. Cazden and Vera P. John. 1972. Prospect Heights: Waveland, 1985.

Locust, Carol. "Wounding the Spirit: Discrimination and Traditional American Indian Belief Systems." *Harvard Educational Review* 58 (1988): 315–30.

Philips, Susan U. "Participant Structures and Communicative Competence: Warm Springs Children in Community and Classroom." *Functions of Language in the Classroom.* Ed. Courtney B. Cazden and Vera P. John. 1972. Prospect Heights: Waveland, 1985.

Reichard, Gladys. *Social Life of the Navajo Indians.* 1928. New York: AMS P, 1969.

Shaughnessy, Mina. "Diving In: An Introduction to Basic Writing." *College Composition and Communication* 27 (1976): 234–39.

Terrell, John Upton. *The Navajo: The Past and Present of a Great People.* 1970. New York: Perennial, 1972.

Valdés, Guadalupe. *Identifying Priorities in the Study of the Writing of Hispanic Background Students.* Grant. No. OERI-G-008690004. Washington, DC: Office of Educational Research and Improvement, 1989.

———. *Language Issues in Writing: The Problem of Compartmentalization of Interest Areas Within CCCC.* Paper presented at the Conference on College Composition and Communication. 21–23 March, 1991.

Vygotsky, Lev. *Mind in Society.* Cambridge: Harvard UP, 1978.

Intellectual Tug-of-War: Snapshots of Life in the Center

Elizabeth H. Boquet _____

FAIRFIELD UNIVERSITY

As Elizabeth H. Boquet illustrates in this article, life in the writing center sometimes goes awry, and conditions often do not reflect anyone's notion of an ideal tutorial or an ideal work situation. She describes several interpersonal conflicts in the writing center — between tutor and student, tutor and coworker, and tutor and accepted tutorial practices — that end in frustration on the part of writer or tutor and, as a consequence, raise issues central to writing center work. Boquet uses "snapshots" of life in the center to examine "moments when tutors are simply at a loss" and "feel that their own progress toward becoming the 'ideal' writing center tutor is jeopardized." As she argues, "Life in the writing center thrives on . . . asymmetry, and on the hope that we can eventually achieve some sort of symmetry, if not harmony." As tutors wrestle with seemingly irreconcilable social or ideological conflicts, experience teaches them to continue to strive to "produce better writers, better tutors, more humane working conditions" without expecting to fully achieve these goals. The article, which originally appeared in the book Stories from the Center: Connecting Narrative and Theory in the Writing Center, *examines several scenarios that tutors will likely confront as they go about their work.*

Just as I sat down to write this paper, a student came up to me for help. She was exasperated, as novice computer workers and uncertain writers often are in the writing center: "My paper won't print out and I need to leave now."

I hurried over to the printer and checked to make sure it was online. Everything seemed to be in order, but still her paper wouldn't print out. Rather than have her wait while I looked into the problem further, I suggested to her that she move to a computer that printed at another station. She replied, "I don't care what you do."

When I asked her what she wanted to call the file so that we could save it, she said, "I don't care what you call it." So I saved it and moved to another computer, yet when I went to call up the file I discovered a maze of subdirectories with no trace of the file that I had just saved. When I asked her if she had been working in a subdirectory, she almost blew up: "Just give me the disk. Just give it back to me. I don't have time to mess with this. I'm just not going to do it."

She grabbed the disk from me, tore through the writing center and slammed into an international student who was waiting to be tutored. Since all the other tutors were busy, I sat down with the ESL student and asked him how I could help him. "Could you check my grammar?"

"Sure," I wanted to reply in my most cynical voice, "Why not." Instead, I mustered up all the charm I had left at 8:30 on a Monday night and sat down to work with what I hoped would be the last of a seemingly endless stream of students that evening. I was tired. I was cranky. I had other work to do. But all those things were not this student's fault. Above all, I had to remember that.

These are scary things to admit. Will my readers think that I'm a bad tutor? Or worse, a horrible person? Should I instead talk about the things I've done right in the center, about the tasks I know I can perform well? That temptation is great, but it is not, for me at least, as necessary as analyzing the moments when tutors do things "wrong," either intentionally or unintentionally. Nor is it as worthwhile as examining moments when tutors are simply at a loss, as I was when the student mentioned earlier stormed away, leaving me standing there in a cloud of dust. So this paper will be about those moments when tutors feel that their own progress toward becoming the "ideal" writing center tutor is jeopardized.

The World as a Stage

For many tutors (including myself), working in a writing center is their first "real" job. In his book *The Presentation of Self in Everyday Life* (1959), Erving Goffmann supplies us with a reading of the world as a stage that might help us to envision life in the center. As tutors, our performers are stepping into a role for which an ideal already exists. As represented in the literature on writing centers, tutors are supportive; they are peers; they affirm; they question. These are formidable expectations for beginning (or for any) tutors to fulfill. Part of the problem seems to be that, with few notable exceptions (*The Writing Lab Newsletter* and the National Conference on Peer Tutoring and Writing being the most obvious), conclusions are drawn *about* peer tutors, information is produced *for* peer tutors, but rarely are these things created *by* peer tutors. Tutors are often objectified and essentialized in the literature devoted to them. In this way, tutors are disallowed a voice in the literature that pertains most directly to them. Even though many tutors have several semesters of training in composition theory and several years of experience tutoring, they cannot, almost by definition, be considered professionals. A peer is *not* a professional; a tutor is *not* a teacher. This is the pro and the con of the job. John Trimbur writes, "[N]ew tutors are already implicated in a system that makes the words 'peer' and 'tutor' appear to be a contradiction in terms. . . . [T]o be selected as a peer tutor in the first place seems only to confirm the contradiction in terms by acknowledging differences between the tutors and their tutees. . . . Appointment to tutor, after all, invests a certain institutional authority in the tutors that their tutees have not earned" (1987, 23). How far such authority extends, however, is not always clear, thereby causing the tutor to sometimes feel torn or confused about her role in the writing center.

In fact, tutors' authority even within the tutoring sessions they conduct has been suspect, as evidenced by the fact that, until recently, tutors have been disallowed a voice in the tutoring sessions they conduct. Much of the standard advice about tutoring, with its genesis in Vygotsky's zone of proximal development and psycholinguistic theories of bootstrapping, emphasizes the need for tutors to "mirror" students' questions back to them so the students can engage in *self*-discovery. Some practitioners, like Brooks in his 1991 article "Minimalist Tutoring: Making the Student Do All the Work," appear downright militant in their insistence that tutors refrain from engaging in meaningful dialogue about a student's text. Interesting that a discipline emphasizing the social nature of knowledge-creation brings us right back to the individual.

Although I certainly wouldn't wrestle authority away from the writers themselves, I also know that simply reflecting student concerns back to the student does not always foster the most productive tutorial environment. I don't want students to perceive me as having all the answers, yet very often I do have the answers they are looking for, and the students themselves know it. While I know that, in the ideal tutoring situation, I (as tutor) would facilitate a student's self-discovery, I also know that real tutorial cases are not always as simple as that. ESL students usually come in looking for help with their grammar, sentence structure, and punctuation. This is often not knowledge that I can help them access, because it is probably not knowledge that they have. By attempting to have them figure it out for themselves, I end up feeling as though I've perpetuated the very notion that I am attempting to dispel — that there is a body of knowledge "out there" that some people (like me) have access to and other people (like them) do not.

In an unpublished essay entitled "Pedagogy of the _____: Resisting Secrecy in College English Classrooms," John Tassoni states, "[A]s teachers we need to avoid moments . . . in which information and opinions are withheld in ways that jeopardize creativity and undermine democratic relations in the classroom" (1). He argues that such secrecy merely serves to "hypostatize knowledge and reinforce unfair power relations between teachers and students" (1). I would argue that such secrecy, particularly as advocated in writing centers, can also be a self-preservation device. It is yet another way of justifying our existence to the faculty and administration, of assuring the powers-that-be (whoever they may be) that we don't "give away any answers." And by engaging in such a practice, we fail to educate our students, our tutors, our colleagues, ourselves. What is the justification for ostensibly creating spaces in which dialogue can occur only to encourage our tutors to be anti-dialogic? What sort of message are we sending to the students we tutor if they perceive us as withholding information vital to their academic success? And to the tutors trained in the writing center, most of whom will take their places (and their philosophies on teaching) into classrooms of their own?

Until now, most of the talk on tutor-training has focused on the overt curriculum — the articles tutors are given to read, the sessions facilitated by directors, the courses designed for tutor development. Much of the training taking place in the writing center, however, falls more in line with Giroux's notion of the hidden curriculum. Tutors are generally intelligent people who quickly learn that the reality of life in the center is much different from that most often depicted in journals. They see that even experienced tutors fade into the woodwork of the writing center (or, as was the case in one writing center, sneak off to the bathroom) when they simply can't face one more student, leaving other tutors to pick up the slack. Through these observations, tutors learn that, when they applied for a job at the writing center, they agreed to join a team whose members are concerned with what Goffmann calls "impression management": "Within the walls of a social establishment we find a team of performers who cooperate to present to an audience a given definition of the situation. . . . Among members of the team we find that familiarity prevails, solidarity is likely to develop, and that secrets that could give the show away are shared and kept" (239).

Breeding a sense of solidarity is crucial to the success of any writing center team, yet, particularly in the writing center, the division between performer and audience is not always clear. Living in our postmodern era of splintered subjectivities, we know that it is not as simple as saying that tutors are performing for an audience of students. Subject and object coexist in a relationship much more dynamic than their binary rhetorical opposition suggests. And tutors themselves are not blank slates. They must negotiate the role of tutor so that it squares with the other roles they play in our society, roles marked perhaps by race, class, gender, and sexual orientation, to name a few. At the same time tutors feel an obligation to back each other up, to make the performance succeed. Tutors defend each other to students, directors defend tutors to professors, and tutors defend professors to students. These are precarious positions, since no one is ever fully a member of any one group. As Goffmann writes, "[W]e must be prepared to see that the impression of reality fostered by a performance is a delicate, fragile thing" (56). The director, for example, is a member of the writing center team, but is also an arm of the administration. The tutors are peer tutors, at once in solidarity with the students and spokespeople for academia. According to contemporary ethnographers, no longer is it fashionable, or useful, to view workers as static, as worked on by their environments. Instead, we need to view workers as dynamic forces within their workplaces, as actively shaping as well as being shaped by their surroundings (Hodson 1991). This tug-of-war can prove to be an enabling force, a means of asserting a self, especially in the writing center.

On Stage with Michael

Learning how and when to assert that self is tricky business. As a graduate student in a rhetoric and linguistics program, I tutored students whose professors frequently had less training in (and less interest in) teaching composition than I did. One of my students, Michael, came in during the first week of classes with a packet of worksheets that his professor put together. It consisted of symbols that stood for propositions, assertions, contradictions, etc. He showed it to me and asked me to help him decipher it. I couldn't. He seemed dismayed. He explained to me that he was to write two sentences per night, following the format described by these symbols, and by the end of the semester he would have a paper.

I was astounded, speechless. There I was, at a university with one of the oldest Ph.D. programs in composition in the country, and that legacy meant very little in terms of pedagogical methods even within our own department.

Michael wondered aloud if all English classes were like that. I smiled weakly and raised my eyebrows. He said, "I have friends who are taking English classes, and they're not having nearly as much trouble as I am." I didn't know what to say. I was caught between my knowledge as a professional, my responsibility to students, and my precarious position as a graduate assistant in an ancillary university service. What would have constituted stepping out of bounds? This student has the right to know that he is not getting his money's worth (literally). I have an obligation as a member of this profession to attempt to effect change within it, yet I feel powerless. And I wonder when I will ever feel power-full. When I have a "real" job? When I have tenure? When I'm a full professor? And I have to ask, along with Carroll, Carse, and Trefzer, "How can we hope to participate in the transformation of the profession . . . when we are ourselves in the process of transformation, struggling to create professional selves in an institution that marginalizes us while dictating the shape of those future selves?" (1993, 64). In this way, perhaps, the profession ensures, by means of subtle (and not-so-subtle) coercion, that its members fall short of the ideal.

In the incident with Michael, I decided to comply with the expectations set out by our writing center directors concerning faculty-tutor-student protocol. In other words, I kept quiet and helped the student as best I could to perform the tasks required of him within the confines of the class. At the time, I justified my actions by reminding myself that the "ideal" tutor is to be neither a student-advocate nor a teacher-advocate. Rather, my job as a tutor was to help Michael learn to operate within the constraints of his rhetorical context. And the instructor, obviously, was a large part of that context.

After a bit of soul-searching, I realized that I hadn't been completely honest, either with Michael or with myself. As a tutor, I was not perched on the fence of neutrality. By failing to speak to this situation in any meaningful way, I was, in fact, aligning myself with the faculty. Politically, I couldn't afford to make an enemy of a faculty member, and I didn't want to put the writing center director in the position of having to defend me (and by default, to defend the writing center) to this faculty member, to the department head, and possibly even to the dean. By comparison, failing to empower a student seemed like a small price to pay. Nevertheless, I don't know how I would have done it differently. I only know that I never felt more acutely that I had fallen short of my own "ideal."

Tutoring as Work

In my interaction with Michael, I acted out the script as it was written for me by the institution — no improvisation allowed. Other tutors with whom I've worked have become quite skilled at quiet subversion. The narrative that I would like to retell involves one tutor who used the very documents intended to record writing center activity to control the ways in which she was written into the center's history.

Tutors, like all workers, strive for situations in which they are able to exert some measure of control, of dominance, over the systems at work on them. Attempting to explore this issue, Randy Hodson conducted an ethnography, the results of which are published in his article, "The Active Worker: Compliance and Autonomy at the Workplace" (1991). Hodson concludes that "workers are active on their own terms and as motivated by their own agendas. These agendas are much more diverse than those theoretically allowed them by management theory or radical social science theory and include both compliance and resistance as well as autonomous creative effort to structure their own work" (47). One of our tutors, whom I'll call Shelly, embodied this compliance and resistance whenever she was faced with recording her tutoring sessions.

Shelly was wonderful with students. Her quiet, calm demeanor drew students naturally to her, and she was quick to tutor any student who needed help. Sometimes in the course of one afternoon she would work with six or seven students. So I found it quite odd that, as I was going through our files, her name rarely showed up as having tutored any of the students that we had on record. When I asked her about this, she replied, "I never fill those sheets out. They take too much time. If the student wants a note sent to her professor, I'll send that, but other than that, I just don't worry about it."

Our writing center is fairly high-tech, with over thirty IBM-compatible computers, but there is one thing that, despite all our technology, we cannot avoid: paperwork. We fill out forms (or we're supposed to) on every student we tutor. At the first staff meeting, we are told that these forms are extremely important to the success of the writing center. They prove our usefulness institutionally. They compose us. The more students we service, the more satisfied customers we produce, the more funding we receive. As is often the case, economics becomes the bottom line, and writing center administrators, like the tutors to whom they serve as mentors, are forced to make decisions and compromises, some of which they are happy with, some of which they merely tolerate.

This emphasis on documentation proves problematic on many levels. As Hurlbert and Blitz write, "[D]ocuments and the literacy demands they contain teach us our place(s) within the institution, institutionalize us, (con)figure us into the autobiography of the institution, incorporate us, make us part of the institution's scene. They tell us what to do and where to do it as they describe, for us, what we *are* doing" (1993, 6). This focus on accountability leaves us subject to the judgments of administrators who may understand little about the idea of a writing center (as North sets it out in his 1984 essay "The Idea of a Writing Center"). Moreover, it places us squarely in the middle of a quantitative tradition of justification that few of us believe in. To perceive ourselves as being "allowed" to exist by some external force as long as we prove ourselves "worthy" is to live with the constant threat of extinction.

To ward off extinction, we use these forms to represent our client base. They write the students that we tutor, reducing a dynamic interpersonal exchange to a mimeographed sheet full of circles and checks. Susan Miller's point about the grading system seems applicable here as well. "In the case of the student, grades and a record of them will be kept to identify and describe that student as an object of the 'grading system'" (1991, 90).

What remains unsaid, however, is that these forms are there for the tutors' protection as well. It is to their benefit to record a particularly difficult session, or one that they feel was significant in any way, in case they need to justify their actions to the student who receives a poor grade, to the professor who feels a particular paper does not represent the caliber of the student's work, and on up the institutional ladder. In other words, they are to note sessions that are less than "ideal" or that stray from the norm in any way, for these are suspect.

Tutoring without Offense

Creating spaces for dialogue arguably does increase the chance for such "suspect" sessions to occur. In my own experience, those students with whom I have abandoned the traditional tutorial model in favor of a more genuine exchange of ideas have frequently been the ones who caused me to question my own value as a tutor. Radical educational and cultural theorists advise us to "teach the debate" (Graff) and to view our cultural spaces (whether in the classroom or the writing center) as contact zones, "social spaces where cultures meet, clash, and grapple with each other" (Pratt 1991, 34). Pratt reminds us that too often we teach with the goal of eliminating confusion, opposition, and discomfort when our goal should be to delve more deeply into these issues. This, of course, does not always make for pretty sessions — struggles rarely are. Certainly, this is a problematic position to advocate for writing center tutors, many of whom are gaining their initial teaching experience in the writing center. But it does seem to be the appropriate time to advocate that tutors interrogate their practice responsibly from the outset and to recognize "pedagogy as a form of cultural production rather than as the transmission of a particular skill, body of knowledge, or set of values" (Giroux 1992, 202).

I learned this lesson the hard way with Tom, a nontraditional student who greeted me every Wednesday night at 6:00 P.M. sharp. Tom was just back from the Gulf War, anxious to pick up where he left off. In his research writing class students were allowed to choose a theme according to their interest and focus all their papers on this theme. Tom chose the death penalty. Tom is a Republican. I am not. We went round and round about his papers, but he kept coming back for more. One typical session began when he said, "This paper is entitled 'Should Juveniles Be Executed?'"

I was offended already, but I suggested that he read the paper aloud to me. As he read, it became apparent that he was not examining whether or not juveniles should be executed. Instead, he was trying to decide whether or not they should be *called* juveniles. In his conclusion, he decided that we should not sentence juveniles to die. Rather, any juvenile who commits a crime severe enough to warrant the death penalty should be *called* an adult and *then* sentenced to die. I began the session by trying to point out to him that the issue he was really debating was a semantic one. After I stated my case, he tried to back off: "Look, it doesn't matter to me one way or the other. All I'm saying here is that we shouldn't kill a kid unless that kid does something so bad that an adult could be killed for it."

I replied, "It's obvious you don't care about the issue, and if you don't care about what you're saying, why should your readers care? Your job as a writer is to make me care about what you're saying." At this, he became furious: "Why should I care? He (the professor) doesn't care. You're saying you don't care. Who does care? All I want to do is get out of this class, and no matter what I do it's not right. Just tell me what I need to do, and I'll do it."

How tempting. And the more difficult a session is, the more I want to just tell the student how I would write the paper. Mark Hurlbert uses Althusser's work to

> [help] tutors become aware that their practices are textured by an institution-alized, educational ideology that sanctions certain discursive forms while excluding others. This ideology can lead a tutor to appropriate a student's text, to make it look and sound like an institutionally sanctioned text. . . . In this case the tutor is no longer offering options, he or she is, despite their best intentions, institutionalizing composing and is reproducing the conditions of production as they are set out by educational ideology: (1987, 6)

Writing tutors, perhaps more than any other students in the university, are the students who have mastered the discourse and internalized the ideology of the institution. To the students they work with, tutors embody the university's ideal. So it is only fitting that those same tutors, often unknowingly, serve as the instruments through which that discourse is enforced. When they are affectionately called the "the cream of the crop," these tutors usually take this appellation as the highest of all compliments, but they should also realize that this makes them among "the most indoctrinated part of the population . . . the ones most susceptible to propaganda." As members of the educated class, they are "'ideological managers,' complicit in 'controlling all the organized flow of information'" (Chomsky, in Olson and Faigley 1991, 19).

The tutor, then, is an arm of the educational establishment, monitoring and regulating production. Tom, by indicating his reluctance to invest himself too heavily in his writing, was questioning the very foundations upon which our discipline rests. Students do this frequently, complaining, "This is stupid. Why do I have to do this?" Yet tutors rarely feel compelled to answer. Is this because they can't? Is this because they want students to question, but only within acceptable limits? Many writing center tutors want students to begin to look at how their subjectivity is constructed, but not too closely. Miller observes, "[This] may involve the student in freely choosing among topics for writing so that questions about the universal requirement 'to write' at all, or about the purposes for 'writing' essays, will be begged" (89–90).

Even though I did not address Tom's question about the purposes behind his writing assignments, I would like to think that, despite our differences, Tom's tutoring sessions with me were, for the most part, productive and engaging.

This has not been the case at all times and with all students. Most tutors are all too familiar with that sinking feeling that indicates a tutoring session gone seriously amiss. My most memorable such encounter occurred with a student whom I'll call Joe.

The phone rang on a Monday morning early in the semester. The student on the other end of the phone asked, "Do I need an appointment to see a tutor?" I replied that no, he did not need an appointment to meet with someone. We take students on a walk-in basis. Ten minutes later, he walked in and we sat down to begin going over his paper.

Joe was a young, working-class kid already embittered by what he perceived to be the injustices involved with being white and male in our society. I took a deep breath and braced myself for the session as he began to read his paper aloud. He claimed that minorities have it easy because all they have to do is shout "Discrimination!" and women have it easy because all they have to do is shout "Sexual harassment!," but white men have no recourse when they are not happy with their situations. He also asserted, in the midst of the Clarence Thomas hearings and the William Kennedy Smith trial, that the court systems are "female based."

Where to begin? I contemplated homing in on the derogatory terms he used to describe certain ethnic groups; but then I realized this approach was just cosmetic. Changing those terms wouldn't change his prejudice, and there were more pressing problems with the organization and content of the paper that I technically should have been worried about. I began to question him about the logic of his paper, faulting him, for example, for only citing one personal instance of his experience in a "female-based" court. I challenged him that for every instance he could think of where the court system was female based, I could give him three instances to prove that it wasn't. At this point, I realized I was out of line and pulled back. I was no longer helping him to grow, either as a person or a writer. In fact, I was on the verge of attacking him.

He looked small and tired as he said, "I had a feeling this would offend you." I told him that I was sorry but I just couldn't help him with this paper. Fortunately (for him), we had a white male tutor who was willing to pick up where I left off. But I was left with the knowledge that I had failed as a tutor. Not only could I not help Joe with his writing, I probably served to reinforce the very prejudices he was clinging to so dearly.

Deciding when, how, and even whether to criticize student opinions has been a constant battle for me. I realize that I ask students with dissenting opinions to offer much more evidence for their positions than I ever expect of students with whom I agree. I, like other composition specialists, see it as my job to encourage students to begin to question their assumptions. Yet I wonder where to draw the line? It's one thing to ask students to look at their values, quite another to force them (by way of a grade) to change their opinions. What have we really accomplished if all of our students become like Tom, so frustrated that they will write anything just to have the grueling process over with? Does writing as discovery still mean discovering what the teacher wants and writing it?

Susan Miller claims, "Society produces fairly well-constrained subjectivities to regulate and map individuals. Regulation includes ways to instill values and responsibilities that best serve the society's maintenance of its particular form of order" (90). Individual variations in subject positions produce my reading and Joe's reading of discrimination, but who am I to say that my reading is "correct," when correctness is so arbitrary? Chomsky would say that my notions of correctness are typical of the "academic left," a term which is truly a misnomer. He asserts that the academic left in America is not left at all. It too is institutionalized, maintaining the appearance of dissent. Consequently, there really exists no radical extreme in America. My reading of an issue is as culturally determined as Joe's is.

From this last incident springs a joke that circulated among the other tutors in our writing center: if a student came in with a paper topic that was particularly offensive to us, we would save that student for Bill, our politically incorrect tutor. Writing in favor of capital punishment? See Bill. Pro-Life? Talk to Bill. And perhaps most importantly, since most of our tutors were female, sexist? You'll have to wait for Bill.

During my tenure in the writing center, Bill served as a frequent reminder that tutor-student relationships are not the only ones that fall short of the ideal; tutor-tutor relationships can run aground as well. Bill often managed to avoid tutoring because he knew so much about the computers, and he would lord this knowledge over the other tutors. When I began working at the writing center, I knew nothing about computers, so I was reluctant to confront Bill about his attitude when I relied so heavily on his knowledge. By the end of the semester, however, I was tired of the way he treated people, women in particular. My anger peaked when I heard him lie to our director about having taught one of the female tutors how to use the graphics program. I confronted Bill, telling him in no uncertain terms that I had been a witness to the initial exchange. He had not taught her anything. He had done it for her. I accused him of behaving this way in order to maintain some measure of control and dominance over other people. I then calmed down enough to explain why this was not only unacceptable but offensive to me. He said that he would try to be more considerate in the future, and he was — to me.

Bill's actions seem to be consistent with sociolinguistic analyses of language, gender, and power. As Tannen points out in her book *You Just Don't Understand: Women and Men in Conversation* (1990), men's communicative strategies are primarily hierarchical while women focus on connectedness. For this reason, women are more likely to involve others in operations involving them, while men are more likely to view a teaching situation like the one described above as an opportunity to assert dominance and control (67). By excluding the female tutor from the process of creating the graphics, Bill was playing directly into this stereotype.

Because he knew so much about computers, Bill did very little tutoring of writing. Those sessions he did concede to do, however, were very directive, and his students were reluctant to ask him for more help when he seemed so impatient with them. Frequently, they would purposefully seek out a female tutor for further clarification, reinforcing the split between domineering male tutors and their more empathetic female counterparts, between the men who are comfortable doing most of the talking and the women who engage in active listening. This reading is consistent with the findings of gender and language studies conducted by researchers such as Fishman and Aries, who found women to be more willing to engage in conversational maintenance work (giving backchannel cues, asking questions, nodding their heads) and men to be more likely to dictate topics, beginnings, and endings. Women fulfill a primarily enabling role, providing an open, supportive environment that is preferable to both men and women. With the female tutors engaged in the more service-oriented work, the male tutors were left to attend to the mechanics of the center's operation — fixing the printers, retrieving lost files, etc — thereby reinforcing the traditional gender stereotypes. Again, Tannen says that we can view this in terms of a hierarchy: "Mutual understanding is symmetrical, and this symmetry contributes to a sense of community. But giving advice is asymmetrical. It frames the advice giver as more knowledgeable, more reasonable, more in control — in a word, one-up" (53).

Life in the writing center thrives on such asymmetry, and on the hope that we can eventually achieve some sort of symmetry, if not harmony. As I look back over these snapshots of life in the center, I realize that the pervasive feeling of often being at a loss, unable to do much good, stems from a desire to foster such connectedness, a goal which, as Miller and others have pointed out, has historically prevented composition practitioners from advancing institutionally (42). We are loath to fill out forms that take our time away from others who are waiting for our help; we are reluctant to talk to computers when we would prefer to talk to people; and we have difficulty working with people who perpetuate stereotypes which we know are damaging to others.

Perhaps the greatest dis-ease I feel is not easily captured in a vignette depicting life in the writing center. It is larger than that, resulting from the perception that writing centers exist on the margin of the margins. The field of composition is marginalized within the university, serving as a gatekeeping device where students must prove they are worthy of higher education (Miller 85), but writing center students are not even considered worthy of composition. This is a view rooted in ignorance, as anyone who has worked in a writing center can attest. Writing centers represent "the marriage of what are arguably the two most powerful contemporary perspectives on teaching writing; first, that writing most usefully is viewed as a process; and second, that writing curricula need to be student-centered. This new writing center, then, defines its province not in terms of some curriculum, but in terms of the writers it serves" (North 1984, 438).

Perhaps North is right; but the goal of the educational institution, as Jeanne Simpson has noted, is often simply one of survival. Helping students as we do in the writing center is the means of achieving what at times seems to be a less than altruistic end. In *Zen and the Art of Motorcycle Maintenance* (1975), Robert Pirsig alludes to a kind of "systematic thinking" that is institutionally pervasive. He writes, "To speak of certain government and establishment institutions as 'the system' is to speak correctly. . . . They are sustained by structural relationships even when they have lost all other meaning and purpose. . . . The true system, the real system, is our present construction of systematic thought itself, rationality itself" (94). Our educational system, based as it is on the industrial model, has production as its ultimate goal. We might not change that. But we can control *what* we (re)produce. We can strive to produce better writers, better tutors, more humane working conditions for everyone involved (tutors and students alike).

Then we can stand back and realize that we have a product we can all be proud of.

Works Cited

Aries, Elizabeth. 1976. "Interaction Patterns and Themes in Male, Female, and Mixed Groups." *Small Group Behavior* 7.1: 7–18.

Brooks, Jeff. 1991. "Minimalist Tutoring: Making the Student Do All the Work." *The Writing Lab Newsletter* 15.6: 1–4.

Carroll, Shireen, Wendy Carse, and Annette Trefzer, 1993. "Fashioning Professional Selves." *Critical Matrix* 7.1: 63–79.

Fishman, Pamela. "Interaction: The Work Women Do." *Social Problems* 25.4: 397–406.

Giroux, Henry A. 1992. "Resisting Difference: Cultural Studies and the Discourse of Critical Pedagogy." In *Cultural Studies*. Ed. Lawrence Grossberg, Cary Nelson, and Paula A. Treichler, 199–212.

Goffmann, Erving. 1959. *The Presentation of Self in Everyday Life.* New York: Doubleday.

Hodson, Randy. 1991. "The Active Worker: Compliance and Autonomy at the Workplace." *Journal of Contemporary Ethnography* 20.1 (April): 47–78.

Hurlbert, C. Mark. 1987. "Ideology, Process and Subjectivity: The Role of Hermeneutics in the Writing Conference." Paper presented at the Annual Meeting of the Conference on College Composition and Communication, Atlanta, 20 March. ED289161. 2–14.

Hurlbert, C. Mark, and Michael Blitz. 1992. "The Institution('s) Lives!" Marx and Rhetoric. Special issue of *Pre/Text: A Journal of Rhetorical Theory.* Eds. James A. Berlin and John Trimbur. 13.1–2 (Spring/Summer): 59–78.

Miller, Susan. 1991. *Textual Carnivals: The Politics of Composition.* Carbondale: Southern Illinois University Press.

North, Stephen M. 1984. "The Idea of a Writing Center." *College English* 46.5 (September): 433–46.

Olson, Gary A., and Lester Faigley. 1991. "Language, Politics, and Composition: A Conversation with Noam Chomsky." *Journal of Advanced Composition* 11.1 (Winter): 1–35.

Pirsig, Robert M. 1975. *Zen and the Art of Motorcycle Maintenance.* New York: Bantam Books.

Pratt, Mary Louise. 1991. "Arts of the Contact Zone." *Profession '91,* 33–40.

Tannen, Deborah. 1990. *You Just Don't Understand: Women and Men in Conversation.* New York: Morrow.

Tassoni, John. "Pedagogy of the _____: Resisting Secrecy in College English Classrooms." Unpublished manuscript.

Trimbur, John. 1987. "Peer Tutoring: A Contradiction in Terms?" *Writing Center Journal* 7.2 (Spring/Summer): 21–28.

ETHICAL DIMENSIONS

Censoring Students, Censoring Ourselves: Constraining Conversations in the Writing Center

Steve Sherwood _____

TEXAS CHRISTIAN UNIVERSITY

In his article, Steve Sherwood examines the potential tutors have for unwittingly censoring student writers' ideas. Although he finds the notion of censorship repugnant, Sherwood acknowledges that the obligation to alert students to language and ideas that are racist, sexist, or in questionable taste may put the tutor in the position of acting as a censor. Before urging a student to suppress an unpleasant idea, he says, tutors must weigh the student's right to free expression against the potential harm the idea could do. At the same time, Sherwood contends that a student's right to express opinions must take precedence over a tutor's own political or social agenda. The article, which originally appeared in 1999 in The Writing Center Journal, *raises compelling ethical questions about the work tutors do in the writing center.*

A few years ago, a student writer came to our Writing Center with a freshman composition paper he planned to present aloud to his class the next day. The paper began, "To me, the biggest turnoff in the world is a woman with a briefcase in her hand." I interrupted him to observe, "You must get turned off a lot." The student nodded and went on reading. Predictably, the essay contended that women should be "barefoot and pregnant" and had no legitimate social role outside the home. As I listened, I reflected that in my professional life, I'd never held a job in which women were not my co-workers and, quite often, my bosses. At the time, my wife was home for a two-month maternity leave with our second child, and would be returning to work soon, for which our joint bank account and I were grateful. Not only did I disagree with the sentiments the student writer expressed, but I also took offense at his assumption that, being male, I must agree with him. And I suspected that my reaction would be mild compared to that of his female instructor and fellow students (he was one of eight males in a class of twenty-seven), who the next day would quite likely have him for lunch. "You're writing this for an audience of young women, most of whom probably plan to have careers," I observed. "What do you think they'll say?" He said he didn't really care what they thought. When I suggested he might want to reconsider making sexist statements that would only reflect badly on him, he said, "I'm supposed to write an argumentative paper. These are my opinions, and I have the right — as an American — to say what I please. No one has a right to tell me what I can and can't say, including my teacher and including you."

As a former journalist, my first impulse when confronted with issues of free speech is to take a strict libertarian view of the First Amendment, which in this case would mean admitting that the student had a constitutionally pro-tected right to voice his opinions, unenlightened as they were. Like Jeanne Simpson, I believe that

> If as educators we do not abide by the First Amendment, if we believe some speech is more equal than other, then all our trumpeting about "academic freedom" is hypocritical rot. The point of the First Amendment is that all ideas will be heard and that the right of the public to make their own judgments will remain unimpaired. (Pemberton 15)

As a teacher of composition, however, bound by National Council of Teachers of English tenets prohibiting sexist speech, I'm caught between this libertarian view and practical concerns about classroom conduct, good manners, and the fostering of community among students — which sexist, racist, offensive, or profane speech tends to disrupt. Already philosophically conflicted, then, I felt appalled at the writer's clear implication that by urging him to avoid sexist statements I was trying to censor him.

At first glance, it seems absurd to talk about censorship in the writing cen-ter because it implies that writing consultants have more power than they actually do. The greater influence a person has over a student writer's life (through grades or approval), the more potential there is for censorship or applying the pressure to self-censor. Therefore, teachers, bosses, parents, friends, and significant others probably have more opportunity to censor stu-dents than we do. Besides, students come to us voluntarily, seeking advice, and we have an obligation to advise them. Principled tutors would not deliberately exercise oppressive authority. Most of us would sooner censor ourselves — refusing to reveal our opinions on issues for fear of being too directive — than censor a student writer. The *Oxford English Dictionary,* though, defines the term censor as, first, the title of Ancient Roman officials who "'had the responsibility of the supervision of public morals'" and, second, as offi-cials of other cultures "'whose duty it is to inspect all books, journals, dra-matic pieces, etc., before publication, to insure that they shall contain nothing immoral, heretical, or offensive'" (qtd. in Jansen 14). So, to the extent that I tried to influence the moral aspects of the student's writing, prior to publica-tion, perhaps I was acting as a censor.

Based on this experience and others like it, I would argue that, perhaps inadvertently, many of us who work in writing centers practice a form of censorship as part of our everyday duties. For the most part, we censor or urge self-censorship in the interest of helping students adjust to and succeed in the academic world. We want to protect students from the practical and political effects of their words. We want to show them that their opinions have consequences, that using sexist or racist terms, espousing particular political causes, speaking carelessly on topics they don't fully understand, and offend-ing their audiences can cost them good grades and the esteem of their teach-ers and fellow students. Sometimes the safe path is the right one, especially if taking it prevents the expression of absurd, rash, or poisonous statements that would only hurt or embarrass the writer and others.

However, by encouraging self-censorship in the early stages of composi-tion, we may prevent student writers from fully developing and expressing valid and valuable ideas and opinions. Often, seeing us as authority figures, students are only too eager to follow our advice. Or, uncertain about the worth of their ideas and unwilling to risk criticism, they censor themselves. One eth-ical quandary we face in advising student writers to suppress controversial or unconventional ideas is that, in spite of all our experience as writers and tutors, we may be guilty of misjudgment. Another quandary comes when we play an ostensibly objective devil's advocate role while responding to student papers, but in reality are anything but objective. Perhaps the most perplexing quandary of all, though, comes in confronting offensive speech like that used by the student with the briefcase-fixation. In such cases, by attempting to pre-serve cherished ideals of equality, civility, and harmony among the sexes and races, we may be asking or coercing students like him to give up their First Amendment rights to free speech and expression.

There are times, of course, when urging self-censorship is almost without question in the writer's best interest. We don't want students to come across as arrogant, naïve, preachy, or wrongheaded. So, depending on the specific pur-pose of a piece of writing, we may ask them to excise portions of their opinions or style that come closest to revealing who they are. Recently, for example, a student came to me for help with a letter of application to Harvard. The letter began, "Greetings!" It was full of witticisms, asides, and winks. At one point, he told the admissions officers that if they found the letter too formal, he would try to be funnier the next time. In parentheses, he added, "By the way that's a joke." When I suggested he take a more formal tone, he objected, saying he wanted to be sure his personality came across on the page. As kindly as I could, I told him I didn't think that was such a good idea. By convincing him to cut the most conspicuous bits of humor from his letter, I may have prevented him from standing out in a way that would have won him a place at Harvard. Even so, the student's best course appeared to lie along a more conventional path, and I led him there out of concern that his audience of admissions officers might find his tone inappropriate and hold it against him.

Although I feel reasonably confident in this bit of advice, what bothers me is how often (in the name of propriety, convention, or audience awareness) I may have encouraged students to write in ways I believed their professors would find more appropriate. By urging them to play it safe, I may have discouraged them from taking the kinds of personal and rhetorical risks that could have led to important insights and interesting pieces of writing. This possibility struck me a few semesters ago when one of my own composition students wrote a parody of an individual conference with me. The parody poked fun at my scraggly beard and large belly, and implied that my vaunted open-mindedness was fraudulent. It also portrayed me in false and unflattering ways — for instance, as succumbing to sudden, explosive bouts of flatulence and taking hits from a hip flask. As it happened, the student ambushed me by reading the piece aloud to the class during a workshop session. The reading was a bold move, calculated to test my dedication to the open marketplace of ideas. She was daring me to censor her — to hold the paper against her — and she judged correctly that I wouldn't do it. The parody was inventive, funny, well written, and relevant to the topic we were discussing (the theories of humor). It was the first piece of creative writing she had done and included a perceptive analysis of how parodies work as well as an analysis of the risks she took by presenting it. The other students understood the joke, and the risks, and they watched my face closely. At least in part out of embarrassment, I laughed along with them. The paper was by far the best work the student writer had done all semester, and I believe that writing it taught her, among other lessons, the value of being so committed to an idea that she was willing to risk disapproval in order to express it.

But what would I say if she came to the writing center for help with such a paper about another professor? Chances are I would have warned her that the professor might find the piece highly offensive and, because of fictitious and defamatory details like the hip flask, grounds for a libel suit. I would have urged her to switch topics or at least talk the paper over with her professor before presenting it. In plainer words, for her own good, I would have urged her to censor herself — to cringe from writing her only "A" paper of the semester.

Depending on her level of self-confidence and determination, she might have disregarded my warning and held to her vision. Unlike the young man who aggressively defended his concepts about women, however, most of the students who come to the writing center are eager to learn how to make their papers more acceptable to their professors. And we can assume that in the face of disapproval, they will give in to the pressure to self-censor. After all, Mark Twain did. Literary critics suggest that Olivia Clemens and novelist William Dean Howells acted as Twain's chief editors and censors, purportedly to protect him from the worst of his literary excesses. Torn between a need to express his heretical views on Christianity and his need for Olivia's and Howells's approval, torn between his urge to morally shock his readers and his need for money and popularity, Twain frequently held his pen in check. Like a student coming to the writing center, Twain sought input from those he hoped could help to refine his writing. It is debatable whether Olivia and Howells (by helping Twain conform to the ideological constraints of Victorian society) ultimately did Twain and American literature more harm than good. It is also debatable, as Nancy Grimm points out, whether writing center tutors do more harm than good by "helping students conform to the regulatory power that resides in assignments, testing, and grading practices" (8).

Grimm contends that, whether they realize it or not, tutors typically act as enforcers of the dominant culture's model of academic literacy. Too often, our conception of what good writing looks like rests on a "fixed notion of literacy, a singular standard" (22) that discourages diversity and independent thinking. Grimm calls on those in the academy to accept diverse definitions of literacy and suggests that writing centers can help by resisting their regulatory role. She urges the adoption of a tutoring practice that "does not seek to suture, to close down understanding, but instead to maintain openness" (22). As she says,

> If writing centers support the idea that literacy is singular . . . and the idea that those who depart from a singular standard of literacy can be "fixed" by assigning them to the writing center, then they contribute to closing the system to difference. (22)

I suspect most of us would claim that we do not support this singular notion of literacy, that we are in fact open to diversity. In practice, though, we may tend to be less than open-minded. Instead, urging students to open *their* minds, we play the devil's advocate, challenging the points of their arguments, calling their ideas, ideals, and lines of reasoning into question. In a 1989 *Writing Center Journal* article, Stacey Freed examines the issue of subjectivity in the tutorial and says, "We would be doing the students a disservice by not voicing our own opinions, forcing them to scrutinize their work" (40). As Freed says,

> We deal with fragile egos, underdeveloped thoughts, unfulfilled promises, and yes, we must not let our opinions get in our way. But in our objectivity, our "respect for the work of the individual," we must make students aware of other points of view that may be "disturbing" to them and may "distress" them; and we should, if we believe an individual case warrants it, overstep the boundaries and be subjective — without being judgmental — in expressing these views. (42–43)

Freed argues responsibly, but the problem is that as human beings we tend to privilege some ideas and approaches to writing over others, and not always because we're looking out for a student's best interest. And if we're intervening in students' ideas and opinions because they offend our sensibilities or run afoul of our political agendas, then such intervention is probably not ethical and may amount to censorship. As one First Amendment scholar, J. M. Balkin, points out,

> In language strikingly similar to that of antipornography feminists, conservative student groups now claim they are silenced by a left-wing consensus about issues of race, sex, and sexual orientation. Whether the actual

phenomenon is overstated or not, the furor over political correctness on university campuses is an excellent example of the American system of private censorship at work. (169)

In an article about working with students who express opinions that writing center tutors find repugnant, Michael Pemberton suggests that in entering into discussions about such opinions, we should view our own motivations with suspicion. As he says, "we rarely seem to tell students to 'think about opposing viewpoints' in conferences when we agree with what they have to say. Most often, we only ask them to consider counterarguments when we disagree with a paper's stance and have objections that quickly spring to mind" (15). In the same article, Joan Mullin reports on a discussion of this issue with her peer tutors. She says,

> Most evident was our own discomfort — ultimately, that is — with our own readiness to oppress others, silence others, in the same ways that we SAY we object to. That is, we SOUND like it's OK to take away the rights of those who don't agree with us: it was frustrating to find ourselves ready to be as aggressively oppressive as those about whom we complain. (16)

Understandably, our readiness to attack ideas we disagree with is most intense when we're confronted with sexist, homophobic, racist, or other forms of hate speech. Hate speech offends us deeply because of the emotional damage and other harm it can cause its victims. Rodney A. Smolla, a constitutional law professor who specializes in free speech issues, says hate speech is "an abomination, a rape of human dignity" that "should be fought by all citizens of goodwill with all the vigor society can muster" (169). Hate speech presents scholars of First Amendment jurisprudence — and society in general — with perplexing challenges because, as Smolla observes, Americans "hate hate speech as much as we love free speech" (169). However, our disgust with hate speech is not enough, by itself, to justify the widespread abridgement of free speech in our society. As Smolla points out,

> Modern First Amendment jurisprudence will . . . permit regulation of hate speech in only a small number of closely confined circumstances. Sweeping prohibitions on hate speech, patterned on . . . group libel notions . . . are unconstitutional. The only prohibitions likely to be upheld are narrowly drawn restrictions on fighting words that present a clear and present danger of violence, or that [cause] physical injury to persons or property, or illegal discriminatory conduct, or that involve purely "private" speech in a context completely removed from the discussion of issues of general or public concern. (167)

There are special settings, including the workplace, public schools, and private university campuses, where the principles of free speech that apply in the open marketplace of ideas are limited. In the workplace, for example, "A racial slur or a verbal sexual advance by a supervisor to an employee is not mere expression of opinion in the general marketplace of discourse" (Smolla 163).

Instead, it is an action that violates laws protecting employees from sexual or racial discrimination. Likewise, referring to public elementary and high schools, Smolla says, "A school need not tolerate student speech that is inconsistent with its 'basic educational mission'" (215). This limitation depends in part on the age of the students, whose First Amendment rights are not equal to those of adults in our society (5). However, Smolla emphasizes that because high school students are in the process of learning to become responsible citizens, they "must still enjoy a very hefty measure of First Amendment freedom — they do not check the Bill of Rights at the schoolhouse door" (64–65).

The same is true of the legally adult students who visit us in the writing center. In fact, most attempts to enforce bans against sexist and racist speech on state university campuses have been found to be unconstitutional, including those that rely on the "fighting words" doctrine, which prohibits speech that "would provoke an immediate breach of the peace" (Balkin 167). A University of Texas policy aimed at disciplining students who aim racial insults at "specific individuals" with the intention of producing "severe emotional distress" (Balkin 168) may be constitutional because it is based on existing tort law. Balkin adds, however, that because this policy covers so narrow a set of circumstances, "it is unlikely to cover many situations of racial harassment. . . . Moreover, by its own terms, the Texas policy does not deal with harassment based on sex or sexual orientation" (168–69).

In view of the complexities and conflicts involved in this issue, those of us working in writing centers would do well to approach hate speech with caution. In fact, we would do well to approach cautiously all attempts to censor student writing or encourage self-censorship. This need for caution does not mean we must censor our own views entirely or shy away from helping students to understand the sometimes harmful effects their words can have on an audience. Despite her own reservations about how to deal with authors of offensive speech, Stacey Freed feels "obligated to tell these students about other worlds, other ways of seeing, thinking, being" (41). Joan Mullin concludes that "to change the vicious cycle of oppression . . . we need to work on listening, questioning, and teaching — both ourselves and those with whom we work" (16).

By allowing my sexist student writer to leave the Writing Center without engaging him in a calm, well-reasoned discussion about the quality of his ideas, perhaps I missed a chance to effect reform. More importantly, though, I missed a chance to teach him crucial lessons about ethos, about how to support one's opinions, about the purpose of academic writing, and about the need to give fair consideration to the perspectives and experiences of others. To explain, for instance, that a primary purpose of academic writing is learning and testing ideas, not simply venting opinions one already holds, would likely not constitute censorship. Neither would it hurt to show the student the need to justify his contentions by presenting evidence or logical reasoning, and to then trace the lack of such evidence in his paper. Finally, it's possible that simply by explaining my own perspective on working women — based on my rather positive experiences with them — I might have prompted the student to reconsider his position.

After all, as a colleague recently pointed out, students who express an unsavory opinion may do so out of naïveté or haste, and might gladly modify the opinion when they understand all of its implications. Not long ago, for example, a young man from New Mexico came for help with a narrative that contained a purportedly humorous anecdote recounted by an older cousin. The young man's cousin told him about a man in their small town who hired "Wetbacks" to beat his dog, so that it would become a perfect watchdog and growl whenever other "Wetbacks" came near the man's house. I had several problems with the anecdote, beginning with its racist content, and I felt obligated to express them. As I told the student, I didn't find the anecdote funny and as a reader it left me with a bad impression of his cousin. "Is that what you intended for the reader to feel?" I asked. When he said no, I told him that when his persona failed to react to, or reflect on, the anecdote, I wondered about his own position on the joke. Did he approve or disapprove of it? Did it affect him at all? The student, who looked appalled, said he was simply reporting what happened and hadn't considered any of these issues.

At the time, I wanted him to realize how readers might react to the anecdote, especially since, as I pointed out, it had little to do with the central theme of his narrative, which was how teens cope with boredom in small towns. The student appeared to understand and accept these objections — at least he did not suggest I was trying to censor him. Suppose, however, that after our calm, logical discussion of audience and rhetorical case building — and my attempts to raise the student's awareness "about other worlds, other ways of seeing, thinking, being" (Freed 41) — he said he fully understood the racist nature of his cousin's joke and had no intention of changing a word. In making a more determined effort to persuade him to self-censor (in telling him, "You simply can't say things like this"), would I be infringing on his First Amendment rights? As I hope I have shown, there's a good chance I would. However, the answer to this question — and whether such infringement is appropriate — will vary with the circumstances that surround each case. Ultimately, then, in deciding whether to urge self-censorship, we must balance the harm students' words might do, to themselves and their audiences, against our respect for their right to hold and express even the most aberrant of opinions. And, I would argue, whatever scale we use in helping us make such a delicate judgment must be heavily weighted on the side of the students' best interests and away from our own political or ideological agendas.

Works Cited

Balkin, J. M. "The American System of Censorship and Free Expression." *Patterns of Censorship Around the World*. Ed. Ilan Peleg. Boulder: Westview, 1993. 155–71.

Freed, Stacey. "Subjectivity in the Tutorial Session: How Far Can We Go?" *The Writing Center Journal* 10.1 (1989): 39–43.

im, Nancy. "The Regulatory Role of the Writing Center: Coming to Terms with a Loss of
   innocence." *The Writing Center Journal* 17.1 (1996): 5–29.
isen, Sue Curry. *Censorship: The Knot that Binds Power and Knowledge.* New York: Oxford
   UP, 1988.
Pemberton, Michael A. "Writing Center Ethics: Directive Non-Directiveness: Readers'
   Responses to Troublesome Scenarios." *The Writing Lab Newsletter* 18.10 (1994): 15–16.
Smolla, Rodney A. *Free Speech in an Open Society.* New York: Knopf, 1992.

Subjectivity in the Tutorial Session: How Far Can We Go?

Stacey Freed

GEORGE MASON UNIVERSITY

*To what extent should writing center tutors confront unpleasant or
politically repugnant ideas of student writers? This is the question Stacey
Freed addresses in her essay, which raises doubts about tutors' ability to
remain objective during tutorials. Although Freed acknowledges the tutor's
obligation to put the primary focus on a student's writing, she argues that it
is often difficult to separate the quality of writing from the quality of ideas
expressed in a piece. Students have a right to hold and state their opinions,
Freed says, and tutors should not let their own opinions hinder the tutor-
student relationship. She adds, "But in our objectivity, our 'respect for the
work of the individual,' we must make students aware of other points of
view that may be 'disturbing' to them and may 'distress' them; and we
should, if we believe an individual case warrants it, overstep the boundaries and be subjective — without being judgmental — in expressing these
views." The essay, which originally appeared in* The Writing Center Journal
*in 1989, raises an issue still being debated by writing center theorists —
one most tutors will confront in their work.*

As a new tutor in a writing center, I find that WHAT students have to say is
often more intriguing than HOW they say it, that the language of their
ideas is intricately tied to their perceptions, that some of them have ideas that
go beyond my capacity for compassion. I must admit I struggle not to lose my
sense of impartiality and get drawn into a moral, political, or religious discussion. But how does one deal with a paper that goes against one's fundamental
beliefs? More importantly, is it our job as tutors to question a student's beliefs
and move from objectivity to subjectivity?

Suppose a student were to read aloud the following from his essay:

> The work of an individual is no longer determined by his character, by the
> importance of his achievement for the community, but solely by the size of his
> fortune, his wealth. The greatness of the nation is no longer measured by the

sum of its moral and spiritual resources, but only by its material goods. All this results in that mental attitude and that quest for money and the power to protect it which allow the Jew to become so unscrupulous in his choice of means, so merciless in their use for his own ends. In the autocratic states he cringes before the "majesty" of the princes and misuses their favors to become a leech on their people. (Maser 214–215)

This example may be far-fetched (as you may have guessed, the author of this work is Adolf Hitler, and not a Comp. 101 student); however, the point I'm trying to make is, do we ignore what this says and focus on "higher-order concerns" of structure? Do we ask this person to back up his argument with examples? Hand this student over to another tutor? How far do we go in discussing the student's views? Teachers do ask students to respond to questions that have no definitive answers and to prepare essays on controversial, emotionally-charged topics such as nuclear weapons, gun control, and capital punishment. We would be doing students a disservice by not voicing our own opinions, forcing them to scrutinize their work.

In grading proficiency exams this past summer, I was given a sample paper by a student who was asked to write a response to the following George Orwell quote: "serious sport . . . is war minus the shooting." The student wrote:

[Mr. Orwell] reveals a misunderstanding on his part about not only sport, but also war, and even, perhaps about human nature itself. For even war, as horrible as it may be, can be viewed in positive and appealing respects: love of country and family and way of life. Does not war produce heroes as well as villains?

Overall, the essay was well-written and presented a fairly clear argument. This student passed the proficiency exam, but had he come into the writing center I wonder how I would have reacted. I am a pacifist, and I do not believe there is anything appealing about war. Yes, this is my view, and I am allowed to have it as much as the student is allowed his or her view. But, am I allowed to voice it in a tutorial session?

I think most tutors would say it is not our job to attack the personal viewpoints of our students, as much as we want to help them to think, and I agree. As Donald Murray points out, "the student comes to conferences to receive the evaluation of the draft and suggestions for future writing behavior" (148). They do not come to argue. But I wanted to find a more definitive answer to my query, a look at the way someone may have handled a similar situation. In searching for answers I went through many of the books on tutoring techniques and writing and found that even those which have sections on problems in the tutorial session, such as Muriel Harris's *Teaching One-to-one: The Writing Conference* and Donald Murray's *A Writer Teaches Writing*, talk about structure or, in Murray's case, problems of office environment. There wasn't much information on dealing with ideas, although many of the books discussed tutoring for analysis or opinion papers, which included asking the student pointed questions about various sides of an argument. (For a good look at this, see *The Practical Tutor* by Emily Meyer and Louise Smith).

I decided to speak with tutors in various university writing centers, mostly in the Northern Virginia/Washington, D.C., area to find out how they may have handled, or think they might handle, this type of situation. Responses varied but I found most tutors had the urge to enter discussion/debate with their students, but saw the writing itself as the first priority and then looked at subject matter in an objective way. I also discovered that many tutors believed themselves to be more liberal than their students. The Assistant Director of Purdue University's Writing Center, Rick Anderson, says he is in constant disagreement with the mostly conservative student body. However, with a student population of 39,000, and a 20-person tutorial staff, there isn't enough time in their 30-minute sessions "to get embroiled in discussions over content." Anderson finds it refreshing when students have different viewpoints, but during a session he works on rhetoric, style, and mechanical problems first. Then, after that, he may deal with other viewpoints.

Most tutors agreed that we must press students about their point-of-view without arguing. Michelle Kayal, a tutor at Georgetown University says, "attacking their point-of-view is not our job. People are entitled to their own views." She believed, however, that a tutor couldn't discuss a paper without discussing the subject but made it clear that she remains objective when doing so. Denny May, a tutor at the Alexandria campus of Northern Virginia Community College (NVCC), says he is very sensitive to this problem. He feels that he personally takes controversial positions and has a great interest in current issues. He works mainly with basic writers and knows he has a tremendous influence on these students, who "are often vulnerable, and without the qualifications to argue social issues." His method is to look at the paper's content and its basic argument and pose questions that make the student probe more deeply. "We can't push our own political agenda on them" he says. May is lucky in a way that many tutors are not — he also teaches a class, and in this way "arms the students with information or facts on a number of viewpoints." Then, he sees these same students in the writing lab.

Another type of problem comes with the student of another culture, who may have a very different value system. I have tutored a number of Hispanic and Latino men who believe that men "make better bosses" than women. I have worked with a young Muslim woman, wearing a veil, whose parents won't allow her to participate in sports. And I've tutored a Japanese woman who writes papers about her new husband — a man she barely knew before marriage and who wants her to quit school, stay home, and be a traditional wife. These are sensitive, personal issues, not hypothetical, esoteric musings on the state of the nation, and they are ones I feel strongly about. I feel obliged to tell these students about other worlds, other ways of seeing, thinking, being. When does my help become interference? At what point am I overstepping the boundaries of being a tutor and becoming either an adversary or a counselor?

In *Teaching One-to-one,* Muriel Harris discusses the roles of the teacher as coach, commentator, counselor, listener, and diagnostician. On being a counselor, she writes:

> Like other counselors, teachers in writing conferences also look at the whole person, not merely the perpetrator of fragments or rambling paragraphs. To move beyond the observable errors on the page, it's necessary to inquire into the writer's previous experience, prior learning, motivation, outside problems, attitudes, and composing processes in order to form an adequate picture of how to proceed. (36)

She focuses on using counseling techniques such as paraphrasing to probe deeper into a student's problems to find out "what might be derailing the student's efforts to write" (38). Might not this type of "off-the-cuff" counseling lead to depression or anger, triggering defensive, frustrated students? But how else can we help students improve their writing without getting a full picture of them ideologically and emotionally? Meyer and Smith in *The Practical Tutor* write that

> Helping a student to develop self-discipline, self-esteem, and confidence can be legitimate forms of assistance. But whenever you feel that the issues raised by a writer are too complex or disturbing for you, that you are out of your depth, then it is time to make a referral as gently as possible. (14)

These authors offer good advice when they remind us that we should always focus on the student's written work. In a tutorial session, no matter how personal it becomes, we must always go back to the task at hand, the writing. But, in the same way that we want to and are expected to deal with personal problems, we should be prepared to question students on their beliefs, to check them on the validity of their arguments. If a student discusses issues in his or her paper, then tutors must act not only as a springboard but also as a foil, a devil's advocate. In *Teaching Tips,* Wilbert McKeachie quotes from a portion of the code of ethics for psychologists published by the American Psychological Association that is relevant to all college teachers:

> Teaching frequently and legitimately involves a presentation of disquieting facts and controversial theories, and it is in the examination of perplexing issues that students most need the guidance of a good teacher. Disturbing concepts should not be withheld from students simply because some individuals may be distressed by them. When issues are relevant, they should be given full and objective discussion so that students can make intelligent decisions with regard to them. However, presentation of ideas likely to be difficult for some students to accept should be governed by tact and respect for the worth of the individual. (254)

Perhaps this sort of code of ethics is needed for tutors, for we too are teachers, perceived by students as authority figures. We deal with fragile egos, undeveloped thoughts, unfulfilled promises, and yes, we must not let our opinions get in our way. But in our objectivity, our "respect for the work of the individual," we must make students aware of other points of view that may be "disturbing" to them and may "distress" them; and we should, if we believe an individual case warrants it, overstep the boundaries and be subjective — without being judgmental — in expressing these views.

More discussion needs to be held on this question of how far we can go in discussing our own beliefs. It is an important issue that seems easily ignored when we view it as a matter of "objectivity." Yet, as teachers, we have an ethical or moral responsibility to face head-on the power of ideas and the written word. We won't be able to change students' minds in one tutorial session, but we can open them.

Works Cited

Harris, Muriel. *Teaching One-to-one: The Writing Conference.* Urbana: NCTE, 1986.
Maser, Werner. *Hitler's Letters and Notes.* New York: Harper & Row, 1973.
McKeachie, Wilbert. *Teaching Tips.* Lexington: D.C. Heath, 1986.
Meyer, Emily, and Louise Smith. *The Practical Tutor.* New York: Oxford UP, 1987.
Murray, Donald. *A Writer Teaches Writing.* Boston: Houghton/Mifflin, 1985.

"The Use of Force": Medical Ethics and Center Practice

Jay Jacoby _____

UNIVERSITY OF NORTH CAROLINA — CHARLOTTE

Although Jay Jacoby discredits most of the comparisons between writing centers and medical clinics, he argues that writing center practitioners would benefit from learning principles of medical ethics. One ethical principle useful in tutoring involves respect for a writer's autonomy — his or her right to make decisions and choices about every aspect of a piece of writing. As Jacoby argues, tutors have no clear right to interfere with a writer's "competent wishes and choices," even when such interference appears to benefit the writer. Often, he says, tutors violate writers' autonomy out of a misplaced allegiance to "the language of academic discourse." To avoid forcing an opinion on a student writer, Jacoby suggests tutors embrace the concept of informed consent, through which tutors "foster in our clients an understanding of the nature of their actions (i.e., the decisions they make as writers), alternative actions (i.e., other decisions that could be made), and their respective consequences." This essay, which originally appeared in Intersections: Theory-Practice in the Writing Center, *is especially useful because it offers tutors an approach to collaboration that emphasizes an ethical sharing of responsibility and decision making between writer and tutor.*

Consider the following case. The paper that appears below was written by a freshman in response to the assignment, "Write about someone who means a great deal to you":

My Grandma Connie is sixty eight years old. It is funny I never think of her in terms of age. When I look at her I do not notice the wrinkles or grey hair — she does not have much gray hair anyway, though she does possess the most calm and understanding grey eyes a grandmother could have.

Once she beat my fifteen-year-old brother at arm-wrestling, disgracing him in front of his buddies.

She lives by herself, now that Grandpa is gone, in a big house that he built himself some thirty odd years ago. Sometimes she will complain about why Grandpa put a window here or why he did not put a door there. Then she will get quiet like she is remembering when they were here together and first moving into their own new house with a door where a window should be.

Before typing a final copy of her paper, the student decides to bring her draft to the writing center. It is her first visit. She hands the draft to a tutor and asks, "What do you think? What should I do now?"

How legitimate would it be — considering the argument that students should "own" the texts they write — for the tutor to return the student's questions: "What do *you* think? What do *you* want to do now?" What if the student unconditionally surrenders the autonomy offered her, saying, "No fair! You're the tutor. It doesn't matter what *I* think." Do we run the risk of playing "hot potato" with authority over the text? Do we damage our credibility — and that of the writing center — if we do not offer pointed suggestions for improvement? Exactly who should control the tutorial session?

Let us now assume that the tutor chooses to be less directive. Through the use of guiding questions, the tutor wants to lead the student to examine her choices. So, the tutor asks, "Is there any part of this paper that you would have developed more if you had had the time?" (kindly implying that lack of time, rather than other considerations, led to what the tutor perceives as an underdeveloped paper). And what if the student does *not* say, as the tutor might have hoped, "Well, I guess I don't say much in the second paragraph"? What if, instead, she says, "Well, I know I wouldn't change the *second* paragraph, the way it just makes a statement and then gets out of the way"? Is it okay to disagree with such a minimalist point of view? And would that simply be a disagreement between two peers? Or does the tutor's authority, based on his or her presumed knowledge about descriptive detail, paragraph development, etc., upset any equality of opinion between tutor and client?

Finally, let us assume that the student comes to the writing center only *after* her instructor has returned the paper with a grade of "D" and a note saying, "This isn't college-level writing. Go to the writing center." Assume that another note comes to the tutor from the instructor saying, "Help this student understand writing expectations in college: introduction-thesis-development-support." What if the tutor feels that such advice is wrong, that the piece will lose something — its artlessness, its ingenuous voice — if those directions are followed? Should the tutor go against what instinct or training suggest and follow the instructor's orders? Does the tutor have any autonomy?

The discussion that follows may not offer many concrete answers to the questions raised here. It should, however, provide a fresh perspective from which to consider those questions, and a theoretical framework upon which possible solutions can be worked out. That perspective and framework draw upon work done in the field of medical ethics during the past twenty-five years. Medical ethics is the process of reasoning that health care professionals use to decide what is right, or what ought to be done, for the physical well-being of their patients and society. Entrusted with the intellectual well-being of our clients and the institutions we serve, writing center tutors can benefit from examining the ethical principles which often inform medical decision-making.

I began this chapter by "presenting a case," an activity engaged in daily by physicians. I should confess, at this point, to considerable discomfort in so clinically presenting the writer of "My Grandma Connie" as a patient to be discussed in a hospital mortality-and-morbidity session. Not long ago, however, it was common to speak of writing instruction using medical metaphors and models. Writing centers were called *labs* or *clinics*. Writers were diagnosed and remedies were prescribed. Tutors emerged from tutorials as interns did from surgery: sweating, talking a writing-center equivalent of doctor-talk; but instead of deviated septums, they dealt with bifurcated propositions, with L_1 interference rather than bowel obstructions. Tutors became the Emergency Medical Technicians of the university, specializing in "Crisis Intervention in the Writing Center" (Ware 1986), and prioritizing concerns through "Triage Tutoring" (Haynes 1988). Perhaps it was thinking along these lines that led Richard Lanham (1979) to recommend a "paramedic method" for eliminating "lard," or wordiness, from writing (a procedure which I suppose could be thought of as a writing center equivalent of liposuction).

Of course, it should not take long for those of us employed in writing centers to recognize the limitations of medical metaphors as they apply to our work. Despite what desperate students tell us, we know that getting an "A" on a term paper, or mastering subject/verb agreement, is *not* a life-or-death situation. Despite what cynical instructors tell us, we know that student writing is not a condition, a disease to be cured. Students coming to the writing center are not patients, a word synonymous with "invalid" and "sufferer." Tutors are not physicians: they swear no oaths to Mina Shaughnessy or Ken Bruffee; their fee scale for consultation differs radically from that of a radiologist or neurosurgeon.

As Mike Rose has cogently pointed out, an "atomistic, medical model of language [and language learning] is simply not supported by more recent research in language and cognition" (1990, 210). In a recent (1991) article, Diane Stelzer Morrow has also identified the limitations of comparing medical practice to writing instruction. She cites Stephen and Susan Judy, who suggest such comparisons lead to "a pessimistic, even fatalistic, view of the student as a learner," and Muriel Harris (1986), who has aptly noted that "the goal of the writing teacher is instructional, not therapeutic" (219). Writing from a unique position of being both physician and writing center tutor, Morrow does recognize, however, the potential value of thinking about what goes on in writing centers in medical terms. Such recognition is based upon certain similarities in the *relationships* between doctors and patients and tutors and clients, relationships in which, Morrow observes, "expectations are not quite so fixed as perhaps they once were" (219).

For the past several years, there has been a rising interest in ethics in the writing center, especially issues of empowerment, tutorial authority, and client autonomy. Entire sessions at professional conferences have been devoted to the subject, offering presentations with such titles as "Authority and Collaborative Learning," "Authority, Gender, and Tutors," "Notions of Authority in Peer Writing Conferences," and "Power Play: The Use and Abuse of Power Relationships in Peer Critiquing." This interest in writing center ethics is reflected by the National Writing Centers Association's awarding of two recent annual best article awards to works focusing upon ethical issues: John Trimbur's "Peer Tutoring: A Contradiction in Terms?" (1987) and Irene Lurkis Clark's "Collaboration and Ethics in Writing Center Pedagogy" (1988). While writing center professionals were turning more attention toward ethical issues involving tutor-client relationships, members of the medical community were growing more concerned about ethical issues that centered upon doctor-patient relationships. From the literature emerging out of those concerns come such titles as "Respecting Autonomy: The Struggle Over Rights and Capacities" (Katz), "Moral Problems in the Medical Worker–Patient Relationship" (McConnell), "The Refutation of Medical Paternalism" (Goldman 1983), and "Ethical Dilemmas for Nurses: Physicians' Orders versus Patients' Rights" (Mappes 1983).

Morrow has suggested that one reason for the rising interest in ethical issues — especially those involving power relationships — among doctors and writing instructors is that "both professionals are moving away from a tradition of authority to one of guide or co-learner" (228). I found these concerns converging two years ago when, as Director of Composition, I received from a first-year instructor an already graded paper on William Carlos Williams's short story, "The Use of Force." Some excerpts from that paper, which I reproduce unedited, follow:

> William Carlos Williams story, The Use of Force, kind of reminded me of the movie The Exorcist, which stars Linda Blair, as Reagan. Mathilda and Linda Blair were very much alike. They both knew something was wrong with them but were afraid to let somebody help them. Just so happens the persons trying to help them were doctors. In Reagan's case there were doctors and priests involve . . .
>
> In both cases it seems like the doctors are fighting a never ending battle and are ready to give up. Mathilda's doctor was just as determine to examine her, as she was determined that he wasn't. In Reagan's case the doctors did give up because her problem was over their heads. That's when the priest took over.
>
> However, Mathilda's doctor finally got to examine her throat and Reagan's priest finally drove the devil out of her. Mathilda was still furious because the doctor had overpowered her, but when the priest drove the devil out of Reagan she didn't remember a thing.

I don't know why I chose the Exorcist to compare with The Use of Force because the Exorcist scared the living hell out of me. I know why, because The Exorcist was a perfect example of a child in need of help but was determined not to let anyone help her . . .

The instructor had given this paper a "D-" and sought from me some confirmation of her judgment that the paper's content and style were "not appropriate or satisfactory for a formal essay." Overwhelmed by the organizational problems and surface errors of a member of what Rose has called "America's educational underclass," this instructor also felt that her student violated rules of academic propriety by her use of colloquial diction and her decision to compare Williams's story to a sensationalistic film. She wrote to the student: "Though I would not have approved this topic, I have to give you credit for originality. . . . If you had come for our scheduled conference, I could have helped you with your topic."

As you may recall, "The Use of Force" is a story about a doctor who suspects that his patient, a frightened young girl named Mathilda, has diphtheria. The doctor exercises his authority — granted to him by his medical knowledge — to force the child's mouth open so he can examine her throat. All of this is done at considerable cost to Mathilda: she is injured during the examination, her privacy is invaded, her trust is shattered. Nonetheless, she is found to have diphtheria, and her life is probably saved as a result of the doctor's persistence in examining her.

What is crucial to us here is the doctor's justification for compromising his patient's autonomy: "The damned little brat must be protected against her own idiocy, one says to one's self at such times. Others must be protected against her. It is a social necessity" (208). Were these the only motives, the doctor might have appeared justified, but there would not have been much of a story. Williams has the doctor reveal yet another set of motives: ". . . the worst of it was that I too had got beyond reason. I could have torn the child apart in my own fury and enjoyed it. It was a pleasure to attack her. My face was burning with it" (207–208). Later, the doctor admits that it is not so much social necessity, "But a blind fury, a feeling of adult shame, bred of a longing for muscular release" (208) that are his operatives.

Keeping the issues of "The Use of Force" in mind, let us now turn to something less dramatic, but no less serious. Do tutors have the right to compromise their clients' autonomy, their opportunities for self-determination? In the interests of "social necessity" (i.e., to maintain university standards and protect academic society from what may be thought of as student "idiocy"), can tutors act on what they perceive to be their clients' best interests (as did the doctor in "The Use of Force") and assume authority over their clients' texts? Are tutors expected to coerce the writer of "My Grandma Connie" into developing her second paragraph? Is the situation any different if tutors subtly lead her into making the choice to expand that paragraph? Must a tutor — who may be fully aware of the problems underprepared writers have in what David

Bartholomae (1985) calls "inventing the university" (i.e., imagining and attempting to reproduce academic discourse) — follow an instructor's orders and convince the writer of "The Use of Force" paper that a comparison with *The Exorcist* is inappropriate? What if that tutor suspects that the instructor's rejection of the student's topic is somehow related to her annoyance about a missed conference? What about cases of L_1 or second-language interference? One tutor, faced with a Vietnamese refugee's paper, wrote that she was having problems forcing herself to point out errors: "Don't tell me I'm doing a sentimental dance around the issue. I know it. But doesn't the error of second language give the essay a quality, a sense of 'heart,' that would somehow be lost in Americanization of the language?"

In encouraging the substitution of our discourse for the student's, we are potentially erasing at least part of that student's identity — some of his or her authenticity — in order to meet the demands of the institution. And often we do so without ever consulting honestly with the student: "Just write the paper this way; this is how it is done here!" In their perceived roles as authorities, even those tutors with the best of intentions take control of what Nancy Allen (1986) calls the "Truth of a paper" (4) and compromise whatever a writer may have intended.

Were peer tutors and others who intervene in the writing processes of others to swear an oath like the one physicians once swore to Hippocrates, that oath might draw heavily upon the ethical principle represented below:

> The dignity of the person commands us to *respect individual persons*. . . . This means that *one human being, precisely as human, does not and should not have power over another human being.* This means that individuals shall not coerce others or limit their activities or impose their will on others. Even society and its instrument, the government, must respect the freedom and privacy of individuals and can interfere only when it is necessary to protect others or for very serious and overriding social concerns.
>
> . . . A little reflection will reveal the fact that neither lawyers, clergymen, teachers, doctors, or nurses have a right to interfere with individuals or force their opinions on them, or even to act on a person's behalf without permission. . . . Specialized knowledge, even a license to practice, does not authorize professionals to control any aspect of another's life, or to limit the freedom of others. (Garrett, Baillie, and Garrett 1989, 27–28)

The principle identified here, *autonomy,* will inform nearly all the discussion that follows.

The central principle of autonomy in contemporary medical ethical theory comes as a reaction to utilitarian ethics which "locates rightness and wrongness in the *consequences* of our behavior" (Arras and Hunt 1983, 7) and has a "tendency to regard the individual as little more than a recipient of good and evil" (Miller 1983, 64). In contrast to utilitarianism, Kantian, or deontological, ethics holds that "the *principles* governing our behavior are of utmost importance" (Arras and Hunt 1983, 7). According to Bruce Miller, the primacy granted to the principle of autonomy in Kantian theory provides "firm ground to resist coercion and its less forceful, but more pervasive cousins: manipulation and undue influence. It also provides a warrant for treating a person's own choices, plans, and conception of self as generally dominant over what another believes to be in that person's best interest" (1983, 64).

Any efforts made to abrogate an individual's autonomy may be considered *paternalism,* which the OED defines as "government as by a father; the attempt to . . . regulate the life of a nation or community in the same way as a father does [for] his children." James Childress has noted, "Because the term paternalism is sex-linked, it is not wholly felicitous" (1983, 18). He would prefer the more gender-inclusive parentalism, but such a term has yet to appear in the literature of medical ethics. In medical practice,

> Paternalism centers on the notion that the physician — either by virtue of his or her superior knowledge or by some impediment incidental to the patient's experience of illness — has better insight into the best interests of the patient than does the patient, or that the physician's obligations are such that he is hampered to do what is medically good, even if it is not "good" in terms of the patient's own value system. (Pelligrino and Thomasma 1988, 7)

There are essentially two forms of paternalism: *Strong* paternalism "consists in overriding the competent wishes and choices of another" and *Weak* paternalism consists of acting on behalf on someone who, for some reason, "is not afforded the full possibility of free choice" (Pellegrino and Thomasma 7).

It is fairly common to see both physicians and writing center tutors engaging in some form of weak paternalism. Such conduct is no doubt activated by the principle of *beneficence,* doing good for others. In their efforts to serve patients and students, doctors and tutors see it as their obligation "to help others further their important and legitimate interests" (Beauchamp and Childress 1989, 194). And, acting upon the principle of beneficence, physicians and tutors may sometimes feel justified in abrogating their clients' autonomy. On these grounds, Bernard Gert and Charles Culver (1979) argue that it is okay to "violate a moral rule" by interfering with another person's autonomy *for that person's own good* (2).

It is difficult, however, to ascertain whether anyone acts solely, or even primarily, out of beneficence. As Childress observes, frequently "the claim to be doing good for others masks the agent's real motives, such as self-interest" (19). In the case of the doctor in "The Use of Force" it was "adult shame" — the desire not to be challenged and defeated by a child — that motivates him. He reflects, "I tried to hold myself down but I couldn't. I know how to expose a throat for inspection" (207). Similar motivations exist in the writing center, as Morrow points out: "I knew how to write and students would be coming to the writing center to learn how to write. They needed advice and I would be able to give it. . . . Medicine, like teaching, has a long tradition of the professional as authority" (223, 227). In the writing center, especially among novice tutors, there is often the irresistible urge to play — not doctor — but professor. It is, as Kay Satre and Valerie Traub have suggested, a "dynamic whereby those who have been put down by a system attempt to gain power by adopting the mode and guise of authority" (1988, 5). If the doctor knows how to expose throats, tutors know how to undangle modifiers. And, if they have read Don Murray's *Write to Learn* (1990), they know all about writing about grandmothers, and they are just waiting for a fresh client upon whom to foist that knowledge.

In addition to the difficulty of acting upon any principle that can be identified as being solely in another's best interests, there is the problem of "the absence of shared beliefs about what is good for persons and what they really need" (Childress 19). It is a problem that surfaces anytime we hand a group of writing tutors a student paper and ask for consensus about what Reigstad and McAndrew (1984) call high-order and low-order concerns (11–19). Not all tutors at my university's writing center felt that the second paragraph of "Grandma Connie" needed further work. And not all tutors were content about persuading the writer of "The Use of Force" paper into dropping the comparison with *The Exorcist*. On this matter, one tutor, Stephen Criswell, wrote:

> I think that the student had at least a germ of an idea in his/her comparison of the Williams story to the movie. . . . the student saw in both stories a child struggling against authority.
>
> It might be that the student would eventually drop *The Exorcist* part of the paper, or reduce it to a very brief mention. But the removal of that part of the paper should be the student's decision — part of his/her process. When the tutor axes that part of the paper, it seems to me that the tutor is sort of cutting off the student writer's ideas in progress. It seems like this writer still needs to work through his/her analysis of the Williams story, and that he/she is using the comparison to do that. The tutor should allow that process to happen and let the *Exorcist* part of the paper fade naturally. Telling the student to lose it seems to artificially put the writer where the tutor wants him/her.

Apparently, Stephen feels that the paternalistic intervention recommended by some of his colleagues — in part to accommodate the writing instructor's comment that the paper topic was inappropriate — would be counterproductive in this particular case.

There are those who might justify such paternalism on grounds other than beneficence. For example, they could propose grounds which the doctor in "The Use of Force" identified as "social necessity": ". . . one is justified in restricting a person's freedom in order to prevent injury or harm to other specific non-consenting individuals. . . . [or in order to] prevent impairment of institutional practices and systems that are in the public interest" by such behaviors as tax evasion, contempt of court, or other actions that "weaken public institutions" (McConnell 1982, 64–65).

Keeping such justification of paternalistic intervention in mind, it may be useful to raise the question, "With whom are writing center tutors collaborators: their student clients or the institution that employs them? Can it be both?" In medicine, physicians who still believe in upholding the Hippocratic oath seem to favor the institution since they swear "to live my life in partnership with him [who has taught me]" (McConnell 267). Frequently, in tutorial practice, though no oaths are sworn, we reveal allegiance to the institution by compromising the autonomy of student writers. That is, with little or no consultation with those writers, tutors compel them to adopt the language of academic discourse, presumably to prevent actions that "weaken public institutions," actions such as using contractions or one-sentence paragraphs, writing literary analyses in the first person, or comparing "classic" texts with those of questionable merit.

Such paternalistic practice, whether consciously intended or not, leads writing tutors to act as gatekeepers for the university. They assume postures that Mina Shaughnessy (1981) has identified as *Guarding the Tower:* "the teacher is in one way or another concentrating on protecting the academy (including himself) from the outsiders, those who do not seem to belong in the community of learners," or *Converting the Natives:* carrying "the technology of advanced literacy to the inhabitants of an underdeveloped country" (63–64). Such postures lead to a kind of mentality whereby writing center clients — by virtue of their allegedly diminished knowledge (after all, most of them are only freshmen!) — are considered as individuals whose decision-making competence can be compromised, for their own protection (we want them to pass, don't we) and that of society.

In a discussion of medical ethics, Samuel Shuman identifies attitudes similar to those expressed above as a form of colonialism:

> Among peers, even those who attempt to influence one another's decision making, there is no colonialism; in the colonial relationship, be it benevolent or malevolent, the keepers and the kept are not peers because the latter can never freely make their own decisions. . . . Englishmen in the last century and earlier in this century justified their colonialism by arguing and even believing that they were bringing the benefits of white civilization to primitive people. In modern medical practice, one finds similar self-serving declarations, which purport to justify society's right to compromise the decision-making autonomy of patients. (75–76).

Shuman's observations apply to problems attending any collaborative effort in the writing center. Collaboration is in danger of dissolving anytime a tutor imposes his or her will upon a client, or when a client surrenders his or her will to the tutor. The latter situation is no less common in tutoring than in medicine: patients often direct their doctors to make all the decisions, to do whatever they think is best. They yield, in other words, to what has been called the "despotism of the expert" (Appelbaum, Lidz, and Meisel 1987, 28). Likewise, in the writing center, as Morrow notes, "most students begin by assuming that the tutor is in charge; most students come into the session taking a passive role" (221). Neither patient nor student demonstrates any desire to become a "knowledgeable participant" (Appelbaum, Lidz, and Meisel ix) in their respective health care or development as writers. In such situations, physicians and tutors may justify the adoption of paternalism on behalf of passive patients or students, using the argument that, "with the development . . . of his rational powers, the individual in question will accept our decision on his behalf and agree with us that we did the best thing for him" (Childress 26). But, as any browbeaten patient or student can testify, this form of acceptance is, like a forced confession, highly suspect.

There may be a way out of some of the ethical dilemmas posed here, a way that guards against the use of force no matter how benevolently intended. The solution I propose derives from the principle of *informed consent*. In medicine, this principle posits that "decisions about the medical care a person will receive, if any, are to be made in a collaborative manner between patient and physician" (Appelbaum, Lidz, and Meisel 12). Moreover, the implementation of the practice of informed consent is seen as both "a central duty of health care professionals and as a right of patients" (Appelbaum, Lidz, and Meisel 26). Garrett, Baillie, and Garrett (1989) note that the following conditions must be present in order for informed consent to take place:

> [1] The patient . . . must be competent or have decision-making capacity. . . . Decision-making capacity is the patient's ability to make choices that reflect an understanding and appreciation of the nature and consequences of one's actions and of alternative actions, and to evaluate them in relation to a person's preferences and priorities.
> [2] Competence requires not only the ability to understand the consequences of one's decisions, but freedom from coercion and such undue influence that would substantially diminish the freedom of the patient.
> [3] The health care professional . . . must have provided the necessary information and made sure that it was understood. . . . [There is] *an obligation to actually communicate and not merely an obligation to spout facts.* A recital of all the technical details and the use of technical language may not only fail to increase comprehension, but may actually destroy understanding. . . . ethics demands that the health care professional make sure the patient understands the consequences in terms of the things that are important to the patient. (28ff)

In applying the principle of informed consent in the writing center, we must foster in our clients an understanding of the nature of their actions (i.e., the decisions they make as writers), alternative actions (i.e., other decisions that could be made), and their respective consequences. Equally important, we must be sure that the decisions our clients make are *their* decisions, informed and deliberate decisions that *they* can justify on grounds that are important to them. Insuring that our clients have such understanding respects their autonomy. Clients given the opportunity for such understanding will make choices about their writing which, in ethicist Bruce Miller's terms, will preserve *Autonomy as Free Action:* choices are voluntary, rather than coerced, and intentional, i.e., the conscious object of the actor; *Autonomy as Authenticity:* choices are in keeping with a person's character, "consistent with the person's attitudes, values, dispositions, and life plans": and *Autonomy as Effective Deliberator:* choices are informed so a person is aware of "alternatives and the consequences of the alternatives, [has] evaluated both, and [chooses] an action based on that evaluation" (67–69).

Following a consultation with a tutor, the writer of "My Grandma Connie" should be able to acknowledge that her one-sentence paragraph violates certain conventions, calls attention to itself, and cries out for details. She should also have the opportunity to speak in support of that paragraph, or to have its potential strengths pointed out to her. In its understatement, the paragraph may communicate something significant about both the writer and her grandmother. Perhaps some of its disjointedness reveals as well a relationship between the writer and her grandfather who put doors where windows should be. Providing an elaborative narrative of the arm-wrestling incident might distract from the naïve tone of the piece. In all probability the writer did not intend the effects spoken of here. For some readers, however, such effects do exist, and they work to strengthen the piece. A tutor should not immediately conclude that the paragraph is simply the result of an "instant-closure" syndrome common to inexperienced writers. Nor should a tutor, upon spotting the paragraph, immediately drag out jargon-laden handbooks, and coerce the writer to modify the paragraph to satisfy the rules of good verbal hygiene.

In a tutorial operating to support the principle of informed consent, the paragraph should be discussed along with the writer's intentions and the possible effects — *both positive and negative* — that the paragraph may have on readers. Ultimately, all decisions for revision must rest with the writer. If, upon conscious deliberation, she opts to expand the paragraph, consenting to certain expectations for college-level writing even though they compromise her original intentions, that consent is still informed rather than coerced. If she opts not to expand, it is also an informed choice. As long as the writer is aware of, and willing to take, the risk of aggravating a reader who demands paragraphs of at least three sentences, she should be able to do so and be able to explain her decision.

To allow for informed consent in the writing center, tutors may again refer to medical ethicists, this time to examine potential models for doctor-patient relationships. Drawing upon the work of Thomas Szasz and Mark Hollender (1956), Diane Morrow identifies three ways in which physicians interact with their patients: "activity-passivity" (the physician assumes responsibility for all decision making on behalf of his or her patient who willingly and absolutely defers to the physician's authority); "guidance-cooperation" (the physician essentially makes decisions which the patient carries out); and "mutual participation" (the physician and patient work together, sharing responsibility for decision making). Robert M. Veatch (1983) notes that the principle of mutual participation prevails in what he calls "The Contractual Model" of the physician-patient relationship. According to Veatch, only in such a model, which imposes obligations on both parties, "can there be a true sharing of . . . authority and responsibility, . . . a real sharing of decision making in a way that there is a realistic assurance that both patient and physician will retain their moral integrity" (50).

Morrow admits that the first two modes she cites are more prevalent in medical practice — perhaps with some justification. She then suggests that mutual participation is the model to which writing tutors should aspire. Comparing it to what Donald Murray has called "the response theory of teaching," Morrow observes, "Central to this model is a kind of balance of knowledge between the two participants: 'But as much as the teacher — the experienced writer — knows about writing, the composition teacher does *not* — and should not know the subject of the student's draft as well as the student writer'" (225). Applied in the writing center, a mutual participation/contractual model obliges clients and tutors to take active roles in the decision-making process. Clients must honestly elaborate their intensions to the best of their ability. Clients must also be prepared to explore actively any alternatives and be responsible not only for making decisions, but also for explaining them. Tutors must be sure that writers are informed of and understand the choices open to them, and that they have made those choices freely.

Under the conditions described above, the writer of the "The Use of Force" paper would first have an opportunity to explain her intentions. Perhaps in high school this student was consistently praised for relating classic texts to works that were more immediately relevant to students' lives. Perhaps her paper represented an effort to repeat her earlier writing successes. The tutor would then have an opportunity to discuss — in terms that her client would understand — expectations and protocols for academic discourse, perhaps differentiating formal and informal diction, and modes of comparison/contrast and critical literary analysis. The tutor might further discuss the importance of carefully ascertaining what the instructor expects from this assignment and the ways in which the paper may frustrate those expectations. Throughout this discussion, the tutor can draw upon her own experiences — what led her to the acquisition of such knowledge.

Imperative to this exchange would be a "mutual monitoring of information disclosure" (Appelbaum, Lidz, and Meisel 1987, viii) so both tutor and client would understand each other's motives and rationales. Equally important is that the exchange be characterized by what Robert Coles calls the "comfortable . . . give-and-take of storytelling" (18). In his *The Call of Stories: Teaching and the Moral Imagination* (1989), Coles urges both physicians and teachers to share stories with clients and to listen to clients' stories with "a minimum of conceptual static" (19). He identifies conceptual static as the abstract theoretical formulation in which professionals engage. Coles further contends that, because such static interferes with the stories clients may be trying to tell, it often gets in the way of ethical practice:

> [T]he story of some of us who become owners of a professional power and a professional vocabulary is the familiar one of moral thoughtlessness. We brandish our authority in a ceaseless effort to reassure ourselves about our importance, and we forget to look at our own warts and blemishes, so busy are we cataloging those in others. (18)

Throughout his book, Coles draws upon his own experience as a psychiatrist who gradually learned of the dangers of hastily applying theoretical constructs without ever really giving his patients the opportunity to tell their stories. Interestingly, this learning process also involved William Carlos Williams, whom Coles visited when he was in medical school, whose "doctor stories" Coles later edited, and who once told Coles, "we owe it to each other to respect our stories and learn from them" (30). Writing center tutors must also respect stories as Coles advocates; his book should stand alongside Harris's *Teaching One-to-One* (1986) and Meyer and Smith's *The Practical Tutor* (1987) as must reading for writing center professionals.

In the tutorial being considered here, both the tutor and the writer of "The Use of Force" paper should have a chance to tell their stories, to express their intentions as fully as possible. They may then be in a better position to collaborate on strategies for revising the paper. For example, perhaps discussion of *The Exorcist* would be subordinated to a more detailed analysis of Williams's story — an analysis which still originates with the similarities the student noted between the two works. Because discussion of *The Exorcist* is not eliminated, the student continues to maintain a stake in the paper, her initial response to "The Use of Force" is not rejected or devalued, and her analysis can remain meaningful to her on her own terms. The student may now be more willing to make certain accommodations — the adoption of more formal diction, for example — so as to become more credible and to present terms that are acceptable to her instructor. Naturally, all decisions about revising the paper are the student's. It is the tutor's responsibility, however, to be sure her client understands those decisions, that she can articulate reasons for the choices she makes (e.g., writing is judged differently in college than it was at my high school; I need to learn to play by a different set of rules). In such a scenario, autonomy is respected. Although it does get compromised, such compromise occurs in ways that the student can understand.

Observing that we live in an age which has undergone a "revolution in our conception of justice," Robert Veatch notes, "If the obscure phrase 'all men are created equal' means anything in the medical context where biologically it is clear that they are not equal, it means that they are equal in the legitimacy of their moral claim. They must be treated equally in what is essential to their humanity: dignity, freedom, individuality" (1988, 47). In the past two decades, attending to the legitimacy of that moral claim has caused profound changes in the field of medical ethics. They are changes that should concern any professional charged with promoting the physical, emotional, or intellectual health of others.

In addition to issues of authority and autonomy introduced here, a consideration of other medical-ethical dilemmas may also have a direct bearing on writing center practice. They include, for example, issues of confidentiality (Should doctors inform employers about the status of the employees' health? Should tutors inform instructors about all that is said in writing consultation?); issues of non-compliance (Are doctors obliged to continue treating patients who do not take prescribed medicine, continue smoking, etc.? Are tutors obliged to work with clients who repeatedly miss appointments, do not revise, do not do suggested exercises, etc.?); and issues of allocation of resources (When time and medicine is limited, should some patients be given priority over others? When tutorial assistance is limited, should some students have priority, i.e., at-risk students before all others?). Because these issues are so morally complex, and because the doctor-tutor analogy will eventually break down, encounters with medical ethical theory may not always illuminate writing center practice. Nonetheless, a working knowledge of such theory certainly can help lead to more ethically sensitive tutors and more informed decision making in the writing center.

References

Allen, Nancy J. 1986. "Who Owns the Truth in the Writing Lab?" *Writing Center Journal* 6.2. 3–9.

Appelbaum, Paul S., Charles W. Lidz, and Alan Meisel. 1987. *Informed Consent: Legal Theory and Clinical Practice.* New York: Oxford University Press.

Arras, John, and Robert Hunt, eds. 1983. *Ethical Issues in Modern Medicine.* 2nd ed. Palo Alto: Mayfield.

Bartholomae, David. 1985. "Inventing the University." *When a Writer Can't Write: Studies in Writer's Block and Other Composing-Process Problems.* Ed. Mike Rose. New York: Guilford. 134–65.

Beauchamp, Tom L., and James F. Childress. 1989. *Principles of Biomedical Ethics.* 3rd ed. New York: Oxford University Press.

Childress, James F. 1979. "Paternalism and Health Care." Robison and Pritchard. 15–27.

Clark, Irene Lurkis. 1988. "Collaboration and Ethics in Writing Center Pedagogy." *Writing Center Journal* 9.1. 3–12.

Coles, Robert. 1989. *The Call of Stories: Teaching and the Moral Imagination.* Boston: Houghton Mifflin.

Garrett, Thomas M., Harold Baillie, and Rosellen Garrett. 1989. *Health Care Ethics: Principles and Problems.* Englewood Cliffs, NJ: Prentice-Hall.

Gert, Bernard, and Charles M. Culver. 1979. "The Justification of Paternalism." Robison and Pritchard, 1–14.

Goldman, Alan. 1983. "The Refutation of Medical Paternalism." Arras and Hunt, 110–18.

Harris, Muriel. 1986. *Teaching One-to-One: The Writing Conference.* Urbana, IL: National Council of Teachers of English.

Haynes, Jane. 1988. "Triage Tutoring: The Least You Can Do." *Writing Lab Newsletter,* 12–13.

Katz, Jay. 1984. *The Silent World of Doctor and Patient.* New York: Free Press.

Lanham, Richard. 1979. *Revising Prose.* New York: Scribner's.

Mappes, E. Joy Kroeger. 1983. "Ethical Dilemmas for Nurses: Physicians' Orders Versus Patients' Rights." Arras and Hunt, 119–26.

McConnell, Terrance C. 1982. *Moral Issues in Health Care: An Introduction to Medical Ethics.* Monterey: Wadsworth.

Meyer, Emily, and Louise Z. Smith. 1987. *The Practical Tutor.* New York: Oxford University Press.

Miller, Bruce L. 1983. "Autonomy and the Refusal of Lifesaving Treatment." Arras and Hunt, 64–73.

Morrow, Diane Stelzer. 1991. "Tutoring Writing: Healing or What?" *College Composition and Communication* 42, 218–29.

Murray, Donald. 1985. *A Writer Teaches Writing.* 2nd ed. Boston: Houghton.

———.1990. *Write to Learn.* 3rd ed. Fort Worth: Holt.

Pellegrino, Edmund D., and David C. Thomasma. 1988. *For the Patient's Good: The Restoration of Beneficence in Health Care.* New York: Oxford University Press.

Reigstad, Thomas J., and Donald A. McAndrew. 1984. *Training Tutors for Writing Conferences.* Urbana, IL: National Council of Teachers of English.

Robison, Wade, and Michael Pritchard. 1979. Medical *Responsibility: Paternalism, Informed Consent and Euthanasia.* Clifton, NJ: Humana.

Rose, Mike. 1990. *Lives on the Boundary: A Moving Account of the Struggles and Achievements of America's Educational Underclass.* New York: Penguin.

Satre, Kay, and Valerie Traub. 1988. "Non-Directive Tutoring Strategies." *Writing Lab Newsletter,* 5–6.

Shaughnessy, Mina P. 1981. "Diving In: An Introduction to Basic Writing." *College Composition and Communication* 27 (1976): 234–239. Rpt. in *The Writing Teacher's Sourcebook.* Eds. Gary Tate and Edward P. J. Corbett. New York: Oxford University Press. 62–68.

Shuman, Samuel I. 1979. "Informed Consent and the 'Victims' of Colonialism." Robinson and Pritchard, 75–99.

Szasz, Thomas, and Mark Hollender. 1956. "A Contribution to the Philosophy of Medicine: The Basic Models of the Doctor-Patient Relationship." *American Medical Association Archives of Internal Medicine* 97, 73–80.

Trimbur, John. 1987. "Peer Tutoring: A Contradiction in Terms?" *Writing Center Journal* 7.2, 21–28.

Veatch, Robert M. 1988. "Models for Ethical Medicine in a Revolutionary Age." Arras and Hunt, 47–51.

Ware, Elaine. 1986. "Crisis Intervention in the Writing Center." *Writing Lab Newsletter,* 5–8.

Williams, William Carlos. 1986. "The Use of Force." *LIT — Literature and Interpretive Techniques.* Ed. Wilfred Guerin et al. New York: Harper and Row, 205–208.

RESPONDING TO TEXTS

Provocative Revision
Toby Fulwiler _____
UNIVERSITY OF VERMONT

Each tutor develops a philosophy of what tutoring should achieve. For Toby Fulwiler, "teaching writing is teaching re-writing" — teaching students how to revise their writing through the techniques of limiting, adding, switching, and transforming. "Early drafts by inexperienced writers try to cover too much territory," and tutors can be effective in helping students keep a topic to a manageable size and depth. In the process, tutors can "make the case that reseeing writing in a different form is . . . generative, liberating, and fun." Fulwiler's essay, which originally appeared in The Writing Center Journal *in 1992, provides insights into revision as a major aspect of the composing process and offers support for the view that modeling the revision process for students can be constructive.*

I have been teaching writing for twenty-four years, first at the University of Wisconsin, later at Michigan Technological University, now at [the] University of Vermont. During the past fifteen years, I have also worked closely with writing centers, watching them evolve from places which emphasize skills and drills to places which provide sophisticated and supportive counseling about the range of writing processes. While my education is far from complete, I have learned what you too must know: that teaching writing is teaching re-writing.

During that same time, however, I have also learned that for novice writers, learning to re-write is an alien activity that doesn't come easily. In fact, many college students, first year and graduate alike, assume that writing is essentially copying down what they've already been thinking — well, maybe with a little spell checking, editing a few awkward sentences, adding a transition or two, and throwing in (get it, throwing in) a few supportive examples.

In contrast, I am convinced that revision is the primary way that both thinking and writing evolve, mature, and improve. So now, when I teach writing, I no longer leave revision to chance, happenstance, or writer whimsy. I not only encourage it, I provoke it, emphasizing where, when, and how to do it. At the same time, I go to great lengths to make sure the writing remains each student's own.

The rest of this paper is concerned with the *where, when,* and *how* of revision. I know how I, a classroom teacher who makes multiple-draft assignments, teach revision. What I am proposing to you who teach by tutoring is a set of provocative suggestions that will help your students learn to take revision seriously These provocations are four: (1) limiting, (2) adding, (3) switching, and (4) transforming.

1. Limiting

Generalization is death to good writing. Limiting is the cure for generality. The problem with generalities is that most people already know the same ones you do. They get bored hearing them repeated again and again. Most people (a generality I make with some trepidation) who read newspapers and weekly news magazines or listen to TV or radio news know general things about famous people and current issues: that the President plays golf, that the crisis in the Middle East won't go away, that communism is on the run in Eastern Europe, as is the natural environment in the United States. What most people do not know about are the close-in details of these same specific issues — the telling details that make subjects come to life. One of the key qualities of writing that we might call "interesting" is that it teaches us something we did not already know — something beyond repetitious small-talk generality. Once a subject — be it a person, place, or problem — is explored through careful research and exposed through thoughtful writing, people are drawn in because they find themselves learning something new.

It's the details that teach. People are fascinated with the details of other people's lives and so biographies and autobiographies frequent the best-seller lists — stories about the details of Presidents and rock stars as well as the assassins who shoot them. In like manner, people are fascinated with details of problems: classic examples include Rachel Carson's detailed exposé of environment-destroying pesticides in *Silent Spring;* Ralph Nader's in-depth investigation of Chevrolet's Corvair in *Unsafe at Any Speed;* and Bob Woodward and Carl Bernstein's minute revelations about the Watergate scandal in *All the President's Men.* Likewise it's the details in the research essays published in current periodicals, from *Rolling Stone* to *The New Yorker,* that make those magazines fascinating to read.

But writers have only so much time to write and space to work with, and so to spend more time and space including details means not including something else — which is where the concept of *limiting* helps out. Here are some specific suggestions for applying the principle of limiting to both narrative and research writing.

Limiting Time, Place, and Action In narrative and personal experience papers, a writer's first instinct is to try to tell or summarize the whole story. Such a generalized approach often gives the writer his or her first sense of what the story is about. As a teacher of first-year and advanced writing classes, I have come to expect — and accept as natural and useful — such overview writing on first drafts. Here, for example, are recent samples of fairly typical openings in first-draft narrative papers:

> This is probably the most heroic event of my childhood. Everyone has their moments, but I believe that this episode is indeed commendable. . . .

Life, it definitely has its ups and downs. Every so often I realize just what stupid, mindless things I've caught myself doing to fill time. . . .

Last summer my mother and I flew to Ireland. . . . This action packed vacation turned out to be more than I could handle. From recalling old memories to falling in love, I helped discover a new side of myself. . . .

In everyday life there are so many things that frustrate us or make us upset that when we find something that makes us truly happy, we should take advantage of it at every opportunity. . . .

This is an experience I hope never to experience again in my lifetime. A friend of my parents committed suicide by shooting himself in the head. This hurt me a great deal because I was close to his children and I felt the pain they were feeling. . . .

These opening lines provide several clues to the problems typical of first-draft narrative writing: first, these writers generalize rather than particularize their experience, putting it into pre-packaged story categories (heroism, action adventure). Second, they evaluate their experience too early, prejudging it, and telling readers in advance to react to it as stupid, frustrating, heroic, etc. Third, though you cannot see this from one paragraph fragment, many writers don't know in a first draft what their final-draft story will be. Consider, for example, this passage from a first-draft essay by Amanda, a first-year student from Scotland, writing a paper entitled "Waitressing":

For most of this summer I again worked on the farm, where I removed rotten, diseased potato shaws from a field all day. But I was in the sun all the time with a good bunch of people so it was quite good fun. But again it was hard work. (As are most jobs!) My waitressing job was nothing to get excited about either. I signed up with an employment agency and got a waitressing job in Aberdeen, a city thirty miles north of our farm. It was only for one week, but I didn't mind — it was the first job that I had got myself and I felt totally independent.

Were Amanda to focus close, this single paragraph could divide into two entirely different directions, one focusing on her title topic, "Waitressing," and a second on "Farming" — in, particular, working the potato fields. In fact, this passage reveals all three features typical of first-draft writing: over-generalizations, pre-judgment, and directional uncertainty. The problem with such writing is not that it is wrong or incorrect, but that it seldom makes good reading. The solution is usually in the writer's returning to the piece, re-seeing it, looking more closely and finding through continued exploration, the story that wants or needs to come out.

Although such revision sometimes happens by itself, especially for writers who are engaged in their task, it does not happen for writers who are not engaged, who are going through the motions of completing somebody else's task — a common predicament in school writing. But there are some ways to begin to create engagement, even in assignments the writer does not yet own. For example, with Amanda's class, I asked all the students to write two new pages about an idea covered in one first-draft paragraph. I was asking them, in other words, to radically and forcibly narrow their focus. Here is a brief portion of Amanda's next draft:

> [Harvesting potatoes] was always in October, so the weather was never very good. It either rained or was windy, often both. Some days it would be so cold that we would lie in between the drills of undug potatoes to protect ourselves from the wind.

In this draft, Amanda's details are helping her tell the story: notice especially the detail about lying "in between the drills of undug potatoes" to keep out of the wind. That's a *telling detail,* the detail that only a writer who has actually dug potatoes on a cold October day is likely to know — the detail that begins to tell the real story for her and to which she ought to listen very closely. Amanda has a lot to say about digging potatoes.

After witnessing the life and energy in the potato field draft, I suggested that Amanda revise again, not about what *usually* occurred in October, but about what *particularly* occurred one day in October. (Aristotle gave this same advice three thousand years ago in his *Poetics* and Robert Pirsig two decades ago in *Zen and the Art of Motorcycle Maintenance.*) I suggested, in other words, that Amanda start her next draft by limiting the *time, place,* and *action* of her potato field story; her next draft begins this way:

> Potatoes, mud, potatoes, mud, potatoes, that was all I saw in front of me. They moved from my right side to my left, at hip level. A conveyor belt never stopping. On and on and on.
>
> I bounced and stumbled around as the potato harvester moved over the rough earth, digging the newly grown potatoes out of the ground, transporting them up a conveyor belt and pushing them out in front of me and three other ladies, two on either side of the belt.
>
> The potatoes passed fast, a constant stream. My hands worked deftly pulling out clods of dirt, rotten potatoes, old shaws, and anything else I found that wasn't a potato. They were sore, rubbed raw with the constant pressure of holding dirt. They were numb, partly from the work and partly from the cold. It was October, the ground was nearly frozen, the mud was hard and solid. Cold. Dirt had gotten into my yellow and yet brown rubber gloves, had wedged under my nails increasing my discomfort.
>
> On and on the tractor pulled the harvester I was standing in, looming high above the dark rich earth, high above the potatoes. . . .

In this, her third draft, Amanda found her story and, in finding it, she found the telling particulars that put us beside her in the potato harvester. The specific suggestion to limit the time frame of her story made all the difference and good writer though Amanda turned out to be, had the revision not been provoked, it wouldn't have happened.

Limiting Scope and Focus   A similar limiting principle also holds true for more analytical or objective writing. *All* first drafts are first explorations and, as such, are likely to be overly generalized, obviously editorialized, and directionally incomplete. As in narrative, so in exposition, argument, and research, early drafts by inexperienced writers try to cover too much territory. It's understandable and predictable. When writers do not yet know a lot about a subject, they see it as if from a distance — and from a distance, even cities and mountains look small and manageable. Writers of such drafts then have the choice of staying far away, letting the generalities stand, and moving on to new subjects (and usually to mediocre papers) or moving in close, narrowing and sharpening the focus, and doing real writer's work — which means exploring the geography up close.

When I assign research projects to my students, I suggest — nay, require — that, in addition to library research, they find some local dimension of their topic, issue, or problem worth investigating. If, for example, they plan to research the abortion question, can they visit the local Planned Parenthood or a pregnancy clinic? If they plan to research something related to the environment, can they visit the local lake, landfill, or development to see the problem first hand?

I need to explain here that when I assign research projects in first-year writing classes, I require that the collecting of information be collaborative, and I strongly recommend the writing be collaborative as well. I do this for several reasons: first, to reduce the harassment of local institutions and people; second, to make the information-collecting process more rapid and efficient; and third, to model collaborative writing so often required of writers in the world outside of college. Though writing center tutors seldom determine whether research writing should be individual or collaborative, be assured that the revision techniques described here work in either situation.

In one first-year writing class, a group of five students researched the rise of *Ben and Jerry's Ice Cream Company* — a local business developed by former University of Vermont students — and, in the following paragraph, described their visit to the original downtown store:

> To the left of the stairs is a long, brown wooden bench with black metal legs that looks like it came straight from Central Park. Above it, on the wall, is a blown-up article from the *Rutland Herald*. To the right of the bench is a white, metal wastebasket, three feet high and two feet wide. On top of the wastebasket is a blue bucket that says "We are now recycling spoons." On every table in the room are napkin dispensers saying, "Save a tree, please take only one napkin."

On the one hand, this is a simple example of on-site descriptive writing meant to give readers the feel of the ice cream store. On the other hand, the recycling signs provide readers with their first clue that "environmental awareness" will be a major theme in the *Ben and Jerry's* research report. Further in the report the authors include library-based research information:

> *Ben and Jerry's* is now looking for an alternative for their pint containers because they are made with a plastic coating for moisture resistance. This combination of materials makes the container non-biodegradable and difficult to recycle. According to their Annual Report, "As a result of this and other recycling efforts, we have reduced our solid waste volume by about 30% this year" (6).

The *Ben and Jerry's* paper concludes by arguing that profit making and environmental protection are not mutually exclusive — a thesis that emerged only gradually as the writers conducted their investigation and experimented with different drafts.

2. Adding

Perhaps the most obvious way to revise a paper is to add new information and more explanation. Most professional writers see adding and revising as synonymous. (They feel the same about subtracting and revising, but that's seldom the novice writer's problem.) However, few of the student writers who visit writing centers are likely to understand what addition could mean, unless an assignment has been made in multiple-draft stages, where proposals, outline, first and second drafts are required over a several week period. In any case, most students can profit by learning about addition, if they seek help early enough so there is time to do it. I want to illustrate this principle by continuing to emphasize local knowledge, this time recommending the addition of "dialogue" — people talking — to both personal experience and research writing.

Adding Dialogue　Having people talk in a paper adds interest by limiting the focus to one or two people or a particular scene. In narrative or personal experience writing, adding dialogue complements Aristotle's suggestion to limit time, place, and action, by putting actors on the sets. Adding talk allows readers to see and hear a story in a dramatic rather than narrative way, increasing reader involvement and interest.

To add talk to narrative writing requires remembering what was said sometime in the past or, more likely, re-creating what was probably or approximately said. Fiction is not allowed, but approximate re-creation is fair game for all experiential or autobiographical writing.

For example, in response to an assignment to draft a personal-experience paper, Karen described her whole basketball season in three pages, concluding with the team playing in the Massachusetts semi-final game in the Boston Garden:

> We lost badly to Walpole in what turned out to be our final game. I sat on the bench most of the time. The coach did not even put me in until the fourth

quarter when there were five minutes left and we were already twenty points behind.

For their second drafts, I asked these first-year writers to work dialogue into their narratives. Karen's second draft includes this scene:

> "Girls, you have got to keep your heads in the game. Don't let them get you down. You've worked so hard all season. You are just as good as them, just look at our record," 18-2-0.
>
> "Coach, they're killing us. They're making us look like fools, running right by us. We're down by twenty with eight minutes to go. It's hopeless."
>
> "I don't want to hear anyone talk like that. You girls have worked too hard to get to this point and give up. You can't quit now."
>
> Yeah, think of every sweat-dripping, physically-gruelling, suicide-sprinting, drill-conditioning Saturday morning practice this year. ("OK girls, for every missed foul shot it's one full suicide!") Oh, yes, I remember those practice sessions just fine.
>
> "Tweet!"
>
> Oh well, I missed another time out. It really doesn't matter, because he won't play me anyway.

Karen has added not only dialogue, but interior monologue as well, turning her paper from a summative to a dramatic telling. In this later version, we learn that Karen's dream changes from hoping her team will win the championship to sinking for herself a three-pointer in the Boston Garden — if only she can get into the game. Karen's second draft has expanded to six pages, but focuses only on the last eight minutes of the basketball game.

Adding Interviews Adding other voices also improves research writing — only now the adding requires actual on-site interviews in place of remembered or recreated dialogue. As a teacher of research, I've long been influenced by Ken Macrorie's notion of *I-Search Papers,* Eliot Wigginton's Foxfire stories — now up to twelve volumes — as well as the practices of investigative reporters who go places, ask questions, and record the results. Adding on-site information from experts increases a paper's credibility and readability at the same time.

One group of four first-year writing students investigated the role of the Ronald McDonald House in providing housing for out-of-town parents while their children stayed in hospitals. In Burlington, a Ronald McDonald House is located between downtown and the University of Vermont Medical Center, within walking distance of the UVM campus. A *Free Press* story turned up through library research reported the following information:

> The McDonald's corporation actually provides about 5% of the total cost of getting the house started. The other 95% of the money comes from local businesses and special interest groups.

For their second draft, however, the group visited the house and interviewed parents, volunteer workers, and the director. In the following passage, Rosemary, the House director, explains the sources of funding:

"Our biggest problem is that people think we're supported by the McDonald's corporation. We have to get people to understand that anything we get from *McDonald's* is just from that particular franchise's generosity — and may be no more than is donated by other local merchants. *Martin's, Hood,* and *Ben and Jerry's* provide much of the food. McDonald's is not obligated to give us anything. The only reason we use their name is because of its child appeal."

Which information, that found in the library or that revealed through live interview, is the most useful for research writers? Which is more interesting or memorable for readers? No need to choose, for in their final draft, the writers included both pieces of information, the one written with statistical authority, the other spoken with personal authority. Adding the voices of real live local experts also holds true for other kinds of objective writing as well: when writers let other voices help them argue, report, and evaluate, their arguments, reports, etc., are both more persuasive and exciting.

3. Switching

Switching involves telling the same story or reporting the same events as the previous draft, but doing so from a different perspective. For example, if a writer has been narrating in past tense, she switches to present. If a writer has been reporting research results in third person, he switches to first person for all or part of a draft. Switching a basic element, such as tense or point-of-view, mechanically provokes writers into re-seeing the content and often into reconceptualizing how to present it with maximum effect.

Switching Point of View In narrative and personal experience writing, the most common first-draft perspective is first person: "Once upon a time I was playing basketball" or something like this. It's only natural that writers tell stories as they experienced them, through their own eyes, perspectives, voices. However, it sometimes helps writers to move deliberately outside of themselves and see themselves as someone else might. This can be done simply by switching pronouns or, in a more complex way, by role-playing a third person. In the following example, Karen continues to tell her story of playing in the Massachusetts basketball semi-finals, but for this draft she adopts the perspective and voice of the play-by-play announcer:

Well folks, it looks as if Belmont has given up. Coach Gleason is preparing to send in his subs. It has been a rough game for Belmont. They stayed in it during the first quarter, but Walpole has run away with it since then. Down by twenty with only six minutes left, Belmont's first sub is now approaching the bench.

Megan Sullivan goes coast to coast and lays it in for two. She has sparked Walpole from the start.

The fans have livened up a bit, but oddly they aren't Walpole's fans, they're Belmont's. Cheers for someone named Karen are coming from the balcony. . . . Number eleven, Karen Kelly replaces Michelle Hayes.

By becoming the announcer, Karen adopts the cadences and spirit of an announcer in the broadcast booth, seeing and reporting the game as she imagines he actually did. Whether the announcer would have paid even this much attention to a substitute player entering in the last few minutes of the game is questionable — but that's not the point. By adding this voice, Karen added more details and a different perspective to her own story. In this draft, she realizes for the first time that her basketball enemies were actually three: the opposing team, the coach who refused to play her, and also her teammates who refused to give her the ball.

Switching Voice Another switch that provides new perspective on exposition or argument is changing the voice that's doing the explaining or arguing. For example, changing the voice that delivers the information from objective third person to subjective first changes the nature of the information as well as the way it is received. Furthermore, if we use as examples the research essays commonly published in leading non-fiction journals, we notice that writers such as Joan Didion, John McPhee, and Jonathan Kozol commonly write in more than one voice — or in one voice, but varying tones, pitches, and registers. Why can't student research writing gain life by using similar techniques?

Here, for example, in the final draft of a thirty-page research report written by a group of first-year writers about pollution in Lake Champlain are four different voices:

> [The Introduction is narrated by an out-of-town male student, who opens the report by meeting an in-town female student.]

> Page 1: We both started to cycle and I followed her down a path near the lake: "I'm just amazed by the beauty of the water. It is great to see the islands out there in front of us. This is paradise," I said.
> "Well, there are some problems with the lake. The sewage treatment plant," she paused and continued, "it's taken a lot of the beauty away."
> "What do you mean?" I asked, and she proceeded to tell me the story. . . .

> Page 3: How do you close down a public beach? You can't barricade the water, can you? *The Burlington Free Press* always used the word "Fecal Coliform," which basically means "shit." But the technological meaning is "a bacteria that indicates human waste." That almost sounds worse than shit!

> Page 7: The sewage treatment plant of Burlington consists of a series of wells, pumps, and tanks. It is built to receive forty million gallons of waste water from the street drainage sewers of private and public bathrooms. During large rainstorms, the amount of water causes difficulties in the plant's ability to treat all the water which enters it.

> Page 18: Some helpful hints for conserving water:

> 1. Take short showers. Get wet first, then turn the shower off, lather up, then turn the shower on and rinse off.

2. Don't keep the water running while you're brushing your teeth.

3. Keep a jug of drinking water cool in the refrigerator instead of running the tap water to get it cold.

In these selected passages, the writers keep reader interest by sometimes switching to unexpected voices. At the same time, the report delivers the goods, describing and explaining the problem of lake pollution from personal and technological perspectives, and offering a range of solutions that include both technological fixes and changing personal behavior.

4. Transforming

My final revision strategy is transforming, where a writer recasts his or her piece into a form altogether different from what it has been. For example, if the piece has been drafted as something called a personal-experience paper, could it be recast as an exchange of letters or a diary? If a piece has been initially drafted as a formal research paper, could it be recast as a speculative or familiar essay? While these moves may seem, at best, superficial or, at worst, inappropriately playful for college-level work, I'd like to make the case that re-seeing writing in a different form is, at the same time, generative, liberating, and fun. Any time writers change around the way they present their ideas and information, they open up new conceptual possibilities in terms of both audience and purpose. In so doing, the staleness that sometimes accompanies routine acts of revision is relieved, and an excitement born of experimentation takes over. Let me give you some final examples.

Transforming Research Reports Research papers are all too often the reports that students hate to write and faculty hate to read. Do they need to be that way — problems for both student writers and faculty readers — with tutors caught in the middle? Some of the students whose work I've already examined have found interesting solutions to this problem.

Remember the Ronald McDonald House? In their final draft, these four writers collaborated to write a script for *60 Minutes*. The form is, of course, fiction, but the content is the hard information uncovered through extensive local research. Here are some of the parts of the script:

[The opening paragraph of the "Editor's Note" which served as a preface to the script.]

In this documentary we had a few problems with getting certain interviews and information. As the house is a refuge for parents in distress, our questions were often limited. We didn't want to pry.

[The opening paragraph of the script.]

Smith: Hello, this is John Smith reporting for *60 Minutes*. Our topic for this week is the Ronald McDonald House. Here I am in front of the

House in Burlington, Vermont, but before I go inside, let me fill
you in on the history of this and many other houses like it. . . .

[Within the script are scenes called a "Camera Eye," set in boldface type, por-
traying the house from the objective view of the TV camera.]

Toward the back of the house, three cars and one camper are parked in an
oval-shaped, gravel driveway. Up three steps onto a small porch are four black
plastic chairs and a small coffee table. On top of a table is a black ashtray
filled with crumpled cigarette butts.

[Smith learns about the house by going on a walking tour with a volunteer
hostess named Robin; most of the information about the Ronald McDonald
House comes from Robin's answers to Smith's questions.]

Smith: Do you always cook dinner for the families?
Robin: Oh no. Most of the time they cook their own meals. However, if we
have free time, we might make something for them. It's really nice
for them to come home to food on the stove.

In other words, rather than writing a report with no audience in mind, in
the generic form of a term paper — which exists nowhere in the world outside of school — these writers posed the hypothetical problems faced by
prime-time TV writers and imagined how they would solve them. Their simple
idea of an "Editor's Note" is itself an interesting move: whereas in typical college research papers authors try to pretend they know everything, in this
format the student writers felt they could be more candid about real problems
they encountered and how it limited their resulting script.

Remember the group researching pollution in Lake Champlain? Their factual report is framed by a narrative story told by a fictional student; the report
itself includes a tour of the waste treatment plant, interviews with merchants
and shoppers to find out the level of public awareness of the problem, and statistical results from a self-designed survey given to Burlington residents about
the pollution problem. The *Ben and Jerry's* report resulted in a feature article
aimed for publication in *The Burlington Free Press,* complete with illustrations.
And another group in the same class reported on the plight of the homeless in
downtown Burlington and wrote their final paper as a short (twenty-page)
book with five chapters, one by each writer, the last one collaborative.

Tutors need to be especially careful here in what you advise. Many professors
who assign research projects will have a specific idea of what such reports should
look like, and tutors need to be careful to counsel the student in those directions.
However, if a student's professor is open to innovative approaches to the assignment, tutors might suggest that re-forming the final draft into something other
than a term paper will be more creative, and fun to do, and interesting to read.

Reforming Narrative Remember Amanda and the story of the potato field? It
turns out that the "mud, potatoes, mud, potatoes" draft we looked at earlier

described her most recent work on her father's farm, after he had replaced manual labor with a mechanical harvester. In a subsequent draft, she wrote about the old days when up to sixty neighborhood people — men, women, children — had harvested the potatoes by hand:

> 1983. . . . I bent down to help Louise finish her stretch of newly uncovered potatoes. It was piece time. We had an hour to devour lunch before the next shift of potato picking began. . . . Martin, who worked alongside me and Louise, had uncovered a nest of field mice, so we saved them from being chopped up by the digger. They were so cute — I hope we got them all. . . .

In her final portfolio draft, Amanda's paper most resembles a drama in two acts, with one act set in 1983 when field hands dug the potatoes, and including large portions of dialogue. The second act, separated by extra white space, is set in 1988 when she worked inside the potato-harvesting machine, and takes place largely as an internal monologue ("Potatoes, mud, potatoes, mud . . ."). However, at the very end she also included a new piece of writing, a coda, set off by extra white space, which explained her final understanding of the story she once thought was about waitressing:

> 1989. This year the potato harvester is still working, the same women on board, with the same bored expressions on their faces. Soon this job will probably not need anyone to work or help the machinery. Labour is an expense farmers cannot afford. There are no tattie holidays anymore, no extra pocket money for the children of the district. Change, technology, development is what they say it is. I say it is a loss of valuable experience in hard work and a loss of good times.

In her final draft, Karen, our basketball player, provides three scenes, two occurring simultaneously and one sequentially: first, the play-by-play from the announcer's point of view; second, her time on the bench and in the game; third, outside the locker room where she finds her father and they have a tearful celebratory conversation. Like Amanda, the third scene was generated only at the time of the final draft, adding a kind of closure to an eight-page story. (And, yes, Karen does make a three-point basket in the Boston Garden.)

It is interesting that Karen made extra copies of her basketball paper at Kinko's to give as Christmas presents to her family. But Amanda, who was equally proud of her potato story, did not send a copy home, so critical had she become of her father's decision to mechanize the harvesting of potatoes on the farm.

In the same class, John, who had been trying to write an essay covering his eleven months in Ecuador, re-formed his essay into a series of cuts from a diary spaced throughout the year — a form that allowed him to show intermittent slices of his growth, but skip long deadly summaries. In like manner, Avy, trying to describe a long-distance friendship over a four-year period, recreated periodic telephone conversations to show the passing of time.

Prior to attending college, many of these writers had been trained to write five-paragraph themes in Advanced Placement English classes; what they discovered as they shaped and reshaped their stories was how much fun it was to write in forms they invented for themselves. Again, tutors need to be cautious in their counsel, but when they discover writers locked into one tedious way of telling their stories, tutors can find out if there is any room in the assignments — or time in their lives — for experimentation and play.

These are the techniques that provoke serious revision in novice writers, showing them specific moves while allowing them to retain ownership of their papers. With a little thoughtful and cautious modification, they may also work for tutors.

Minimalist Tutoring: Making the Student Do All the Work

Jeff Brooks _____

SEATTLE PACIFIC UNIVERSITY

In presenting the philosophy of minimalist tutoring, Jeff Brooks argues that "the goal of each tutoring session is learning, not a perfect paper." In contrast to those who view the tutor as a proofreader and editor, Brooks sees the tutor as a commentator and guide and contends that "fixing flawed papers is easy; showing the students how to fix their papers is complex and difficult." Like Stephen North, he believes that the tutor's job is to improve the writer, not the writer's text; "our primary object in the writing center session is not the paper, but the student," he says. For tutors to achieve the goals of minimalist tutoring, Brooks advocates a hands-off approach to students' papers — one that avoids editing the papers for errors in favor of emphasizing structure, organization, logical reasoning, and stylistic control. He explains the assumptions that guide this model and describes the techniques and strategies of forms of minimalist tutoring that he terms "basic," "advanced," and "defensive." This essay first appeared in 1991 in Writing Lab Newsletter.

A writing center worst case scenario: A student comes in with a draft of a paper. It is reasonably well-written and is on a subject in which you have both expertise and interest. You point out the mechanical errors and suggest a number of improvements that could be made in the paper's organization; the student agrees and makes the changes. You supply some factual information that will strengthen the paper; the student incorporates it. You work hard, enjoy yourself, and when the student leaves, the paper is much improved. A week later, the student returns to the writing center to see you: "I got an A! Thanks for all your help!"

This scenario is hard to avoid, because it makes everyone involved feel good: the student goes away happy with a good grade, admiring you; you feel intelligent, useful, helpful — everything a good teacher ought to be. Everything about it seems right. That this is bad points out the central difficulty we confront as tutors: we sit down with imperfect papers, but our job is to improve their writers.

When you "improve" a student's paper, you haven't been a tutor at all; you've been an editor. You may have been an exceedingly good editor, but you've been of little service to your student. I think most writing center tutors agree that we must not become editors for our students and that the goal of each tutoring session is learning, not a perfect paper. But faced with students who want us to "fix" their papers as well as our own desire to create "perfect" documents, we often find it easier and more satisfying to take charge, to muscle in on the student's paper, red pen in hand.

To avoid that trap, we need to make the student the primary agent in the writing center session. The student, not the tutor, should "own" the paper and take full responsibility for it. The tutor should take on a secondary role, serving mainly to keep the student focused on his own writing. A student who comes to the writing center and passively receives knowledge from a tutor will not be any closer to his own paper than he was when he walked in. He may leave with an improved paper, but he will not have learned much.

A writing teacher or tutor cannot and should not expect to make student papers "better"; that is neither our obligation, nor is it a realistic goal. The moment we consider it our duty to improve the paper, we automatically relegate ourselves to the role of editor.

If we can't fix papers, is there anything left for us to do? I would like to suggest that when we refuse to edit, we become more active than ever as educators. In the writing center, we have the luxury of time that the classroom teacher does not have. We can spend that time talking and listening, always focusing on the paper at hand. The primary value of the writing center tutor to the student is as a living human body who is willing to sit patiently and help the student spend time with her paper. This alone is more than most teachers can do, and will likely do as much to improve the paper as a hurried proofreader can. Second, we can talk to the student as an individual about the one paper before us. We can discuss strategies for effective writing and principles of structure, we can draw students' attention to features in their writing, and we can give them support and encouragement (writing papers, we shouldn't forget, is a daunting activity).

Assumptions

All of this can be painfully difficult to do. Every instinct we have tells us that we must work for perfection; likewise, students pressure us in the same direction. I have found two assumptions useful in keeping myself from editing student papers:

1. The most common difficulty for student writers is paying attention to their writing. Because of this, student papers seldom reflect their

writers' full capabilities. Writing papers is a dull and unrewarding activity for most students, so they do it in noisy surroundings, at the last minute, their minds turning constantly to more pressing concerns. It is little wonder that so much student writing seems haphazard, unfocused, and disorganized. A good many errors are made that the student could easily have avoided. If we can get students to reread a paper even once before handing it in, in most cases we have rendered an improvement. We ought to encourage students to treat their own writings as texts that deserve the same kind of close attention we usually reserve for literary texts.

Our message to students should be: "Your paper has value as a piece of writing. It is worth reading and thinking about like any other piece of writing."

2. While student writings are texts, they are unlike other texts in one important way: the process is far more important than the product. Most "real-world" writing has a goal beyond the page; anything that can be done to that writing to make it more effective ought to be done. Student writing, on the other hand, has no real goal beyond getting it on the page. In the real world when you need to have something important written "perfectly," you hire a professional writer; when a student hires a professional writer, it is a high crime called plagiarism.

This fairly obvious difference is something we often forget. We are so used to real-world writing, where perfection is paramount, that we forget that students write to learn, not to make perfect papers. Most writing teachers probably have a vision of a "perfect" freshman paper (it probably looks exactly like the pieces in the readers and wins a Bedford prize); we should probably resign ourselves to the fact that we will seldom see such a creature. Most students simply do not have the skill, experience, or talent to write the perfect paper.

Basic Minimalist Tutoring

Given these assumptions, there are a number of concrete ways we can put theory into practice. Our body language will do more to signal our intentions (both to our students and to ourselves) than anything we say. These four steps should establish a tone that unmistakably shows that the paper belongs to the student and that the tutor is not an editor.

1. Sit beside the student, not across a desk — that is where job interviewers and other authorities sit. This first signal is important for showing the student that you are *not* the person "in charge" of the paper.
2. Try to get the student to be physically closer to her paper than you are. You should be, in a sense, an outsider, looking over her shoulder while she works on her paper.

3. If you are right-handed, sit on the student's right; this will make it more difficult for you to write on the paper. Better yet, don't let yourself have a pencil in your hand. By all means, if you must hold something, don't make it a red pen!

4. Have the student read the paper aloud to you, and suggest that he hold a pencil while doing so. Aside from saving your eyes in the case of bad handwriting, this will accomplish three things. First, it will bypass that awkward first few moments of the session when you are in complete control of the paper and the student is left out of the action while you read his paper. Second, this will actively involve the student in the paper, quite likely for the first time since he wrote it. I find that many students are able to find and correct usage errors, awkward wording, even logic problems without any prompting from me. Third, this will help establish the sometimes slippery principle that good writing should sound good.

I am convinced that if you follow these four steps, even if you do nothing else, you will have served the student better than you would if you "edited" his paper.

Advanced Minimalist Tutoring

Of course, there is quite a bit more you can do for the student in the time you have. You can use your keen intelligence and fine critical sense to help the student without directing the paper. As always, the main goal is to keep the student active and involved in the paper. I have three suggestions:

1. Concentrate on success in the paper, not failure. Make it a practice to find something nice to say about every paper, no matter how hard you have to search. This isn't easy to do; errors are what we usually focus on. But by pointing out to a student when he is doing something right, you reinforce behavior that may have started as a felicitous accident. This also demonstrates to the student that the paper is a "text" to be analyzed, with strengths as well as weaknesses. This is where the tutor can radically depart from the role of editor.

2. Get the student to talk. It's her paper; she is the expert on it. Ask questions — perhaps "leading" questions — as often as possible. When there are sentence-level problems, make the student find and (if possible) correct them. When something is unclear, don't say "This is unclear"; rather, say, "What do you mean by this?" Instead of saying, "You don't have a thesis," ask the student, "Can you show me your thesis?" "What's your reason for putting Q before N?" is more effective than "N should have come before Q." It is much easier to point out mistakes than it is to point the student toward finding them, but your questions will do much more to establish the student as sole owner of the paper and you as merely an interested outsider.

3. If you have time during your session, give the student a discrete
    writing task, then go away for a few minutes and let him do it. For
    instance, having established that the paper has no thesis, tell the
    student to write the thesis while you step outside for a few minutes.
    The fact that you will return and see what he has accomplished (or
    not accomplished) will force him to work on the task you have given
    him probably with more concentration than he usually gives his writ-
    ing. For most students, the only deadline pressure for their paper is
    the teacher's final due date. Any experienced writer knows that a
    deadline is the ultimate energizer. Creating that energy for a small
    part of the paper is almost the best favor you can do for a student.

Defensive Minimalist Tutoring

So far, I have been assuming that the student is cooperative or at least open to
whatever methods you might use. This, of course, is not a very realistic
assumption. There are many students who fight a non-editing tutor all the
way. They know you know how to fix their paper, and that is what they came
to have done. Some find ingenious ways of forcing you into the role of editor:
some withdraw from the paper, leaving it in front of you; some refuse to write
anything down until you tell them word for word what to write; others will
keep asking you questions ("What should I do here? Is this part okay?"). Don't
underestimate the abilities of these students; they will fatigue you into submission if they can.

To fight back, I would suggest we learn some techniques from the experts:
the uncooperative students themselves.

1. Borrow student body language. When a student doesn't want to be
    involved in his paper, he will slump back in his chair, getting as far
    away from it as possible. If you find a student pushing you too hard
    into editing his paper, physically move away from it — slump back
    into your chair or scoot away. If a student is making a productive ses-
    sion impossible with his demands, yawn, look at the clock, rearrange
    your things. This language will speak clearly to the student: "You can-
    not make me edit your paper."
2. Be completely honest with the student who is giving you a hard time.
    If she says, "What should I do here?" you can say in a friendly, non-
    threatening way, "I can't tell you that — it's your grade, not mine," or,
    "I don't know — it's *your* paper." I have found this approach doesn't
    upset students as it might seem it would; they know what they are
    doing, and when you show that you know too, they accept that.

All of the suggestions I have made should be just a beginning of the ideas
we can use to improve our value to our students. I hope that they lead to
other ideas and tutoring techniques.

The less we do *to* the paper, the better. Our primary object in the writing center session is not the paper, but the student. Fixing flawed papers is easy; showing the students how to fix their own papers is complex and difficult. Ideally, the student should be the only active agent in improving the paper. The tutor's activity should focus on the student. If, at the end of the session, a paper is improved, it should be because the student did all the work.

A Critique of Pure Tutoring[1]

Linda K. Shamoon and Deborah H. Burns _____
UNIVERSITY OF RHODE ISLAND

In a counterpoint to Jeff Brooks's minimalist approach, Linda Shamoon and Deborah Burns examine and critique the student-centered, nondirective practices espoused by university writing centers. These practices, they argue, generally begin as guidelines but often harden into orthodoxy. While nondirective tutoring can help students learn to depend on their own resources as writers, Shamoon and Burns point out that advanced graduate students tend to write, and learn, under the directive tutoring of thesis and dissertation advisors. Such advisors "seem authoritative, intrusive, directive and product-oriented. Yet these practices created major turning points for a variety of writers." In a similar way, master musicians often teach through a process of demonstration and directive critique, first showing student musicians how to perform a piece and then guiding the students through a performance of their own. This article, which originally appeared in The Writing Center Journal in 1995, is important in unambiguously stating that directive tutoring, particularly when it involves discipline-specific pieces of writing, is often an effective teaching strategy. In view of these insights, Shamoon and Burns argue that writing center practices need to encompass both directive and nondirective tutoring strategies.

In our writing center and probably in yours, graduate teaching assistants and undergraduate peer tutors conduct student-centered, one-on-one tutoring sessions. We train these tutors to make use of process-centered writing pedagogy and top-down, writer-centered responses to papers. During the tutoring sessions, tutors are always careful not to appropriate the students' writing and not to substitute their ideas for those of the students. Thus, tutors let students set the agenda, and they resist word-by-word editing of any text. While this cluster of practices has helped us establish a growing clientele and a good reputation, we have begun to wonder about the *orthodoxy* of these practices, especially as we reflect upon our personal experiences and upon stories from faculty in writing across-the-curriculum (WAC) workshops who tell us that they "really" learned to write during one-on-one tutoring sessions which were directive and appropriative. In an effort to understand these experiences more clearly, we have turned to research on expertise, social and cognitive development, and academic literacy. These sources have convinced us that directive tutoring, a methodology completely opposite our current tutoring practices, is sometimes a suitable and effective mode of instruction. As a result, we are currently struggling with radically oppositional practices in tutoring, and we are contemplating the places of these oppositional practices in our writing center.

The Orthodoxy of Current Practice

The prevailing approach to writing center tutoring is excellently explained and contextualized in several texts, among them Irene Clark's *Writing in the Center: Teaching in a Writing Center Setting* and Emily Meyer and Louise Z. Smith's *The Practical Tutor.* From these sources tutors learn to use a process approach, to serve as an audience for the student writers, and to familiarize students with the conventions of academic discourse (Clark, *Writing* 7–10; Meyer and Smith 31–32, 47). This approach emphasizes a student-centered, non-directive method, which suggests that "in order for students to improve in their writing, they must attribute their success to their own efforts and abilities, not to the skill of the tutor" (Clark, *Writing* 7). To encourage active student participation, tutors learn about "legitimate and illegitimate collaboration" (Clark, *Writing* 21). True collaboration occurs when the participants are "part of the same discourse community and meet as equals" (21). Tutors learn that illegitimate collaboration happens when the tutor takes over a student's writing by providing answers rather than by asking questions. Illegitimate collaboration, says Clark, creates dependency: "[T]utor dominated conferences, instead of producing autonomous student writers, usually produce students who remain totally dependent upon the teacher or tutor, unlikely ever to assume responsibility for their own writing" (41). These ideas and others from books about tutoring, along with related concepts from articles in *The Writing Center Journal* and *Writing Lab Newsletter,* provide the bases for current writing center practices.

Upon reflection, however, we find that sometimes these sources become more than simply the research backdrop to writing center practice; sometimes they form a writing center "bible." This bible contains not only the material evidence to support student-centered, non-directive practices, but also codes of behavior and statements of value that sanction tutors as a certain kind of professional, one who cares about writing and about students, their authentic voices and their equal access to the opportunities within sometimes difficult institutions. These codes and appeals seem less the product of research or examined practice and more like articles of faith that serve to validate a tutoring approach which "feels right," in fact so right that it is hard for practitioners to accept possible tutoring alternatives as useful or compelling. For example, Jean Kiedaisch and Sue Dinitz, in "'So What?': The Limitations of the Generalist Tutor," note that while those tutors who know the discipline and can supply special information for students' papers may be effective, such tutors may not always be available. Kiedaisch and Dinitz conclude, "If we can't ensure that students writing for upper level courses can meet with a knowledgeable tutor, should we be alarmed about relying on generalist tutors? We think not" (73). Kiedaisch and Dinitz may be drawn to this conclusion because the alternative model examined in the study — that of a knowledgeable tutor supplying "special information" — is simply too far outside orthodox writing center practice to be acceptable.

The power of this orthodoxy permeates writing center discourse, where we sometimes find statements that come more from a range of assumed values rather than from researched findings. For example, we read online a writing center tutor's "confession" that she showed a model essay to a student rather than let the student get frustrated at having no readily available, familiar written format to help tame his chaos of ideas. Well over a hundred entries followed assuring the tutor that models have a place in tutoring, as long as they do not transgress upon the authentic voice of the student ("Imitation/Modeling"). These assurances could be interpreted as obviating the sin of appropriating the student's paper. In addition, Evelyn Ashton-Jones, in "Asking the Right Questions: A Heuristic for Tutors," argues that to promote cognitive growth of students, tutors must engage in a version of "Socratic dialogue" and not "lapse into a 'directive' mode of tutoring" (31–33). Quoting Thom Hawkins, she labels the directive tutor as "shaman, guru, or mentor," and Socratic tutors as "architects and partners" (31). In our culture who would not rather be an architect than a shaman? Finally, in discussing the need for students to be active learners during a tutoring session, Clark asserts that students should never be "disciples sitting in humility at the feet of a mentor" (*Writing* 7).[2] The language and tone here forbid challenge. The idea that one cannot be extremely appreciative of expertise and also learn actively from an expert is an ideological formation rather than a product of research.

In these instances and others, ideology rather than examined practice ("things that go without saying") seems to drive writing center practice. First, writing is viewed as a process tied to cognitive activities occurring in recursive stages. Although these stages have been labeled in numerous taxonomies, Jack Selzer finds that most enumerations include invention, organization, drafting, and revision (280). As a result, tutoring sessions often follow a ritual that begins by noting where a writer is with a text and proceeds by "walking" through the remaining stages. Second, writing center practice assumes that process strategies are global and transferable (Flower and Hayes 365–87). The extreme nonhierarchical, presumably democratic version of this assumption is that anyone who is familiar with the writing process can be of help to anybody. In practice, tutors from any discipline who seem to be good writers help all students, allowing for peer tutoring across the curriculum (Haring-Smith 175–88). A third assumption is that the students possess sole ownership of their texts ("Teaching Composition"; Brannon and Knoblauch; Sommers

149–50). In practice, then, the tutors' mission is to help clarify what is in the text and to facilitate revision without imposing their own ideas or their own knowledge and, in so doing, without taking ownership of the text. Thus, tutors follow a script that is question-based and indirect rather than directive. Fourth and closely related, the prevailing wisdom assumes that one-on-one conferencing can best help students clarify their writing to themselves (Murray, "Teaching" 144). In practice, then, tutoring is conducted in private. Finally, there is the assumption that all texts are interpretive and that the best writing contains statements of meaning or an authentic voice (Schwegler; Murray, *A Writer;* Elbow). In practice, then, much of the tutors' discussion and indirect questioning aims at getting students to voice and substantiate overall statements of meaning. Once this has been achieved, students are often sent home to revise their texts in light of this understanding. In sum, tutoring orthodoxy is: process-based, Socratic, private, a-disciplinary, and nonhierarchical or democratic.

Many points in this characterization of writing have been challenged by social-constructionist views. Social-constructionists characterize writing as a social act rather than as a process of personal discovery or individual expression. Kenneth Bruffee calls writing displaced conversation, implying that writing occurs not in isolation but in response to ideas found in other texts and other forms of communal conversation (*Short Course* 3). Furthermore, Bruffee cites Oakeshott's belief that education is primarily an "initiation into the skill and partnership of this conversation in which we learn to recognize the voices, to distinguish the proper occasions of utterance, and in which we acquire the intellectual and moral habits appropriate to conversation" (638). Patricia Bizzell sharpens the critique by adding that students

> need composition instruction that exposes and demystifies the institutional structure of knowledge, rather than that which covertly reintroduces discriminatory practices while cloaking the force of convention in concessions to the 'personal.' The cognitive focus of process-oriented composition studies cannot provide the necessary analysis. (112)

In these ways, social-constructionists challenge the private, a-disciplinary nature of writing, but according to Robert J. Connors there is little in the *practice* of teaching or tutoring writing that has changed because of social constructionist views. Connors maintains that, in the classroom, social constructionists still base teaching and tutoring upon stages in the writing process. Thus, the social constructionist critique has broadened our understanding of the contexts of writing, but it has not formed an alternative set of practices.

The Challenge from Experience and from Writing Across the Curriculum Faculty

The more serious challenge to current tutoring orthodoxy starts for us with some of our personal experiences as we learned to write in our discipline. When

Deborah Burns was completing a thesis for her M.A. in English Literature, she was tutored by her major professor. She reports the following experience.

> The most helpful writing tutoring I ever received at the university came from the director of my Master's thesis. I wrote what I thought was a fairly good draft of my thesis, then shared it with my director for comments. I remember, at first, being surprised at the number of problems my director found with my draft. He added transitions when needed, showed me how to eliminate wordiness, and formalized my vocabulary. In addition, he offered specific suggestions for rewriting entire paragraphs, and he always pointed out areas where I had lost focus. The most important thing he did for me was to write sentences that helped locate my work in the field of Dickens studies. For example, Dickens critics had thoroughly examined family relationships in the novels, but few worked on alcoholism and its effects on children, the central idea of my thesis. My director's specific suggestions helped me to foreground my unique way of examining some of Dickens's novels. I learned that I was so immersed in the research and articulation of the new ideas I wanted to explore in my thesis, I had neither the time nor the experience to fully understand how to write an extended piece of scholarly work in the discourse community. At first, I was confused about my perceived inability to write like the scholar I was supposed to be, but I soon realized (especially at my thesis defense) that I was fortunate to have my director as a person who *showed* me how to revise my draft so that it blended with conventional academic discourse. After I watched my director work with my text, and after I made the necessary changes, my thesis and other academic writing was much less of a mystery to me.

For many years Burns puzzled over the direct intervention made by her director while she composed her Master's thesis. The intervention had been extremely helpful, yet it went against everything she had learned in composition studies. Her director was directive, he substituted his own words for hers, and he stated with disciplinary appropriateness the ideas with which she had been working. Furthermore, Burns observed that other graduate students had the same experience with this director: he took their papers and rewrote them while they watched. They left feeling better able to complete their papers, and they tackled other papers with greater ease and success. Clearly, several features of the graduate director's practice violated current composition orthodoxy. His practices seem authoritative, intrusive, directive, and product-oriented. Yet these practices created major turning points for a variety of writers. For Burns and for others, when the director intervened, a number of thematic, stylistic, and rhetorical issues came together in a way that revealed and made accessible aspects of the discipline which had remained unexplained or out of reach. Instead of appropriation, this event made knowledge and achievement accessible.

This challenge to current tutoring practices has been further extended by conversations with faculty from a variety of disciplines during our WAC workshops. We have held faculty workshops semiannually for the last three years, and it is not unusual for faculty members to remember suddenly that at some point late in college or in graduate school, during a one-on-one conference, a professor they respected took one of their papers and rewrote it, finally showing them "how to write." During our first workshop, a colleague from animal science reported that in graduate school his major professor took his paper and rewrote it while he watched. In the colleague's own words, "He tore it to shreds, but I sure learned a lot." When he made this statement, there were looks of recognition and sympathetic murmuring from others in the room. Just recently, in a WAC faculty writing circle, a colleague from nursing reported that in order to complete her doctoral proposal she has sat through numerous revising sessions with the most accessible member of her doctoral committee, each time learning more about writing, about critical theory, and about how to tie the theory to her research methods. In these examples and others, professors were acting like tutors, working one-on-one with student authors to improve their texts, but their methods were hardly nondirective. Over and over in the informal reports of our colleagues we find that crucial information about a discipline and about writing is transmitted in ways that are intrusive, directive, and product-oriented, yet these behaviors are not perceived as an appropriation of power or voice but instead as an opening up of those aspects of practice which had remained unspoken and opaque.

While we do not pretend that these informally gathered stories carry the same weight as research data, we are struck by the repeated benefits of a tutoring style that is so opposite to current orthodoxy. As we discuss these revelations further with WAC faculty, we find that the benefits of alternative tutoring practices are frequent enough to make us seriously question whether one tutoring approach fits all students and situations. Surely, students at different stages in their education, from beginning to advanced, are developing different skills and accumulating different kinds of information, thus making them receptive to different kinds of instruction and tutoring. In fact, in "The Idea of Expertise: An Exploration of Cognitive and Social Dimensions of Writing," Michael Carter sets forth a five-stage continuum of cognitive learning that characterizes the progress from novice to expert. Carter explains that novices and advanced beginners utilize global, process-based learning and problem-solving strategies; that intermediate and advanced students shift to hierarchical and case-dependent strategies; and that experts draw intuitively upon extensive knowledge, pattern recognition, and "holistic similarity recognition" (271–72). If students are exercising different cognitive skills at different stages in their learning, it makes sense that they may be responsive to different kinds of information and tutoring styles at different stages, too. Our personal and WAC experiences suggest that, at the very least, for intermediate and advanced students, and perhaps on occasion for beginners, too, one tutoring approach does not fit all.

An Alternative Mode of Practice: Master Classics in Music

Since we have encountered so many positive alternative representations of the tutoring of writing, we have started to ask ourselves when such practices are helpful and exactly how they can be best characterized. Interestingly, in order to find answers we have had to look outside the discipline. This is not surprising since, according to Michael Agar, most of us sometimes have difficulty seeing alternatives to our own ways of thinking, especially to everyday notions that seem based on common sense.

> There are two ways of looking at differences. . . . One way is to figure out that the differences are the tip of the iceberg, the signal that two different systems are at work. Another way is to notice all the things that the other [system] lacks when compared to you[rs], the so-called *deficit theory* approach. . . . The deficit theory does have its advantages. But it's a prison. It locks you into a closed room in an old building with no windows. . . . (Agar 23, emphasis in original)

In other words, within a strong system generally held notions and behaviors so permeate our lives that only they seem legitimate or make sense, while all other notions and behaviors seem illegitimate. In order for alternative practices to look sensible, they must be appreciated from within another strong system. One such system that may be found outside of writing instruction is the practice of master classes in music education. Master classes are a form of public tutoring that is standard practice in music education (Winer 29). The circumstances and conduct of master classes are almost totally opposite those seen in nondirective tutoring practices.[3]

During a master class an expert music teacher meets with a group of students studying the same specialty, such as piano, voice, strings, brass, etc. The students vary in their achievement levels, from novice to near-expert. Several students come to the session prepared to be tutored on their performance of a piece or a portion of a piece, while others may come as observers. The tutorial typically begins with one student's performance; then the master teacher works over a section of the piece with the student, suggesting different ways to play a passage, to shape a tone, to breathe, to stand or sit, or even to hold an instrument. On occasion, the master teacher will play the passage herself and ask the student to play it with her or immediately after her. Then, as a typical end-of-the-tutorial strategy, the master teacher has the student play the whole passage or the piece again. At this time it is not unusual for those who are observing to respond with a new sense of understanding about the music or the technique.

When a master class is at its best, the emotional tone is compelling. The atmosphere is charged with excitement, with a sense of community, and with successive moments of recognition and appreciation. Excitement comes from the public performances, which are often anxiety provoking for the performer; but there is relaxation, too, for no one expects the perfection of a formal performance. Instead, a sense of community animates the participants, who are willing to have their performances scrutinized in order to improve, and everyone recognizes those moments during the tutorial when increased mastery passes into the hands of the student. Indeed, all the participants have a sense of high expectation, for they have access to someone who has mastery, who wants to share this knowledge with them, and who, by showing them about a limited passage of music, reveals a world of knowledge, attitude, and know-how.

Examples of such master classes can be found in the documentary *From Mao to Mozart: Isaac Stern in China,* a film about violinist Isaac Stern's 1979 visit to China. The film, which won an Academy Award for the best documentary of 1980, includes several excerpts from master classes on the violin offered by Stern to a variety of students in China. In one scene, Stern works with a young, extremely able violinist who is having trouble following his precise suggestions. Suddenly, Stern says he will share a secret with her. He plays a passage from her solo piece and then pulls out an extra shoulder pad hidden under his suit jacket. This extra padding enables him to hold his violin in a position that facilitates his playing. Later, the student replays the passage while Stern pushes up and positions her violin as if she, too, were wearing the secret padding. Her performance suddenly improves so much that the audience recognizes the change and bursts into applause. Throughout this episode, there is a sense of delight, of the sharing of important information, and of appreciation.

What strikes us as important about master classes is that they feature characteristics exactly opposite current tutoring orthodoxy. They are hierarchical: there is an open admission that some individuals have more knowledge and skill than others, and that the knowledge and skills are being "handed down." This handing down is directive and public; during tutoring the expert provides the student with communally and historically tested options for performance and technical improvement. Also, a good deal of effort during tutoring is spent on imitation or, at its best, upon emulation. Rather than assuming that this imitation will prevent authentic self-expression, the tutor and the student assume that imitation will lead to improved technique, which will enable freedom of expression. Finally, there is an important sense of desire and appreciation. The students have sought out the expert because they already have recognized the value of her knowledge and skills, and because she seeks to share this expertise with students, both to preserve and to expand the discipline and its traditions. Mutual appreciation and mutual desire seem to be at the center of this kind of teaching. In music master classes, sitting at the feet of the master is one way of learning.

Reflections upon Alternative Tutorial Practices

Although the master class model has much to offer writing centers, it is not immune to abuse. History is littered with examples of directive, authoritative "tutoring" gone awry, from sports coaching to religious cults. Nor are all music master classes as successful as those portrayed in the documentary about Isaac Stern. The famous German conductor Wilhelm Furtwangler, for example, was known to belittle and physically abuse his students and orchestra members (Fenelon 116). But such cases represent alternative practices run amok, when authoritative has become authoritarian, when directive has become dictatorial, and when imitative has become repressive. The challenge for writing centers is to know the best features of these alternative pedagogies in order to broaden current practice. We need to know enough about these practices to prevent abusive application and to secure their benefits for students and their tutors.

Music is not the only discipline to use alternative tutoring practices. In art education, the studio seminar is an important and widely practiced form of public tutorial. According to Wendy Holmes, a professor of art history at the University of Rhode Island, studio seminar is the crucial intermediate course for art majors, when they start exploring, locating, and solving artistic problems on their own, whether in sculpture, painting, or other media. During studio time, students work on their own projects, and the instructor "visits" and tutors each student individually, suggesting ideas, options, or techniques for the project; and during seminar time, students display their work to each other and to the instructor for public commentary, analysis, and reflection. Studio seminar is a mix of private and public tutoring that is directive. In pharmacy practice internships, senior pharmacy majors are placed in real-world settings to observe their professors in action, to apply their newly acquired professional knowledge, and to receive guided practice in a mix of private and public tutoring (Hume). Nursing students take "clinicals," courses which provide the same combination of observation and guided practice as do medical internships and residencies (Godfrey). All these examples include practices that are more similar to the music master class than to nondirective writing tutoring. Emulative learning is conducted in a hierarchical environment to facilitate new information or masterly behavior within a domain. While these examples of alternative practices are most commonly found at intermediate or advanced levels, they are sometimes usefully applied with novices, too (as we explain below).

These instances of public tutoring that are the norm within certain disciplines provide an opportunity to reflect upon the constellation of conditions that make directive tutoring fruitful. Three strands of research are important: research on the development of expertise (including connections to imitation and modeling) helps explain the links between directive tutoring and cognitive development; theoretical explanations of subjectivities help us understand directive tutoring and social development; research on academic literacy helps us understand directive tutoring and disciplinary development.

As we have already noted, research about expertise helps elucidate the connections between cognitive skills development and alternative tutoring practices for all learners, from novice to near-expert. Specifically, Carter explains that experts have extensive "repertoires" for problem solving, repertoires built on domain-specific knowledge and experience. He points out that chess grand masters have about "50,000 meaningful chess configurations in their repertoires" (269). Carter argues that novices in all domains build up such repertoires, gradually shifting their modes of thinking from global, general purpose strategies to the hierarchical, domain-specific strategies used by experts in the field (269). Similarly, in her review of the literature on the cognitive aspects of expertise, Geisler points to students in physics solving "thousands of word problems" as they build up domain-specific problem solving repertoires (60). Geisler explains that the changes which characterize the cognitive move from novice to expert include the development of abstract representations of specific cases, the replacing of literal description with abstract discourse, and the rehearsal of extended arguments to support solutions to problems (9–54).

With this research in mind, we turn first to intermediate stages of development, followed by a look at the needs of novices. We find that master classes, studio seminars, clinicals, and other representations of directive tutoring enable committed intermediate and advanced students to observe, practice, and develop widely valued repertoires. When the studio instructor turns the student's attention away from the student's own painting and toward the painting of a master, the student sees how an expert has solved the same problem of light, color, and form. When the studio instructor dabs some pigment on the student's canvas and transforms the impact of the picture, the student observes how experts handle the major elements of the discipline. Throughout the studio seminar, the student has time to practice similar solutions and try out others. Thus, directive tutoring provides a particularly efficient transmission of domain-specific repertoires, far more efficient and often less frustrating than expecting students to reinvent these established practices. At its best, directive tutoring provides a sheltered, protected time and space within the discipline for these intermediate and advanced students to make the shift between general strategies to domain strategies. This cognitive shift seems to depend upon observation and extensive practice — often in emulation of the activities of the tutor-expert — leading to the accumulation of expert repertoires and tacit information.

Novice writers can also benefit from observing and emulating important cognitive operations. In "Modeling: A Process Method of Teaching," Muriel Harris explains that for novice writers, too, composing skills and writing behaviors may be learned through imitation, and that productive patterns of invention or editing may come to replace less useful ones through observation and "protected" practice. In fact, using some of the same techniques that we are arguing for in this article, Harris reports a case study in which she turned to modeling after observing the nonproductive composing habits of a novice writer named Mike.

> Scrambling for a better technique [than free writing], I seized on modeling. . . . In preparation I explained [to Mike] the strategies we would use for the next few sessions. We would begin by having him give me a topic to write on for fifteen to twenty minutes. I would begin by thinking about the rhetorical situation, the "who," "what," "why," plus a few operators to achieve my goal. After these few minutes of planning, I would start writing and keep writing. . . . When I was done, we would reverse roles, and I would give him a topic. As much as possible, he would try to copy the behavior he had

observed. All of these instructions were preceded by brief explanations of what he would observe and the principles he would try to use. My intent was to model a pattern of behavior for Mike to observe and try out and also to monitor his attempts by listening to his protocol and observing his actions. (78)

After three such sessions, Harris reports that "Mike's writing improved noticeably." We note that in these sessions Harris was being directive, telling the student what to observe, what topics to write on, and what behaviors to imitate. We note, too, that the modeling continued for several sessions, with Harris providing a repeated, fixed focus upon specific writing repertoires, and that the student engaged in several learning activities — observing, imitating, and practicing — always guided by Harris' supportive words. We take this to be a version of directive tutoring at its best, with periods of observation and protected practice focused upon important skills development. As Harris says, "And what better way is there to convince students that writing is a process that requires effort, thought, time and persistence than to go through all that writing, scratching out, rewriting and revising with *and for* our students?" (81, emphasis ours).

Cognitive development, however, is not the only change students undergo as they engage in formal education. Recent work in cultural criticism suggests that as students strive to attain academic knowledge or a new understanding of a profession or a career, they inevitably occupy a new subject position, one that may be well-served by directive tutoring practices. These points are most easily explained with respect to intermediate and advanced students, but the ideas apply to beginners as well. Most intermediate or advanced students are highly motivated, active learners, already working with a significant amount of domain knowledge and with the representations of the field given to them by their instructors. As they master this information, they typically start to see themselves as members of a domain community. For example, Faigley and Hansen note that students who successfully completed an advanced course in psychology "felt confident that they could write a publishable report, suggesting that they viewed themselves at the end of the course as fledgling members of the field, able to think and write like psychologists" (144). Similarly, Geisler states, "Professional identity becomes part of personal identity" (92). Bizzell notes that admission to the "academic discourse community is as much social as cognitive, that it is best understood as an initiation" (125). In other words, as intermediate and advanced students get a sense of a domain, they start to occupy a subject position as a *participant* in the domain that is both confirmed by others and assumed by the student. But, as Robert Brooke suggests, this experience of shifting subjectivities and the transformation of identity is *not* necessarily limited to intermediate or advanced students. Brooke found that students in an *introductory* level English class who were encouraged to imitate the drafting processes of their teacher were also receptive to other aspects of being a writer, including the expressions of attitudes, values, and stances towards experiences that lie at the heart of a writer's identity. By the end of the semester several of the students in Brooke's study came to view themselves as writers, and they accepted this identity as new and exciting (32–5). All of these researchers draw attention to the social dimensions of learning and to the important connections between domain processes and social identity.

Directive tutoring supports these connections. Not only does directive tutoring support imitation as a legitimate practice, it allows both student *and* tutor to be the subjects of the tutoring session (while nondirective tutoring allows only the student's work to be the center of the tutoring session). For example, when the master musician rephrases a passage for the intermediate or advanced violin student, the tutor's phrasing, tone, and body language become the subject of the session — her skills *and* her way of being a musician — but the student does not necessarily feel that his musicianship has been appropriated. Instead, the student, too, will have his turn as musician in this master class, and this confirms his musicianship. The interaction with the master teacher establishes that he, too, is a musician. The social nature of directive and emulative tutoring serves to endorse the student's worth as an emerging professional. Similarly, directive tutoring of writing presents more than a demonstration of steps in the writing process. It models a writer's attitudes, stances, and values. In so doing, it unites the processes of writing with the subjectivity of being a writer. As Brooke points out, not all students, particularly not all novices, would choose to assume the subjectivity of their writing tutor or teacher, but when they do, they encase writing processes in the values, attitudes, and acts of interpretation that make writing a socially meaningful experience (37–8). There is much to be gained by unifying the processes of writing with the writer herself. Directive tutoring displays this unity, even for novices.

Finally, in light of research on academic literacy, we speculate that directive tutoring lays bare crucial rhetorical processes that otherwise remain hidden or are delivered as tacit knowledge throughout the academy. According to Geisler, academic literacy and achievement of professionalism are tied not only to domain content and personal identity but also to mastery of rhetorical processes (88–92). These processes of reasoning, argumentation, and interpretation support a discipline's socially-constructed knowledge base. Those students who learn to recognize these rhetorical processes seem also to come to understand a discipline. Geisler argues that the current system of education is constructed to keep these rhetorical processes hidden from students, usually until sometime during graduate school, thus creating a "great divide" among those who have mastered such processes and those who have not (89–90). Geisler charges that academicians and professionals are complicit in hiding these crucial rhetorical processes from most students and the public, thus ensuring their own social status and power over others. Her book is an attempt to place before the public the argument that rhetorical processes must be made more prominent in education if we are to give all students access to academic literacy and a share in the wealth of our society. Although Geisler does not present a method for revealing rhetorical processes earlier in education, she does present a fascinating case study in which such processes were made public (214–29). In a philosophy class, students had a chance to hear their instructor build an argument for a comparative reading of several texts, tear down that structure, and then rebuild it. When the teacher honestly shared his rhetorical processes in this manner, Geisler found that the students gained both a wide appreciation of a discipline and also an ability to express themselves within it (226–27).

We argue that directive tutoring, at its best, is similarly empowering. Directive tutoring displays rhetorical processes in action. When a tutor redrafts problematic portions of a text for a student, the changes usually strengthen the disciplinary argument and improve the connection to current conversation in the discipline. These kinds of changes and the accompanying metalanguage or marginalia often reveal how things are argued in the discipline. Thus, directive tutoring provides interpretive options for students when none seem available, and it unmasks the system of argumentation at work within a discipline. In fact, we speculate that when faculty have not developed an appreciation of the connections between the social construction of disciplinary knowledge and related rhetorical processes, they treat knowledge of the discipline as self-evident and absolute rather than as changing and socially negotiated. Directive tutoring is based upon the articulation of rhetorical processes in order to make literate disciplinary practice plain enough to be imitated, practiced, mastered, and questioned.

Implications for the Writing Center

Alternative tutoring practices are provocative for the writing center, especially if it is to develop into the kind of writing community Stephen North calls for in "The Idea of a Writing Center," a place where all writers — novices and experts — receive support for their writing. We need to keep in mind the crucial cognitive, social, and rhetorical changes students undergo as they strive to become proficient writers in the academy. The writing center could better help to facilitate these developments by serving as a site where directive tutoring provides a sheltered and protected time and space for practice that leads to the accumulation of important repertoires, the expression of new social identities, and the articulation of domain-appropriate rhetoric. Furthermore, if the crucial difference between novice and advanced expertise is the development of rhetorical practices, then writing centers could be the site where instructors from a variety of disciplines articulate and demonstrate these practices, so that students may observe, emulate, question, and critique them.

Many writing centers are already providing elements of these practices. For example, Muriel Harris reports that professors from across the curriculum participate in writing centers, talking about the features of domain-specific writing ("Writing Center and Tutoring" 168–69.) Kiedaisch and Dinitz, as well as Leone Scanlon, supply examples of knowledgeable students from a variety of domains tutoring in writing centers. At the University of Rhode Island a writing center tutor is present during a physics laboratory, on hand for conversation and consultation as students gather and record data in their lab notebooks, as they write up their lab reports, and as they revise their drafts in light of the instructor's responses. Finally, Louise Smith describes two writing programs that draw on experts for writing instruction. One program at Queens College pairs faculty members with advanced undergraduates, and another at the University of Massachusetts/Boston fosters collaboration between faculty and tutors to disseminate theory and research about composition.

Although these applications of public and domain-based tutoring are interesting and impressive, they are piecemeal and seem prompted by concerns other than critically broadening orthodox tutoring practices. We probably do not know the best systematic application in the writing center of directive, public, and emulative tutoring; we probably do not yet know the writing center equivalent of master classes. We do know, however, at least some of the features that should be part of this application. The writing center can be a site where ongoing conversation about the rhetoric of a domain occurs *in* the rhetoric of the domain. For example, the writing center can be a site where professors work occasionally and *publicly* on their writing and on others' writing. Also, the writing center can be a site where the proficient (such as graduate students and seniors) and the novice converse about "intersubjective knowledge" (Geisler 182), or that kind of discourse which externalizes and argues for domain-appropriate abstractions, which externalizes and argues for domain-appropriate linkages to case-specific data, and which provides opportunities for reflection and critique. This is exactly the kind of discourse now hidden from the novices; the writing center is the place to make it public, directive, and available for imitation, appreciation, and questioning. Finally, the writing center can be a site where experts and novices meet often to externalize tacit information — those values, assumptions, and options that inform all texts within a discipline.

Unless writing center research and methods are enlarged to include these practices, writing centers are in danger of remaining part of the social arrangements which, according to Geisler, encourage the a-rhetorical accumulation of domain knowledge and which keep expert rhetorical processes at a distance from the lay public and the novice:

> Our current educational sequence provides all students with a naïve understanding of the more formal components of expertise but withholds an understanding of [the] tacit rhetorical dimension. In this way . . . a great divide has been created — not a great divide between orality and literacy as literacy scholars originally suggested, but rather a great divide with experts on one side with a complete if disjoint practice of expertise, and lay persons on the other side. (89–90)

Current writing center and tutoring practices support this social arrangement by making an orthodoxy of process-based, Socratic, private, a-disciplinary tutoring. This orthodoxy situates tutors of writing at the beginning and global stages of writing instruction, it prevents the use of modeling and imitation as a legitimate tutoring technique, and it holds to a minimum the conduct of critical discourse about rhetorical practices in other fields. If writing center practices are broadened to include *both* directive and non-directive tutoring, the result would be an enrichment of tutoring repertoires, stronger connections between the writing center and writers in other disciplines, and increased attention to the cognitive, social, and rhetorical needs of writers at all stages of development.

Notes

[1] The authors wish to thank Meg Carroll, Rhode Island College, and Teresa Ammirati, Connecticut College, for the use of selected resources from their writing centers.

[2] Clark does not universally dismiss imitation, modeling, or other directive techniques. In "Collaboration and Ethics in Writing Center Pedagogy," she suggests that "imitation may be viewed as ultimately creative, enabling the imitator to expand previous, perhaps ineffective models into something more effective which ultimately becomes his or her own. . . . Sometimes a suggestion of a phrase or two can be wonderfully instructive" (8–9).

[3] The term "master class" may lead to some confusion about the differences between teaching and tutoring. We are referring to "tutoring" as one-on-one instruction, coaching, and responding; and "teaching" as one-to-whole group instruction, coaching, and responding.

Works Cited

Agar, Michael. *Language Shock: Understanding the Culture of Conversation.* New York: Wm. Morrow, 1994.

Ashton-Jones, Evelyn. "Asking the Right Questions: A Heuristic for Tutors." *The Writing Center Journal* 9.1 (1988): 29–36.

Bizzell, Patricia. "College Composition: Initiation into the Academic Discourse Community." *Academic Discourse and Critical Consciousness.* Pittsburgh: U of Pittsburgh P, 1992.

Brannon, Lil, and C. H. Knoblauch. "On Students' Rights to Their Own Texts: A Model of Teacher Response." *College Composition and Communication* 33 (1982): 157–66.

Brooke, Robert. "Modeling a Writer's Identity: Reading and Imitation in the Writing Classroom." *College Composition and Communication* 39 (1988): 23–41.

Bruffee, Kenneth A. "Collaborative Learning and the 'Conversation of Mankind.'" *College English* 46 (1984): 635–52.

———. *A Short Course In Writing: Practical Rhetoric for Teaching Composition through Collaborative Learning.* 3rd ed. New York: HarperCollins, 1993.

Carter, Michael. "The Idea of Expertise." *College Composition and Communication* 41 (1990): 269–86.

Clark, Irene. "Collaboration and Ethics in Writing Center Pedagogy." *The Writing Center Journal* 9.1 (1988): 3–11.

———. *Writing in the Center.* Dubuque: Kendall/Hunt, 1985.

Connors, Robert J. Address. URI/Trinity College Second Summer Conference on Writing. Kingston, May 1994.

Elbow, Peter. *Writing Without Teachers*. New York: Oxford UP, 1973.

Faigley, Lester, and Kristine Hansen. "Learning to Write in the Social Sciences." *College Composition and Communication* 36 (1985): 140–49.

Fenelon, Fania. *Playing for Time*. New York: Atheneum, 1977.

Flower, Linda, and John R. Hayes. "A Cognitive Process Theory of Writing." *College Composition and Communication* 32 (1981): 365–87.

Geisler, Cheryl. *Academic Literacy and the Nature of Expertise: Reading, Writing, and Knowing in Academic Philosophy*. Hillsdale, NJ: Erlbaum, 1994.

Godfrey, Deborah. Professor of Nursing. University of Rhode Island. Personal interview. 29 July 1994.

Haring-Smith, Tori. "Changing Students' Attitudes: Writing Fellows Programs." *Writing Across the Curriculum: A Guide to Developing Programs*. Ed. Susan H. McLeod and Margot Soven. Newbury Park, CA: Sage, 1972. 177–88.

Harris, Muriel. "The Writing Center and Tutoring in WAC Programs." McLeod and Soven. 154–74.

———. "Modeling: A Process Method of Teaching." *College English* 45 (1983): 74–84.

Holmes, Wendy. Professor of Art History. University of Rhode Island. Personal interview. 15 July 1994.

Hume, Anne. Professor of Pharmacy Practice. University of Rhode Island. Personal interview. 15 July 1993.

"Imitation/Modeling as a Teaching Method." Writing Center Discussion List [Online]. 19–30 May 1994. Available e-mail: WCENTER@UNICORN.ACS.TTU.EDU

Kiedaisch, Jean, and Sue Dinitz. "So What? The Limitations of the Generalist Tutor." *Writing Center Journal* 14.1 (1993): 63–74.

Meyer, Emily, and Louise Z. Smith. *The Practical Tutor*. New York: Oxford UP, 1987.

Murray, Donald M. *A Writer Teaches Writing*. Boston: Houghton Mifflin, 1968.

———. "Teaching the Other Self: The Writer's First Reader." *College Composition and Communication* 33 (1982): 140–47.

North, Stephen. "The Idea of a Writing Center." *College English* 46 (1984): 433–46.

Scanlon, Leone. "Recruiting and Training Tutors for Cross-Disciplinary Writing Programs." *The Writing Center Journal* 6 (1986): 37–41.

Schwegler, Robert A. "Meaning and Interpretation." URI/Trinity College 2nd. Summer Conf. on Writing. Kingston, May 1994.

Selzer, Jack. "Exploring Options in Composing." *College Composition and Communication* 35 (1984): 276–84.

Smith, Louise Z. "Independence and Collaboration: Why We Should Decentralize Writing Centers." *The Writing Center Journal* 7.1 (1986): 3–10.

Sommers, Nancy. "Responding to Student Writing." *College Composition and Communication* 33 (1982): 148–66.

Soven, Margot. "Conclusion: Sustaining Writing Across the Curriculum Programs." McLeod and Soven. 189–97.

Stern, Isaac. *From Mao to Mozart: Isaac Stern in China*. Dir. Murray Lerner. Harmony Film Group, 1980.

"Teaching Composition: A Position Statement." *College English* 46 (1984): 612–14.

Winer, Deborah G. "Close Encounters: Pros and Cons of Master Classes." *Opera News* 54 (1989): 28–31.

Constructing Each Other:
Collaborating across Disciplines and Roles

Joan Mullin, Neil Reid, Doug Enders,
and Jason Baldridge _____
UNIVERSITY OF TOLEDO

As a result of the intersection of writing centers and writing-across-the-curriculum programs, peer tutors sometimes find themselves serving in unanticipated roles — for example, as classroom writing instructors and graders. This article, which came out of the collaboration among a writing center director, a geography professor, a peer tutor, and a geography student, examines some of the dilemmas that developed due to a lack of clear understanding of the tutor's role. As Joan Mullin points out, one of the keys to a successful integration of a peer tutor into a writing-intensive classroom is to establish a clear definition of the tutor's role. But in spite of good intentions on the part of the director, tutor, and professor — and attempts at clear communication — the tutor soon found himself serving not simply in his stated role as writing consultant, but also as paper grader. Also, the tutor discovered that his grading criteria and interpretations of writing assignments differed markedly from those of the professor. This article, which originally appeared in the book Weaving Knowledge Together: Writing Centers and Collaboration, *chronicles insights the director, professor, tutor, and student gained from attempts to understand their differences and work together effectively — insights peer tutors should find helpful as they attempt to work with the students and professors of writing-intensive courses.*

EDGES OF THE MAP[1]

Recently, a geography course at the University of Toledo served as a writing-intensive class in which the director of the writing center, a writing center tutor, the professor, the graduate assistant, and a selected student from the class collaborated. This essay, examining how a collaboration works within such a writing-intensive situation, is the result of our experiences as taken from journals and conversations.

My voice (Joan Mullin) will frame this collaboration for several reasons:

- *the audience we are writing for is basically within my disciplinary area;*
- *I organized everyone from the start;*
- *supposedly I have the time for and most stake in this (disciplinary) publication; and*
- *the others are unsure of "what exactly the issues of collaboration are here."*

The naming of these reasons already points to definitions of and positions within the collaboration. For our purposes here, I (uncollaboratively) want to direct attention to the way in which we worked and to how balances were or were not struck within the contexts in which we worked and as a result of the perspectives we held. The previous sentence makes obvious that success or failure of collaboration has to do with the expectations we bring to collaborative situations, with how well we negotiate these expectations, and with whether we reach some kind of agreement or consensual action.

Negotiation of this sort is no simple task. Layered amid these expectations are the images we take on and project within our classes, tutorials, and interactions, many of which we are unaware of or unwilling to negotiate, especially if they are deeply ingrained. The following narrative of this project reveals how the process of negotiation fared; it includes missed opportunities to learn from each other or to communicate, and it points to the successes which led to understanding and positive change.

On the one hand, this project resembled those defined by Lunsford and Ede in that our "collaborative efforts need[ed] to be carefully organized or orchestrated" (64); I was the orchestra leader. On the other hand, when we met together, the group's shifting positions during discussions resembled a "more loose, fluid mode" of collaboration, "one that focused more on the processes of collaboration rather than on the end products, one that emphasized dialogue and exploration rather than efficiency and closure" (67). So that even as I put these words down, I am moved by the voices and tangible artifacts from our quarter together. We have all been changed by our conversations, if only in ways that nonetheless preserve and reinforce our own perspectives; however, I do not think any of us will think the same way about Population Geography 344.

Diffusion Barriers

The collaboration occurred among five principals: me (Joan), as director of the writing center; Doug, as writing center tutor linked to this writing-intensive class; Neil, as assistant professor and teacher of the geography class; Jason, a student in the class; and an unexpected addition, Trish, Neil's graduate assistant, who also worked with him in the classroom. The class itself was an upper-division, writing-intensive course in population geography taken by some geography majors, but most often taken as an elective by those outside the department who need to fill writing-intensive or social studies requirements. The class met two times a week, and all principals (except me) attended class.

As with all tutor-attached courses, Neil, Doug, and I met to discuss the role the tutor would play in the class. I believe it is my role to protect the tutor from being used as a gopher or paper filer, but I also use this discussion time to encourage a re-visioning of the syllabus (if necessary), and to discover the assumptions that guide the instructor's pedagogy. Since attitudes about writing are tied to attitudes about learning, this discussion provides a short hop to a discussion of how learning is conducted in a classroom, how a syllabus looks to students, and how assignments are constructed.

I looked forward to working with Neil because he has impressed me as a straightforward, open, and reflective professional whom students seem to like. During this initial discussion, I wrote that

> (JM) I'm pleased that Neil and Doug seem to get along well, as I thought they would. Neil already has demonstrated the ability to think [about teaching] and the willingness to do so. Doug is as easy going, thoughtful, and up-front about asking questions as I expected him to be too. This will be a great combination!

Doug had worked in the writing center and I knew that he could respond appropriately within many different contexts; I trusted that the tutorial role would, as I had seen in other tutor-attached classes, evolve to meet the needs of the class and instructor. Early on, I noted that

> (JM) Doug's responsibilities as a tutor are to attend the class, work with Neil and the students on writing assignments and their completion, participate as agreed upon in class activities, and take over a class now and then when Neil wants him to talk about particular aspects of writing. Trish's role is apprentice teacher: she is someone to whom students can go for clarification of course material. Neil is a very easy going, although demanding, instructor (with an engaging Scottish accent), who is genuinely interested in a collaborative course.
>
> It will be made clear to the students that each of the three facilitators in the class is available to help them with their writing, but that Doug in particular is an expert in this area. It will also be made clear that each will comment on students' papers, although Neil will be responsible for assigning a grade.

Neil wrote that his "preference was to have Doug take a very active part in the class [and that Doug] was amenable to this." Neil, like me, seemed to think that during our discussion we all agreed on how each would function; he later wrote that

> (NR) Doug was available for student consultation. Each student was required to meet with Doug to discuss the first draft of the first assignment. This allowed the students to get to know Doug and to become familiar with the ways in which he could help them. It also allowed Doug to make students aware of any writing problems that [they] had.

However, what directed Neil's understanding of Doug's role was his previous experience with another writing center tutor. This tutor's interaction with students was quite minimal; she did not pursue opportunities to become an active member of the class or of a teaching team.[2] On reflection, I would say that I did not closely follow that tutor's interaction with the class either, assuming (since she had worked with a geographer before) that she would take on an active role. She did not, and, as a result, Neil's expectations for the tutor in this situation were quite minimal; Neil presumed that Doug's role would be limited to dealing with issues of writing such as grammar and punctuation. Doug's response to the meeting hints at hidden conflict embedded in our assumptions:

> (DE) Initially, my role in Neil's class was not clearly defined. Neil, Joan, and I met to establish my role before the course officially began. In the meeting, we discussed the course and looked at various assignments, and Neil made clear he welcomed my input. And that was that — my role was to provide welcomed input. It was clear to me from what I knew about other attached tutors that I would provide consultation for students similar to that performed within the writing center, but with the advantage of being present in class, being privy to lectures, handouts, assignments . . . I should have an advantage over the traditional tutor in the sense that I would be familiar with the assignments and perhaps their intent . . . While the meeting made me feel welcomed and interested, it did little to define my role, especially as I began to ask myself questions.
>
> I am not sure if I am a tutor or a teacher. For the writing center director, I feel I have one agenda and that is to find out how this class is or is not suited for the attached-tutor program. In this sense, I am to record which aspects of the course lend themselves to tutoring and which do not. Also, as a tutor, I should be nondirective for the most part. From the standpoint of the host teacher, I feel like I am something more than a tutor, something slightly more directive. Being an instructor, this pulls on my "teacher" strings. Conflicting agendas is something I will have to observe.

Likewise, Doug's response to the first class indicated far more confusion about his role than Neil or I anticipated.

> (DE) Neil's introduction on the first day of class did little to clarify my role, at least in my mind. In fact, it confused it. In introducing me in class, Neil emphasized that I was a resource for students to use for writing purposes. He made it clear that he and Trish would handle matters of content. Setting up this division may have limited my role and effectiveness in working with the students. . . . To make matters worse, in introducing me, Neil focused on my ability to help students with writing mechanics, in particular with punctuation. Only briefly did he suggest I might be of service to them in organizing their papers.
>
> In introducing myself, I explained how the writing center can be useful for writers who find themselves at any stage of the writing — prewriting, discussing assignments, generating ideas, drafting, and revising. In contrast to Neil, I focused on the role I might have in helping them deal with content and its organization. . . . Conflicting agendas seemed present.

> The different views of my role were apparent. Since it was my first time as an attached tutor and since I had not worked with Neil before, I did not feel it appropriate to discuss these differences with him.

Later, Neil pointed out that one factor in his caution regarding Doug's role was due to the fact that he did not know who Doug was. He did not know what Doug would be like to work with or what Doug's commitment level would be. As Neil worked with Doug, however, he began to see that this tutor was much more open to working with students in ways that went beyond the previous tutor's role. When we later discussed all the time it took to iron out our roles, Neil pointed to the issue that kept resurfacing in the project: "My prior experiences determined my caution and my expectations."

When Doug discussed concerns about his role, I was surprised. I assumed I had been clear about what his role would be — but the only clear part was my assumption. I also began to fear the surfacing of the one problem that plagued some of the tutor-attached situations: that the tutor would not be used as effectively as was possible. Sometimes that came from the composition of the class: students were just not mature enough to seek assistance, or they were reluctant to seek help from anyone not in absolute authority (i.e., the grade giver). Sometimes, though, it came from the gap all of us contend with as teachers or tutors or directors: the one between what we say we believe and what we say in class. In the interests of this writing project, and because I have found it more useful to let a first-time tutor-attached experience run its course, I tried to be a listener and supporter of Doug — I was also confident that he would know what to do and that things would work out (the optimistic director). Yet, I was concerned about what I began to see as Doug's role as a grader. I feared that the writing component was being again separated from the content. Would this project turn into a "one grade for writing and one for content" situation? Since that is so antithetical to what I practice, I hope not. Should I say something to Neil about my fears? Should I let Doug figure it out? Should I keep my composition-trained perspective out of Neil's geography class? I remained silent and waited.

The missteps — those that resulted from what was spoken, not spoken, not heard, or not fully articulated — continued throughout our conversations and written responses about the class. But all these misses and near misses seem a necessary part of the process of engagement. The following scenes and excerpts demonstrate the way in which those who collaborate make assumptions relating to disciplinary perspectives, motivations, and purposes. They also show the roles we adopt or project onto others as teacher-tutor experts or the role played by the student-in-difficulty or the student-as-learner (depending on the situation, the role changes). Clearly, we need to be aware of each as we negotiate our positions. Doug wrote,

> (DE) Fortunately, my role expanded (although it did so without clarifying my initial concerns) as I reported to Neil about students who came to me for a mandatory meeting for the first paper. Neil required each student to meet with me to establish a working relationship between us that, hopefully, would lead to continued visits. Perhaps my interest and insights caught Neil's attention for soon he increased my role.

Although Doug was pleased with this turn of events, when he told me one of his new responsibilities was to grade papers, I wrote,

> (JM) Although tutors attached to classes often do read papers, I am a little nervous about the idea that Neil wants Doug to actually put a grade on his copy of the student's paper. This was never our policy, and I believe it should not be. Neil assured me that he wants that kind of feedback and that he alone will decide what grade to give. In the interests of this project — and out of curiosity — I let the issue slide.

Grading — and the criteria that determine grades — gradually became the central issue in our discussions about the class while it was in session; despite our writing center tendency to revel in process, product is the bottom line that motivates and frustrates teachers, tutors, students, and directors. The remainder of this chapter will focus on the ways in which grading criteria proved problematic and eventually served as the locus around which more of our expectations and assumptions emerged.

Fault Lines

Typically speaking, the class was organized the following way. Each of the eight writing assignments was based on lectures, videos, assigned readings, and group discussions. On the day of the assignment, Neil passed out the writing prompts, explained them, and asked for questions. Then he broke the class into small discussion groups so that students could talk about the assignment and their responses to it. The class then reconvened and discussed any further questions. Although Neil says this collaborative practice — especially small-group discussions — produced better results than in situations without groups, he admitted that student responses were still not altogether satisfying. Neil said, "While the level of commitment and enthusiasm [are] higher, the difficult thing for students is to answer the question that is asked on the exam. Are students looking at an ulterior motive? Are they trying to read the professor's mind?"

Students may have difficulty meeting a professor's expectations when they enter a discipline like geography from another disciplinary or cultural background and import assumptions that do not belong to the new discipline. If an instructor's expectations are unclear or if they differ from students' past experiences, the result is a variety of responses, none of which may satisfy present demands.

Our first conversation since our initial meeting began with a discussion of the diagnostic writing done the first day in class: the students wrote to the prompt, "Overpopulation is one of the most difficult problems facing the world today." Jason, the student in our project, commented on the diagnostic:

> (JB) I enjoyed writing this one. I just sat down and wrote. It came out quite naturally with very little deliberation over what to say. I think this is largely because it was not defined and limited the way other papers are.

Doug wrote,

> (DE) I asked students if this was a difficult thing to write. The vast majority said no. . . . I was surprised because it would be difficult for me. In English, we teach students to manipulate questions into the students' own answers, showing what they know. A good percentage tried to scan the field — which the question lent itself to. Would it have been better for them to focus on one or two ideas rather than write about everything? They [purposefully] never had any direction for the assignment; although some said that they saw they should focus, only a couple of them did. Most felt that was an appropriate response — to cover the field. People worked from three hours to twenty minutes — some went to the library and researched the diagnostic!

The diagnostic was "our" idea; that is, one that is traditionally proposed in English classes to determine what students know about writing. It asked for students' opinions about a population issue; it gave freedom of composition to the student. Such a beginning diagnostic may not be appropriate for a geography class; it only tells us how well students can respond to an opinion-based question. Yet that is not the kind of assignment they will initially receive in geography. The first few assignments demand a level of interpretation within the parameters of particular sets of information. What is worse, besides not providing the information we need about students' abilities to write in the discipline, the form of the diagnostic may have given students the wrong impression about the nature of future assignments in the class. A better diagnostic would measure students' abilities to process a piece they have read for the geography class.

One of our conversations hints at the disciplinary differences evident in our expectations of students' responses:

> *Doug:* But that brings me to that gray area again. Their answers might come in a package that is more familiar to me than it is to another. Do you want a paper that follows a particular format; do you want to see what they do?

Neil: What do you do?

Doug: Well, I let them go their own way, but I think that might put some students at a disadvantage; they will say the same thing but not put it in a way — in a package — that is familiar.

Doug wrote,

> (DE) One student had written a paper that tried to cover too many areas and, as a result, did so at a very superficial level. We talked about this. His thought was to cover as many areas as possible to show what he knew. I suggested he might have more success if he had chosen only one of the areas to discuss in this one-to-two-page assignment. We talked about his audience — Trish and Neil — and how, after reading many papers, they might not respond well to a superficial discussion and that an essay with a tighter focus that discusses its subject in more depth might be better received. This seemed like sound advice at the time, but now, I see I was inserting my own notion of what good writing is, taken from the discipline of English. I still feel my advice was good, but maybe Neil will privilege a broader approach to these writings.

Yet, Neil never indicated to Doug his dissatisfaction with his classroom or paper comments. Neil commented,

> (NE) As each assignment and exam was handed out in class, I gave Doug the opportunity to give the class his advice as to how they might tackle the assignment from a writing perspective. As I handed each assignment and exam back to the class, I asked Doug to make any statements on generic problems he had noted regarding the assignment.

Doug wrote,

> (DE) Upon handing out and explaining assignments to class, Neil began to refer student questions to me. This practice was a test in improvisation for, especially toward the beginning of the course, I was not sure if my answers were the same as those that Neil would have given. It often proved difficult to comment on assignments informatively, especially when I might have only seen the assignment just before class.

The assumptions here on Neil's part seem very clear from his own disciplinary stance, whereas Doug, now debating the differences between English and geography, finds himself in a student's position constructing criteria from class evidence. During our reflections on the class, Neil pointed out, "I try to be restrictive with my assignments for a reason. I want students to incorporate the readings and to force students to read. The first three assignments are like that; I want to know if they have read the material."

In conversation again:

> *Doug:* There was a nice moment in class the other day. . . . You showed your hand there [during a video]. You mentioned that it is not the facts you use, it is what you do with those facts. The one [speaker] was using absolute numbers and the other was using percentages. They [students] asked which was right, and you said, "That's the point — that is for you to decide. It is not so much that they have to know facts, is it? They have to be aware of how those facts are used. Not that they discount facts, but this is not a course where they memorize only."
>
> *Neil:* Two things I have done that have been significant: one is to break down in groups, and the other is to give them take-home exams. It gives them time to bounce around ideas, to make sure their thinking is on the mark, or to get ideas; sometimes it gives them a chance to filter major points from minor points.

Later, Doug wrote,

> (DE) Neil explained to the class how he graded . . . He explained that he tries to be fair and that he receives input from Trish and me. He claimed that part of his judgment came from an absolute scale: he knew which paper was best, and all papers had to be judged according to that. The other part of his judgment was more relative — here, he was treading on tricky ground. He reiterated that he would try to be fair and that just because one paper was much better than the others did not mean that other papers deserving an A wouldn't also receive an A. Neil's answer did not satisfy me. I do not know if it satisfied the class. He also emphasized the importance of answering the question.

But "answering the question" soon called for a different kind of response because the type of paper required had shifted. Jason noted that the

> (JB) Big difference in geography is that the papers define what I must write about — in anthropology, the area is broad and I choose the subject [like English composition?]. I am being defined by the geography assignment.

Jason, Doug, and I talked about the assignments:

> *Doug:* On that Simon paper, you came off at a different slant on the issue.
> *Jason* (*who admittedly is not really pleased with a grade less than an A*): It was one very pleasing to me (I got a B+ or A), and I was happy with it.

But then I realized I was not analyzing Julian Simon as much as I was supposed to. Then I realized that I am not going to explore my personal issues; I am not going to put in my opinion. . . . I am just going to follow what they ask for.

The problem for me was that Dr. Reid said, "Look at some of these things and talk about it." Then I got docked for not addressing some issues, but he did not say I had a particular number to address. I got comments saying, "Well, what about this, or that?" I got an A- but that means something was not there. He said to pick a few to discuss, and I thought I picked more than I had to do. I got the Julian Simon [paper] back and then I realized what he was looking for — I had to use quotes and citations.

The writing task changed slightly for the third assignment. Students were asked to comment on the population pyramid — a seemingly simple assignment — but one that called for strict adherence to the pyramid — interpreting facts by using facts. Jason reflected on his confusion over the assignment's expectations:

> (JB) I wrote this paper very nonchalantly. The directions seemed to indicate that not much was expected — just write a bit about what was apparent in the U.S. population pyramid, make sure to mention the big things, and everything would be fine. I wrote this one very quickly because of this and also because I was not horribly interested in the topic. I was surprised to discover that all three of the reviewers were left either with questions or with suggestions about what I did not mention. Dr. Reid said that one page would be sufficient — I wrote two and was rather perturbed to discover how picky he was when he graded it. The presentation of what was required and the grading did not jive.

Jason believed he eventually worked all this out. He began comparing the way previous English compositions were graded for improvement over the whole of the quarter. He preferred these because "teachers were letting me write what I thought"; but in geography, Jason told us, "Each paper was graded in isolation. So for the second and third papers I received an A- and B+, and I feel that this is because I did not really know what was expected."

And yet, I wondered when Jason made similar comments in our conversations, whether he was not fooled into thinking that composition instructors were "letting him write what he thought." I noted that he really believed that

> (JM) If one messed up the first few papers [in English], significant improvement on subsequent ones could override the less adequate initial attempts. This meant, as Jason wrote, that "the student is not penalized for not knowing what the professor expects." Yet we in composition and as tutors, by our very

> guidance, by our very presence, by the name of our discipline, assume an expertise; we do guide, control, and demand that disciplinary expectations be met. The way we do it may feel better to students than what is felt by them in another class — perhaps we mask our authority better! But dismiss our authority? I do not think so. We cannot really, can we? Not without stepping out of our culture and the institution in which we operate. . . . We may change the way we exercise our authority or expertise, but students will look to us for those qualities nonetheless — as well as other professors.

Doug was still figuring out disciplinary differences:

> (DE) Much of what I had to say about the assignments came through the students. Those that came to office hours made it clear if an assignment was or was not clear. For example, many of Neil's assignments asked students to discuss the validity of claims. On the surface, such a request appeared harmless, especially since Neil defined in class what he meant by the term. He explained that to discuss, one looks at all sides of an issue and presents each side carefully. Neil suggested that the term forces one to consider the subject under discussion expansively. Neil also explained that the purpose of the prompts was not to get students to regurgitate information but to think about issues. Student essays should not be limited to a presentation of facts but should discuss ideas and concepts using factual support. Neil also emphasized that students should make use of the readings, suggesting that students should also draw from lectures, the videos, and discussions, and synthesize the material into a cohesive, logical, well-organized essay. He made it clear that students could not get by on lecture notes alone, stressing the importance of synthesis.
>
> Yet more than one student claimed confusion. Brain, who attended my hours religiously, really was stymied by the term discuss. The word seemed to take his freedom away — he felt like he could not speak his mind, that he had to relay information only. Discuss meant to him that he was to talk about both sides of an argument but was forbidden to take a side. I asked him why; he said he talked to Neil who told him to keep his opinion out of the paper.

Doug brought up the use of the term discuss, and we began wondering if it meant something different to Neil than to us. I suggested we "discuss" it at our next meeting. At that time, Trish joined us, and we began immediately to talk about the take-home midterm exam. Neil pointed out that students still did not answer the question, ignoring it either entirely or partially. If they were comparing views, one side might be represented but then the other was totally ignored. This was especially frustrating because in anticipation of the ways he might use language on exams, Neil handed out the list of essay terms, explained what they meant, and, in groups, students talked about potential essay questions. On the take-home exam, Neil tried to give explicit directions, most of which asked students to discuss the validity of a topic, and then he referred to the definition of the essay terms on the handout. Nonetheless, when asked to "Discuss the one-child policy in China," students often just summarized the issue, loading it with emotional response (unethical, immoral, etc.). At best, their arguments implied but did not state the other side. We wondered out loud if they learned this method in their college composition classes.

Relative Locations

Doug, Joan, Trish, and Neil in conversation:

> *Doug:* One of the problems on the exam may still have to do with their understanding what they need to do.
> *Joan:* Like . . .
> *Doug:* In composition class, discuss means talk about what you want to talk about; discuss means give an opinion.
> *Trish:* Really? I never thought about it like that.
> *Doug:* I'm afraid of that word because of where I come from [i.e., English and Writing Studies].
> *Neil:* (reflecting) If they did not answer the question as I thought they should answer the question, they were really hammered in terms of the grade.
> *Doug:* If this would have been an English class, some of those papers that got Ds or Cs would have gotten As. In fairness to Neil, he went out of his way to explain his terms and their places in the discipline. But to me, discuss invites a lack of discipline — it means just talk.
> *Trish:* I guess that is what I did when I was an undergraduate — for English classes.
> *Neil:* Maybe discuss should not be used. Instead of discuss the differences, if I said "analyze," would that change the response?
> *Doug:* Brian knew it all and had all of his argument yet would stop and say, "There is that word, 'discuss.' Is this discussing?"
> *Neil:* Until I had this discussion this morning, I never tied this kind of writing to the term discuss.

Even as we spoke, we seemed unaware of the role discuss had already played in the class. Initially, the diagnostic asked students to discuss overpopulation as a serious world problem — a broad subject that elicited papers, as Jason said, that "Came out quite naturally with very little deliberation over what to say." Following this diagnostic, students were given a narrow topic such as the Julian Simon debate in which they discussed points of view, but had to understand the assumptions behind the speakers' facts. Discuss meant focus on the speakers, not only on your opinion. The pyramid paper and the exam narrowed the field by asking for an interpretation of a closed set of facts — to discuss the facts in students' own ways.

> *Neil:* In regard to the exams, we should treat them just like a paper. Students should take a broader approach to the material. Exams make them think in bigger terms.
> *Joan:* It puts the emphasis on writing?

A nod of confirmation. But my comment moved our discussion away from where it should have gone — what does "broader approach" mean to Neil? I was assuming that by emphasizing writing, Neil wanted students to carefully construct their perspectives and to focus on their composition, as Jason had discovered.

> *Doug:* When I worked with students — I had a person miss the question each time, although he is a good writer. We sat down and looked at the question step by step; I just saw this tendency to drift off. He never thought, "Should I bring this in? Is this relevant?"

By now, Jason was figuring out what he had to do but not why he had to do it:

> (JB) I found I had to limit my focus much more than ever before. Previously, like in anthropology classes, I had more freedom to write about a topic of my choice and take it to where I wanted. In many ways, those papers are very exploratory — you do not even know the questions until you have done the research and have written your introduction. It was not uncommon for me to write a paper and then have to go back and rewrite the introduction so that it related to what I actually wrote about and concluded. The writing process was largely a thinking process that allowed all of the information and ideas about the subject to coalesce and make a coherent whole.
>
> In this geography course, however, I found that I needed to be much more mechanical about writing — stick to the basics, research what you are told, and do not stray so far from the question (which has been asked for you, not by you). In many ways, this stifled me and left me uninterested in the papers. The more leeway I had, or the more leeway I gave myself (even when I should not have given it to myself), the more I enjoyed writing. However, it was intellectually useful to force myself to write in the way expected by the course. I do emphasize the word force, by the way.

Jason had pinpointed the position in which many of us in writing centers find ourselves: we are faced with students' assignments that we do not like or cannot understand the construction of or with assignments wherein we question the

objectives of the instructor. We know that students write best when they are
interested in the assignment, when they can write from what they know. Yet that
is not possible in many of our colleagues' classes in which students do not have a
mature disciplinary knowledge base.

When Neil asked students to discuss the one-child policy in China, he was
using a familiar term, "discuss," whose meaning he had attempted to explain
to students. However, students (even when they were as bright as Jason) may
not have been ready to hear or understand the purpose of their discussion, to
analyze the facts from their perspective in order to substantiate their interpretations. Jason writes,

---

(JB) [The first exam was] the most carefully written of the quarter. By this
time, I had gotten the input on the first three papers. I discovered from the
second one that I had to pay close attention to the question being asked and
limit myself to that and that I should include quotes from the readings. I
learned from this that I could not write the papers with little care.

In conversation, I asked Jason,

Joan: What kinds of skills does this call for?
Jason: Pay attention in class, take one side of the issue, and your argu-
ment is done for you.
Joan: Is that because of the way the assignment is posed?
Jason: No, it is because the information is given to me; I can go beyond,
but I do not really have to — I still get an A.
Joan: So, standing back from the course, is its purpose to provide you
with basic knowledge more than it is to analyze?
Jason: It is not so much that you have to come up with your own
insights: you are not saying aha! That is fine for the purpose of the
course.
Joan: Which is . . . ?
Jason: To give people a form they can use to learn how to write about
population geography. I see a lot of people whose writing sucks.
So, for the next exam paper, I put in citations and did not go off
on my own thing. I just stayed within the limits of the exam and
got glowing feedback.
Doug: So, in this class, it is writing for regurgitation? facts? arguments in
the discipline?
Jason: Hmm. . . . Dr. Reid gives them [facts], and you take them and slap
them together. How you slap them together is probably how your
grade goes.

Zone in Transition

Although students received three sets of independent comments, they received only one grade — from Neil. Students did not see the grades awarded by Trish or Doug, but they did see their comments, which the grade finally awarded by Neil did not always seem to reflect. This undoubtedly caused some confusion. Jason, for example, received praise from Doug for his original thought, whereas Neil graded him down for not sticking to facts.

Earlier, Doug had written in his journal,

> (DE) It often proved difficult to comment on assignments informatively, especially when I might have seen the assignment just before class. When I did comment, I urged students to consider their audience. Sometimes my comments would be drawn from a recent grading session, and I would try to emphasize the problems that Neil, Trish, and I noted.

Doug began to come to terms with Neil's requirements, and Jason saw the evidence:

> (JB) Doug's comments on the first two papers both remarked on their original insights — he never made such a comment again in any subsequent papers (which I tried to write with an eye for what was wanted by the professor).

We all talked about grading:

Joan: How did you manage to grade all these together?

Neil: Well, we would all grade a set and then compare them. The person who was most divergent is asked why he or she did what was done. The grade will move toward the low end if there are two Bs and a D; there will be a compromise most of the time. Sometimes, the person with the high grade admits he or she was tired or will look at it again and say, "You're right." We really enjoy spending time together, so we try to make these sessions last as long as they can [general laughter]. It is kind of fun and kind of interesting, enjoyable [general agreement all around].

Trish: I am always surprised at how much we agree. It surprises me because I think I am not as qualified as [Doug and Neil] are. I wish I had this kind of help; I give these papers back, and I feel very confident about the grades. I tell students that although they get three copies of the exams back with our initials on them, the grade should be discussed with Neil. He gives them a week to appeal, but they get all three copies and must make a case for their review.

> *Neil:*   They are getting much more feedback here than they would get anywhere else.
>
> *Joan:*   What do you learn from the discussions over grading?
>
> *Doug:*   We begin to look at the papers in similar ways. We begin to think of the others when we go through the papers because we know one or the other of us will attack it in a particular way. You think, "These guys won't like this, but they will like that."
>
> *Neil:*   Right from the beginning, I expected Doug to be the person who made most of the comments.
>
> *Doug:*   And how long did it take before that was thrown out?
>
> *Trish:*   No, I think this has all been helpful; it has made me look at how I write. I never even thought about that before.

And later from Jason's final reflections:

> (JB) I did like the fact that the papers were read by three people and that their input was taken into consideration. I found Doug and Dr. Reid's comments the most helpful — they told me what I did good, but they also made clear what needed to be improved (although, at times I did not agree with their comments). Tricia usually just had nice things to say, which were good (and necessary) pats on the back, but did not help me much. I think that the three together probably helped Dr. Reid assign more accurate grades.

Mapping the Future

Despite our misinterpretations of each others' agendas, expectations, and meanings, we worked together surprisingly well. As Lunsford and Ede point out in their study, successful collaboration hinges on an agreement to reach for desired goals, and we agreed on those goals. However, as we review this report of our collaboration, we find contradictions throughout all of our statements. As director, I felt that I had defined Doug's role, but he felt undefined. I thought that I had made clear that Doug was not to be a grader, whereas Neil proposed that he grade. Neil believed he had explained assignments clearly, yet Jason felt he had to guess what Neil wanted, and Doug decided that he had to create the grading criteria. Doug gave writing advice to students only to discover that Neil and Trish were using different criteria. Jason claimed the writing sometimes was not fairly assessed, but he acknowledged that disciplinary differences might create the disparity between these grades and his previous ones — between what he thought he should write and what was acceptable in this context; he also felt confused by all the comments, even though he recognized that he benefited from them.

As instructors, we believe that we maintained our commitment to our common desired goal by assuming a role of agreement, an agreement built on continual self-reflection. Doug's questioning, my remaining silent or setting up a meeting, Neil's reassessment of his pedagogy, Jason's evaluation of his learning process — all of these enact a reflective pedagogy critical to success in writing center tutorials, in writing center–teacher interactions, and in individual classrooms in which we are the primary facilitators.

In this particular case, we needed to agree on what an assignment should do, how we should respond to it, and how it should be evaluated. We listened carefully to each other and reflected on our own practices. Although it would have been easy for Doug or me to claim our writing center/composition/rhetoric expertise as the most accurate maps for students' thinking and writing, we were keenly aware that these were not all-terrain maps, that we could not superimpose them at will over all disciplinary or pedagogical contexts. What we learned from these encounters was what all seasoned tutors come to know: writing experts become so only in response to specific situations, to acceptable practices and forms, to audience expectations, and to agreements about knowledge and its constructions.

Likewise, from our collaboration, Doug and Trish learned the value of reflective practice, something that they already may have known but now named with a new vocabulary — ours. Jason, on the other hand, had his abilities to "invent the university" corroborated in a way most students do not. He learned that writing in his discipline — in this context — was different from writing in other disciplines; he also learned, as did we, that his own repertoire expanded as he asked questions and viewed solutions from others' perspectives.

Doug, Neil, Trish, Jason, and I each still believe (I would say, rightly) in our inherited, surmised, and useful perspectives, but we also see that our learning, theorizing, and researching is evolutionary and recursive. Clearly, both the difficulties and the solutions within our own collaborations (as well as in writing center tutorials) emerged from assuming, sharing, or relinquishing authority as we worked to move on to the next challenge. As tutors, we recognize this negotiation as that narrow line over which we weave like drunken rhetoricians, reading our own situations and making decisions as we participate in them. This quite human endeavor is the space in which we learn as much from our apprehensions as we do from our misapprehensions, where we collaborate not toward consensus but toward understandings that allow us to reach a common goal.

This negotiation supports a culture of reflectivity. During our last conversation, Neil, Doug, and I talked a lot about the assignments: how they might be recast; how Neil might clarify their various purposes; how evaluation criteria might be designed. As we ended this discussion, Neil summed up the relationship that needs to characterize writing center/WAC collaborations: *"I don't think in terms of what kind of writing I ask for — that's why I need a writing tutor who does think like this."* Although Neil has gained that insight from us, I have begun to think about how the notion of diagnostics might be reconceived for different disciplines. I will also continue examining my more global assumptions about writing in the disciplines and about the ways 1 interact with writers, faculty members, and writing center tutors. Doug has sought outside observers to provide feedback on his own classroom practices, while, with Neil, he continues examining ways to work with the current geography class; the two hope to carry what they learn into next fall's writing intensive classes as well. Thus, while engaging in a social constructionist collaboration, we managed to respect and value each others' perspectives and trust each others' reflectivity. What resulted was a positive evolution of our own perspectives and practices.

In the future, our collaborative ventures will include frequent face-to-face meetings in which we foreground all of the participants' assumptions about writing, terminology, and disciplinary expectations. The first several weeks of the quarter will demand weekly meetings (possibly electronic) of the writing center director and tutor and the faculty member; after that, every other week may suffice. During those meetings, we will discuss and, I suspect, negotiate the assignments, their objectives, and their evaluation criteria, giving priority to the disciplinary faculty member's voice. However, in these sessions, as was true in this project, it is likely that the negotiation will take the form of education moving both ways. Our work with this project shows some of the ways in which writing centers must be flexible in WAC collaborations. Although in one sense, the center's ways of thinking about and working with students is not negotiable, in other ways, by opening up to other disciplinary ways of thinking, writing center staff expand their own definitions and practices. As much of the literature on collaboration and writing center research suggests, we need to continually negotiate as these collaborations proceed in order to reach agreed upon, even if shifting, goals.

Notes

[1]When we discussed the writing of this chapter, Neil explained his own assumptions about how he initially perceived Doug's role.

Works Cited

Lunsford, Andrea, and Lisa Ede. *Singular Texts/Plural Authors: Perspectives on Collaborative Writing*. Carbondale: Southern Illinois UP, 1990.

AFFIRMING DIVERSITY

Cultural Conflicts in the Writing Center: Expectations and Assumptions of ESL Students

Muriel Harris _____

PURDUE UNIVERSITY

To help tutors better understand the perspectives of ESL students, Muriel Harris compares and contrasts the theory and pedagogy that inform most writing center tutorials with the attitudes expressed by student writers from other cultures. What Harris has found, by asking ESL students to respond to a questionnaire, is that the students' ideas about what should go on in a tutorial often differ from tutors' ideas. For example, ESL students tend to see a tutor as someone whose primary role is to answer questions and solve problems. ESL students often do not expect a tutor to ask them questions aimed at facilitating collaboration or returning the burden of problem solving to the students, and these conflicting expectations can impede learning. An especially useful portion of the essay involves ESL students' advice to tutors as to how to most effectively interact with students from different cultures. Among their recommendations, ESL students suggest that tutors be patient, try to learn something about students' cultures, and realize how hard the students must work in order to thrive in an unfamiliar environment. As Harris says, keeping in mind that the assumptions and expectations of ESL students may clash with our own assumptions and goals is a first step toward avoiding misunderstandings and facilitating effective collaboration. This essay was originally published in the book **Writing in Multicultural Settings** *in 1997.*

When students learning English as a second language enter writing-center tutorials, they bring along not only their papers but also their culturally conditioned notions about what to expect in a nonclassroom instructional setting. Too often they enter a learning environment that seems bewildering, threatening, frustrating, or antithetical to their prior experiences. Similarly, tutors, having been trained in the theory and pedagogy of writing centers, are often just as bewildered and frustrated by these students, who may resist the roles tutors want to assign them. The tutor and the student, if they are unaware of culturally determined differences in how they expect the tutorial to play out, are likely to begin working at cross-purposes. When this happens, the outcome is not usually very productive. Without shared assumptions about what will happen, the tutor and ESL student can proceed on opposite tracks and spend their tutorial time trying to get the other person to move in their direction. But tutors — as well as teachers who meet in collaborative, one-to-one settings with their ESL students — can remedy this lack of overlap by becoming more sensitive to cross-cultural differences that may impede ESL students' ability to profit from writing tutorials.

To help us learn more about these possible conflicts, I focus here on differences between the theory and pedagogy of collaboration in the writing center and the assumptions and expectations of students from culturally diverse backgrounds who seek tutorial help with writing skills. With such awareness, I hope, we can help ESL students step more fully into — and profit from — the collaborative world of the tutorial.

Tutors' Perspectives on Collaborative Learning

The writing-center approach that tutors are trained to use puts the student in a collaborative, interactive, individualized setting. Collaboration is viewed as empowering because it returns ownership of the piece of writing and responsibility for learning to the writer. Tutors are there to guide, ask questions, listen, and make suggestions, but they are neither authority figures nor evaluators. As Art Young has written:

> Collaboration . . . is fundamental to who we are and what we do. . . . Writing centers have been places for collaboration from their beginnings; for tutoring, for conferencing, for the talk that brings clarity to purpose and ideas, for the listening that empowers those who write and speak. Writing centers were founded on an alternative vision of the way many people learn and develop facility with language. . . . they were founded on the deceptively simple principles of human interaction, social negotiation, and contextual language development. (4–5)

Tutors, then, are trained to move writers into the active role of making decisions, asking questions, spotting problem areas in their writing, and finding solutions. Tutors are taught how to keep from seizing control and how to avoid identifying problems and offering solutions for students. Tutors may initiate tutorial talk about aspects of the paper, but they expect to be collaborators, not teachers. The tutor's goal is not to fix the individual paper but to help the student become a better writer. The tutor hopes that the writer will internalize the tutor's questions and use them from then on and will adopt as practices the strategies the tutor demonstrates. Tutors provide answers and information, of course, but that is merely one of the ways they help writers. But do ESL students share these assumptions? When they sit down next to their tutors and launch into the session, how likely are they to respond as tutors expect them to? If they are not inclined to share their tutors' perspectives, what do they expect will happen? What do they want to happen? What role do they expect their tutors to play? How willing are students from other cultures to enter into the kind of collaboration that requires them to answer questions as well as ask them? Or, acculturated to treating teachers as authority figures, can they enter into collaboration with tutors who, despite their age and level of education, situate themselves as peers?

ESL Students' Perspectives

To learn more about what ESL students expect when they come to tutorials, I asked eighty-five international students at my university to respond in writing to a lengthy list of questions. These students were enrolled in writing courses ranging from low-intermediate to more advanced composition, and the length of the time most had spent in the United States varied from a few months to several years. Although a few had been here most of their lives, many retained citizenship in other countries, pending future plans. While immigrants or refugees are more likely to come to this country with little or no formal instruction in English, the majority of the ESL students answering the questionnaire had learned at least some English in their home countries, a factor that may have influenced their answers to questions about what they want to

learn about writing in English. Their national origins reflect the ESL population in my university and are not particularly different from the general per-
centages for ESL students nationwide. Over sixty percent of the group were
from East Asia — the People's Republic of China, Taiwan, Korea, Hong Kong,
Japan, and so on — but there were also students from the Middle East, Europe,
Central and South America, Africa, and the Indian subcontinent. Two-thirds
were male.

To see how their written responses might differ from interviews, I did a trial
run with six students, asking them the kinds of questions I planned to include
in the questionnaire. Their answers in person were more minimal, more
guarded, and less critical of anything American than their anonymous
responses to the questionnaires. Anonymity and the privacy of writing seemed
to free some of the students, and the fuller responses on paper were most likely
the product of the students' being able to take the questionnaire home for a few
days, reflect on what they wanted to say, and then write for a while. The written responses are indicative only of the group surveyed, but the comments
should caution us to be wary about creating learning environments in which
we assume students from other cultures share our perspectives and goals.

Tutors versus Teachers

Several questions about the differences between tutors and teachers and
between classrooms in their home countries and in the United States invited
these ESL students to describe their perceptions about tutors and teachers.
Despite their cultural diversity, they were remarkably consistent in stating that
teachers teach and tutors help. They described teachers as those who work
with large groups, lecturing on general concepts and course content. Teachers
are the experts and authorities on the subject, and their role is to deliver information. Tutors are "not as advanced," lower down on the ladder of authority,
prestige, or knowledge. Tutors work individually with students to help them
solve their problems and improve their abilities, give more detailed advice and
answers, and deal with specifics. "A teacher can tell that you got a problem
but is not to work with you to solve them," one student wrote. "Tutor works
with you to fix mistakes or solve your problems." Thus these students view
the tutor as the appropriate person to bring their problems to and as the person who deals with specifics, that is, with individual examples of larger principles explained by the teacher. This perception can impede tutors who want
to help students gain greater insight into larger rhetorical issues of writing as
well as mastery over various writing processes and can frustrate the student as
well. Tutor and student may have different goals but both perceive the tutorial
environment as informal and helping; these ESL students see tutors as more
understanding, more personal, more adept at helping each student, and easier
to talk to than teachers. A number of these students noted that they feel freer
to ask tutors questions. "Teachers tell you what to do, tutors give advice,"
wrote one student; "The teacher lectures, the tutor discusses," noted another.

ESL students, then, perceive tutors to be more immediately helpful, more approachable, more practical, and more personal than teachers are, but the students expect tutors to work on errors and difficulties in specific pieces of discourse, not on the larger, more abstract level of writing skills and processes. A few students also said that the tutor is supposed to help with writers' concerns. Typically, they indicated that the tutor should encourage and/or motivate the student. One Puerto Rican student noted that the tutor should "help and encourage students to 'keep it up.' That with a little effort, people can reach their goals and do well in college." Another Puerto Rican student saw the tutor as someone who "encourages the students to improve their work." Similarly, an Indonesian student wrote that the tutor's major responsibility is "to motivate the students to study the subject." There were several other similar responses, but all were from non-Asian students. The Asian students all responded that the tutor's job is correcting errors, showing mistakes, and "giving clear understanding," not providing motivation or encouragement.

While many students noted that in their countries students do not ask questions in class, all the students responded that they are willing (and eager) to ask tutors questions. None expressed any reluctance, to do so, and many wrote that they see tutorials as their opportunity to ask the kinds of questions they hesitate to ask in class or cannot ask elsewhere. "I have many questions but few opportunities to do asking," wrote one student. Since all these students are enrolled in courses in which teachers set aside several hours each week for conferences, they apparently do not see that time as the appropriate opportunity. Asking questions is how they check their mistakes, give the tutor a better idea of what kinds of problems they have, and clear up their doubts. "I should know what I want to know, so I must ask a tutor," one wrote. Many echoed one student's succinct comment: "How else to learn?" Given this expectation, it may surprise some ESL students that tutors have long lists of their own questions to ask writers. Tutors, trained to work from the top down, from higher-order concerns such as clarity, focus, and organization to lower-order concerns of sentence-level correctness, might well want to open a tutorial by asking what the student liked best in the paper, what the main point was, which part was troublesome, who the audience is, and so on. For the student who wrote that he sees the tutor's role as "answering my questions about hard points like right verb tense," such broad questions about more general matters might be disconcerting indeed. Moreover, the student may well enter the tutorial prepared to ask questions, not to answer them.

While students from other cultures enter tutorials expecting to take an active role in asking questions, the students have a concomitant expectation that tutors deliver information, that tutors are in control of the situation and do the work of finding problems and offering solutions. Numerous responses on the questionnaires repeated the point that the tutor's task or responsibility is to help students — to point out weaknesses, to correct errors, to answer questions, to help improve their writing, to show students how to make their papers better, and to help them understand what they need to know. These responses all use active verbs, describing actions that the tutor is to take. ESL students expect the tutor to take control of the session — to diagnose and convey to the student what needs to be learned, much as a teacher is expected to lecture and deliver information. The tutor's responsibility is "to solve my problems" or "to explain my errors." A few students, however, did recognize that their role in the learning process is also active: "A tutor helps people to find their own style of writing and know how to check our mistakes" and "The tutor gives hints and lets the thinking to me." More generally, though, these students think their role is to listen, remember, and ask questions that will clarify their understanding. Thus there may be strained silence in a tutorial when a tutor asks and then waits patiently for answers to standard tutors' questions intended to give the student an active role, such as "How would you fix this paragraph?" or "What do you see as the problem here?" The tutor may interpret this silence as an indication that the student doesn't have an answer, but it may more likely be that the student is also sitting patiently, waiting for the tutor to fulfill her or his function of providing such answers. Some discussion is then necessary to help the student see that he or she really is being given an opportunity to learn by offering an answer.

Nonnative students' passivity in tutorials may stem from behavior learned in classrooms in other countries. When the ESL students I questioned described classrooms in their native countries, they noted that students listen and teachers lecture. Students are expected to accept what the teacher says and not to raise questions. The student's role is to study hard and to learn — sometimes by memorizing — what is presented. When asked to describe differences between American classrooms and those in their own countries, they often commented on the freedom in our classrooms to ask questions. One student wrote that "students in America are more involved in the learning process," and another wrote that in her country "the student is not so active." Yet another student commented that in his country students spend their class time copying down what the teacher writes on the board and their time outside of class memorizing what they have copied. (See Tateya for a description of the student as note taker in the Japanese classroom.)

These very different approaches to education should help us realize what a leap we are asking some students to make in the tutorial. Students who have not had lengthy conditioning to classroom discussion and question asking are less likely to take control in tutorials, even when invited, because they are not familiar with how to become the active learners that tutors want to develop. For ESL students, finding their own answers rather than being told what the answer is or what they must learn can be a new process. As tutors, we have to suppress any discomfort with ESL students who seem to want us to tell them how to fix their papers. There is a cross-cultural problem in the clash between

ESL students who sit with pencil poised, waiting to write down what we tell them, and us, as we keep trying to return responsibility for revision to the writer. When the tutor asks, "What is the connection between these two sentences?" or "Is there a word missing there?" and the polite student waits for the tutor to answer the question, the two parties are acting out assumptions and expectations from very different worlds. If we want to break this mold, we need to backtrack and address the differences, to think about how to help the student adopt a mode of learning that can seem foreign and difficult at first — even impolite or disrespectful. Sometimes we can do so by stating at the beginning of the tutorial that we expect and look forward to having students answer their own questions and that answering will make them better writers. Judith Kilborn suggests an alternative approach for nonnative students who are used to hearing directive statements from teachers: When appropriate, tutors can begin their questions with "Please explain" instead of "Why" or "How." An answer to a relatively open-ended request might be more useful and enlightening for both the ESL student and the tutor.

We need not to be hesitant about introducing ESL students to new learning environments. These students are already astute observers of how things operate in this country. Even if they are not comfortable embracing our approaches, they recognize some of the differences. When asked to compare student-teacher interactions in the United States with those in their countries, the ESL students frequently commented that the relations here are more informal, casual, or relaxed. In their home countries, students do not criticize teachers and students show more respect than these students see exhibited here Repeatedly, ESL students commented on the freedom in American classrooms to challenge the teacher, to interrupt with questions, to sip drinks, to call teachers by their first names. Some ESL students are likely to change their modes of interacting with teachers and tutors in an effort to conform. They may, then, start acting more like American students, but we must realize that their adaptation may not be very deep. ESL students can still find it difficult to interrupt us, to slip easily into the informality of the tutoring setting. Other cultural factors may be at work as well. Xiaomin Cai, an Asian tutor in an American writing center, cautions us that Asian students prefer to be indirect and may agree or nod rather than challenge or confront those they disagree with. They may also pretend to understand when they don't, to save face.

Just as ESL students adopt some behaviors to cope with our culture, our behaviors may be irritating or offensive to them. For example, a number of students responding to my questionnaire expressed strong feelings of discomfort at American habits such as engaging in discussion after the teacher answers a question, smoking and joking around in class, even putting their legs up on tables or other informal means of slouching. One European student was angry about being called by his first name. He wrote that he expects us to use appropriate titles and expects in return not to be treated like a child and called by his first name. His discomfort was echoed by a student from Pakistan, where students also do not call teachers by their first names. We may not easily recognize such students and their resistance to behavioral norms and standards in American learning environments, but we can at least be aware that the ESL students who come to our writing centers may be trying to move from very different perspectives on the teacher-student relationship or are not comfortable with our assumptions or ways of interacting. A peer tutor in training recently commented to me that she wished the ESL student with whom she had been working would stop agreeing with her all the time. "He just needs to stop that and to concentrate on what is going on," said the irritated tutor, obviously unaware that all the vigorous head nodding and verbal affirmatives were likely the result of a deeply felt need to show respect, which was no doubt inculcated in his native country.

ESL Students' Attitudes

Because tutoring pedagogy emphasizes the need to establish a comfortable relationship at the beginning of the tutorial, tutoring manuals often advise starting a session with a few minutes of friendly chatter. This getting-acquainted time can have several benefits. It can send students the message that the environment will be collaborative and helpful and will not sustain whatever anxieties they entered with. As they relax, they will feel freer to ask questions, and tutors, as a side benefit, can learn some useful information about things that interest the students, about their levels of motivation, about classroom or time-management problems, even about their levels of verbal ability. Students who speak easily and comfortably but have some diction problems in writing will probably benefit from proofreading. But students who exhibit problems with verb endings or prepositions in speaking will probably require more than proofreading practice.

These benefits can also apply to ESL students. But I find they occasionally seem very businesslike when we begin a tutorial. Are they uncomfortable or reluctant to enter informal conversations because learning environments in their cultures are very formal? Do they even want to converse with a tutor in this second language with which they are struggling?

On the questionnaire I asked the ESL students whether they want to spend a few minutes in friendly conversation with a tutor before beginning to work together, and I encouraged them to explain their answers. Overwhelmingly, these students wrote that they very much do. Most explained that they are nervous at the beginning of a session and need to relax. As one student wrote, "Most of foreign students have the anxiety and fear about conversation. So it will soothe them or warm them up." Another student wrote, "I get nervous when I must speak in English at this time. Therefore, a friendly conversation can make me relaxed." John Parbst, a tutor, described using such off-topic conversation in a session with an ESL student who initially was too shy or nervous to speak. Over about twenty minutes of conversation, the student slowly relaxed and eventually became interested in talking. The few remaining minutes of the tutorial were focused and productive: "That five to ten minutes of a true exchange of ideas was better than the alternative: me talking at an uninvolved audience for thirty minutes" (2).

Some of the students also recognized that their sessions would be more effective if they could get to know the tutor first: "I like friendly atmosphere while learning as I always have a better result." Other students expressed a need to be comfortable with the person who would be their tutor — or at least comfortable enough to discuss their problems. Still others considered it important to break the student-teacher barrier through conversation, and a few welcomed the opportunity to chat with a native speaker because they rarely have occasion to do so. Two ESL students also recognized this as a chance for the tutor to do some diagnostic work: "[Conversation] can make more understand between tutor and students and make the tutor know what level the student is," and "The tutor can understand me more, e.g., how long have I been learning English." In addition, as Cai reminds us, there is an Asian preference for making friends before getting down to business; this practice can mystify or confuse American businesspeople when dealing with their Asian counterparts (L. Young). But a few ESL students did not prefer to open a tutorial with friendly talk, mainly because they did not want to waste time or because they felt uncomfortable chatting while other students were waiting to see a tutor.

The questionnaire contained an open-ended question that invited the ESL students to offer advice to tutors. Many of the students — from a variety of language groups — responded with a plea: ESL students, they wrote, need sympathy and understanding when they ask what they perceive to be dumb questions or when they think they are making foolish mistakes. "International students make silly mistakes that native speakers never will," wrote one student. "Don't be scared by the stupid mistakes that we made," noted another. "Please do not laugh at what you see. They already have had a feeling that their writing is not good," wrote another student. It is important, then, for tutors to remember that the ESL students elbow to elbow with us may feel inept or uncomfortable, that they see themselves as objects of ridicule. As we talk with them, we may be awed by their ability to function in an institution of higher learning in a second language, though we rarely say anything. Those of us who have tried to negotiate our way in foreign countries with a smattering of the local language know the humbling feeling of incompetence or childlike dependence that we sink into when we try even simple tasks such as finding the appropriate bus or purchasing tickets. ESL students have to negotiate far more complex tasks in English while learning the language. It is our responsibility to be sensitive to their discomfort and to help them restore their sense of self-worth as they go through this process. If nothing else, we can do more to allay their fears of being objects of derision because they make mistakes and have to ask questions that native speakers do not ask.

ESL Students' Expectations about Learning

The ESL students I questioned usually commented that what they most want from writing tutors is help in improving their writing. This response is not specific enough to be very informative. But I also asked them to characterize good writing in their first language, and their answers offer clues about what qualities they want their writing to have. Most of the students, from a variety of language groups, noted the significance of "good organization" or "well built structure." They cited grammatical correctness as important almost as often, indicating perhaps a rationale for ESL students' emphasis on eliminating sentence-level errors in the papers they write in English. If they continually request help with grammar, it may be that, in addition to having focused on sentence structure, mechanics, and spelling when learning English, they view correct grammar as integral to good writing. Some Asian students also cited the importance of clarity and vivid description in writing in their languages, and Asian and non-Asian students alike rated vocabulary, the use of "good and broad" words, as a major quality of good writing in their first language. Use of "nice words," "beautiful vocabulary," and "good choices of words" were frequent answers, which indicates that we need to pay more attention to ESL students' requests for help with vocabulary. We may dismiss these requests or put them on back burners when the student seems to be capable of adequate expression in a paper, especially when there are other problems to address. But we should listen more closely, understanding that perhaps vocabulary building is a pressing concern for the student, even if it is not high on our agenda. Similarly, we must respond to requests for help with synonyms when students express unhappiness that they are repeating words. The Chinese students I have tutored are particularly interested in synonyms; they often cite repetition (sometimes of a word that has appeared several times in a three- or four-page paper) as something that detracts from the quality of their drafts. In our rush to help nonnative students master the elements of American academic writing, we need to be sensitive to their goals as well.

Although work on grammatical correctness and vocabulary is not simple, obvious, or quick, working on rhetorical qualities of good writing is even more difficult because we are less aware that some are culturally determined, not universal. For example, while Americans value conciseness, directness, and clarity, work in contrastive rhetoric has shown us that these qualities are not necessarily valued in the discourse of other languages. We have learned about the Asian preference for indirection, which contrasts with the American preference for clear, overt announcement of a topic in an introductory paragraph (Eggington; L. Young), about the difference between languages in which the reader is responsible for making meaning from the text and languages, such as English, in which the writer is responsible for making the meaning obvious to readers (Hinds, "Reader"), and about some languages' higher tolerance for digression (Clyne; Kachru, "Writers").

The students who responded to my questionnaire generally seemed unaware that there might be differences between rhetorical values in American academic writing and writing in their first language, though a student from Switzerland noted that in the United States "content can be directly read out of the text passage" while in Switzerland "content is more implied." Because most of the respondents did not indicate an awareness of the need to learn about rhetorical values of American academic discourse, a tutorial with an ESL student may be a tug-of-war, as the tutor may, for example, see a great need to have the student work on specificity while the student feels no such need but has a strong desire to learn how to use articles or prepositions, Cai notes that because Asian students are less likely to see the need to work on documentation, tutors need to help them understand its importance in American discourse. As Cai explains, in Asian cultures there is a strong sense of putting the group first, as opposed to the American sense of self that leads to a strong sense of ownership of ideas. Americans more easily understand the importance of citing sources, providing documentation, and avoiding plagiarism. Citing sources is less important to Asian students, says Cai, and may even, for some, be an unknown art, resulting in the ready mixing of ideas from various sources and the use of few if any citations. Furthermore, as William Eggington explains, in Korean prose writers may use a "some people say" formulation when taking a controversial stand, in order to protect their positions by enlisting anonymous support or to avoid appearing too direct when criticizing another's position. Student writing that features this approach might look as if it needs citation but may actually present the writer's own ideas. (For a further discussion of cross-cultural rhetorical differences, see M. Harris, "Individualized Instruction.")

While contrastive rhetoric has helped us identify some of what nonnative students may need to learn about English, it is also useful to uncover what they feel is important and what they perceive as stumbling blocks on the way to better writing skills. Therefore I asked respondents to note the characteristics of good English that are difficult or puzzling for them. The responses most often were lists of items at the word or sentence level. Vocabulary was the most frequently listed item: "Sometimes I know the meanings of some words but I don't know how to use them"; "Sometimes, there are different words that can be translated by a same word in our language, but they will be used in different positions in English." The students also frequently cited verbs, colloquialisms and idioms, prepositions, and sentence structure. Larger discourse concerns appeared occasionally, though infrequently: "Be specific or concrete is difficult for Chinese," "how to develop my argument in American way," "how to express my ideas in an American way," and "use American language not [my] language." With this kind of knowledge we can be more aware of what the ESL student really wants — or expects — when she or he comes to a tutorial with a paper and asks that familiar question, "Can you please help me with my writing?"

ESL Students' Advice to Tutors

Finally, another area of concern for tutors working with ESL students is the students' response to American habits that help or interfere with tutoring. What pleases these students? What annoys them? Asked to offer advice to American tutors, the student respondents did so at length. They most often cited American friendliness as a characteristic they appreciate; many also respond favorably to American helpfulness. Other qualities of American tutors that the students cited favorably were enthusiasm, eagerness, energy, ability to make jokes and to speak humorously, willingness to offer encouragement, and ability to motivate. A few respondents seemed puzzled by the American preference for informality, but some thought that an informal atmosphere makes tutorials more "agreeable" or "happy." Among the American habits that annoy them are showing impatience with students who don't know answers or who catch on slowly, covering too much material in too short a time, "looking down on students," speaking too quickly, using slang, approaching students as if they don't know English at all, displaying uneasiness in talking with ESL students or listening to "poor English proficiency." Other habits that annoy ESL students may result from the tutors' lack of understanding about what is acceptable to ESL students in tutoring situations or lack of awareness of cross-cultural differences. Exhibitions of American informality in tutorials, such as drinking coffee or putting one's feet on a table, may not bother most American students, but some ESL students listed these acts as annoying. One ESL student, not used to the frequency or type of compliments Americans bestow so easily, suggested that American tutors refrain from comments that may seem like insults to students from other cultures. "If I am look nice in my new coat, I very much wonder if my tutor is mean I am not look nice before," explained the student.

Mainly, though, in their advice to tutors, ESL students asked for patience and some understanding of them and their cultures. The following responses (presented in their own words) indicate that the students are acutely aware of how different they are:

- Tutors need to be quite patient because international students may come from a country with different cultural background.
- Learning little background of the country and difference in writing will help much.
- Please try to understand problems faced by international students.
- Try to understand how hard they have to work to study in the foreign country and language.
- Be more patient since the way we think sometimes is so different from the way American people do.
- Do not think of them as foreigners.
- Try to enjoy getting to know different persons from different cultures; don't be frightened or look down to us.
- Try to learn from those cultures.

Because my exploratory conversations with ESL students indicated their concern for showing respect to and receiving respect from teachers and tutors, I included a question about how students, teacher, and tutors show respect. The many lengthy responses made me realize that this is a topic that we as tutors do not consider much. Many of the ESL students expect that teachers and tutors, as a sign of their respect for the student, will be patient, polite, and helpful; will treat the student as an adult; will make an effort to understand the student; and will not laugh at the student's mistakes. The students indicated that they could show respect to their teachers and tutors by arriving on time, following instructions and having all assignments finished, having pen and paper ready to take notes, listening closely and paying attention to what the teacher or tutor says, working hard, and expressing appreciation for what is being taught.

The ESL students' responses to my questionnaire may differ in some details, but I came away from their pages of writing with a strong sense of their commitment to learning. Despite the different written accents in their English and the variety of their comments and suggestions, they all are determined to learn how to write in English. They come to writing-center tutorials (and classrooms and office conferences) ready to learn, and we are equally eager to help them become fluent in our confusing language. In the interaction that follows, then, we need to remain conscious of the assumptions we work under in the learning environments we create. Tutors, particularly new initiates to the collaborative environment that frees them from the red-pencil world of finding errors and telling writers how to correct them, tend to forget that many of the students sitting next to them, particularly ESL students, do not necessarily share their goals or methods. The writing-center commitment to working with individual differences in the tutorial should therefore extend to seeking out and understanding the expectations and assumptions of students from other cultures. When tutor and student are headed in the same direction, they are more likely to get there together.

Works Cited

Cai, Xiaomin. "Behavioral Characteristics of Oriental ESL Students in the Writing Center." *Writing Lab Newsletter* 18.8 (1994): 5–6.

Clyne, Michael. "Cultural Differences in the Organization of Academic Texts: English and German." *Journal of Pragmatics* 5 (1981): 61–66.

Eggington, William G. "Written Academic Discourse in Korean: Implications for Effective Communication." *Writing across Languages: Analysis of L2 Text.* Ed. Ulla Connor and Robert Kaplan. Reading: Addison-Wesley, 1987. 153–68.

Harris, Muriel. "Individualized Instruction in Writing Centers: Attending to Writers' Cross-Cultural Differences." *Intersections: Theory and Practice in the Writing Center.* Ed. Joan Mullin and Ray Wallace. Urbana: NCTE, 1994. 96–110.

Hinds, John. "Reader vs. Writer Responsibility: A New Typology." *Writing across Languages: Analysis of L2 Text.* Ed. Ulla Connor and Robert Kaplan, Reading: Addison-Wesley, 1987. 141–52.

Kachru, Yamuna. "Linguistics and Written Discourse in Particular Languages: Contrastive Studies: English and Hindi." Ed. Alan C. Purves. *Writing across Languages and Cultures: Issues in Contrastive Rhetoric.* Newbury Park: Sage, 1988. 50–69.

Kilborn, Judith. "Tutoring ESL Students: Addressing Differences in Cultural Schemata and Rhetorical Patterns in Reading and Writing." MinneTESOL Conference. Saint Paul. 2 May 1992.

Parbst, John R. "Off-Topic Conversation and the Tutoring Session." *Writing Lab Newsletter* 19.1 (1994): 1+.

Young, Art. "College Culture and the Challenge of Collaboration." *Writing Center Journal* 13.1 (1992): 3–15.

Young, Linda Wai Ling. "Inscrutability Revisited." *Language and Social Identity.* Ed. John J. Gumperz. Cambridge: Cambridge UP, 1982. 72–84.

Reassessing The "Proofreading Trap": ESL Tutoring and Writing Instruction

Sharon A. Myers _____
TEXAS TECH UNIVERSITY

Sharon A. Myers explores the practical and ethical challenges tutors face when working with second-language writers. Although Myers acknowledges the writing center profession's deep roots in nondirective (or minimalist) tutoring, she argues that tutors cannot expect ESL writers to learn in the same ways or at the same rates as native writers. She calls for tutors' recognition that so-called "sentence-level" errors actually involve deeper levels of creating and processing meaning. By helping ESL students correct these errors, then, tutors can help students gain deeper insights into English syntax — an important step in becoming better readers and writers of the language. Such learning often takes a long time — "years, not months" — and may not become immediately apparent to either the student or the tutor. Myers takes particular issue with writing center scholars and others who view sentence-level revision for ESL students as unethical. As she says, "The central insight in foreign language pedagogy in the last thirty years is that, in fact, language acquisition emerges from learners wrestling with meaning in acts of communicating or trying to communicate. That is exactly what ESL students are doing in writing centers, person to person." This article, which first appeared in The Writing Center Journal *in 2003, serves as a thought-provoking challenge to tutors who attempt to apply nondirective approaches to ESL students. It may also provide theoretical support for tutors who tend to take a more directive approach in working with second-language writers.*

ESL writers present a common dilemma to writing centers — the desire for sentence-level interventions from their tutors. Our staff often experience such interventions as contradicting the aim of writing centers, formulated by Stephen North as making "sure that writers, and not necessarily their texts, are what get changed by instruction" (438). The job of writing center tutors, North stated, "is to produce better writers, not better writing" (438). The sentence-level demands of ESL students, however, are seen as "editing." Eric Hobson expresses this attitude in an article about writing center pedagogy in which he complains that during the period between the late 70s and early 80s,

> writing courses dealt with writing (e.g., invention, drafting, revision, development of authors' voices, etc.) while writing center staff were allocated the demanding and ethically questionable task of "cleaning up" writers' editing skills, of eradicating minority dialects . . . and of "dealing with" non-native writers. (155–166)

It is easy to understand why, faced with cutting through the confused syntactic and lexical tangles entwined in the sentences of second-language texts, writing specialists might much prefer to discuss issues of content and organization. Giving students correct grammar or more appropriate vocabulary is perceived as "fixing" the paper, something understood to violate the autonomy of the writer and the integrity of the work's authorship.

As someone who has worked with ESL writers for more than fifteen years, the attitude that sentence-level errors are mechanical, relatively unimportant ephemera has always seemed problematic to me, though I have heard it expressed or implied by conscientious tutors many times. It is a good example of the professional disjunction between composition specialists and ESL specialists that Paul Matsuda has described in *College Composition and Communication,* and a good example of the need to go outside of composition studies to improve what Matsuda refers to as "institutional practices" appropriate to second-language learners. It is wrong to assume, he explains, "that ESL writing can be broken down neatly into a linguistic component and a writing component and that the linguistic problems will disappear after some additional instruction in remedial language courses" (715). I want to show, in this article, that it is indeed the "linguistic" component (vocabulary and syntax) as much or more than what is considered the "writing" (rhetorical) component that ESL students need most, and that their "errors" are persistent evidence of normal second-language learning and processing, not some failure on the part of students. Many international graduate students, in particular, usually have a good idea of what they want to say, but are often at a loss as to how to say it. That is, they may have fewer whole-essay problems than native English speaking students, but still need a great deal of support. Even in cases in which a student is producing multiple drafts, the organization of such drafts may require macro-organizing language such as "Arguments against phenomenon X depend on four assumptions," or "The perspective that informs most research on X is . . . ," or "I would like to discuss two alternatives and their implications . . . ," or other language to signal sequencing of information across a text, provide background for contrast, or announce the dimensions in which the topic will be presented (e.g., whether the writer is going to evaluate, analyze, report, or critique). The language and the writing are inseparable.

There are a number of causes underlying the frustrations felt by both ESL students and tutors in writing centers. These include the unrealistic expectations about language learning embedded in our institutional arrangements for ESL students; the historic de-emphasis of sentence pedagogies; a conception of culture which excludes the structure of languages; ethical confusion; the understanding of errors as something to be eliminated rather than as artifacts of processing (and often of developmental progress); and the failure to recognize the depth of the "sentence-level" problems involved in second-language processing.

Unrealistic Expectations

Writing is arguably the most advanced and difficult of the modes, and usually the last acquired. Even among first-language learners, relatively few achieve the ability to write good formal academic prose at the university level. While the ability to speak a given language does not necessarily predict a person's ability to write in it, it is useful to note something about the time involved in spoken second-language acquisition in order to adjust the dimensions in which we need to perceive our students' struggles. The Foreign Service Institute has estimated that a minimum level of professional speaking proficiency (entailing the ability to fluently support opinions, hypothesize, and explain complex phenomena) in a foreign language relatively remote from English may require a native English speaker 2,400 hours of intensive training under the ideal conditions provided by the Foreign Service. A superior level may entail hundreds of hours more. According to Liskin-Gasparro, attaining a superior level in a more closely related language, such as Spanish or French, is estimated to take 720 hours (qtd. in Omaggio-Hadley 26). By comparison, four semesters of foreign language classes in a U.S. university provide 200–300 hours of instruction. Assuming that these estimations of the time it takes English learners to learn to speak foreign languages at professional levels would at least approximate the time it takes for speakers of other languages to speak with the same proficiency in English, it is not realistic to expect that many ESL students will speak fluently at advanced levels. I don't believe the ability to write at advanced levels is achieved much faster or that writing center tutors should be led to believe that students should. Writing is denser than speech and in academic settings requires very high levels of reading comprehension, a formal register, sophisticated paraphrasing ability and a specialized vocabulary. Very few ESL students who walk into a writing center are likely to have such high levels of proficiency. As Williams notes, it is not realistic to believe that they "should have put their second language problems behind them and be ready to take on the challenges of the composition classroom without further support" (qtd. in Matsuda 715). Students from China and Korea, for example, may have "studied" English for as long as eleven years in their home countries, but that "study" may have consisted of rote memorization of isolated words in vocabulary lists and "grammar" tests based on discrete items conforming to "rules" whose limitations are unknown to them. Immigrant students who enter U.S. high schools may never have had their needs to understand English as a foreign language attended to adequately, given the patchwork of requirements and variable quality of ESL teacher-training programs across the states and the strong political resistance to funding the needs of bilingual students. Even now, very few TESL or Applied Linguistics teacher preparation programs offer full courses in second-language composition. As a result, immigrant students often come into writing centers with second-language issues in addition to all the problems associated with "basic" writers in other populations.

The acquisition of a second language is a major achievement in a human life. It takes years of work. The depth and scale of the achievement are not always appreciated by U.S. writing tutors, few of whom have ever mastered any language other than their own at the level of sophistication demanded of ESL writers in academic settings, and who may actually, therefore, consider the control of agreement conventions in language, for example, a minor problem (more about agreement conventions further on).

The Historic Turn from Sentence-Level Pedagogies

In his history of "The Erasure of the Sentence" in composition studies, Robert J. Connors attributes the fall of the sentence as a focus of instruction to the strong movements away from formalism, behaviorism, and empiricism that have defined much of composition theory for the last twenty years. He laments the loss of useful sentence pedagogies as many writing specialists rejected everything about all three *isms* (or what they associated with those *isms*) with the kind of extremism unfortunately typical in education. With good reason, form was dethroned and meaning crowned. No one wants a return to the bad old days of the five-paragraph jello mold garnished with topic sentences, but like Connors, I think that ignoring the sentence, which is a central feature of writing in the texts of both native and non-native speakers, is a disservice to both populations. In the case of ESL students, whose greatest and most consistent difficulties are baldly manifested in the boundaries of the sentences itself, it seems like an eerie kind of denial.

More problematic than the historic de-emphasis of the sentence, however, is the separation of instruction in vocabulary and syntax with instruction in rhetoric. An article representative of dichotomizing sentence-level errors ("language") from "writing" in work with ESL students is "Avoiding the Proofreading Trap: The Value of the Error Correction Process" by Jane Cogie, Kim Strain, and Sharon Lorinskas published in *Writing Center Journal* (Spring/Summer, 1999). Constructing their analysis in just that framework, they interpret the persistence of the primary problems of ESL students and the persistence of the student need/demand for help with them (articulated or not) as a source of frustration and stress. Student demands for direct help in what the authors seem to consider a secondary level of writing are actually construed, as their title indicates, as a "trap" which must be "avoided" through techniques of indirect error correction. But there is no getting away from the fact that students need control of a great deal of lexis and syntax in the first place. They need a lot of vocabulary and a lot of experience, both in comprehension and production, to get to any level where "ideas" even become comprehensible. Meaning does not flow from such knowledge and experience, but the ability to express meaning does.

Language and Culture

Jane Cogie introduces the article by noting her appreciation of Judith Power's interpretation of the role of writing center instructors as "cultural informants":

> The cultural informant role endorsed by Powers gives writing center tutors flexibility for meeting specific needs of ESL students not met by the nondirective writing center ideal. With their many cultural, rhetorical, and linguistic differences, ESL students often lack the knowledge to engage in the question and answer approach to problem-solving used in most writing centers. . . . the read-aloud method for discovering sentence-level errors, frequently productive for native speakers, provides little help to ESL students who lack the ear to hear their own errors. The value of the cultural informant role, then, is that it validates sharing information about English that these students have no way of knowing on their own. (7)

Over time, however, Cogie feels disillusioned, as "too often this role, at least when sentence-level errors were concerned, tended to translate into the tutor editing and the student observing" (7). Like Purcell, whom she cites, she wishes to "shift the focus of the ESL session from difficult-to-resist, sentence-level errors to more meaningful idea-related issues . . ." (8). Cogie describes a tutor who felt that in her role as "cultural informant," she was merely editing, giving the student her "language," but not her "ideas" (8). But just as instruction in vocabulary and syntax ("language") cannot be separated from instruction in rhetoric ("writing"), language and culture are inseparable.

Writing instructors are indeed cultural informants. Culture refers not only to the contours of personal space, the educational roles of teacher and student, the sense of time, the politeness conventions and the discourse conventions of a given group, but to language and its forms. Culture includes the way that a given language determines, subordinates, complements, coordinates, pluralizes, counts, modalizes, interrogates, lexicalizes. In fact, the greatest problem many ESL writers have is in controlling the syntax and lexis of the English language. By "lexis," I mean not only words — what we usually think of as "vocabulary" — but multi-word units such as "in some ways," "on either side of," phrases such as "make arrangements for," and frequently co-occurring words such as "highly significant" or "closely linked." If we want to help non-English speakers write in English, we need to acknowledge the central role of language in writing — including all the redundant syntactic forms needed for "ideas" to take shape. Writing instructors and tutors schooled in modern composition theory, well aware of the failings and absurdities of traditional writing instruction reifying form over content, are wary of reducing the concept of writing to "good grammar." But what "English grammar" means to a native speaker of English, even one who grows up with a dialect of English unused in formal instruction, is very different from what it means to a second-language learner. The need to learn the many complex ways a language determines, subordinates, coordinates, lexicalizes and so on are often demeaned in composition literature, pooh-poohed as mere "sentence-level grammar" resulting in "sentence-level errors." These language structures should not be somehow divorced from culture or our roles as cultural informants. Errors in vocabulary and syntax occur within the structural constraints of a language and constitute "culture" just as much as every other feature of language below (phonetic) or above (rhetorical) the sentence level. Enabling the members of a different culture to express themselves in a new culture is work that cultural informants do. Being a culture informant includes being a language informant.

Ethical Perspectives: Writing Process and Language Learning Process

One concern of writing tutors is expressed in the area of Cogie et al.'s article subtitled "Ethical Rationale" (9). The authors cite an example in which a writing tutor (Kate Gadbow) "helps a Japanese M.A. student more than she intends" on a master's thesis (9). After graduating, the student interviewed for U.S. jobs and was rejected. As a result, Gadbow believes, the student had to relinquish her "career goals" and go back to Japan. Gadbow reports that her student "was harmed by her focus as a tutor on helping her to graduate rather than on helping her become more proficient in English" (10). Cogie then comments: "Certainly not all ESL sessions that fail to promote independence in the writer have such momentous consequences" (10). It may not be the case that Gadbow's editing role resulted in the student's failure to find work in the U.S. An alternative explanation could be that the student failed on the basis of her oral proficiency and/or listening comprehension, rather than her writing. In any case, second-language learners are inevitably dependent on people who know how to speak and write the second language, in order to learn how to speak and write it themselves. The learning takes a very long time and very, very many engagements with the language, not just a series of sessions with a writing tutor. In fact, the tutor may have provided much of the input the student will finally need to make particular vocabulary or structures available for spontaneous production at a later date when the student's growing and changing inner version of the language (often characterized as "interlanguage") is ready to absorb them.

While I would interpret the case of the Japanese student differently than Gadbow, fear is understandable in tutors who believe that such consequences might be possible if, according to their best lights, they "fail to promote independence" in the ESL writers they work with. But what does independence

mean? Learning is slow and occurs through processes neither entirely understood nor under the control of either the tutor or the learner. It is frustrating
for ESL students to have a native informant of the language resist informing
them, particularly one who is employed, ostensibly, to pay attention to their
language and help them write. And not only resist, but suggest through this
resistance (even though it may not be intended) that it is somehow dishonest
or lazy to expect the tutors to do so. This resistance is confusing, but most
second-language learners are insecure about their language learning themselves and not in a position to question their tutors' methods.

If an ESL student's text is corrected by a tutor who flags an error and then
offers alternatives, the fact that the student returns on another day and makes
the same mistake is not evidence that the student is irresponsible nor is it irresponsible of the tutor to correct it again. Some features of language are learned
before others. Students are not uniformly ready at all times to internalize
everything pointed out to them, and much of language acquisition — that is,
language that is internalized and available for production, takes place at an
unconscious level. There are far too many things to remember to hold everything in conscious memory. Moreover, although we don't understand exactly
how they work, there is substantial evidence for the existence of developmental patterns in second-language learning, which may well supersede the dictates of formal instruction (see Rod Ellis's *Study of Second Language Acquisition*).
It is also important to keep in mind that students may require many expo-
sures to words or patterns, and perhaps multiple communicative engagements
with them as well, before they are internalized. Repeating a correction is not a
capitulation to some stubborn student trait; it is simply acknowledging the
real nature of what is a genuinely long and messy process. It may appear to
the tutor that the student is passive, that is, not "responding to instruction,"
but the student is not necessarily passive at all. A great deal of language learning is receptive. Nor can the student necessarily fully learn features of the language in the time dimension in which the tutor is teaching. Checking writing
samples across periods of six months or a year may show improvement barely
noticeable over a thirteen week semester — and some language features and
levels of fluency do take years, not months, to achieve. This or that exposure
to some language feature may be just one or two frames in the time-lapse
movie in which the human brain captures the unfolding contours of a foreign
language. The students can't be rushed into an exclusive focus on the issues of
mature language use we have come to consider the "writing process." Some of
the ethical tension writing tutors experience also seems to be a result of under-
estimating how much idiosyncrasy is embodied in every human language.

Treatment of "Error"

Cogie et al.'s article is intended to provide student "tutors and their trainers a
collection of practical strategies for developing bit by bit the error awareness
ESL students need to self-edit" (10). In fact, students are very often painfully

aware of their errors, but are not sure or simply do not know how to fix them. I don't think tutors need to spend a lot of time to develop "strategies" to increase the students' (already sometimes paralyzing) awareness of their errors, or that doing so necessarily enables students to self-edit. (To give Cogie credit, she does appreciate the importance, in the affective domain, of assessing a student's proficiency and level of confidence, and advises restraint accordingly.) Most student "errors" however, are lexical, and if they don't have the appropriate word or lexical phrase, no editing will provide it. A great many tangles in "syntax" are a result of circumlocutions — vocabulary problems, not grammar problems. While I agree that there is a place for helping students self-edit, insofar as they can, I think that so much focus on errors is only helpful in proportional relation to the students' proficiency (the lower the proficiency, the less useful it is) and that for any level of proficiency it is not as important as learning more and more language in the first place. Accuracy, as Michael Lewis has often pointed out (*The Lexical Approach,* 164–172), is the last thing any second-language learner ever acquires, and then it is relative. I don't find any shame in directly helping students identify what is not working, but even then, that is only a small part of what they need and what we can provide, which is a repertoire of things that do work. They are not engaged merely in "editing" but in learning a new language.

Before discussing other ways we might help ESL students with "sentence-level" problems, I would like to consider the four suggestions offered by Cogie et al.: using a learner's dictionary, minimal marking, error logs, and self-editing checklists. They write that their rationale is to provide, in the absence of "native-speaker-like-intuitions," these "'more mechanical proofreading strategies' Muriel Harris and Tony Silva suggest are 'necessary'" (9). What Harris and Silva actually wrote, however, was "Therefore, some recourse to more mechanical rule-based proofreading strategies *or to outside help, such as a native speaker reader, will probably be necessary*" (535, emphases mine). Comments on the four strategies Cogie et al. suggest follow:

Learner's Dictionaries   The use of learner's dictionaries (see Appendix) is the least controversial of Cogie et al.'s suggestions. Such dictionaries are aimed at the needs of non-native speakers. They use phonetic spellings and information about how to stress lexical items such as compounds and idioms. They also provide a great deal of lexical grammatical information, such as the countability or non-countability of nouns and the gradability of adjectives. They may have a limited vocabulary for definitions so that learners don't have to continually look up new words. Kim Strain points out to a student that a learner's dictionary can provide information, for example, about what verbs are transitive or intransitive (16–17). The dictionary can indeed be useful if the student knows that a violation of the verb's transitiveness or intransitiveness has occurred. If this is pointed out, then the student can look to the dictionary for some examples. If it is not, then the only way a student could "edit" his or her paper would be to look up every single verb. Strain writes that the student may need "a firmer sense of the grammatical pattern for transitive and intransitive verbs." But there is no "grammatical pattern" to get a sense of. You just have to know what verbs are transitive and what verbs are not. There is no rule establishing this pattern.

Minimal Marking Minimal marking (in this case, two checks by a text line with two errors and one check by a line with one error) doesn't seem very helpful. It tells the student, "There are two errors here." What kind of errors? Nouns? Verbs? If verbs, is it a problem with tense? Aspect? Person? Valency (patterns of transitivity)? Agreement? Register (formal/informal)? Mode (a spoken rather than written form)? Are my errors concerned with articles? Pronouns? Word order? Lexical choice? The possibilities for a non-native speaker are a veritable black hole. I think we owe it to the student to at least identify the nature of errors and not just to enumerate them. Whose independence does this minimal marking really support? Richard Haswell's minimal marking scheme (which Cogie et al. cite) is intended for "regular freshman composition sections" (603). Such sections are primarily made up of native speakers of English. Haswell proposes that "[b]ecause the teacher responds to a surface mistake only with a check in the margin, attention can be maintained on more substantial problems" (601). But what may be a minor problem for a native speaker can be a substantial problem indeed for a second-language student. One rationale he gives for this minimal marking is that "[i]t shows the student that the teacher initially assumed that carelessness and not stupidity was the source of the error" (601). However, this rationale does not necessarily apply to the errors of non-native speakers either quantitatively or qualitatively, as it is not carelessness that accounts for most of their problems.

Error Log Bogs The value of error logs may be the most questionable of all Cogie et al.'s recommendations because, given the extremely long time it takes to learn a language, the cost/benefit ratio seems much more likely to be enhanced by spending more time learning more language (meaning more words and lexical phrases) than on the study of errors. The number of times a student is asked to have recourse to a dictionary, for example, has to be embedded in a realistic estimate of how many times it will actually be useful and at what point the student will become so frequently and hopelessly distracted from the flow of the text that he or she just chucks it. Time estimates have to be based on how much time the student has to spend on a piece of writing in the context of everything else the student has to do, and not only on the time available for individual instruction in the writing center. Sometimes it is simply more economical to point out an error and supply a correction or an alternative way to express something. A lexical notebook, such as those proposed by Michael Lewis (*Implementing* 75–85), would probably be more valuable than an error log and more likely to be referred to in the future. Lewis recommends having students keep notebooks of collocations such as "population increase/decrease"; polywords such as "in accordance with"; and phrasal verbs such as "look up to," that are clustered around themes and topics of importance to each student. If there is no time, the same thing can be done verbally, with the student repeating examples from a dictionary or examples supplied by the tutor. There is substantial evidence that phonological memory influences both grammar and vocabulary acquisition (see Nick C. Ellis).

I refer to error log "bogs" because I think it is easy to get bogged down in spending time and attention to the nature and analysis of wrong use of language when that time and attention could be employed in the service of learning correct use that eliminates errors in a much more productive way. Most learner errors are quite predictable, without the need for logs of them. They are either lexical, in which case they are tied to word idiosyncrasies and not amenable to "sentence-level" grammar anyway, or predictable in the sense that they are the same errors all second-language learners make while they are learning English. A great deal of variation is predictable on the basis of first languages, described in *Learner English: A Teacher's Guide to Interference and Other Problems* by Michael Swan and Bernard Smith, who list and discuss the sources of common problems typical of English learners from nineteen different language groups. Students who come from languages that do not have articles, for example, strongly tend to omit articles; students whose first languages have articles tend to use them too much in English. Writing down "missing definite article" under a column labeled "Name/Description of Error" could get pretty redundant for Korean students, for example. There are so many dimensions of article use that govern whether or not an article belongs in front of a given noun in a given context that simply putting it in front of the noun in the "Correction" column, even in the context of a phrase, is not always guaranteed to elucidate anything for the student except that he or she should have used it in that place in that sentence in the context of that paper. Why not just correct it in the paper in the first place?

Very often, not having the English necessary to express something, students simply translate directly from their mother tongues. Filling up an error log with all the infelicities this produces does not address the cause of the error, which is simply lack of the language needed in the first place. Such "errors" cannot be reverse engineered in an error log.

Self-editing Checklists The authors propose self-editing checklists, handouts given to students which ask them to record their three most frequent errors (to check against their current paper) and to check all verbs for subject-verb agreement, modals, tenses, and voice (all extremely complicated phenomena from a second-language perspective). While I am skeptical of such checklists for the same reasons I question the value of error logs, I think there may be a place for self-editing checklists for very advanced students, but only for certain problems which can be simply defined and identified. One that comes to mind is the comma splice. A list of example comma splices which have appeared in the student's own texts, matched by a corresponding repair might be useful to list, contributing to the sense of what comma splices look and "sound" (read) like. Probably the most useful suggestion on the checklist provided by the authors is the final one, which advises the ESL student to "ask a knowledgeable friend to read over your paper and look for problem areas" (22). The authors note that this should be a friend outside of the writing center. I would note that that such friends would be very likely to provide the vocabulary and grammar correction that the tutors in the writing center are not comfortable providing.

Looking Below the "Surface" of the Sentence

The major question for writing instructors and for tutors is always, first of all, where to begin on ESL papers full of errors in syntax and vocabulary. The authors advise distinguishing between "local errors" and "global errors," a distinction which usually refers to prioritizing errors that obscure meaning (global errors) over "errors that do not significantly hinder communication of a sentence's message (local errors)" (Hendrickson 360). This is a useful distinction and a legitimate instructional strategy, but the distinction cannot be made mechanically through an a priori definition of errors, such as "Global errors include incorrect verb tense, verb incorrectly formed, incorrect use or formation of a modal . . . awkward word order . . . ," and so on (Cogie et al. 15), while "Local errors include incorrect subject-verb agreement, incorrect or missing article, problem with the singular or plural of a noun, wrong word choice . . ." (Cogie et al. 16). Whether or not an error is global or local depends first and foremost on its context. "Awkward word order" in the sentence of a given text does not necessarily interfere with meaning at all; it may be, simply, awkward. On the other hand, the distinction between singular and plural in a noun phrase could very much affect meaning, and "wrong word" choices probably obscure meaning more than any other single mistake. Rather than refer to these arbitrary and misleading categories, a tutor would be better advised to simply ask herself or himself, during the reading of a text, what, if anything, most confuses meaning here? Or, what, if anything, makes the meaning most difficult to process, even if it is recoverable? In some contexts, it may indeed be even the misuse or omission of a single definite or indefinite article.

Related to these distinctions is the practice of waving away what native speaking tutors or instructors define as "local" or "surface" errors, "minor irritants" that the students should be able to clear up relatively easily. In reality these errors often reflect extremely complex problems for second-language learners. Subject-verb agreement often falls into this category. Isn't it strange how, despite all the times they are shown and told, the students, even very advanced ones, just keep failing to make their subjects and verbs agree? It appears to be so simple.

The belief that it is simple is an instance of what Paul Westney points out as instructor (not student) error in teaching pedagogical "rules," which is the assumption that because they look simple to us, they are simple to a non-native speaker (80–83). Subject-verb agreement is a difficult feature of English. First of all, the student has to know whether a given noun is countable in order to make it agree with a verb. The "countable/non-countable" distinction made of English nouns is bizarre to students whose languages do not contain it. A furniture is a furniture is a furniture. On what basis is the student supposed to be able to figure out that it is not? Again, it is lexical, something particular to a word, not "sentence-level" grammar that determines what to do. There is nothing about words that flags their countability, and the semantic concept is so alien it is hard to remember even if the countability of a particular noun has been brought to the student's attention on some other occasion. In addition to this pitfall, the tricky English anachronism of the third person "s" lies in wait to ambush subject-verb agreement in the sentences of even the most advanced students. On one level, the third person "s" is probably hard to keep in memory precisely because it doesn't affect meaning very much; it is a redundant feature, since the noun clause has already declared its identity and number. Meaning has already been established, so there is no strong semantic demand for the information, only the abstract grammatical convention of repeating it. This is not natural or obvious to non-native speakers at all, nor is it easy to keep in mind. Compounding the problem of subject-verb agreement are both the phonological and orthographic properties of the "s" inflection. The "s" is often deemphasized in the speech of natives, from whom students get much of their input. Because it is deemphasized, it is often not heard, and as a result, not imitated. If students tend to drop it in speech, they tend to drop it in writing. The "s" inflection is realized in three different morphemes: /s/, /z/, and /ez/. These have to be rendered as "s" or "es" in writing independent of their pronunciation, and are sometimes confounded with the apostrophed "s" and "es" forms of the possessive incarnation of the "s" inflection. Unless, of course, the noun takes an irregular plural. This is a feature of individual nouns, and not a rule-governed phenomenon. Compound nouns, too, are a real minefield for non-native speakers trying to produce agreement. Zalewski illustrates the difficulties with compound nouns by noting that sometimes there is no formal singular or plural distinction at all, as in the word "Japanese" in an example where a writer explains that Americans shrug to express "I don't know," followed by the sentence, "On the other hand, Japanese shakes the head from side to side" (695). The ambiguity of this and other problems in number and person, she writes, "constitute a serious textual breakdown not only because trying to solve them costs the reader a lot of processing effort but also because ultimately their disambiguation turns out to be impossible" (697). Such problems, she writes, "have all too often been viewed as *local* and thus de-emphasized in form-focused instruction" (697, emphasis added).

As for "incorrect or missing articles," insofar as they embody anaphoric relations (those which refer back to previous discourse), their significance (and therefore the choice of whether or how to use them) can span across hundreds of pages or years of shared knowledge; their use is not at all confined to the insides of sentences or to the local demands of a noun phrase. Using "a" in front of the word "experiment," for example, may obscure the fact that the writer is referring to the one known to the addressee and the writer, which was described six pages ago. Another one of Zalewski's student texts illustrates extrasentential links expressed by articles at the paragraph level. The student is writing about arranged marriages (notes in italics are mine):

> There is a go-between who take care of between a boy and a girl. Before they meet, they can get personal histories of each other. Then, a go between (*In native discourse the "a" here would be "the" since the go-between has already been introduced in the previous sentence*) gives them a meeting. In a meeting (*again, this would be "the," because the meeting has already been mentioned*), a go-between (*should be "the," previous mention*) introduces a boy and a girl (*as before, previous mention: should be "the boy" and "the girl"*) to each other. In almost case, meetings are dinner parties. Their parents often go with them to a meeting (*the meeting previously described, not just any meeting: should be "the" meeting*). (694)

These are not sentence-level links. Importantly, they are also errors which seriously hamper the ability of a reader to process meaning.

I mention each of these different issues concerning subject-verb agreement and definite/indefinite articles to illustrate how deeply complex they are for non-native speakers. And they represent only two features of syntax that are often misconstrued as merely "surface" or "local." In fact, both connect to very large regions of language structure and use.

Teaching Language Versus Documenting Errors

I think it is both possible and desirable for writing center staff to fill the role of "foreign/second-language teachers" as well as writing instructors. In fact, writing tutors are perfectly positioned to facilitate the language learning these students need in order to develop their ability to write in English. The central insight in foreign language pedagogy in the last thirty years is that, in fact, language acquisition emerges from learners wrestling with meaning in acts of communicating or trying to communicate. That is exactly what ESL students are doing in writing centers, person to person.

What needs to occur is a shift in emphasis from carving up whatever language the students have managed to summon up for their texts and then asking them to autopsy it, to giving the students more and more language from which to make choices, establishing more and more links for them from the language they have to new language they need. Facilitating learning by providing correct language input rather than focusing on incorrect language can be done in a principled way, informed by insights into writing processes staff already have, but conditioned by an understanding of language-acquisition processes that are no less real or important, such as the time dimension in which acquisition takes place and the many layers of complexity learners face such as those illustrated above.

Writing tutors need to acknowledge and respond to the central role of lexis in language learning. They should also be equipped with much better knowledge of the pedagogical grammar of English as a second/foreign language. It is not the same grammar used to teach native speakers. Rather than just pointing out an error, tutors can provide alternative language: "Another way to say that is . . ."; "One way of putting it is . . ."; "Some other phrases you can use are. . . ." Much of writing (and much of speech, for that matter) consists of stringing together lexical phrases, not filling in grammatical slots. We use, and learn, much of language in words and word "chunks," not in abstract rules (Nick C. Ellis; Kirsner; Lewis; Little; Nattinger and DeCarrico; Tschirner). Language can be given verbally (asking the student to repeat), dictated with the student taking it down in writing, or offered through the use of a collocation dictionary (see Appendix). In some contexts, a lexical notebook might be appropriate; in another, just inserting a correction directly into the student's text as a reformulation might be the best course of action (see Myers for one version of using reformulation as composition feedback).

Modern corpus linguistics and discourse analysis provide interesting language frames that can be used to help writers. Nattinger and DeCarrico, for example, advocate acquainting students with written discourse forms at both global and sentence levels. In formal essays, for example, these frames include lexical phrases for topic nomination such as "[T]he goal of this paper is to . . ."; phrases for agreement and disagreement ("X does not support Y . . ."); or contrast (". . . is unlike . . . with respect to . . .") (172). Learning sentence heads (such as "It is possible that . . . ," or "The research suggests that . . .") enrich the writing repertoire, as do frames, such as "Evidence of . . . indicates . . . ," or "One interpretation of . . . is . . . ," or "An alternative interpretation is. . . ."

Reporting verbs (e.g., suggest, imply, point out, note) are used much more in writing than in speech, and can be presented to students as alternatives in sentence-level contexts. Consciousness-raising exercises can be advised, such as suggesting that a student note reporting verbs they find when they read English text outside of the writing center. Subordination and coordination, the bane of ESL students, can be practiced in sentence combining exercises such as those popular in the 1970s and 80s (de Beaugrande; Broadhead; Strong).

Much of the language students need is writing-specific, and the writing center is an ideal place to give it to them. Most of all, showing is better than telling: "Here are some examples of acceptable student essays written by students in your field," or "Here are some examples of acceptable texts written by students who have been given assignments similar to yours." With the permission of student writers, writing centers could have files of such examples. Students need to get a sense of what such texts look like and "sound" like. This would be especially useful to international students, who are often even less familiar with what they are expected to produce than are the U.S. students.

Grammar instruction needs to be based on a principled examination of what is genuinely teachable and learnable, not just shunted off to traditional reference grammars based on Latin language paradigms aimed at native speakers that so many writing specialists just assume are useful (see Appendix for a recommendation). Tutors need to relinquish the attitude that giving second-language students the language they need is "unethical" or "immoral." Filling in an article somewhere it is needed and pointing out the context is one drop in the waves of the language ocean carving out its shape on the shoreline of the student's memory. One drop, or even fifteen, are not all that significant. Likewise, repeating some words or other instruction is not a sign of pathological student "dependence." Repetition plays an important role in language learning. Nor should native English speaking students be used as models in designing instruction for ESL students.

I am well aware that there are students who would be happy to let writing tutors do all their work for them; that there are students who are lazy or manipulative or both. Members of this minority show up regularly in my classes, and while I give everybody the benefit of the doubt to begin with, it doesn't take very long to identify them. Tutors who have multiple sessions with such students soon identify them, too. I just flatly tell these students that they need to go home and work on the text more before I will be willing to help them with it, or I point out a few "global" errors and note that it is sloppy in regard to X, Y, and Z, too, and to come back after they have paid more attention to it. But most students, especially ESL students, genuinely want to learn and are willing to work hard. I think we owe second-language students second-language writing instruction more broadly conceived than error documentation. There is indeed a "trap." It is created by the contradictions between what ESL learners need and are capable of and what an uninformed perspective leads us to suppose they need and are capable of. Nancy Grimm's admonition in regard to students with different backgrounds (in her example, an African American student and a young woman from a conservative Christian background) could apply as well to ESL students who enter the writing center:

> When the proofreading issue is contextualized within an ideological model of literacy, it becomes . . . complicated. Rather than refusing to engage in this task because individual writers are supposed to be able to do it for themselves, writing centers need more complex understandings of the issues involved. (20)

A much more relaxed attitude about "error," one reflecting an appreciation of second language acquisition processes, and better training in the pedagogical grammar of English as a second language would go a long way toward preventing either students or tutors from feeling frustrated or "trapped" in any part of the tutoring process.

Works Cited

Biber, Douglas, Stig Johansson, Geoffrey Leech, Susan Conrad and Edward Finegan. *Longman Grammar of Spoken and Written English*. Essex: Longman, 1999.

Broadhead, Glenn J. "Sentence Patterns: Some of What We Need to Know and Teach." *Sentence Combining: A Rhetorical Perspective* Ed. Donald A. Daiker, Andrew Kerek, and Max Morenberg. Carbondale: Southern Illinois UP, 1985. 61–75.

Cogie, Jane, Kim Strain, and Sharon Lorinskas. "Avoiding the Proofreading Trap: The Value of the Error Correction Process." *The Writing Center Journal* 19.2 (1999): 7–31.

Connors, Robert J. "The Erasure of the Sentence." *College Composition and Communication* 52:1 (2000): 96–128.

de Beaugrande, Robert. "Sentence Combining and Discourse Processing: In Search of a General Theory." *Sentence Combining: A Rhetorical Perspective*. Ed. Donald A. Daiker, Andrew Kerek, and Max Morenberg. Carbondale: Southern Illinois UP, 1985. 61–75.

Ellis, Nick C. "Sequencing in SLA: Phonological Memory, Chunking, and Points of Order." *Studies in Second Language Acquisition 18* (1996): 91–126.

Ellis, Rod. *The Study of Second Language Acquisition*. Oxford: Oxford UP, 1994.

Gadbow, Kate. "Foreign Students in the Writing Lab: Some Ethical and Practical Considerations." *The Writing Lab Newsletter 17.3* (1992): 1–5.

Grimm, Nancy. "The Regulatory Role of the Writing Center: Coming to Terms with a Loss of Innocence." *The Writing Center Journal* 17.1 (1996): 5–29.

Harris, Muriel and Silva, Tony. "Tutoring ESL Students: Issues and Options." *College Composition and Communication 44.4* (1993): 525–37.

Haswell, Richard H. "Minimal Marking." *College English 45* (1993): 600–04.

Hendrickson, James M. "Error Correction in Foreign Language Teaching: Recent Theory, Research, and Practice." *Methodology in TESOL: A Book of Readings*. Ed. Michael H. Long and Jack C. Richards. New York: Newbury House, 1987. 355–69.

Hill, Jimmie, and Michael Lewis, eds. *Dictionary of Selected Collocations*. Hove, England: Language Teaching Publications, 1997.

Hobson, Eric H. "Writing Center Pedagogy." *A Guide to Composition Pedagogies*. Ed. Gary Tate, Amy Rupiper and Kurt Schick. New York: Oxford University Press, 2001. 165–182.

Huckins, Thomas N. and Leslie A. Olsen. *Technical Writing and Professional Communication for Nonnative Speakers of English*. 2nd ed. New York: McGraw Hill. 1991. 514–530.

Kirsner, Kim. "Second Language Vocabulary Learning: The Role of Implicit Processes." *Implicit and Explicit Learning of Languages*. Ed. Nick C. Ellis. San Diego: Academic Press, 1994, 283–311.

Leki, Ilona. *Understanding ESL Writers: A Guide for Teachers*. Portsmouth, NH: Boynton/Cook, 1992.

Lewis, Michael. *The Lexical Approach: The State of ELT and a Way Forward*. Hove, England: Language Teaching Publications, 1993.

———. *Implementing the Lexical Approach: Putting Theory into Practice*. Hove, England: Language Teaching Publications, 1997.

Liskin-Gasparro, Judith E. *ETS Oral Proficiency Testing Manual*. Princeton, NJ: Educational Testing Service, 1982.

Little, David. "Words and Their Properties: Arguments for a Lexical Approach to Pedagogical Grammar." *Perspectives on Pedagogical Grammar*. Ed. Terence Odlin. Cambridge: Cambridge UP, 1994. 99–122.

Matsuda, Paul Kei. "Composition Studies and ESL Writing: A Disciplinary Division of Labor." *College Composition and Communication 50.4* (1999): 699–721.

Myers, Sharon. "Teaching Writing as a Process and Teaching Sentence Level Syntax: Reformulation as ESL Composition Feedback." *TESL-EJ* 2.4 (1997): 11–16.

Nattinger, James R. and Jeanette S. DeCarrico. *Lexical Phrases and Language Teaching.* Oxford: Oxford UP, 1992.

North, Stephen M. "The Idea of a Writing Center." *College English* 46.5 (1984): 433–46.

Omaggio-Hadley, Alice. *Teaching Language in Context.* 3rd ed. Boston: Heinle & Heinle, 2001.

Powers, Judith K. "Rethinking Writing Center Conferencing Strategies for the ESL Writer." *The Writing Center Journal* 13.2 (1993): 39–47.

Purcell, Katherine. "Making Sense of Meaning: ESL and the Writing Center." *The Writing Lab Newsletter* 22.6 (1998): 1–5.

Strong, William. *Sentence-Combining: A Composing Book.* New York: Random House, 1973.

Swan, Michael and Bernard Smith. *Learner English: A Teacher's Guide to Interference and Other Problems.* Cambridge: Cambridge UP, 1987.

Tschirner, Erwin. "From Lexicon to Grammar." *The Coming Age of the Profession: Issues and Emerging Ideas for the Teaching of Foreign Languages.* Ed. Jane Harper, Madeleine Lively, and Mary Williams. Boston: Heinle & Heinle, 1998. 113–28.

Westney, Paul. "Rules and Pedagogical Grammar." *Perspectives on Pedagogical Grammar.* Ed. Terence Odlin. Cambridge: Cambridge UP, 1994, 72–96.

Williams, Jessica. "ESL Composition Program Administration in the United States." *Journal of Second Language Writing* 4 (1995): 157–79.

Zalewski, Jan P. "Number/Person Errors in an Information-Processing Perspective: Implications for Form-Focused Instruction." *TESOL Quarterly* 27.4 (1993): 691–703.

Appendix: Resource Recommendations

LEARNER DICTIONARIES

Collins Cobuild learners' dictionaries are good references and can be found on the Cobuild website: <http://www.cobuild.collins.co.uk/>. They provide information about whether a verb takes a gerund and/or an infinitive, for example, and about how common or uncommon a word is (information much appreciated by students who do not want to sound old-fashioned or weird). They are based on a corpus of over 250 million words taken, not from traditional definitions and examples, but from real-world speech and writing. Word pragmatics are noted, explaining word function (advising or agreeing, for example). Discourse organizing functions are noted, along with attitudes the words express, or whether they are used for emphasis. Style is described (American or British, rude, journalistic, literary, technical, spoken or written, technical, formal or informal), and authentic examples are given in complete sentences. All nouns are identified as count or non-count, and adjectives as graded or not and how (that is, inflected for comparison, as in "slow, slower, slowest"). Verbs that only occur in the passive voice are noted, and transitive and intransitive verbs are noted as is information, for example, about whether an intransitive verb is followed by a prepositional phrase or by a specified adverb. Patterns in the use of titles are given, as well as the patterns in which number and other word classes are expressed. Such an advanced learner's dictionary is also a good reference for tutors, who need to learn "word grammar" themselves, or at least know where to find it if they are not familiar with the pedagogical grammar of English as a foreign language. The advanced learner's dictionary is now on CD-ROM with a thesaurus, grammar information, and a five million word wordbank for examples.

An online dictionary much favored by my ESL university students is *Wordsmyth:* <http://www.wordsmyth.net/>. Examples of how English expresses things, whether found in a dictionary or provided by a native speaker, are the most useful. The students need to learn the right way to use the language to express their meanings, not just how to recognize (in the cases where recognition is even possible) that they have used some word or expression in the wrong way.

COLLOCATION DICTIONARIES

Another good resource for ESL writers is the *Dictionary of Selected Collocations* edited by Jimmie Hill and Michael Lewis. This is a resource enabling students to learn what is often of most use to them as writers: what words go with what words. This collocation dictionary is based on contemporary work in corpus linguistics. Our ability to analyze the patterns of language has been boosted many orders of magnitude over traditional analyses by the use of computers, and it is only recently that these findings are emerging into dictionaries and grammars. The collocation dictionary does not define words, but gives students probable combinations based on frequency studies of huge corpora of authentic written and spoken language. This book is of great value to second language students. Entries are given on the categories of nouns, verbs, adjectives, and adverbs (mostly nouns). For example, if a student is writing about a career, the dictionary provides a list of words and phrases which most commonly cluster around that word, including a list of verbs that come before the noun, a list (in the most common tense) of which come after it, and a list of adjectives and phrases which contain the noun. Here is their example entry (11) ("sb" is an abbreviation for "subject"):

CAREER

V: abandon, be absorbed in, be destined for ~ in, boost, carve out, change, choose, concentrate on, cripple, cut short, damage, determine, develop, devote oneself to, embark on, end, enter upon, further, give up, hamper, have a ~ in (banking), help, hinder, interrupt, launch out on, launch sb on, map out, plan, predict, promote, pursue, put an end to, ruin, sacrifice, salvage, set sb on, spoil, start, take up, wreck ~

V: ~ blossomed, had its ups and downs

A: amazing, brilliant, chequered, colourful, demanding, difficult, disappointing, distinguished, entire, fine, flourishing, glittering, golden, good, great, honourable, ill-fated, meteoric, modest, promising, splendid, steady, strange, successful, turbulent, unusual, varied ~

P: outset of, peak of, pinnacle of, springboard for, summit of ~, a ~ change

In a different example, starting from a verb or adjective, the student would find, after the word "convinced": "absolutely, almost, easily, half-, more or less, not altogether, not entirely, practically, totally _convinced_ about/of . . ." (230).

Another useful reference for collocations is the Collins Cobuild English Collocations on CD-ROM, available through the same website of the Cobuild dictionaries noted above.

GRAMMAR REFERENCE

A good modern resource grammar for tutors is the *Longman Grammar of Spoken and Written English* by Douglas Biber et al. Unlike descriptions in traditional grammars, those in the *Longman Grammar* are based entirely on empirical data.

Learning Disabilities and the Writing Center

Julie Neff ————————————————————————
UNIVERSITY OF PUGET SOUND

In order to assist students with learning disabilities, writing center tutors need to understand the challenges these students face in writing academic papers. As Julie Neff points out in her article, students with learning disabilities often score above average on intelligence tests and do excellent work in some courses, but they may not perform well in courses that emphasize particular skills, such as math, reading, or writing. Students with learning disabilities may amass a wealth of specific knowledge about a discipline but have trouble accessing that knowledge without assistance. Such students may need help brainstorming about topics, with the tutor asking probing questions and writing down the students' answers. Others may have difficulty at the strategic level. Because of the variety of learning disabilities, Neff suggests, tutors must remain open-minded and modify tutoring techniques to meet individual student writers' specific needs. This essay, which first appeared in Intersections: Theory-Practice in the Writing Center, *provides a place for tutors to start building an understanding of students with learning disabilities.*

Since September 1984, when Stephen North's now famous article, "The Idea of a Writing Center" appeared in *College English,* a picture of the writing conference has developed: the writer and the writing advisor sit side by side, the writer holding the pencil, the writing advisor asking probing questions about the development of the topic; or the student types text into a computer as the writing advisor fires questions designed to help the student think through the writing problem; or, in a revising session, the advisor points to a word or phrase that seems to be "wrong" for this particular paragraph as the student jots notes so she can later correct the text. In these conferences, the writing advisor tells the student to check punctuation and spelling and gives the student a handout to help with the process. After all, the writing center is not a "fix-it" shop for student papers; it is a place for writer to meet reader in order to receive a thoughtful response.

Behind these pictures of writing center conferences lie some basic assumptions: students can improve their ability to invent, organize, draft, revise, and edit based on the responses of a thoughtful reader. Even though the conference is in many ways collaborative, most of the responsibility for composing and transcribing is placed on the student writer. Recent theory and pedagogy in rhetoric and composition support these pictures of the collaborative writing conference, e.g., Bruffee, Harris, Ede, and Lunsford.

But one group of students does not and cannot fit into this pedagogical picture: students with learning disabilities. Though their particular disabilities vary, these students need a different, more specific kind of collaboration than the average student who walks through the doors of the writing center.

What Is a Learning Disability?

Although there is still some disagreement about the precise definition, learning disabilities are generally a varied group of disorders that are intrinsic to the individual.

The Learning Disabilities Act of 1968, which has only changed in small ways since it was drafted, defines a learning disability as "a disorder in one or more of the basic psychological processes involved in understanding or in using spoken or written languages." Individuals with learning disabilities are likely to experience trouble with "listening, thinking, talking, reading, writing, spelling, or arithmetic." Learning problems that are primarily due to a physical condition, like visual or hearing impairment, retardation, emotional dysfunction, or a disadvantaged situation, are not considered to result from learning disabilities. While these other problems sometimes accompany a learning disability, they are not the cause or the result of the disability. Nor are learning disabilities the result of social or economic conditions. People who have learning disabilities are born with them, or they have acquired them through a severe illness or accident, and the disability will continue to affect them over their lifetimes. Although many people overcome their learning disabilities, they do so by learning coping strategies and alternate routes for solving problems. People with learning disabilities cannot be "cured." However, with help, those with learning disabilities can learn to use their strengths to compensate for their weaknesses.

A learning disability is the result of a malfunction in the system in one or more areas. We cannot look into the brain and see the malfunction, but we can see the results in a student's performance on a discrete task. The Woodcock-Johnson Test of Cognitive Ability, one of the most widely used tests for measuring learning disabilities, uncovers discrepancies between capacity and performance. Although the requirements differ from state to state, two standard deviations between potential and performance on the Woodcock-Johnson test (or similar tests such as the WAIS-R, TOWL, or WRAT) suggest that a student is learning disabled, as does an extreme scatter of subtest scores.

Some learning disabilities are truly debilitating in that the individual is unable to cope with or overcome the problems. However, many people with learning disabilities are able to function at the highest levels in one area while having difficulty in another. In fact, many people who are learning disabled in one area are gifted in another. Dyslexic and slow to read, Albert Einstein was learning disabled, as was Thomas Edison (Lovitt 1989, 5). Although these are two of the most well-known cases, they are not exceptional ones. According to specialists at a learning disabilities clinic, Another Door to Learning, one successful businessman claimed his learning disability has contributed to his success because it allowed him to view problems from a different perspective.

Often learning-disabled students who come to college score in the above-average range of standard IQ tests and have finely honed skills for compensating for and adapting to their particular disability.

What Do We Know about the Brain?

While no one yet knows the precise causes of a learning disability, the materials drafted by the National Joint Committee on Learning Disabilities presume that the disability, which manifests itself in problems with the acquisition and use of listening, speaking, reading, writing, reasoning, mathematical or spatial skills, grows out of some sort of brain dysfunction.

Although researchers know much more now than they did a decade ago, the debate over just how the brain works continues. Some scientists believe that the brain is bicameral, with the left side responsible for language and reason, and the right side responsible for nonverbal, intuitive activities — the mystical if you will (Bergland 1985, 1). Others believe that the bicameral model oversimplifies the workings of the brain and is more misleading than it is useful.[1]

Richard Bergland (1985) explains that in the last several years a new "wet model" of the brain has emerged, one that is based on the theory that the brain runs on hormones. The idea that the brain is a gland run by hormones has resulted in a new, burgeoning field of medicine known as neuroendocrinology which gives credence to the idea that the learning disability has a physiological basis.

Meantime, over the past decade, cognitive psychology has moved away from the Platonic idea that human rationality grows out of pure intelligence. Instead, researchers are seeing the brain as "a knowledge medium," a storehouse for great quantities of knowledge about the world. This view of the brain represents a paradigm shift from the Platonic view, which asserts that only by reasoning with formal rules we can come to general understanding: if worldly knowledge is more important than pure reason, we have a model of human rationality that relies on information in the brain and vast associative connections that allow the human mind to turn a fragment of information into a considerable amount of knowledge. Human cognition consists not of pure reason but is instead composed of the information stored in the brain and the brain's ability to connect those pieces of information. Worldly knowledge, according to Jeremy Campbell (1989), has become far more important than pure logic.

How Does This Theory Help Us Understand a Learning Disability?

The idea of the brain as a knowledge machine, and as an organ run by hormones, can help us understand a learning disability. The brain processes enormous amounts of information. The brains of learning-disabled persons have these same properties; but often learning-disabled persons have trouble accessing and retrieving the information, and occasionally gathering and storing it.

This is not because they are unintelligent but because of a physiological problem. Judy Schwartz, author of the book *Another Door to Learning,* says that individuals not only have to have basic information, they have to know they have it. The substance and assumptions are inside the learning-disabled person's brain, but he or she may not know the information is there. To access what is known, he or she must consciously learn how to tap the information through self-cuing or other methods. In these circumstances, the writing center can be helpful.

Misconceptions about Learning Disabilities

Although brain theory and research support the idea that a learning disability has a physiological basis, many people, including educators, continue to have a number of misconceptions about people with learning disabilities. Some see the learning-disabled students as "special education" students who are now being mainstreamed. Some see them as manipulative individuals looking for an excuse for bad spelling and punctuation. Some see "learning disability" as a euphemism for "retarded." Others claim that learning disabilities do not actually exist.[2]

Since a learning disability has a physiological basis and is not due to low intelligence, social situations, or economic conditions, a learning disability is not unlike other kinds of disabilities that have a physiological basis. Renee must use a wheelchair because she was born with an imperfect spine. This defect, not caused by low intelligence, social situation, or economic factors, is a physiological problem that Renee overcomes by taking a slightly different route to accomplish her goals. Renee can reach the second floor, but she won't use the stairs; she'll use the elevator. Similarly, the learning-disabled student can master the material; but she may need to write the exam on a computer, and she may also need extra time to access the information she has.

A Case Study

Although learning disabilities vary widely, it may be easier to understand how a learning disability affects an individual by looking at a specific student with a specific disability. When Barb was in middle school, her mother asked her to take a roast from the refrigerator and put it in the oven at 350 degrees so it would be ready when she got home from work. The roast was in the baking dish, seasoned, and covered with plastic wrap. At the appropriate time, Barb did exactly as she was asked. The roast was done perfectly when her mother came home, but it was coated with melted plastic.

Why hadn't Barb removed the plastic? She had taken cooking in school and often baked cakes and cookies at home. Even though she has 20/20 vision, Barb couldn't comprehend the plastic. Because the plastic exists in space, Barb's spatial problems kept her from seeing it until her mother tied it to language by saying, "This roast is covered with melted plastic." Barb replied, "I'm sorry. I didn't notice it."

Barb has a disability that affects her ability to access and create reliable images and thus to understand things spatially. She understands and gains access to her world and spatial relationships by building and shaping images with language, which in turn gives her access to images.

Barb needed written or oral directions to remove the plastic. As soon as she had words, Barb could grasp the situation and accomplish the task. According to Carol Stockdale of Another Door to Learning, the image was recorded, but Barb only had access to it through language. Barb often said, "Well, I know that," but, in fact, she did not know it consciously until she had the language to refine the image.

In middle school, Barb was placed in an English class that taught grammar as a discrete subject: two weeks for literature, two weeks for grammar. Barb's spoken English was excellent; her speech included sophisticated syntax and vocabulary, and she was most successful with the reading and discussion of the literature. But the spatial quality of the grammar drills confounded Barb. Because she failed to grasp the spatial task of retrieving the mechanics of written English, spatial labels like "adverb" meant nothing to her. While she could use an adverb correctly in spoken and written English, she could not "see" the term "adverb" any more than she could see the plastic wrap.

When Barb started high school, her classes were content rich; they stressed worldly knowledge. Although she continued to have difficulty with math and chemistry, she found that her writing and especially the mechanics improved as she took courses in history, literature, and art and music history. In these courses, she was learning the language that would allow her to store and retrieve information. The more information she had the better she became at making connections, and these connections were as apparent in the classroom as in the kitchen.

Because Barb was coping well with her reading and writing in her high school classes, she did not anticipate that "driving class" would be a problem. But as Barb sat behind the wheel of the family sedan to have a practice session with her mother, her mother realized that learning to drive, a spatial task, would be much more difficult than learning art history.

Barb edged the car toward the pavement from the gravel shoulder of the road. "Turn the car a little to the left, Barb, and as you pick up speed, ease onto the pavement," her mother said patiently. Barb eased the car onto the grey cement at about 20 mph. But soon she was back on the gravel, and then a minute later she had drifted to the left side of the road. Many novice drivers drift, but Barb remained unaware of both the drift and resulting position. "Barb, you're driving on the wrong side of the road! Do you realize what could have happened?!" Barb's mother exclaimed.

"I'm sorry," Barb replied calmly; "I didn't notice." And indeed she did not notice, even though she saw. Barb had not yet used language which "uncovered" the images before her eyes to build and access the images that would allow her to drive safely.

Though she had never thought much about it before, Barb's mother realized that driving is in many ways a spatial task. According to Jeremy Campbell's theories, Barb's brain was capable of storing and connecting great amounts of information; her learning disability kept her from accessing it.

Carol Stockdale, a learning-disabilities specialist who had worked with Barb, suggested several strategies for conquering the problem. Barb walked around the car, touching it and measuring it against herself to see how big it was, all the time having a conversation with herself that translated the spatial into verbal dimensions. She went back to the country road near her home to look at the lines that marked the road and to touch the road and the gravel on the shoulder of the road and to say, "These are the lines that mark the lane, and these are the rocks that mark the side where I do not want to drive." As she found her way to all of her usual spots — the store, the school, the hardware store — she developed an internal conversation: "Turn right at the Exxon sign; turn left at the blue house on the corner."

Navigating through Space

And so Barb learned to use verbal clues to navigate through space. Understanding how to learn to drive gave Barb insight into conquering all kinds of spatial problems. Although she continued to have difficulty with mathematics and foreign language in high school, her ability to write academic papers about topics in her language-based academic courses — history, literature, and art history — continued to improve.

When Barb went to college, she needed help with kinds of structures that were new to her, and she needed specific models to understand the shapes of analytical papers particular to certain courses. She also needed these models translated into language. For Barb, looking at something was not seeing it, at least not until she had shaped and refined the image with language.

More and more confident of her ability to know the world through language, Barb was increasingly comfortable with difficult ideas, for instance, in her college philosophy class: "Plato uses serval [sic] arguments to prove the existence of the forms: the first argument occurs in the Meno when Socrates shows that learning is merely a recollection of previous knowledge of forms by questioning a slave boy about the Pythagorean theorem." Despite the misplaced letter in the word "several," and the misplaced first phrase, the sentence involves sophisticated content communicated in an equally sophisticated sentence structure. This sentence is not the work of a basic writer or a person unable to deal with the intellectual challenges of higher education. Still, because of her difficulty accessing spatial information, Barb needed help with organization, mechanics, and new kinds of writing tasks.[3]

The Role of the Writing Center

Although learning-disabled students come to the writing center with a variety of special needs, they have one thing in common: they need more specific help than other students.

Often writing center directors do not know what kind of a learning disability the student has, but because the spatial systems and language systems overlap and act reciprocally, students who are dyslexic and students who are spatially impaired may demonstrate many of the same problems with spelling, grammar, development, and organization.[4] Therefore, they will need similar kinds of assistance.

By changing the picture of the writing conference, the writing center director can ensure that learning-disabled students, no matter what the disability, are being appropriately accommodated. The writing advisors still need to be collaborators, but they also may need to help the students retrieve information and shape an image of the product. They may be called upon to demonstrate organization or to model a thesis sentence when the students cannot imagine what one might look like. The advisors may have to help the students call up detail in ways that would be inappropriate for the average learner. They may need to help with the physical production of texts. And they may need to help with correcting mechanics when the papers are in their final stages.

Paradoxically, and at the same time, the writing advisor must help the students be independent through self-cuing; creating a dependent atmosphere does not foster the students' ability to cope, does not develop the students' self-esteem, and does not help the students become better writers. The writing advisor must treat learning disabled persons as the intelligent, resourceful persons they are. Conferences without respect and understanding are seldom successful.

Prewriting

Many of the discovery techniques commonly used in the composition class and in the writing center may not be productive for students with learning disabilities because, though these students may have the information, they may have no way to access it. The picture of the eager student freewriting to discover ideas needs to be amended when one works with learning-disabled students. Freewriting is almost impossible for most because they do not know, and can't imagine, what to write. Students with language retrieval problems may not be able to call up any words at all to put on the paper. This holds true for students with either spatial impairments or language difficulties.

For learning-disabled students, freewriting leads from one generalization to another or from one specific to another. Because they do not see the relationship between the specific and the general, without intervention they are locked in a non-productive cycle, unable to succeed unless it is by accident. And if they do succeed by accident, they do not understand their success. According to Carol Stockdale at Another Door to Learning, many learning disabled students have no way of intentionally creating order.

Freewriting is also frustrating for persons who are learning disabled because it requires them to write without knowing where they are going. Just as Barb had trouble understanding the road, other learning-disabled students need to know where they are going so they will know when they get there. Unable to recognize what is relevant and what is not, they find the freewriting an exercise in futility, while other students may find it a way to create knowledge.

In the writing center, directed conversation can take the place of freewriting. Because these students have trouble accessing what they know, they are unlikely to realize they know great amounts of information. Here, the writing advisor plays an important role. Nowhere else on most campuses can writers find an individual who will ask the leading question that can unlock trapped information.

In some cases, the writing advisor may need to ask students like Barb specific, seemingly obvious questions to help them unlock the ideas in their minds and then take notes for them as they generate ideas for their papers. In essence the writing advisor is helping them see the plastic wrap.

Here is an example of a writing conference that respects the student's intelligence and at the same time helps him gain access to what he knows, and helps him find an organizational pattern for it.

> *Writing Advisor:* Hi David, how are you? Have a seat.
> *David:* Not good. I have another paper to write for my Intro to Fiction class.
> *Writing Advisor:* Hmmm, you did well on your last paper, didn't you?
> *David:* Yes, but this time I don't have anything to write about.
> *Writing Advisor:* Now just think back to that first paper. As I recall, you didn't have a topic for that one either the first time we talked.
> *David:* I guess you're right, but this time I really don't know what to write about.

The writing advisor knows that David has a learning disability. Understanding the brain as Jeremy Campbell explains it, as the great storehouse of knowledge, she suspects that David knows a great deal about the potential topic; she knows she will need to help David gain access to the tremendous information he does have.

> *Writing Advisor:* What is the assignment?
> *David:* To write a 3–4 page paper about *The Great Gatsby.*
> *Writing Advisor:* David, I know you're worried about this paper, but I also know from the last paper we talked about how smart you are and how much you actually know. So let's just chat for a few minutes about the book without worrying about the paper.

The writing advisor turns her chair toward David and takes off her glasses. She realizes that despite David's high scores on standard I.Q. tests and good study habits many of his teachers have considered him "slow," careless, or lazy. She wants to be sure she treats him as the intelligent person he is. She begins with the obvious questions that will help him focus on the book and what he knows.

> *Writing Advisor:* Who wrote *The Great Gatsby?*
> *David:* F. Scott Fitzgerald. He was married to Zelda. And he also wrote *Tender Is the Night.* Some people think he stole his stories from Zelda's journals. Don't you think that's right?
> *Writing Advisor:* I do think it's "right." I did know she had a big influence on him. . . .
> *David:* I mean he was drunk a lot and Zelda was the one who was writing all this stuff about their life. It's not fair.
> *Writing Advisor:* I agree. This whole idea of fairness . . . was there anything in *Gatsby* that wasn't fair?
> *David:* Yes, I don't think Tom was fair in the way he treated Daisy. He had an affair and he lied to her. Gatsby wasn't all that good either. He made his money illegally.
> *Writing Advisor:* Do you think that was fair?
> *David:* I guess not, at least not for the people he took advantage of.
> *Writing Advisor:* I wonder if a word like "honesty" or "integrity" might help get at what we're talking about.
> *David:* "Integrity," that's it.

When the writing advisor saw David lean forward, his eyes bright, she knew it was time to write something down. She took out a piece of paper and a pencil, wrote "integrity" in the middle of the page and showed it to David. She continues to take notes so that David can work at connecting the information without worrying about the physical production of text.

> *Writing Advisor:* Tell me who has it and who doesn't.
> *David:* Tom doesn't and Gatsby doesn't. [The writing advisor wrote "Tom" on the left side of the page and "Gatsby" under it and connected each word to "integrity" with a line.]
> *Writing Advisor:* Tell me why you don't think they have integrity.

David recounted example after example and the tutor noted each one under the appropriate name. As he talked, David included other characters and decided whether each had integrity or not and gave appropriate examples. In each case the tutor noted the information David produced and drew lines around similar information.

> *Writing Advisor:* This is going to be a wonderful paper. Can you see the development taking shape? Look at the connections you've made.
> *David:* Yes, but I'm not sure how to start the introduction.

Writing Advisor: Well, what kinds of things will your reader need to know in order to follow you through the paper?

By the time David had listed the kinds of things that he would include in the introduction, almost an hour had passed. The writing advisor wanted to conclude the session on a reassuring note, and she wanted David to know that he could teach himself to self-cue.

Writing Advisor: David, you know so much about your topic, and you have really good ideas. All I did was ask you questions. Eventually you'll be able to ask yourself those same questions. But now, why don't you do some writing, and then we'll have another appointment, if you like, to look at transitions, mechanics, and those sorts of things. It's fun seeing the connections in your mind unfold.

David: I think I can write a draft now. Will you be able to help me with spelling later in the week?

Writing Advisor: Sure, I'll see you when the draft is done, and we'll look at all kinds of things.

Because the act of calling up the words and getting them onto paper is so difficult for some learning-disabled students, the student may be unable to concentrate on the ideas and instead only focuses on the production of text. The writing advisor may need to do the typing or the drafting so the student is free to concentrate on answering the fairly specific, sometimes leading, questions proposed by the writing advisor. The writing advisor will know when to do the typing by asking the student, "Would you like me to record so you can work on generating the words?"

Organization

Even after generating a page or two of material, students may still not be able to distinguish the important information from the supporting detail. Again writing advisors should understand that they must help the student over or around the problem. The advisors will probably say what they think is the most important element; once they say it, the students may be able to agree or disagree even though they cannot invent or articulate the idea on their own. The writing advisors might draw a map of the ideas and support for the student, or color-code the information to help with organization. The writing advisors should always be doing and saying at the same time. With learning-disabled students, just pointing seldom helps.

The writing advisor might need to model a thesis sentence for the student, asking simple questions like "What is your paper about?" "Rice," the student replies. "What about rice?" Students are often delighted and surprised when they come up with the single statement that will set the paper spinning.

The advisor may need to be just as explicit about the paper's development: "What is your first point going to be?" As the student responds, the advisor takes down the information, and then asks, "And what is your second point?" "And your third?" Showing students how to create an overview of the information and then teaching them how to categorize information will help the students manage the spatial qualities of organization.

Simply using a model like the five-paragraph essay to teach organization is unlikely to produce successful writing. Since structure grows out of content, the students may be successful one time with a five-paragraph essay, but when they try to apply the formula the next time, the formula may not work. They may be further hindered by being unable to let go of the formula or image.

A student like Barb may not be able to see paragraph breaks until the writing advisor says, "Notice how long this paragraph is," while at the same time pointing to the too-long paragraph. She may even need to say, "This is a paragraph." But the instant the advisor points it out, Barb will say, "Well, I know that." And after saying so, she does indeed know it.

Proofreading and Editing

Frank Smith (1982) makes the distinction between composition and transcription, between the composing of thought and the mechanics of getting the language down on paper according to certain conventions. Spelling and punctuation need to be done with the students so that they feel part of the process; most importantly, the editing must be specific and hands-on and must involve detailed explanations of what the advisor is doing. The writing advisor cannot expect the students to make the changes based on a rule or principle. The explanation must be specific, and it may need to be written as well as said: "Look at the beginning of this sentence. You have five words before your subject. How about a comma?" Students may agree that something is so, but they may be unable to hold the thought in their minds or recall it later.

Encouraging students to be independent through the use of a spell checker and grammar checker is essential, but the writing advisor may need to sit at the computer with students explaining how it works and its limitations. Telling students to put text through a spell check is seldom enough. The advisor may need to read the paper aloud to the students so they can catch errors: a final proofreading by the writing advisor is also appropriate for the learning-disabled students because these students may not be able to see the mistakes until they are pointed out to them.

Wheelchair-bound students can get to the third floor, but they may not be able to take the stairs. Their only routes are the elevator or the ramp. It's not that students with a learning disability can't get it, it's that they can't get it the same way the normal learner can.

Other Kinds of Organization That Affect Writing

Learning-disabled students sometimes have as much trouble coping with the organization of the writing and research time as they do with the organization of the text. Writing advisors can help by showing the students how to use a study planning sheet that contains small but regular accomplishments, and which will lead to the accomplishment of a larger task. It is not enough to tell students to do it; the writing advisors need to demonstrate the strategy, especially the first time. They should also ask the students to refer to the list on a regular basis; the markers of accomplishment need to be tangible.

Social Interaction

Many, but not all, learning-disabled students have trouble in social situations. A visit to the writing center may be one of these social situations. The student's behavior may be inappropriate: he interrupts another conversation, she stands too close or talks too much. Many people with learning disabilities are unable to "read" the nonverbal behavior of others. So even if the writing advisor frowns or looks away, the inappropriate behavior continues. Being explicit but positive will help the individual change this behavior: "Marty, please stop talking; I have something important to tell you." "Glad to see you, Sara. I'll sit here; you sit across from me; that will be a comfortable distance. I'll be ready to talk to you in a minute."

Despite the need for specific instructions and clear questions, the writing advisor must remain positive and encouraging. Often teachers and others misunderstand learning disabilities and accuse students of being lazy or dumb. As a result, college students with learning disabilities often have low self-esteem and may be defensive or uncertain of their own academic ability. Writing advisors can make a major contribution to a learning-disabled student's success if they are positive, encouraging, and specific about the writing, the revision, and the writing process.

Working with these students in the writing center is sometimes difficult because it means modifying or changing the usual guidelines, and it may mean more and longer appointments, for instance, appointments that last an hour instead of a half hour, and a writing advisor may need to proofread. Writing centers may need to change the rules and policies that govern these sessions and change the training that staff receive. But the students have a right to services, and writing centers have a responsibility to help learning-disabled students succeed.[5] Writing centers have always been places that help students reach their full potential, and this philosophy should extend to students with learning disabilities.

Most learning-disabled students need more support and help rather than less. And writing centers can provide that assistance. For these students, writing center professionals need a new picture of the writing conference that includes the writing advisor's becoming more directly involved in the process and the product. With adequate help and support, students with a learning disability can produce better papers, and they can also become better writers.

Notes

[1] At the October 1991 meeting of the International Conference on Learning Disabilities, the debate over the left brain–right brain model continued in the conference sessions. The

debate is interesting in that writing center professionals often use the model to explain parts of the composing process.

[2] The same law that defines a learning disability guarantees the rights of the learning-disabled person. It is just as illegal to discriminate against a learning-disabled person as it is to discriminate against a person of an ethnic minority or a person with a physical disability. Recently a professor at the University of California Berkeley refused to accommodate a student's request for untimed tests. The student filed suit, and the faculty member was required to pay monetary damages to the student. Faculty members and institutions can be held accountable for blatant discrimination. (Heyward).

[3] Barb's is not an unusual case. As the diagnosis of learning disabilities has improved, students can be helped sooner and can be taught compensatory strategies that lead to success in high school as well as in college. In 1978 when statistics on learning disabilities were first kept, 2.6 percent of all freshmen reported having a disability. In 1988, it was 6 percent. In ten years of record keeping, the number had more than doubled. Still, many experts in the field believe that 6 percent is much too low and the number of learning disabled students is actually between 10 and 20 percent. Many cases have gone undetected.

[4] Because problems with spelling and mechanics are the easiest to recognize and fix, many educators have believed that these are the only problems that learning-disabled students have with writing. But a University of Connecticut study showed that 51 percent of the students had trouble with organization compared to 24 percent who had trouble with proofreading (McGuire, Hall, Litt).

[5] In 1993, the American Disabilities Act (ADA), which makes discrimination against a learning-disabled person illegal, became law.

References

Bergland, Richard. 1985. *Fabric of Mind.* New York: Penguin.

Brinkerhoff, Loring. 1991. "Critical Issues in LD College Programming for Students with Learning Disabilities." International Conference on Learning Disabilities. Minneapolis, MN: October 11.

Campbell, Jeremy. 1989. *The Improbable Machine.* New York: Simon & Schuster.

Hammill, Donald D., James E. Leigh, Gaye McNutt, and Stephen C. Larsen. 1981. "A New Definition of Learning Disabilities." *Learning Disability Quarterly* 4.4, 336–42.

Heyward, Lawton & Associates, ed. 1992. *Association on Handicapped Student Service Programs in Postsecondary Education Disability Accommodation Digest* 1.2, 6.

Heyward, Salome. 1991. "Provision of Academic Accommodations." *Postsecondary LD Network News* 12, 7.

Levy, Nancy R., and Michael S. Rosenberg. 1990. "Strategies for Improving the Written Expression of Students with Learning Disabilities." *LD Forum* 16.1, 23–26.

Lipp, Janice. 1991. "Turning Problems into Opportunities." *Another Door to Learning Newsletter,* 1–3.

Longo, Judith. 1988. "The Learning Disabled: Challenge to Postsecondary Institutions." *Journal of Developmental Education* 11.3, 10–12.

Lovitt, Thomas. 1989. *Introduction to Learning Disabilities.* Needham Heights, MA: Allyn and Bacon.

McGuire, Joan. 1991. "Access and Eligibility." International Conference on Learning Disabilities. Minneapolis, MN: October 11.

McGuire, Joan, Debora Hall, and A. Vivienne Litt. 1991. "A Field-Based Study of the Direct Service Needs of College Students with Learning Disabilities." *Journal of College Student Development* 32, 101–108.

National Clearinghouse on Postsecondary Education for Individuals with Handicaps 8.2 (1989), 4.

Philosophy take-home exam. Smith College, 1991.

"The Rehabilitation Act of 1971." 1977, May 4. *Federal Register,* 93–112.

Schwartz, Judy. 1991. Personal interview. October 13.

Schwenn, John. 1991. "Stereotyped Football Players: Poor Students or Undiagnosed Learning Disabilities?" International Conference on Learning Disabilities, Minneapolis, MN: October 12.

Smith, Frank. 1982. *Writing and the Writers.* Hillsdale, NJ: Lawrence Erlbaum Associates.

Stockdale, Carol. 1991. Personal interview. October 13.

U.S. Congress, 1969. *Children with Specific Learning Disabilities Act of 1969.* Washington, D.C.: U.S. Government Printing Office.

Woodcock, Richard, and M. Bonner Johnson. 1989. *Woodcock-Johnson Tests of Achievement.* Allen, TX: Teaching Resources.

Centering in the Borderlands:
Lessons from Hispanic Student Writers

Beatrice Mendez Newman

UNIVERSITY OF TEXAS – PAN AMERICAN

Based on experience gained as a student, graduate student, and faculty member in universities along the United States–Mexico border, Beatrice Mendez Newman takes a close look at how writing centers can help Hispanic students achieve academic success. Hispanic students at "borderlands" institutions often find themselves torn by the conflicting demands of and affiliations to both home and institutional cultures. As Newman says, "When family upbringing, social expectations, acknowledgement of authority, and marginal entry into a traditional academic environment come together in the university setting, Hispanic students find themselves in antagonistic relationships with traditional institutional structures. . . ." Too often, the result of these antagonistic relationships is students' failure, withdrawal from the university, or marginal success. As institutional borderlands themselves, writing centers offer Hispanic students struggling to both retain their cultural identity and succeed at the university "a welcome contrast to the authoritative environments of the traditional classroom and the instructor's office." In this article, which first appeared in The Writing Center Journal *in 2003, Newman examines specific challenges Hispanic students face as writers of English and suggests how tutors can help them meet these challenges. Tutors who seek to help Hispanic students become better writers, she says, may have to abandon the traditional nondirective approach to tutoring and help students "construct sentences in a more appropriate form."*

> Things fall apart; the center cannot hold;
> Mere anarchy is loosed upon the world.
> — *William Butler Yeats, "The Second Coming"*

As a metaphor for writing center work, carnival frames this work as, to bor-
row Susan Miller's words, a "relation between high and low discourses,"
in this case, between frequently marginalized writing centers and the larger
university or academic "structures" that contain — and depend on — these
centers.

– Angela Petit

In Chapter 1 of *Noise from the Writing Center*, Elizabeth Boquet examines the
metaphors used in reference to writing centers — clinic, laboratory, center,
workshop — and connects these metaphors to perceptions of the writing center's place in the institution. Her own metaphor, noise, situates the writing
center as a vibrant component of the institution with the capacity for having a
significant impact on a student's journey through the academy. In drawing
connections among the writing center's label, locale, and function, Boquet
continues the discussion begun in Nancy Grimm's *Good Intentions: Writing
Center Work for Postmodern Times*. For Grimm, the writing center is far more
than a campus location and an institutional unit: she sees the writing center as
an agent for institutional change particularly in the institution's response to
difference, to alternative discourses, and to non-mainstream literacy. Angela
Petit's metaphor — the writing center as carnival where "normal rules, authorities, and boundaries do not disappear but are temporarily relaxed or inverted"
(43) — fits comfortably with Grimm's and Boquet's observations about the
apparent disruption that writing centers create for institutional authority.
Boquet, Grimm, and Petit focus our attention on the way that writing centers
work both as partners and as "adversaries" to traditional institutional structures particularly in our work with students who in any way deviate from the
"norm." Such students could be non-traditional, non-mainstream, foreign,
at-risk, disabled, or ethnically and linguistically different from the "typical"
(competently and confidently literate, well-prepared) student. Yeats' coup-
let provides the metaphor I would like to adapt for my discussion of the way
that writing centers help institutions respond to a particular type of non-
mainstream student: the Hispanic student at borderlands institutions, institutions on the U.S.–Mexican border in California, Arizona, New Mexico, and
Texas.[1] Boquet writes about noise, Petit about carnival, Grimm about agency
— types of disruptions in the institutional status quo that cast the writing
center as a challenge to the norm, as an inducer of a sort of institutional
"anarchy." For the students I will focus on in this discussion, usual types of
institutional "centers" — the classroom, the professor's office, advisors, etc. —
do not "hold." In fact, as these writers have pointed out, the very component
that disrupts institutional norms — the writing center — is what helps borderlands Hispanic students center themselves in the institution.

Writing center scholarship has examined interactions with several types
of non-mainstream students — ESL students, learning disabled students,
physically disabled students, members of non-Anglo ethnic groups, and
non-traditional students (Edlund; Neff-Lippman; DiPardo; Powers; Neff;

Friedlander; Powers; Gardner, Lyman, and McLean). Little has been written, however, about Hispanic students and writing centers, and nothing has been written about Hispanic students at writing centers in borderlands institutions. These students fit neither the traditional ESL nor non-traditional student definition,[2] yet they pose specific challenges to writing center workers at borderlands institutions and at institutions in other parts of the country where these students are recruited in an effort to diversify student bodies. For borderlands Hispanic students — whether they attend borderlands institutions or institutions in other parts of the country — the writing center offers, in a twist of Yeats' phrase, a "center that holds," an agency that helps them understand and join in the conversation of the academy.

Statistics: Hispanic Student Populations at Borderlands Institutions

Given the recently released U.S. Census Bureau figures showing that Hispanics are now the nation's largest minority group (numbering 37 million compared to 36.2 million African-Americans [Clemetson; U.S. Census Bureau]), this is an appropriate time to examine how writing centers respond to the special educational needs of Hispanic students. There are no "historically Hispanic" institutions in the United States (as there are historically Black institutions); instead, institutions with Hispanic student enrollments of 25% or more are designated by the U.S. Department of Education as "Hispanic-serving" institutions (National Center for Education Statistics, "Completions"). My comments and observations are based on my experiences with students at The University of Texas–Pan American, whose 89% Hispanic enrollment (10,950 Hispanic students in a 12,569-member student body) positions it at the top of four-year, Hispanic-serving borderlands institutions.[3] The University of Texas–El Paso, another borderlands institution, stands just below UTPA with a 77% Hispanic enrollment, 10,005 Hispanic students in a 14,695-member student body (National Center for Education Statistics, "Completions").

An important aspect of my ability to conduct a discussion on Hispanic students at borderlands institutions is the fact that I am Hispanic: I grew up in a borderlands area, attended a borderlands institution for my undergraduate work, and, after venturing into areas beyond the borderlands for my graduate degrees, I have been privileged with opportunities to work with students who remind me of myself when I was their age. My interpretation of the academic conduct of Hispanic borderlands students is based on first-hand, personal experience reinforced by years of watching students work as hard as I did — at their age — to find a place in academia.

Hispanic students at borderlands institutions have been overlooked in part because many of the instructional and support staff at such institutions simply do not know enough about these students to understand how their academic experiences are affected by home-life, culture, and limited fluency in the institution's dominant language. The students at the center of this article are of Mexican descent (at least one parent is of Mexican origin; their strong cultural and familial ties "interfere" with academic expectations and situate them in borderland institutions within driving distance of their homes rather than at institutions far removed from their home environment). Because they do not leave their homes and families to attend college, the family creates a special type of on-going "interference" with their assimilation into the academy. (Let me provide an example: I have a student in one of my classes right now who missed three consecutive classes recently. He told me, although I did not ask him the reason for his absences, that his grandmother was in the hospital and, since his mother does not drive, he took care of getting his mother to and from the hospital. For Hispanic students, such situations do not create a dilemma; when family calls, the call must be answered regardless of academic obligations. A professor unfamiliar with Hispanic culture might see this behavior as academically irresponsible and see the family connection as "interference" in the quest for academic success when in fact the behavior is a manifestation of the student's identification with family.) Because their parents have minimal levels of education, only functional literacy in Spanish and English, and literally no urgency to assimilate into the American culture, borderlands Hispanic children acquire neither English nor Spanish at a level of competence that could classify them as literate in either language.

For many borderlands students, literacy in English develops in school settings and is not reinforced in homes where grandparents, parents, other relatives, and family friends speak some version of border Spanish; where books, newspapers, and other reading materials are rare; and where family comes above everything else — including school attendance and school work. Thus, when these students arrive at borderlands institutions, they lack the literacy skills to succeed in college, and because they are still tethered to families with whom they continue to live (as opposed to moving into the far-from-home-on-campus-dorm-living-environment), they are unable to acculturate themselves into university life. Instead, they feel the pull of every family situation and/or crisis far more urgently than they feel the responsibility of showing up in class or completing class assignments.

An added wrinkle in the academic tapestry is the fact that national statistics about teenage moms are realities in our borderlands university classrooms. It is not at all unusual at my institution for at least one quarter of the 18–20 year-olds in freshman classes to be parents (usually single parents) of one or more children. So, whether the family "interference" comes from parents and siblings or from their own children, many students at borderlands institutions cannot privilege education above family responsibility. Acknowledging this situation does not require that we approve of it; we just need to understand that family is a significant disruption in a borderland student's attempt to achieve a college education.

The aggressively bicultural ambience of borderlands communities cancels the pragmatic effectiveness of the "total immersion" approach to assimilating into a different/"dominant" culture. Borderlands businesses require employees who regularly interact with customers to speak Spanish and English. Service workers are almost exclusively Mexican citizens or Hispanic Americans with little or no knowledge of English. (Those of us who live on the border know that we must be proficient enough in Spanish to deal with plumbers, waiters and waitresses, gardeners, carpenters, and other workers on whom we rely daily.) But the mix of cultures seems to work politically, socially, and economically. U.S. borderlands communities celebrate Mexican holidays like Cinco de Mayo (May 5, the day Mexican soldiers overthrew Maximillian's French forces), Diez y Seis de Septiembre (September 16, Mexican Independence Day), and Día de los Muertos (November 1, Day of the Dead). Easter, Christmas, and New Year's take on Hispanic touches in borderlands communities, with *cascarónes* (dyed egg shells filled with confetti) being as popular as traditional hard-boiled Easter eggs; *luminarias* (small paper bags — or these days, empty milk jugs — partly filled with sand to hold lit candles) lining sidewalks at Christmas; and *buñuelos* (paper thin, fried pastries dusted with sugar and cinnamon) more common than black-eyed peas on New Year's Day.

Then there are social expectations and regulations. Mexican parents teach their children to be extremely respectful of authority: grandparents, parents, and other authority figures are always addressed in the formal second person (*usted* — roughly equivalent to addressing an authority figure as "Sir" or "Ma'am"). Girls are expected to cater to male relatives, to observe curfews, and to learn to do housework so that they can take care of a husband when the time comes. In many Hispanic borderland families, a high school education is considered a terminal degree, and going on to college is viewed as delayed entry into the workforce. Hispanic young people are expected to contribute to the household; when they have jobs, part of their salary goes into the family *coffers,* no questions asked. When Hispanic students from lower socioeconomic homes enroll in college, financial support from the family is limited or non-existent.

It is out of this milieu that Hispanic students at borderlands institutions emerge, and it necessarily impacts their ability to integrate themselves successfully into the institutional setting. This is where the writing center comes in — not as a solution to all the problems of Hispanic borderlands students but as an agent of access to the institution and to the avenues of success and acceptance an institution of higher education represents.

Lessons from Hispanic Students: Rosa, Dahlia, and Leo

In many ways, writing centers at borderlands institutions provide the "center" that Hispanic students need in order to hold on to the institution. Borderlands Hispanic students, like non-traditional, non-mainstream students at universities and colleges throughout the country, lack strategies for negotiating an institutional environment dominated by traditional mainstream authority, a lack of preparedness exacerbated by literacy problems and by insufficient support mechanisms from the institution. Although addressing the problems of non-traditional students in writing centers. Eric Cardner's observation that "to lots of educators [non-traditional students] have been invisible" (7) aptly describes the presence of the Hispanic student in borderlands institutions, an invisibility sustained by institutional reluctance (?), inability (?), failure (?) to adapt traditional educational practices to the needs of changing student populations.

Narratives about specific non-mainstream students have shown writing center workers how we can better serve our clients by listening and noting the problems they face as they try to integrate themselves into the institution (DiPardo's Fannie, Grimm's Joe, Boquet's Todd ["Disciplinary Action"]). I would like to add the voices of some of my writing center students to Fannie's, Joe's, and Todd's voices. Rosa, Dahlia, and Leo — students with whom I worked at my writing center — are excellent representative examples of how a writing center at a borderlands institution can help Hispanic students position themselves in the institution when traditional means for such centering have proved ineffective. Rosa's. Dahlia's, and Leo's stories show how writing centers can be advocates of students whose voices are ignored (or not even heard) by traditional institutional entities.

Rosa Rosa brought me graded Freshman English essays that included error counts (30 in one essay, 31 in another, 33 in the next, etc.) and sarcastic comments — "Don't you know how to write a thesis???" — but never any encouraging comments about what she was doing right or how to improve her next essay. Despite my insistence that she arrange a conference with her instructor, she refused to approach him. To a traditional instructor. Rosa was resistant to strategies intended to foster communication between student and professor. To a writing center director who works daily with students with strong ties to their Hispanic culture, Rosa was acting in the way dictated by her culture: she had to accept her authoritative instructor's judgment about her writing even though she knew that her writing was far more competent than the steady stream of D's indicated.

Working with Rosa required far more than knowing how to help her become a better writer. Her papers had numerous language use errors but none which significantly interfered with her message. As I looked over the graded papers she brought me, I could tell that the instructor had violated all principles of effective response to student writing. Instead of using his comments to "guide learning," he was offering snide comments and apparently demonstrating his prowess as an error-hunter (Lindemann 230). Writing in *Response to Student Writing*, Sarah Warshauer Freedman points out that response to student writing should be "collaborative problem-solving" with the responder guiding the student writer toward increased competence and toward independence from the instructor/responder (7). For Rosa, her instructor's response was making her increasingly dependent, not on her instructor but on writing center tutors, and she was losing confidence in her writing competence.

My response to Rosa was two-fold: first, I worked with her to identify areas of competence in her writing. Rosa's instructor had failed to acknowledge to what extent she had fulfilled the requirements of the assignment. Every one of Rosa's papers did in fact have a thesis: her instructor required that she underline the thesis and topic sentences in every essay. And, objectively, I could point out to her that every thesis statement, every topic sentence met the requirements of such structures. All of her essays were appropriately and effectively developed. The only recurring problems were language use and grammar errors that stemmed from her Spanish language background, and these relatively superficial errors became the focus of the instructor's evaluation. When Rosa worked in the writing center with plenty of time to produce multiple drafts, she could write effectively. However, her instructor required that all essays be written in class in a 55-minute period; unfortunately, he did not allow students to work from a draft. By focusing on the errors, her instructor had caused Rosa to feel not incompetent but hopeless: she knew that her classroom instructor would never acknowledge that she had any understanding of essay format, unity, voice, development, or audience awareness since all he noticed was the errors.

The second part of my response to Rosa dealt with training my tutors to handle similar situations. Clearly, Rosa needed much more than "help with commas." So I held a training session in which I showed tutors how to help students like Rosa, whose instructors had failed to use effective response strategies, to recognize what works in their writing. While tutors cannot possibly respond the way instructors do to student writing, we can recognize that tutoring is in fact a type of response. To move students toward independence as writers, we need to inspire confidence in them about their own writing. Thus, saying, "I see you've written a thesis that clearly states your topic and that asserts a point you can defend throughout the paper" may work better than saying, "Can you show me where your thesis is?" The declarative statement shows the insecure student writer that we recognize his/her competence; the question suggests that there might not be a thesis in the paper, and even if the student thinks he/she wrote a thesis, the question leads to second guessing and to diminishing confidence.

I did not help Rosa earn higher grades in freshman English, but I did serve as a centering mechanism for her: by the end of the semester, she realized that her impending failure in freshman English did not mean she was a failure as a writer or as a student. The following semester she came back, smiling and confident, to tell me how well she was doing in her second attempt at freshman English. I had advised her to enroll in a class conducted in a computer lab where the instructor conferenced with students as they worked and where multiple drafts and peer conferencing defined the approach to writing.

Dahlia Dahlia did attempt a student-teacher conference but could not find her political science professor during his office hours. When she lingered after class to speak to him, she was dismissed with unspecific, unsubstantiated encouragement — "Don't worry; you'll do all right" — despite the consistent low C's on her essays. As a young Hispanic woman, Dahlia's academic involvement was regulated by her husband's work schedule and by the demands of her toddler, so she had very limited opportunity to seek out her instructor for individual conferencing. Although our writing center does not have synchronous conferencing or any type of formalized, online conferencing, I encouraged her to send me her drafts via email. We exchanged emails throughout the semester following several visits to the writing center: she sent me her drafts; I embedded comments in her text designed to direct her toward her instructor's expectations and focused on helping her achieve clarity and logic in her writing. Working with Dahlia "after hours" on my own time called for a type of disruption: because of her deadlines and family responsibilities, I had to make time for email tutoring late at night or very early in the morning while I was at home. She did not consult me as she finalized her last essay for this class; instead, she sent me an email message saying she felt good about her writing now and could complete the paper on her own.

Dahlia's role as a mother and wife obviously superseded her role as student, but a student like Dahlia must be able to find an entity somewhere on campus that does not penalize or criticize her for that choice. She came to our writing center because her professor was inaccessible during his posted office hours, because his written evaluation of her writing did not match his expressed optimism regarding her chances for success, and because she genuinely wanted to improve her writing. In working with Dahlia, I again had to compensate for what the instructor failed to do. Like Rosa, Dahlia's "writing problems" extended to areas beyond her writing: she felt that her professor's inaccessibility was hurting her chances for success in that course. Not only did contact with our writing center help her improve as a writer, it also helped her develop confidence as a student in the institution.

Leo Leo was writing a research paper on the death penalty. His freshman English instructor had turned the pedagogically powerful individual conference into an opportunity for disparaging his students' efforts. Leo told me that as he and about five other students waited in the hall for their research paper conferences, he grew increasingly nervous: "We could hear him, and all he was telling the students was how bad the papers were." He showed up at the writing center convinced his paper was worthless. With Leo, my task was to help him understand what his instructor meant by a lack of coherence as well as to help him develop confidence as a writer. (At my first session with Leo, he was despondent over his inability to please his instructor.) Unlike Rosa, Leo did go back to his instructor, but he came back to the writing center still puzzled about what was wrong with his paper. Initially, I took a non-directive approach: I asked Leo what he wanted to say about the death penalty, how he could back up his position, what evidence he had to support it, etc. Then I ventured into more directive tutoring: I had him write a new outline that began with a thesis statement (elicited after I pointedly asked him to state in one sentence the most important thing he wanted to say about the death penalty) supported by several sections that the instructor would recognize as evidence for the thesis.

Leo was one of many students with whom I've worked who need a somewhat "visual deconstruction" of the writing they have produced. After he wrote his outline, I sat at a computer with him and showed him how to use the highlight feature on Microsoft Word to match what he had written to specific sections of his outline. For example, I helped him find everything related to death row inmates who were later proved innocent, and I had him computer highlight all those sentences in one color. Everything related to the death penalty in other countries was highlighted in a different color, etc., etc. By the time our conference ended. Leo thoroughly understood that "lack of coherence" was not an insurmountable problem (plus he had a very colorful draft!). I helped him see his draft as a text that was disorganized but which could be "fixed" with the cut-and-paste editing tools. The despondence with which he had entered the writing center was replaced with enthusiasm to cut and paste sections of his text to achieve coherence.

In response to my experience with Leo, I devoted a tutor-training session to recognizing the features of effective writing (significance, unity, clarity, economy of language, grammatical acceptability, vigor, and authentic voice) as presented in Maxine Hairston's *Successful Writing* (7–15). I taught our tutors how to talk about global writing concerns with clients and how to "salvage" papers such as Leo's — in other words, to recognize what works in the paper and to give the clients terminology for discussing their writing.

At the end of the semester, I received this email message from Leo:

> This is Leo, the guy you helped out with the death penalty paper. Just writing to say thanks and to tell you how I did. I was sort of disappointed because I got an 80, and that's because he had given me a 70 but changed it, I guess he knew how hard I worked on it. I was expecting like an 85 or 90 but not an 80. He wrote some comments I can't even understand. Thanx A lot I appreciate it.

Through his visits to the writing center, Leo learned more than how to organize his material. Leo's message suggests he approached his instructor ("he had given me a 70 but changed it") and negotiated a higher grade for his essay because he felt confident about the work he had produced, a confidence which, I believe, he developed as a result of his contact with the writing center.

Rosa, Dahlia, and Leo are evidence that, at borderlands institutions, our contacts with Hispanic students in the writing center extend far beyond their writing competence. Although they show up at the writing center to improve their writing ("I just need help with my commas"), before long, their conversations turn into conversations about instructors that seem oblivious to the academic barriers Hispanic borderlands students face. In the process of working with their writing, we help students learn to negotiate those academic barriers. Although they have been allowed entry into the institution, they lack strategies and resources for ensuring their academic success.

When family upbringing, social expectations, acknowledgment of authority, and marginal entry into a traditional academic environment come together in the university setting, Hispanic students find themselves in antagonistic relationships with traditional institutional structures; in other words, they find that traditional academic centering mechanisms "will not hold." In an article that articulates the problems of Hispanic students in academia with a depth of analysis heretofore unseen in scholarly discussions of these students, Michelle Hall Kells writes:

> The failure to recognize the fine linguistic and ethnic distinctions of Mexican-origin individuals has hastened the exodus of culturally and linguistically complex students from the American educational system. Furthermore, the language attitudes, myths, and polarizing biases reflected in the college English classroom constitute a potentially alienating domain. (16)

Kells' discussion focuses on the composition classroom, but her assessment of the obstacles, lack of understanding, and student response to such problems reinforces my assertion that Hispanic students at borderlands institutions must seek alternative avenues to success once they have gained nominal entry into the institution. The "exodus . . . from the American educational system" does not have to occur if students find centering mechanisms that provide the support they need to negotiate academia successfully.

Faced with impending academic defeat, students seek the safety of a "borderland," a term that Carol Severino applies to writing centers. She writes,

> [T]he writing center's mission is a borderland one — to help students articulate the cultural and rhetorical similarities and differences they observe and confront; to help them "grapple with" or negotiate between and among intersecting and clashing cultures, languages, literacies, discourses, and disciplines; to help them decide when to follow organizational and stylistic conventions . . . and when to take risks and violate them — instead of being violated by them. (231)

"Borderland" takes on a particularly appropriate application for writing centers at institutions on the border: our students live both on the metaphorical borderland that Severino describes and on a geographical borderland (the U.S.–Mexico border) where cultural dictates significantly influence student-teacher interactions and their assimilation into the academic community.

Lisa Gonsalves' recent study of interactions between Black male students and white faculty points to some of the same issues that impact the academic experiences of Hispanic borderlands students. Gonsalves identifies interactions over student writing as "the first, and sometimes only contact between faculty and student" (437) and connects the success of such interactions to retention. This study of writing conference narratives provided by white faculty and Black male students shows how both parties' misunderstandings contribute to non-productive student-teacher interactions, misunderstandings exacerbated by cross-racial differences in communication styles. Gonsalves ends with suggestions for increasing faculty awareness of ethnic and cultural issues so as to improve students' educational experiences. However, the solution to the problem seems to rest with the faculty: what happens when institutions do not sanction initiatives to improve cross-cultural communication in student-faculty transactions? Students fail, students drop out, students have less than productive academic experiences — unless they find ways to overcome obstacles created by faculty who are non-responsive to ethnic difference.

Pedagogically, writing centers fill gaps created when Hispanic borderlands students lack the strategies and confidence to function productively in an academic environment. Students who are ill-prepared for academic life and who see teachers as "authorities" that are not to be challenged use neither conferencing nor classroom interactions productively. Even when educators try to impose the new paradigm Xin Liu Gale describes in *Teachers, Discourses, and Authority in the Postmodern Composition Classroom* — inviting student interaction through collaborative activities, through conferencing with the professor, through teaching approaches that make the professor a member of a learning community rather than the dispenser of authority — Hispanic students have difficulties participating because of their culturally-ingrained respect for authority. Hispanic students from Mexican families — in which age, experience, and position establish authority — cannot position themselves as members of a community of learners in a college classroom. On the other hand, when they sit in classrooms in which the professor chooses a traditional lecturer-listener approach, Hispanic students do not ask questions lest they be considered resistant to the teacher's authority. Neither do they approach professors during office hours, fearing that they are "disturbing" the professor during his/her "time off."

When Hispanic borderlands students show up at the writing center, they find the encouraging environment created by tutors and other staff a welcome contrast to the authoritative environments of the traditional classroom and the instructor's office. The one-on-one contact, the effort to find in their writing what is effective, the learner-centered discussion of what could be changed to improve the writing enables Hispanic borderlands students to envision themselves as members of the academic culture. In short, writing centers are places where barriers to institutional access are eliminated or at least significantly reduced: in Irene Clark's words, they are "comfortable, non-threatening places for learning" (7). When those barriers are significantly reduced — as they are at writing centers — students can concentrate on the real work of being in the academy: accessing knowledge, enhancing skills and competencies, and sustaining the quest for knowledge that originally brought them to the institution.

Writing Center Work and Hispanic Students: The Center Holds

The responsibility of guaranteeing safe passage through the institution for historically underprivileged Hispanic students should not fall solely on the shoulders of writing center workers, but I do believe that we are in a position to make that passage less turbulent, less traumatic, and less damaging. It's time to come back to all the metaphors I began with: carnival, clinic, laboratory, nois(y) site — and my metaphor: the center that can hold. The writing center is uniquely positioned to help Hispanic borderlands students find a center that enables them to "hold" on to institutional expectations, to meet institutional requirements, to exit the institution with the skills and knowledge to be productive citizens of America.

To help writing centers work as centers that hold, I offer the following guidelines for working with Hispanic students, with the caveat that even when they manage to leave the borderlands, Hispanic borderlands students retain their borderlands orientation, so these guidelines can help writing centers in all parts of the country.

Guideline 1: Recognize the types of writing produced by Hispanic borderlands students and "deconstruct" what the writer has done in order to help him/her move to higher levels of literacy. At the outset, we need to acknowledge that the writing of borderlands students is not ESL writing. These students do not fit the usual second-language acquisition paradigm, where the speaker moves gradually from the native language through interlanguages toward the target language and where the speaker — or writer — "monitors" constructions to ensure comprehensible output (Edlund 206–209; Krashen 21) because their "native" language is usually a mixture of Spanish and English that exists only in oral form. Edlund's application of Krashen's monitor is on target when the speaker metacognitively evaluates and filters output, but such awareness requires significant understanding of the grammar of both the native language and the target language. I know that when I am trying to speak in Spanish, I am very aware of the grammatical structures I am producing, of the not-quite-right accent, of the mispronunciation of certain constructions, of the significantly slower pace at which I speak compared to a native speaker — all evidence that I am using Krashen's and Edlund's monitor. However, the students I am writing about lack facility in English and Spanish; thus, there is no monitor for them. When Hispanic borderlands students start school, they are acquiring a formal language for the first time, and language use problems persist through college because of the lack of reinforcement for the new language (English) that they receive at home. (As I pointed out earlier, their parents don't read either English or Spanish publications, and Spanish, usually some version of border Spanish, is the language spoken by parents, grandparents, family friends, and the students' peers.) Thus, English, for many borderlands students, is exclusively the language of school, and because they can function economically, socially, and personally with limited mastery of

English, their motivation to become fully literate in English is low. As John Edlund explains it, "Another way to look at the issue of motivation is to say that the input must not only be comprehensible, but also socially meaningful. An individual may live and work in an environment rich in input in the second language, but if this potential input is defined as being directed toward some social group the individual does not belong to, it may not be attended to" (207). Many Hispanic borderlands students literally learn only enough English to get by in school. This should be an important consideration for us as we work with these students in our writing centers.

The errors seen in the writing of borderlands students are so numerous that they can easily overwhelm a tutor: it is easy to conclude — erroneously — that such writers know nothing about English. For example, the following excerpt from an essay written by Esteban presents challenges for writing center workers that simply do not exist when we work with students who have developed literacy in their native language and whose grammatical knowledge in that language can be used to build their literacy in English. The prompt was to describe a memorable meal:

> My mom was just putting the new roof in our house. We just had come from Illinois we were working to help my mom make some money. For she could pay the work of the persons who were going to do the new roof in our house and for she could buy all the materiel that we were going to need for the roof. It was November and it was cool almost thanksgiving day and my brothers and me decided to work for the person who was doing the roof of our house he used to give us $40 dollar per day. We knew that we were not going to have a turkey for Thanksgiving Day that year because we were going to be working. Three of my ants won a turkey each one on a raffle that they went in on the television they were giving away 48 turkeys on those day and my ants were ones of the 48 persons who won a turkeys those day. . . . My mom was going to do some eggs with beans for dinner again but my ants call my mom and told her not to do anything so we thought my mom was mad with us and she was not going to do our dinner for that night. But my brother and me were just thinking about how to go sleep with all the hungers we had and we were too tired to do something to eat. My ants finally go to the house with the turkeys we were on a room but we could smell the good of the turkey. (Newman)

This is one of those passages that evokes a dual response in a tutor: on one hand, the tutor (in this case, me) is saying to herself, "Wow! There are so many errors in this that I don't know where to begin. Can I do anything to help this writer? How do I keep from making him feel that almost every word, every phrase is an error, that his writing is worthless?" On the other hand, the tutor can get a grip and say to herself, "Okay I need to hear what the writer is trying to say even if I don't understand the 'rules' behind his writing. Esteban needs to leave our session understanding how to turn his writing into a text his instructor will understand and accept."

I read through the paper to get a sense of Esteban's rhetorical intentions and then suggested we work on structure and rhetoric first and worry about language on the next draft. I was forthright with him: I told him that he had language use errors in every sentence and that he would be demoralized if we attempted to identify every error. I showed Esteban how to build and maintain suspense for his surprise ending (the fact that his aunts had won a turkey and shared the meal with his family, which in his first draft he had given away almost immediately). I did what writing center pedagogy advocates: I praised the student for what he had accomplished (I told him it was a great story) and showed him how to make the text ready for a reader. I had him write notes in the margins of his draft to ensure that he would remember what we were saying about his writing, particularly the global aspects. I had him highlight in different colors the parts of the essay related to the problem (no money for a Thanksgiving meal), the "build up" (he and his brother were working on the roof to help their mom), the surprise ending (his aunt had won a turkey in a raffle), the description of the meal (family and friends gathered around the table on a symbolic occasion). Once he realized he could cut-and-paste chunks of his writing to achieve a more effective rhetorical order, we began addressing the language use problems, which at that point seemed relatively minor to him given his grasp of the global problems in the essay.

Esteban's essay is a "worst case scenario" for writing center workers who interact with Hispanic students. My next excerpt illustrates structures and practices common in Hispanic borderlands student writing. The task was to write a short summary of a *National Geographic* article on sharks:

> (1) Scientist have made studies on the great white to find that they are not we think they are but just themselves. (2) An author by the name Peter Benchley wrote a book called *Jaws* saying that this creatures like to eat us humans but actually it's just the mistake that the sharks does, confusing us for his real prey. . . . (6) Now that they learn more about sharks are interested on the life of the creature. (Newman)

This passage demonstrates several relatively "common" errors seen in the texts of Hispanic borderlands students who are not directly translating but are being influenced by structures that they hear in their oral border Spanish language. (Recall my earlier point that Hispanic borderlands students are fluent neither in Spanish nor English and thus cannot rely on strong grammatical knowledge of either language to moderate their constructions in writing.) In sentence 1, *made* substitutes for the all-purpose Spanish *hacer,* a verb that can mean, among many things, make, have, hold, commit. Sentence 2, although only a Spanish speaker would know this, uses *does* as a different form of the verb *made* in sentence 1. Sentence 2 also shows the influence of inflections in Spanish: *sharks does* in Spanish would be *tiburones hacen* with both the noun and the verb inflected with plural markers (-es for the noun and -en for the verb), where in English only the noun has an obvious plural marker. Also in sentence 2, this is not a pronoun error; it is a phoneties error: in Spanish, *i* is pronounced like the long *e* in English. Thus, for someone whose language is influenced by Spanish phonetics, *these* and *this* are indistinguishable sounds. Finally, in Sentence 6, the verb choices show a common phenomenon (error) among speakers of Spanish: because Spanish is an inflected and completely conjugated language, the verb frequently includes the subject; thus, there is no need for the Spanish speaker to reiterate the pronoun subject. For this writer, *are*, the verb in the main clause, includes the pronoun subject *they* as it would in a Spanish version of this construction.

Because of my knowledge of Spanish, I can actually contrast the construction the student shows in the writing to what he or she intended. However, tutors who do not know Spanish can still explain the cause of the error (much the way I do when I work with Japanese, Middle Eastern, or Russian students). When syntactic constructions are extremely aberrant, we can guess that certain, incorrect structures are influenced by the students' knowledge of another language and use that hypothesis to help the writer become aware of such potential pitfalls in future writing.

Guideline 2: Adopt a more directive approach to tutoring. Because of their limited facility with English, borderlands Hispanic students frequently do not respond well to non-directive tutoring. Thus, asking questions aimed at helping the writer decipher problems in a text leads to frustration and to the student's suspicion that tutors are "withholding information" about grammar and writing. I discovered very early in my work with Hispanic borderlands students at the writing center that they do not feel comfortable with questions such as "What are you trying to say here?" They do not understand why, when they finally approach an institutional representative (the writing center tutor), that authority figure "refuses" to help. I frequently got responses such as "I don't know." While directive tutoring may violate a writing center's objective to help writers develop independence, sometimes the special conditions of the writer's situation warrant a temporary departure from non-directive tutoring. For example, instead of asking what the writer intended to convey through certain constructions, I describe what he/she seems to be saying and explain why that message is not getting across, and I help the writer construct sentences in a more appropriate form. Or, let's say the writer is having difficulty maintaining consistent verb tense, a far more common problem among borderlands Hispanic students than it is in mainstream student writing. One thing I've done in this situation is to have the student highlight all the verbs in a short passage (sometimes I have to help the student figure out which are the verbs). Then I'll ask the student to notice the form of the verbs and to notice context clues that he or she has included to mark the time as past, present, or future.

I certainly am not suggesting that we simply tell the student what the problem is and how it can be corrected. Neither am I suggesting that we create situations where writing center clients become dependent on our tutorial help. Judith Powers discusses the pragmatics of adopting directive tutoring techniques with ESL writers because they lack sufficient discourse and linguistic knowledge to respond well to a non-directive approach (370–373). My suggestion stems from the Hispanic student's cultural directives that require they assume a quiet, passive role in learning. It is very difficult for a student who has been taught to revere his teachers and to respect authority (even a "pseudo" authority figure such as a writing center tutor) to be assertive about what he/she wants to do in a piece of writing. Imposing a non-directive approach on such students is risky: rather than endure a tutor's well-intentioned questioning, they will simply quit coming to the writing center — an outcome that I have witnessed far too many times.

Guideline 3: Remember the context from which Hispanic borderlands students' academic problems emerge. Most borderlands Hispanic students sense their marginalized status in the institution. They cannot participate in the day-to-day life of the institution because of the family responsibilities they have. When I realize that a student's writing problems are due to family-related limitations, I try to "teach" the student strategies for success as I tutor. I might say something like, "These are good sources, but notice that you can't use this source because you didn't jot down all the bibliographical information you need. You don't have time to go back and get the information you need for this source, so why don't you find something similar in a source that is complete." When a student brings in a draft that needs more than a 15-minute "quick fix," I point out areas that we could have worked on if we had more time, but I make clear to the student that I am willing to do what we can in the short time we have before the paper is due: "Okay, we have only a few minutes, so I'll just help you make sure that you get rid of the really noticeable problems. If we had a bit more time, we could work on your sentences to make your paper sound more sophisticated. But perhaps we can do that with your next paper." And I listen. Many times when I've worked with Hispanic students, I've realized that they really need to tell someone about the non-productive student-teacher interactions they have had. While it may seem easy for me to tell the student, "Go talk to your instructor; that's why he or she has office hours," it is not easy for a Hispanic student to move from a mindset where the instructor is always right to an attitude that permits questioning of authority, which is how most borderlands Hispanic students perceive an office visit with the instructor. For students like Rosa, approaching an instructor to ask for a justification of a grade requires the repudiation of everything her family has taught her.

I never cut off a student if he or she just wants to talk about school or about the problems he or she is having in a particular class. Such talk may seem tangential to the writing problems we need to work on, but, in fact — as I tried to demonstrate in my narratives of Rosa, Dahlia, and Leo — this talk is what helps students see the writing center as the center that can help them hold on to their academic goals. When our tutoring session is over, I always invite students to come back — or to email me — to tell me how they fared on the assignment. I hope such interest demonstrates that my investment in them is only partly associated with their writing: I am working with the student rather than with the writing.

Centering the Borderlands Student in the Institution

Despite the growing presence of Hispanics in the general population, they continue to be an underrepresented population in higher education: statistics from the U.S. Department of Education show that only 9% of the total student enrollment in two and four-year institutions is Hispanic (NCES, Digest). Unfortunately, when Hispanic students arrive at institutions of higher learning, whether in the borderlands or elsewhere in the country, those institutions tend to be unable to respond to the impact that the students' ethnicity has on their success in the institution. Kells notes that she is "concerned by a gap in our literature [composition/rhetoric studies] that leaves unexamined the implications and consequences of the prescriptivist practices of English studies among sociolinguistically marginalized student populations" (7). Kells' study focuses on the experiences of South Texas Hispanic students in college classrooms, but her observations certainly extend to other arenas in the institutional setting, including the writing center, where students' written texts come under even closer scrutiny than they do in the typical classroom.

It is time for writing centers to claim their place in the institutional environment as agents of access: because of our totally student-centered orientation, we are able to work with students in ways that seem to oppose the pedagogical authoritativeness of the classroom and that challenge the somewhat schizophrenic orientation of the institution ("we'll allow you in but succeeding is your business"). According to Kells, "the most obvious response by Mexican-origin students to the linguistic sanctions historically imposed by the United States' formal educational system is their eventual and total withdrawal" (12). While writing centers cannot right all of the problems endured by Hispanic college students, they can provide support that enables them to persist within institutions of higher learning.

Grimm's view of the writing center as an agent for institutional attitudes toward difference, Petit's view of the center as carnival, and most recently, Boquet's view that the center creates noise that disrupts institutional silence suggest that writing centers threaten the status quo on our campuses: writing centers enable non-mainstream students to position themselves in our institutions and eventually succeed despite obstacles inadvertently or indifferently created by institutional authority. Regardless of the circumstances responsible for their marginalization, non-mainstream students must find a center that holds as they journey through our institutions. Adapting Yeats' image, the writing center is both a locale and a mechanism that keeps "things" from falling apart — in other words, it helps non-mainstream students (in my discussion, Hispanic borderlands students) center themselves in the institution. The writing center centers students by helping them find a voice in the academy and by empowering them in ways that traditional institutional authority does not. The writing center can help Hispanic students: (1) understand that the classroom is only one of the settings in which teaching and learning occur in a university; (2) realize that linguistic and ethnic difference should not be a liability, that such difference can work to change the institution's response to non-mainstream students; (3) appreciate linguistic and ethnic diversity as assets to the institution and to society in general; and (4) recognize that although success may seem unattainable because of obstacles created by the institution, it is in fact accessible.

The students whose stories I've told are changed students because of their contact with the writing center. They came from classrooms where their voices, their ideas, and their identities were mediated by teacher authority and modulated by cultural expectations. Because of their contact with the writing center, each has moved closer to meeting academic goals that could have been thwarted by institutional authority manifested in classrooms and in the overall institutional environment. The writing center, operating as facilitator of student learning and achievement, can enable Hispanic borderlands students to negotiate institutional barriers and to center themselves in the institution. Functioning as an agent for access, the writing center enables marginalized students of all types to maintain their dignity as student members of the academy by helping them find and grasp the center that holds.

Notes

[1]I am using the designation "Hispanic" (instead of "Mexican-American," "Latino/a," or "Chicano/a") primarily for consistency since I am using Census Bureau and Department of Education documents that use the term to refer to the population at the center of my discussion.

[2]According to Susan Choy, writing in the U.S. Department of Education's Condition of Education 2002, a student is defined as "non-traditional" on a continuum based on the number of non-traditional characteristics met: delayed enrollment following high school graduation; part-time college attendance; full-time work; financial independence; dependents other than a spouse; single parenthood; no high school diploma.

[3]Florida International University has a higher Hispanic enrollment (16,495 out of 31,293 students for a 57 % Hispanic enrollment) (National Center for Education Statistics, "Completions"). While its proximity to Cuba puts Florida International in a different type of "borderland," I am focusing on Hispanic students of Mexican heritage attending institutions on the U.S.–Mexico border.

Works Cited

Boquet, Elizabeth H. "Disciplinary Action: Writing Center Work and the Making of a Researcher." *Writing Center Research: Extending the Conversation.* Eds. Paula Gillespie, Alice Gillam, Lady Falls Brown, and Bryon Stay. Mahwah, NJ: Lawrence Erlbaum Associates, 2002, 23–37.

————. *Noise from the Writing Center.* Logan, UT: Utah State University Press, 2002.

Choy, Susan P. "Nontraditional Undergraduates." The Condition of Education 2002. U. S. Department of Education: National Center for Education Statistics. May 2002. 4 August 2002 <http://nces.ed.gov/programs/coe/2002/pdf/2002_special2.pdf>.

Clark, Irene. *Writing In the Center.* 3rd ed. Dubuque, IA: Kendall/Hunt Publishing Company, 1998.

Clemetson, Lynette, "Hispanics Now Largest Minority, Census Shows." *New York Times Online* 22 January 2003. 22 January 2003 <http://www.nytimes.com/2003/01/22/national/22HISP.html?todaysheadlines>.

DiPardo, Anne. "Whispers of Coming and Going: Lessons from Fannie." *The Writing Center Journal* 12.2 (1992): 125–44. Rpt. in *The Allyn and Bacon Guide to Writing Center Theory and Practice.* Eds. Robert W. Barnett and Jacob S. Blumner. Needham Heights, MA: Allyn and Bacon, 2001. 350–367.

Edlund, John R. "Working with Non-Native and Dialect Speakers in the Writing Center." Chapter 10. *Writing in the Center.* 3rd ed. By Irene Clark, Dubuque. IA: Kendall/Hunt. 1998. 203–234.

Freedman, Sarah Warshauer. *Response to Student Writing.* NCTE Research Report No. 23. Urbana, IL: National Council of Teachers of English, 1987.

Friedlander, Alexander. "Meeting the Needs of Foreign Students in the Writing Center." *Writing Centers: Theory and Administration.* Ed. Gary A. Olson. Urbana, IL: National Council of Teachers of English, 1984. 206–214.

Gale, Xin Liu. *Teachers, Discourses, and Authority in the Postmodern Composition Classroom.* Albany, NY: State University of New York, 1996.

Gardner, Eric, Cynthia Lyman, and Kambria McLean. "Writing Center Ethics and 'Nontraditional Students.'" *The Writing Lab Newsletter.* 26.6 (February 2002): 7–11.

Gonsalves, Lisa M. "Making Connections: Addressing the Pitfalls of White Faculty/Black Male Student Communication." *College Composition and Communication* 53.3 (February 2002): 435–465.

Grimm, Nancy Maloney. *Good Intentions: Writing Center Work for Postmodern Times.* Portsmouth, NH: Heinemann, 1999.

Hairston, Maxine, *Successful Writing.* 4th ed. New York: Norton, 1998.

Kells, Michelle Hall. "Linguistic Contact Zones in the College Writing Classroom: An Examination of Ethnolinguistic Identity and Language Attitudes." *Written Communication* 19.1 (January 2002): 5–43.

Krashen, Stephen D. *Writing: Research, Theory, and Applications,* New York: Pergamon Press, 1984.

Lindemann, Erika. *A Rhetoric for Writing Teachers,* 4th ed. New York: Oxford University Press, 2001.

National Center for Education Statistics, Integrated Postsecondary Education Data System (IPEDS). "Completions, 1999–2000" and "Fall Enrollment, 1999" surveys. Table 219 — Enrollment and Degrees Conferred in Hispanic Serving Institutions, by Institution, Fall 1999 and 1999–2000. 8 February 2003 <http://nces.ed.gov/pubs2002/digest2001/tables/dt219.asp>.

National Center for Education Statistics. Digest of Education Statistics, 2001. Chapter 3. Postsecondary Statistics. 2002, 15 February 2003 <http://nces.ed.gov//pubs2002/digest2001/ch3.asp#1>.

Neff, Julie. "Learning Disabilities and the Writing Center." *Intersections: Theory-Practice in the Writing Center.* Eds. Joan A Mullin and Ray Wallace. Urbana, IL: National Council of Teachers of English, 1994, 81–95.

Neff-Lippman, Julie. "Dealing with Learning Disabilities in the Writing Center." Chapter 7. *Writing in the Center.* 3rd ed. By Irene Clark. Dubuque, IA: Kendall/Hunt Publishing Company, 1998. 147–164.

Newman, Beatrice Mendez. "Mi Lengua No Es Su Lengua: Decoding Alien Structures in Student Texts," Paper delivered at the 2002 Conference on College Composition and Communication. 22 March 2002.

Petit, Angela. "Removable Feasts: The Writing Center as Carnival." *Composition Forum* 12.1 (Winter 2001): 41–58.

Powers, Judith K. "Rethinking Writing Center Conferencing Strategies for the ESL Writer." *The Writing Center Journal* 13.2 (1993): 39–47. Rpt. in *The Allyn and Bacon Guide to Writing Center Theory and Practice.* Eds. Robert W. Barnett and Jacob S. Blumner, Needham Heights, MA: Allyn and Bacon, 2001. 368–375.

Severino, Carol. "Writing Centers as Linguistic Contact Zones." *Professing in the Contact Zone.* Ed. Janice M. Wolff. Urbana, IL: National Council of Teachers of English, 2002. 230–239.

U.S. Census Bureau. National Population Estimates — Characteristics. Table US-EST2001-ASRO-03. Released 21 January 2003. 7 February 2003 <http://eire.census.gov/ popest/ data/national/tables/asro/US-EST2001-ASRO-03.php>.

Yeats, William Butler. "The Second Coming." *Literature: Reading, Reacting, Writing.* 3rd ed. Eds. Laurie G. Kirszner and Stephen R. Mandell, Fort Worth, TX: Holt, Rinehart and Winston, 1997, 1033.

"Thirty-something" Students: Concerning Transitions in the Writing Center

Cynthia Haynes-Burton _____

THE UNIVERSITY OF TEXAS AT DALLAS

As companies "downsize" and various industries lay off workers, many adults are returning to school to pursue a second career. To help them face their new challenges, tutors must recognize that "thirty-something" students have needs that differ from those of traditional students. Nontraditional students often suffer anxiety when confronted by a loss of the stability and identity their previous careers gave them. Most will likely balance multiple family and work roles in addition to assuming their new roles as students. They may also be reluctant to ask for help with their writing, and, when they do, they may tend to focus on basic problems with grammar and mechanics rather than on overall structure or support for their ideas. Writing centers are well suited to help nontraditional students make the transition back to school, Cynthia Haynes-Burton says. When such students "establish a solid relationship with the writing center," they can regain a sense of security they have lost. Tutors can help reduce the anxieties of nontraditional students by "showing them how to channel the confidence they possess in other areas of their life and apply it to writing problems." Her essay demonstrates the sensitivity to different circumstances and life experiences that a successful collaborative relationship between tutor and nontraditional student requires. This essay originally appeared in Writing Lab Newsletter *in 1990.*

It would not be exaggerating to say that there has been an enormous growth in the *industry* of composition instruction; yet, until recently, we often defined our field in terms of static theories and practical pedagogies rather than across the fertile chaos that this industry has spawned. Ironically, the effects of dynamism and flux in composition theory have produced a backlash of centrism, or the nostalgia for a stable "center." In contrast, the realities of writing instruction, and writing centers in particular, cry out for affirmation of change, of drifting in and out of stable centers. In their collection of essays, editors Ray Wallace and Jeanne Simpson note the common thread that "writing centers are dynamic, not static, that change and adjustment to new problems come with the territory" (xiii). I am interested in isolating this notion of change in terms of the effect on the writing center of one particular subculture within the composition field, the growing population of older college students — people who are living models for the process of change.

One of the most extreme effects of this process of change is the feeling of displacement, whether physical or conceptual. For example, in the past twenty years, due to the advent of corporate mergers, lay-offs, hiring freezes, staff contractions and realignments, consolidations, and attrition, we have seen a rapid growth in career transitions. When these forced displacements occur, many people return to college, or choose to begin their post-secondary education for the first time. As these individuals enter college, the demographics of our student populations change drastically. While this growing diversity in age creates the need for new strategies in the classroom, it also represents an immediate challenge for the writing center.

An important first step in addressing the needs of older students in the writing center would be to recruit tutors from all age groups. Not only is it important to hire or appoint tutors with diverse disciplinary backgrounds and good writing skills, it is equally important to mirror the ethnic, gender, and age differences of the general student population of any institution. There are, however, other models for consideration. For example, Susan Kleimann and G. Douglas Meyers created a unique program in their writing center in which senior citizens volunteered to work as writing tutors. According to Kleimann and Meyers, these tutors bring their experience in the non-academic world to bear on the students' writing. Many of them were retired professionals such as former librarians, professors, engineers, etc. Their practical experience introduced a level of maturity and authenticity that traditional-aged "peer tutors" often do not yet possess. If we look at the reverse of this situation, we must also ask how traditional-aged peer tutors and older student writers work together. The answer lies in redefining the "peer" relationship.

The concept of peer tutoring has recently come under scrutiny, most notably in John Trimbur's essay, "Peer Tutoring: A Contradiction in Terms?" Trimbur's concerns center on the tutor training process which he claims can often send contradictory signals to tutors who are being trained as "little teachers" while also being encouraged to identify themselves as "peers" of other student writers. Trimbur argues that "if peer tutoring programs are efforts by educators to tap the identification of student with student as a potentially powerful source of learning, peer tutoring can also lead to the further identification of peer tutors with the system that has rewarded them, underscoring the tutors' personal stake in the hierarchical values of higher education" (24). Trimbur suggests that the conflict between the "apprentice" model and the "co-learner" model of tutor training reproduces the contradictory experience of "peer" and "tutor" that students "experience at a gut level" (26). His solution is a "sequence of tutor training that treats tutors differently depending on their tutoring experience — in short, that treats tutors developmentally" (26).

I agree with Trimbur in principle, that "peer tutoring" is a contradiction in terms; but, the contradiction goes deeper than this when tutors face older student writers. Rather than introduce new terminology to describe the "peer tutor," I suggest that we need to ask ourselves whether, given these dynamics, peer tutoring as a concept is capable of properly characterizing what it is that goes on in the writing center; and, more importantly, we need to redefine the relationship between tutor and writer across different bases. The issue of tutor training, like any pedagogical contact, immediately introduces theoretical disputes, socialization concerns, and pragmatic challenges. Writing center practitioners have struggled with these issues in great detail. I am suggesting that we also need to define the role of the writing center tutor in terms of transitional concerns.

In his recent book, *Transitions,* William Bridges reminds us that "every transition begins with an ending" (11). When people go back to school there is an anxiety associated with "starting over" so late in life. Bridges argues that this is part of a mentality that says the earlier part of our life was a mistake or that now it is time to catch up to everyone else. In addition, Bridges claims that it is harder to teach older adults "process" because the world is so mechanistic, so product-oriented. We see ourselves as something not-yet-finished. In the writing center this is often why older students perceive their writing errors as "malfunctions." Against this, Bridges encourages us to view transitions as a time of readjustment and renewed commitment, rather than as "the confusing nowhere of in-betweenness" (5). He sees life as "unfolding," as a series of alternating periods of stability and change. According to Bridges, transitions in career signal a change from being motivated by the chance to demonstrate competence to being motivated by the chance to find meaning.

One manifestation of this difference in motivation is the difficulty that older students experience when faced with the "freedom" to choose their own topic for writing assignments. The problem is that in addition to its positive effects, *freedom is also something we fear.* Yet, in the writing center, freedom is often a banner under which we march to justify and tout our non-directive tutoring philosophies. We must be aware that the effect of unexpected freedom is sometimes the loss of structure, whether it is the structure of a job or a piece of writing. The implication of this for tutor training is to maintain a delicate balance between freedom and structure for both tutors and writers. The experiences of older students teach us that the involuntary loss of structure is a lesson we all need to heed in order to qualify our writing center theories and pedagogies.

Some of my older students tell me that when they enter the writing center, they do so with additional motives and different assumptions about what writing and tutoring can accomplish. Often returning students come to the writing center asking advice about which freshman writing courses to take to help them "brush up" on their grammar. They explain that it has been ten, fifteen, or twenty years since their last English course, and they are no longer confident of their grammar and style skills. In some cases, they appear in a panic and highly insecure about their chances for a successful re-entry into college. It is not difficult to imagine visions of red ink in their memories of freshman composition or diagramming sentences in a code they no longer remember. I do not discourage these students from taking such courses now. I do, however, encourage them to consider their options. For example, I explain that most freshman composition programs actually integrate reading, writing, and critical thinking skills. They will be reading essays in order to respond with an expository or argumentative essay of their own. I explain how their writing will be evaluated in terms of organization, support for their ideas, and clear and cohesive prose rather than strictly on the basis of grammar and style. I suggest alternative courses that focus on grammar and style, but these often do not count toward their degree. The best alternative, and the one they choose most often, is to establish a solid relationship with the writing center. I assign a specific tutor to work with them on a regular basis. Sometimes the student and tutor work together on specific writing projects, sometimes the tutor creates an assignment for them, and sometimes they just talk. The result is that students gain the confidence in writing that matches the confidence they possess in other areas, like jobs or families.

In some ways these students are no different from traditional-aged students. That is, they face identical assignments and harbor similar anxieties about writing and grades that a large dose of confidence will often help to resolve. On the other hand, they face these anxieties with a different set of experiences and expectations. For example, many of them are more organized in their approach to assignments, yet they are less confident of their ability to convey their thoughts. In these instances, it is simply a matter of showing them how to channel the confidence they possess in other areas of their life and apply it to writing problems.

One returning student, I'll call him Steve, came to the writing center because he was having trouble understanding his teacher's assignment to write an interpretive paper on a poem the class was studying. Steve had received a "C" on his paper. His teacher claimed he had not supported his conclusions. Steve did not understand his instructor's expectations, and he simply could not see what he was doing wrong. Prior to coming to the writing center, he had made an appointment elsewhere to test for [a] learning disability, thinking that he had some dysfunction. Steve had convinced himself that he was impaired because he did not understand his assignment. In addition, Steve seemed embarrassed to ask for help; yet, Steve's reluctance to seek help is typical of adult learners who have shifted from dependency to independency. Unlike most traditional-aged students, older students are no longer dependent upon their parents for support and encouragement. In fact, many of these students are working parents who balance multiple roles in their family and at work. I encouraged Steve often to keep this in mind when his lack of confidence in writing seemed overwhelming.

After Steve and I worked together for an entire semester we both learned some valuable lessons about writing and learning. I learned that older students have unique needs and have a great deal of experience to bring to their writing and to the tutoring session itself. Each time Steve came in the door, I threw caution to the wind and looked for ways to encourage the elements of transition and change I witnessed in his writing, as well as the confidence I could see gradually emerging. Steve did not improve his grade on the "C" paper, but he worked hard on subsequent papers and eventually improved to his own satisfaction. The following semester Steve became president of *Encore,* our university organization for older and returning non-traditional students over the age of twenty-one.

Since my first session with Steve, I have worked with many older student writers, hired several older "writing assistants," and set up an office for *Encore* in the writing center, and I am working on a proposal for a major grant to develop an organized writing center program to meet the needs of older non-traditional students. With the defense spending cut back, many military support personnel will soon be displaced. These events are also part of a general trend in local business to "downsize" companies through staff "realignments." In light of these alarming trends in job elimination in the United States, all American universities and community colleges face new challenges as these displaced individuals re-enter the education process. I believe writing centers can move to the front line of responding to the needs of older students. Christina Murphy puts it best: "if writing centers are to become true 'centers' of outreach amongst disciplines, they must also become true centers of outreach for communities and whole regions" (284).

Works Cited

Bridges, William. *Transitions: Making Sense of Life's Changes.* Reading: Addison-Wesley, 1980.

Kleimann, Susan, and G. Douglas Meyers. "Senior Citizens and Junior Writers: A Center for

Exchange." *Writing Center Journal* 2.1 (1982): 57–60.

Murphy, Christina. "Writing Centers in Context: Responding to Current Educational Theory." *The Writing Center: New Directions*. Ed. Ray Wallace and Jeanne Simpson. New York: Garland, 1991. 276–88.

Trimbur, John. "Peer Tutoring: A Contradiction in Terms?" *Writing Center Journal* 7.2 (1987): 21–28.

Wallace, Ray, and Jeanne Simpson, eds. *The Writing Center: New Directions*. New York: Garland, 1991.

Transcending "Conversing": A Deaf Student in the Writing Center

Margaret E. Weaver

SOUTHWEST MISSOURI STATE UNIVERSITY

In this essay, which originally appeared in JAC: A Journal of Composition Theory *in 1996, Margaret Weaver questions the "conversing" metaphor of writing center theory, arguing that it excludes deaf writers. By working with Anissa, a deaf student whose professors blamed her "poor writing performance" on a lack of motivation, Weaver discovered that Anissa processed information differently from members of the "audist" culture. As she says, deaf students often are second-language students, having first learned American Sign Language — "a highly structured system with its own vocabulary and syntax."*

One realization Weaver and Anissa have during their tutorials is Anissa's aversion to using such "audist" verbs as "stated," "said," and "articulated" and her preference for verbs such as "claimed," "indicated," and "suggested," which do not imply oral speech. Thus, as Weaver points out, one of the keys to helping deaf students in writing tutorials is to understand the hidden assumptions underlying the students' "center of reference" and how these assumptions differ from those of the hearing community. This article is valuable in helping tutors understand the need to examine the sources of misunderstanding between members of the majority population and particular minorities — including the assumption that interactions with student writers rest on a foundation of conversation.

Writing centers developed in the 1970s to provide an alternative to the traditional classroom environment. Whereas the traditional classroom presupposes on the hierarchical relationship between teacher/student, the writing center changes the social context of learning by creating an environment of peer collaboration. Writing center tutors facilitate this environment by encouraging students to enter what Kenneth Bruffee calls "the conversation of mankind." Rather than remaining passive recipients of knowledge, students are encouraged to collaboratively articulate their understanding with their peers. As such, the writing center serves as a place for individuals to converse. Bruffee views conversing (not writing) as the writing center's primary purpose:

> What peer tutor and tutee do together is not write or edit, or least of all proof-read. What they do together is converse. They converse about the subject and about the assignment. They converse about, in an academic context, their own relationship and the relationships between student and teacher. Most of all they converse about and pursuant to writing. (10)

Like most writing staff members, I had accepted this characterization of our work place. Conversing was the activity which best described my tutoring sessions with students. I accepted speaking and hearing as necessary criteria for participation in the writing center. When I began working with Anissa, though, I was forced to re-examine these criteria. Conversing did *not* describe the activity of our tutoring sessions. Very few of our sessions involved speaking and none involved hearing. Rather, we relied on seeing. We watched each other's facial expressions, we read each other's written words, and we observed each other's nonverbal gestures. These methods of communication allowed Anissa and me to have productive tutoring sessions without speaking or hearing — a necessity as Anissa is congenitally deaf.

What follows is a narrative of my interactions with Anissa. Working with her led me to question the writing center's purpose as "conversing." Bruffee's metaphor continues the bias of a society of hearing individuals. An "audist" society inhibits those without speech or hearing from full participation. So although the writing center has historically viewed itself as an inclusive place — a place which encourages multi-culturalism and different learning styles — it also sends messages of an exclusive nature to those who are hearing-impaired. By assuming the "conversing" metaphor, the writing center excludes people like Anissa whose linguistic abilities are founded on different principles of social interaction.

A Student Who Needs to Be "Pushed"

Last Spring an Art History faculty member called my attention to Anissa. She prefaced her remarks by stating, "this student will probably not pass my class without some significant assistance in writing." During the phone conversation, she revealed that Anissa is a Graphic Design major who has been deaf since birth. She has no hearing in either ear, but can occasionally hear vibrations with hearing aids. Despite being a superb lip reader, Anissa still needs an interpreter and note-taker in all of her classes.

After providing these preliminary facts, the faculty member asked if I thought the student's hearing loss could be a factor in her poor writing performance. Not knowing anyone in Anissa's situation, I suggested that she contact a specialist in the Communication Disorders Department. During the next day, I received the following e-mail message:

> I talked with a woman in Communication Disorders and she confirmed that it is often difficult for hearing impaired individuals to write very well. She indicated that the type of sign language that they use can greatly affect how they write. I think Anissa's problem has more to do with conceptualizing than it does with ability to express. (I checked this out with another faculty member who had her as a student in Graphic Design.) This faculty member indicated that Anissa had a very hard time — that she took criticism very, very hard, but that the faculty member had pushed Anissa hard enough to get her to the level of most students in the class by its end. (Anissa had to do one project over 8 times.) My inclination would be that she needs to read others' ideas and then try to express them in her own words.

Regardless of the advice from the woman in Communication Disorders, this faculty member identified Anissa's problem as "having more to do with conceptualizing than with the ability to express." That is, according to this teacher, Anissa had the ability to write but just did not put enough thought into her writing. The faculty member's decision to mention Anissa's experience last semester suggested that she concurred with her colleague in Graphic Design who believed Anissa's poor writing performance was a result of her lack of motivation. Anissa needed to be "pushed."

This characterization of Anissa reflected both faculty members' audist perspectives. Accepting the majority paradigm, Anissa's poor writing performance could not be attributed to her hearing loss because she had, it seemed, learned English. Anissa lipreads and "speaks" English. Whereas non-native speakers of English are beginners, Anissa was not considered a beginner. If she made a grammatical error, it had to reflect carelessness because, unlike ESL students, she should have already learned the concept through years of using "English." However, Anissa uses American Sign Language (ASL). These faculty members erroneously identified English as Anissa's language. English is the language she speaks within the larger audist society; she uses ASL, which she acquired as her first language, to communicate with other deaf individuals. In short, these faculty accepted the audist assumption that a language must be spoken for it to be recognized as a language.

Disregarding ASL as the basis of Anissa's use of language performance, the faculty members perceived her writing difficulties erroneously. They concluded Anissa had reduced ability to conceptualize/think, thus showing their assumptions. Traditionally, hearing-impaired individuals have been labeled as deaf and "dumb." One connotation of "dumb" is that to be without a spoken language is to be without intelligence — without the ability to think. Yet this inability has not been recognized as a biologically-grounded mental deficiency. Rather, it is often taken to be a sign of moral character. In *Deaf in America: Voices from a Culture,* Carol Padden and Tom Humphries discuss the public image most associated with deaf people. This is an image of individuals who are "lazy" (46). The image has developed as a result of the increasing number of able-bodied deaf peddlers who solicit donations from the public. These peddlers often serve as the only form of interaction between the hearing public and the deaf community. They alone are taken as representative of the work ethic of those who are hearing-impaired. As a result, the hearing community assumes that the deaf need to be "pushed." Without being "pushed," they will remain unmotivated. As the faculty member explained to me, Anissa was able to pass her Graphic Design class last semester only because a hearing teacher pushed her to the level. Furthermore, Anissa would only be able to pass her Art History course this semester if I (the Director of the Writing Center) pushed her hard enough.

A Student with "Weak Thoughts"

During our first tutoring session (March 8), Anissa shared all of her writing thus far in the Art History course: her diagnostic essay and her first nine journal entries complete with teacher comments. At the bottom of her diagnostic essay, the professor had written, "Anissa — You're going to need to work on your writing in order to do well in this class. I strongly encourage you to use the writing center. I'll be glad to help you in any way that I can." Following this written comment, the faculty member had given Anissa my name and told her that she should see me for help with her journal. The diagnostic essay was dated January 31, so despite the faculty member's recommendation, Anissa had chosen not to seek my help until she had already completed nine entries and received feedback from the professor.

Anissa's journal began with an entry which articulated what she saw as the role of the journal in her learning: "Today is the beginning of my journal as a major assignment for this Art History class. I hope this journal will help me to stimulate my thoughts." By defining the journal as a method to *stimulate* her own thoughts, Anissa had added credibility to the faculty member's assumption that she was unmotivated and, thus, needed to "read others' ideas and then try to express them in her own words." However, although Anissa confirmed that the journal entries were to be her thoughts, she neglected to mention the role of books and articles in her thinking. This was not surprising, though, as the only place the faculty member actually mentioned books and articles was in a parenthetical phrase in the syllabus: "Since the purpose of this assignment is to encourage you to think, each entry must evidence thinking on your part about the ideas you are writing about. You will not be 'graded' on the correctness of your thoughts (with the exception of the entries on books and articles)."

Because Anissa recognized the emphasis on her thoughts, her second journal entry began, "I spent most of the day asking myself why art is so important in everyone's lives." In this short one-page entry, almost every sentence began with the phrase "I believe." This was followed by a third entry which began "I spent most of the hour thinking how much information from the lecture that I was going to miss in class since it was the day of my grandmother's funeral." The entry discussed something that Anissa's grandmother said to her about art before she died, and again, the entry included many sentences which began "I remember," "I asked," "I came," and "I believe." In the fourth entry, Anissa attempted to discuss something she had read in the class textbook: "While reading the 'High Renaissance' section in the book, I was fascinated by Michelangelo's remarkable works." This entry had a reduced number of sentences beginning with "I." Only four sentences began "I was amazed," "I would never have thought," "I'm referring to," and "I believe."

Anissa received no feedback on these first four entries. It was not until the fifth entry that she received a written comment from the faculty member. In the fifth entry, Anissa compared two artistic styles. None of the sentences in this entry used "I." Unfortunately, she did not provide any clue as to the origin of the ideas as she had in the previous entries. The originator was apparent, however, upon reading the faculty member's comment written at the bottom of the entry: "careful — getting close to rehashing lectures."

After this comment, Anissa's journal entries reverted back to her earlier style of writing. The sixth entry made four references to "I'm asking," "I can," "I have to remember," and "I need to," followed by two more journal entries totaling fifteen sentences of "I feel," "I believe," "I think," "I guess," and "I wonder." These three entries received only one comment written at the end of the eighth entry: "very weak entry; not much thought apparent."

Apparently dismayed by this faculty comment, Anissa chose not to discuss an issue related to art in her ninth entry. Instead, she discussed her concern over progress thus far in the class: "It seems to me I tried to explain my answers; however, they didn't come out as clear as I wanted them to. I hope I'll do better . . . because I can't afford to fail." This entry prompted the faculty member to observe, "I don't understand the purpose of this entry; info isn't part of class."

Evidence of Thought

After examining these first nine journal entries and the faculty member's comments, it appeared that Anissa and the faculty member were assuming, respectively, different things about what shows evidence of thought. Anissa equated thought with personal reflection while the teacher viewed personal reflection as evidence of little thought. The more the faculty member criticized Anissa's writing as not showing much thought, the more Anissa used "I" in subsequent journal entries. Similarly, the more Anissa used "I," the more the faculty member viewed the entries as "weak." Their miscommunication centered around how Anissa chose to discuss ideas in her journal. Based on the information in her journal entries, Anissa had read the assigned readings. What was in question was the way she wrote about the material. She presented information in her journal entries without any clear indication as to the originator of the idea or by prefacing the idea with a first-person singular pronoun. Only in the third entry did Anissa indicate the originator of the ideas (e.g., grandmother), and this then was followed by no other references. All subsequent information was presented in the context of "I believe." In the fourth entry, Anissa mentioned that she was responding to something in the text, but she does not indicate an author. This same difficulty was present in her newest journal entry — the entry she wanted to revise during our tutoring session.

In her newest journal entry, it was clear that Anissa was struggling with the concept of authorship. In particular, she had written three sentences which illustrated the difficulty she was experiencing when incorporating written texts into her own writing:

> This writer believes that even the best artists do not use the hands following one's own mind.

> In the first reading of "The Model and the Statue," the poem stated that Michelangelo claimed that artists should carve or design a figure or sculpture from one's own mind.

> In the second reading of "The Model and the Statue," indicates that often artists sketch a figure down on paper.

In the first sentence, the subject suffered from ambiguity. It was unclear as to whom "the writer" referred: Anissa? Michelangelo? In the second sentence, Anissa assigned the poem rather than a subject credit for the information. In the third sentence, Anissa left out the subject. Because all three sentences revealed problems with the subject, it was clear that Anissa was not simply lazy. These ways of referring to the subject were not careless or typographical errors. Anissa had made deliberate decisions.

First Language Interference

Prior to my first tutoring session with Anissa (following the e-mail request), I had briefly investigated American Sign Language (ASL). ASL is not a set of individual gestures used by hearing-impaired individuals, as suggested by Anissa's professor, but is a highly structured system with its own vocabulary and syntax. ASL is not based on, nor derived from, English. Signs and words may have overlapping meanings, but the sentence structure into which they are placed differs dramatically. As Peggy Marron identifies in "Tutoring a Deaf Student: Another View," "sign language is very different from written English. Articles are not used; tenses are usually not shown; plurals are shown by repeating a sign or are indicated by context" (15). Because ASL has a distinctive structure, some universities give foreign language credit to students fluent in ASL. In a practical sense, ASL is considered to be a spoken language. The deaf acquire ASL, not English, as a first language (Padden and Humphries 58). Consequently, Anissa's first language is not English. Her first language is ASL. Like other non-native speakers of English, Anissa has learned English but has yet to reach a level of mastery equivalent to a native English speaker. She still must rely on an interpreter who translates the faculty member's spoken English into "spoken" ASL.

The most obvious distinction between ASL and English is the means by which each language is used. While ASL and English are both spoken, only English can be written. At the present, no method exists for recording ASL in written form. It is not surprising, therefore, that ASL has features associated with oral speech communities.

Shirley Brice Heath investigated the characteristics of oral communication patterns. She discovered that story-telling followed a similar structure regardless of community. The story-teller/author tells stories only about him/herself or someone else who was present at the time of the storytelling. Heath explains, "stories 'told on' someone other than the story-teller are never told unless the central character or someone who is clearly designated his representative is present" (149). As the author or subject is always present, no method of identification is needed for the author. Similarly, ASL does not have a sign for "author." "Author" is not included among the 4,400 signs listed in the *American Sign Language Dictionary*. No particular sign exists for pronouns either. According to Humphries and Padden's *A Basic Course in Sign Language*, "if the person or object is visible or nearby, the signer points in the direction of that person or object. If the person or object is not present, the signer can point to a location on either side" (6). Consequently, if a signer is telling a story about someone who is not present, the author is forced to use an unclear referent — pointing off in another direction. No mechanism exists to indicate if this "pointing" refers to he, she, or it. Thus, the concept of pronouns in written English presents some difficulty for fluent speakers of ASL.

In *Deafness, Development, and Literacy*, Alec Webster concludes, "the most important feature [in the writing of the deaf] is the difficulty in linking sentences together." Webster attributes part of this difficulty to the deaf's use of pronouns in written English. Rather than substituting a pronoun to refer back to words used earlier, hearing-impaired individuals assume that the redundancy is self-evident; therefore, they often do not restate the subject. ESL specialist Alice Horning suggests that this lack of redundancy is common among those learning written English.

In Anissa's case, she recognized the need to rearticulate the subject but struggled with the appropriate means. Each one of the problematic sentences in her newest entry (see page 279) attempted to imply the subject without actually stating it (e.g., Michelangelo). This was necessary because the subject/author was not present. If Anissa was to follow proper etiquette within her oral-based culture, she could not tell Michelangelo's "story" without his presence. Therefore, Anissa resorted to telling the "story" from her own vantage point because she was present. Unlike her earlier journal entries, though, Anissa chose in the first problematic sentence to use "this writer believes" rather than "I believe" to refer to herself. Based on the comment she received from the faculty member on her ninth journal entry ("info isn't part of class"), Anissa chose to replace the personal pronoun with a third-person subject. This increased the likelihood that her audience would interpret the text's meaning through their own experiences and, thus, see the meaning as relevant. Each reader could situate him/herself into the generic category of "writer" whereas "I" limited the referent to Anissa. Characteristic of the oral tradition, Anissa reshaped the written text so that it was guided by communication assumptions of ASL speakers.

On glancing at the third problematic sentence, it appeared that Anissa had accidentally left out the subject. However, this structure actually reflected interference from her first language. In ASL, statements such as "My wife has a new job" and "My wife, she has a new job" are spoken using the identical signs. The only variation occurs in the accompanying facial expressions. The second statement uses a topic marker to restate the subject. This topic marker is represented by raised eyebrows (Humphries and Padden 92). Without being able to use eyebrows, Anissa's written sentence structure in English appeared to leave out the subject. However, if translated into ASL, the noun of the initial phrase ("The Model and the Statue") would automatically become the subject of the sentence. Thus, this reflected the same structure as her second sentence. Within the second problematic sentence, Anissa used "the poem" as her subject. In both sentences, she attributed the ideas to the poem rather than to Michelangelo. Not only did she attribute the idea to the poem, she also endowed the poem with speaking ability.

An Audist Center of Reference

For people immersed in an audist culture, this personification of the poem may seem "unthoughtful." Anissa neglects the fine distinctions between the abilities of an inanimate object and an animate subject. She does not acknowledge spoken language as the distinguishing characteristic of humankind.

For the audist community, the oral form of discourse (conversing) is at the center. The mouth is typically recognized as the originating point of language and the ear as the receptive point of language. Everything is interpreted in relationship to this framework. For example, while reading may not appear to be tied to an aural culture, buried assumptions exist about the process of reading/writing. In "Deafness and Insight: The Deafened Moment as a Critical Modality," Lennard Davis points out that "the way we discuss reading and writing has in fact implied the ostracism of those who are differently-abled linguistically" (883). Reading and writing are perceived as processes dependent upon hearing and vocalizing. The most obvious indication of these buried assumptions is the way the act of reading is defined. The *Merriam-Webster Dictionary* defines reading as an activity "to understand language by interpreting written symbols for speech sounds; to utter aloud written or printed words." This definition promotes the idea that people read by imagining words into sound. In fact, when children first learn to read, emphasis is placed on phonics. They are told to "sound it out" in their oral reading groups. Even the whole language movement encourages students to first "tell" their stories. In more advanced classes, students are encouraged not only to imagine words into sound, but also to imagine or pretend authors into presence. Because presence/participation in an audist society is predicated on an individual's ability to speak and hear, students learn how to use words such as "states," "says," and "articulates" to create a subject's presence within a written text. These audist assumptions are further magnified in the writing center where a prerequisite for improving writing is the ability to "converse." Writers in the writing center are encouraged to read their papers aloud so as to "hear" problems.

DEAF as a Center of Reference

Anissa forced me to re-examine the epistemological bases the audist community has imposed on hearing-impaired individuals. Edward Sapir, an important modern linguist, hypothesized that if people speak a different language, they also live in a different world. Having grown up within a deaf household, Lennard Davis explains, "the Deaf feel that their culture, language, and community constitute a totally adequate, self-enclosed, and self-defining sub-nationality within the larger structure of the audist state" (881). As a result, the deaf often have a different center of reference for interpretation than an audist culture. Padden and Humphries provide an example of how this center of reference can result in different interpretations. For audists, A LITTLE HARD-OF-HEARING means a person who can hear quite well and VERY HARD-OF-HEARING means someone who cannot hear well at all. For the hearing-impaired, A LITTLE HARD-OF-HEARING means a person who has slight hearing and VERY HARD-OF-HEARING means someone who can hear quite well. This deviation in meaning occurs because both cultures are using a different center of reference. In many cases such as this one, the deviation can result in a complete reversal of meaning. Padden and Humphries explain,

> In ASL, as in English, HARD-OF-HEARING represents a deviation of some kind. Someone who is A LITTLE HARD-OF-HEARING has a smaller deviation than someone who is VERY HARD-OF-HEARING . . . yet the terms have opposite meanings in the two languages. . . . DEAF, not HEARING is taken as the central point of reference. A LITTLE HARD-OF-HEARING is a small deviation from DEAF. (41)

Padden and Humphries discovered this deviation by observing a football game between two deaf schools. Members of the home team kept referring to the opposing team as HEARING despite the team's lack of hearing. For them, HEARING did not refer to a physiological condition as much as a recognition that the other team was the opposite of them: the "Other."

A Tutoring Session

Recognizing that Anissa uses a different center of reference, I began our session by showing Anissa reviews of texts. I emphasized that these reviews were written by hearing individuals. I pointed to the places where the authors of the texts were mentioned, phrases like "the faculty who speak in this book." I also pointed to the place in her third journal entry where she had referred to a speaking subject (e.g., her grandmother). Next, I took a pencil to her second sentence and crossed out "the poem stated." This left the sentence to read, "In the first reading of 'The Model and the Statue,' Michelangelo claimed that artists should carve or design a figure of sculpture from one's own mind." I then pointed to the next problematic sentence, inserted a blank line to indicate that the subject was missing ("In the second reading of 'The Model and the Statue,'_____ indicates that often artists sketch a figure down on paper."), and asked Anissa "who?" Almost immediately, Anissa wrote "Michelangelo" in the blank space. In reference to the first sentence ("This writer believes that even the best artists do not use the hands following one's own mind."), I asked Anissa if "this writer" referred to her. Vehemently she shook her head and changed "this writer" to "Michelangelo" and "believes" to "suggested."

What fascinated me was Anissa's decision to change both the subject and the verb in this sentence. Upon re-examining the previous journal entries, I noticed that she only used the verb "believe" in conjunction with "I." She had continually used this particular verb when discussing others' ideas. Using "I believe" provided Anissa with a means to express someone else's ideas without having the person present. Ironically, Anissa was actually doing exactly what the professor had told me she wanted Anissa to do: "read others' ideas and then try to express them in her own words." Attaching "I believe" was the only method Anissa had for expressing others' ideas in her own words.

Unfortunately, this form of overtaking others' ideas was interpreted as if she had authored the ideas. Once she recognized that in an audist society ideas are attributed to an author even if s/he is not present, Anissa added a subject. But instead of using audist verbs like "stated," "said," "articulated," all of the verbs she chose to use ("claimed," "indicated," "suggested") referred to not necessarily oral activities. So although Anissa had inserted a subject, she had not endowed the author with the ability to speak. This method allowed her to bypass the audist assumptions of the author "speaking." Taking DEAF, not HEARING, as the central point of reference negated the need for an author who speaks because readers like Anissa do not hear. I could not hide my excitement; neither could she. We both realized that she had discovered a method for acknowledging the author which did not rely on the "conversing" metaphor. She could make the necessary distinction between an author's ideas and her own ideas without feeling ostracized by an audist culture.

Because the distinction between self and other is determined by the scene rather than language in her first language (ASL), Anissa had to discover a method to distinguish between self and other in written English. Unlike native speakers of English who are members of an audist culture, Anissa had no linguistic habit of making the distinction between self and other comprehensible in English. Her conversations all occur face-to-face rather than by aural means (i.e., on the phone, from another remote location). Therefore, Anissa had to develop a way to mark the distinction in her writing. For her the ways of acknowledging the distinction were not self-evident as they were for writers immersed in an audist society. Hearing individuals assume that the writer is the originator of the ideas in the text, so "I believe" is not necessary to include. For Anissa, though, "I believe" is necessary.

Out of curiosity, I asked Anissa to write another sentence stating what *she* believes. She wrote the following: "I believe that Michelangelo and other sculptors are not identical because Michelangelo used his own ideas to create sculptures of beauty while the other sculptors used their own sketches to create their works." This was the first statement Anissa had written that used both "I believe" and a subject. She acknowledged both presences within the same sentence. As a result, "I believe" was transformed into a marker for Anissa's thoughts rather than a linguistic substitute for a subject.

Afterthoughts

Throughout the semester, Anissa and I continued to explore the hidden audist assumptions in the reading/writing process. Rather than resisting the assumptions, she and I deliberately attempted to transcend our different centers of reference. As a result, Anissa's writing became more like the writing of native speakers of English and my tutoring focused less on conversing. Anissa concluded her journal by suggesting that the writing center (a place which has historically magnified the hidden assumptions of the audist community by privileging "conversing") can provide "wonderful encouragement to deaf students in the years to come." The faculty member concluded the semester by sending me the following e-mail message: "After talking with you, it seems very likely that her [Anissa's] hearing impairment was affecting her performance."

Works Cited

Bruffee, Kenneth. "Peer Tutoring and the 'Conversation of Mankind.'" *Writing Centers: Theory and Administration,* Ed. Gary A. Olson. Urbana, IL: NCTE, 1984, 3–15.

Davis, Lennard. "Deafness and Insight: The Deafened Moment as a Critical Modality." *College English* 57 (Dec. 1995): 881–900.

Heath, Shirley Brice. *Ways with Words: Language, Life, and Work in Communities and Classrooms.* Cambridge: Cambridge UP, 1983.

Horning, Alice S. *Teaching Writing as a Second Language.* Carbondale: Southern Illinois UP, 1987.

Humphries, Tom, Carol Padden, and Terrence J. O'Rourke. *A Basic Course in American Sign Language.* Silver Spring, MD: T. J. Publishers, 1980.

Marron, Peggy. "Tutoring a Deaf Student: Another View." *Writing Lab Newsletter* 17 (1993): 15–16.

Padden, Carol, and Tom Humphries. *Deaf in America: Voices from a Culture.* Cambridge: Harvard UP, 1988.

Sternberg, Martin L. A. *American Sign Language Dictionary.* New York: Harper, 1994.

Webster, Alec. *Deafness, Development and Literacy.* New York: Methuen, 1986.

ONLINE TUTORING

The Anxieties of Distance: Online Tutors Reflect

David A. Carlson and Eileen Apperson-Williams _____

CALIFORNIA STATE UNIVERSITY AT FRESNO

In wrestling with the benefits and difficulties of online tutoring, David Carlson and Eileen Apperson-Williams use the concept of distance — literal and figurative — to highlight several concerns. One form of distance they discuss is the geographic distance between student writers and writing centers. As Carlson and Apperson-Williams point out, "Time constraints, proximity, and introverted personalities often keep students from attending tutoring sessions. Computer technology can bring students and tutors closer together, overcoming the distance that may exist." At the same time, the geographic distance between tutors and writers can translate into a social distance if tutors fail to establish an interpersonal relationship with the students they help online. One of the strengths of face-to-face tutorials, after all, is the warm and productive relationship some tutors and writers develop. As the authors point out, however, interpersonal distance sometimes develops even in face-to-face tutorials, and the benefits of online tutoring tend to outweigh the drawbacks. Tutors who are anxious about online tutoring will find sympathetic voices in this essay but may also come to understand how to bridge the social distance between tutor and student writer. This essay first appeared in Taking Flight with OWLs: Examining Electronic Writing Center Work.

The premises for online tutoring are noble — to improve access to campus writing centers and to narrow distances between students and tutors. Time constraints, proximity, and introverted personalities often keep students from attending tutoring sessions. Computer technology can bring students and tutors closer together, overcoming the distance that may exist.

The desire to span this distance prompted the writing center staff at California State University at Fresno (CSUF) to develop an online tutoring program. However, thinking about how to overcome obstacles between tutors and students via the Internet opened new challenges. In particular, the idea of distance becomes more complex when writing centers support both face-to-face and online tutoring. As distance is lessened by increasing access, what happens to the relationship between student and tutor? What happens as tutors respond through a faceless, expressionless computer screen? For us, the face-to-face relationship is one of the joys, as well as a reason for success, in a tutoring session. With online tutoring, this relationship is severed. The tutoring table is replaced with a computer screen: cold, sterile, and, to many, uninviting.

Methodology

In this chapter, we listen to tutors who work in the CSUF writing center; we share dialogue with other tutors and dialogue with students seeking writing assistance online. Dialogue and distance complicate and complement one another. Philosopher David Bohm (1996) reminded us of how we might view the nature of dialogue:

> "Dialogue" comes from the Greek word *dialogos*. *Logos* means "the word," or . . . we would think of the "meaning of the word." And *dia* means "through." . . . The picture or image that this derivation suggests is of a *stream of meaning* flowing among and through us and between us. This will make possible a flow of meaning . . . out of which may emerge some new understanding. It's something new, which may not have been in the starting point at all. It's something creative. And this shared meaning is the "glue" or "cement" that holds people and societies together. (p. 6)

In distance tutoring, particularly faceless tutoring, the nature of dialogue is especially pronounced. Traditionally, gesticulation, tone of voice, and facial expression contribute to meaning and understanding. In e-mail tutoring, almost all meaning is carried through words alone.

For tutors accustomed to gesticulation, tone of voice, and facial expressions as an aid to Bohm's "flow of meaning," becoming comfortable using e-mail may take time, but it can be done: E-mail is a medium that allows more than is readily apparent. As seen in the quotations throughout this chapter, e-mail incorporates both formal and informal styles of writing, often in the same messages. Chesebro and Bonsall (1989) explained that with the proliferation of personal computers and modems, "personal 'messaging' was the most popular choice of the personal computer owner. . . . In virtually every test, home-computer owners seem to enjoy communication with other users more than any other computer-using activity" (p. 100). E-mail has quickly become a medium of friendships and alliances; hence, informal styles of writing (e.g., personal letters with fragments, idiomatic expressions, inside jokes, and allusions) are standard. At the same time, e-mail is often used by academics, who are trained to communicate in formal styles. Without showing faces, perhaps without stating credentials, people form e-mail groups, which put people using varied levels of formality in dialogue with each other.

E-mail style, then, tends to be an amalgam of styles. Conveying meaning becomes more difficult as intentions can be easily misinterpreted. Chesebro and Bonsall (1989) expressed this difficulty as a problem of how to maintain an interpersonal relationship: "the development of a [relationship] typically includes physical intimacy as one of its most important features. . . . If computer users claim that they have developed [relationships] solely through electronic connections, how must interpersonal specialists readjust their conceptions of [relationships]?" (p. 103). As "interpersonal specialists," tutors must readjust their conceptions of how to develop interpersonal relationships when tutoring online.

Important principles can be learned from the numerous listservs that continue to form rapidly around various academic subjects. Casal (1998), the list-owner of an e-mail discussion group, regularly reminded the group of the following rules:

- No personal attacks or flame wars.
- No lengthy discussion of movies or other nonprint media.
- No arguing about list policies on the list. (Address all concerns privately to list-owner.)
- Clear labeling of messages.
- No gushing about or bashing of characters or authors.

Although most of these rules do not literally apply to online tutoring, the spirit of them indicates how to maintain relationships over e-mail between tutors and students. These rules emphasize the constant need to exhibit courtesy and patience in a medium that does not allow for physical gestures and tone of voice. Words alone can seem cold and distancing even when not meant as such.

Rules meant to promote courtesy in dialogue are developed through practical experience. Elvira Casal (personal communication, June 4, 1998) mentioned her experiences with the discussion group as revealing "[a]nother problem[:] . . . online communications seem to encourage some people to imagine an 'ideal audience' that often isn't there. . . . [and that online audiences] also have expectations . . . and we feel irritated when these expectations are not met." Casal noted that e-mail users can easily offend others unintentionally. Bohm (1996) reminded us that distance is an element of every discussion, even face to face, and, in particular, he suggested that "[t]he people who take part are not really open to questioning [these] assumptions" (p. 7).

Online writing labs need to study interpersonal communication. Tutoring is most successful when dialogue occurs: "[i]n a dialogue . . . nobody is trying to win. . . . There is a different sort of spirit to it. In a dialogue, there is no attempt to gain points, or to [demand that] your particular view prevail" (Bohm, 1996, p. 7). Even though the tutor may have more knowledge and experience than the student, the student and tutor should engage in a dialogue about writing rather than have the tutor lecture the student about writing. Through e-mail tutoring, words may often seem cold and insistent. We should learn how to communicate over e-mail in such a way that courteous and patient dialogue becomes the norm when physical appearance and tone of voice cannot convey such qualities.

Because interpersonal communication differs from individual to individual, the study of how distance affects communication between tutors and students must focus on actual online dialogue between tutors and students. In the discussion that follows, we explore the interpersonal communication of our online tutors; our particular emphasis is on how distance transforms or otherwise affects the relationships among them and between them and their students.

A Dialogue of Tutors

The unnerving loss of face-to-face interaction keeps some tutors and writing centers from tutoring online. New and experienced tutors alike may feel anxious responding to an impersonal computer screen. This section demonstrates the anxieties of tutoring online as well as underscores that many of the skills used in face-to-face tutoring can aid online tutoring: "Solid writing center theory applies in cyberspace as it does in the traditional center. Students still need to be put at ease and made to feel comfortable. They still need special attention on particular writing problems" (Jordan-Henley & Maid, 1995b, p. 212). Although anxiety toward online tutoring is understandably daunting — it certainly has been for us — online tutoring is not an entirely new experience despite the different tutoring environment.

Tutors continually expressed concern about venturing beyond the familiar environment of the face-to-face tutorial, fearing that distanced relationships would inevitably result from geographic distances. The semester before we began online tutoring we e-mailed our tutors with this question: "What are your expectations and/or anxieties as you approach online tutoring for the first time?" The first person to respond was Ginny, a three-semester tutor: "I guess the only worry I have is that I think it would be easy to lose the personal touch you get when tutoring face to face. This kind of personal interaction, I feel, has really helped me and my tutees to become better at writing." The e-mail dialogue that followed Ginny's post indicates that most tutors agreed. Used to forming trusting relationships with their students, tutors worry about altering the situation. John, a four-semester tutor, offered his concerns:

> First of all, I rely HEAVILY on the interpersonal communication that tutoring offers me. I use my own personality to build a relationship with my students that enables me to push them farther and farther with their work as the semester progresses. I do agree that there is tone and voice in writing but I also think that they can be easily misinterpreted, misunderstood, or simply missed when talking online. The relationship I generally have with my students is one built on trust and one that takes more than just a 25 minute session to cultivate, (personal communication, August 7, 1997).

John brought up an important aspect of face-to-face tutoring: the development of the tutor/student relationship. In a traditional tutoring session, the first challenge to this relationship involves agreement over interpersonal distance. Although many students welcome personal interaction with their tutors, others keep a safe distance, a distance that usually decreases with time. This agreement on space creates favorable working conditions. With online tutoring, however, this space is already defined. A computer screen not only becomes a shield for those who are wary, but also creates a safety zone by virtue of anonymity. Such students may find what a student in Jordan-Henley and Maid's study (1995b) reported: "the computer [seems] as just another 'appliance' like a 'telephone, TV, or VCR'" (p. 213). Although dialogue occurs, the separation of the parties allows each a sense of control (Jordan-Henley & Maid, 1995b, p. 215). Thought is transmitted, whereas the lack of physical presence promotes the sense that each party chooses to receive information. One chooses to log on to e-mail much the same way that one chooses to turn on a television.

Some distances are fiercely maintained in face-to-face tutorials. At what point does a paper pass from being the student's work to the tutor's? Although this same opportunity for issues of distance occurs with electronic tutoring, the computer's presence between tutor and student poses as a guard against becoming too close. The tutor only knows what the student decides to present; the tutor cannot see the look in the student's eye, hear the emotion in the student's voice, or read the student's body language. Such privacy can be empowering to the student. In "Online Writing Labs (OWLs): A Taxonomy of Options and Issues," Harris and Pemberton (1995) stated:

> All dialogue in online configurations will be text driven, eliminating the subtle voice and body clues to composing processes. . . . Although tutors, thus, have to learn to rely on other clues as to who writers are, meeting onscreen will also mean meeting in a world where gender, ethnicity, and race are not immediately evident except through lexical and social cues. Voices normally shy may be stronger and clearer, and stereotypes are less likely to impact the tutorial. (p. 156)

Although some tutors like John worry that tutoring without face-to-face presence increases misinterpretation and misunderstanding, Harris and Pemberton (1995) reminded us that face-to-face interaction is not free of misunderstanding. Online communication alleviates some of the baggage that accompanies physical bodies. Perhaps, then, embedded within anxieties about the effects of distance on online tutoring is a positive result: that discussions foreground students' texts instead of the mediated relationships between tutors and students.

Justin, a three-semester tutor, began searching for ways, not unlike Harris and Pemberton, of making the best of this new interaction:

> I just finished reading Ginny's mail and I do agree that it would be strange to not have the close personal interaction that we have dealt with in our groups, but at the same time, distance allows us to avoid our own biases, judgments, etc., at least to a point. I think that communication could also be aided if, in contrast to our groups, we did not intimately know the student, and therefore there would be no worries on their parts of embarrassments when asking questions or discussing topics. Sometimes it is easier to open up to someone

when you know that you won't be seeing them on Thursday, (personal communication, August 9, 1997).

Here, Justin suggested that although distance may prevent the familiar personal interaction, it can bring us closer to our goals and to the student's goals too. In traditional writing centers, relationships between tutors and students are often close, with tutors becoming coaches, confidants, and even friends. Without question, much can be gained by this type of relationship. However, this interpersonal relationship sometimes prejudices both the tutors' and the students' views of writing. Online tutoring, as a result of distance, can alleviate some of this prejudice. Tutors and students still work on student texts, but the absence of face-to-face interaction causes the interpersonal relationship to develop through words about the writing rather than through physical presence. Online distance is an advantage for students, too, allowing them to raise questions that they may feel uncomfortable asking face to face. Some aspects of the power dynamic between tutors and students are flattened online.

Another tutor, Libra, argues that online tutorials place more responsibility on students:

> No, there won't be face to face interaction, but there will definitely be something to work on (this isn't always true when you're face to face with your students). I hope online tutoring presses the importance of planning ahead of time. Maybe students will learn to be more aware of the writing process by observing how many times a paper can be changed or reworked, (personal communication, August 10, 1997).

Libra made good points. The Website requires the students, first, to include the prompts and, second, to pinpoint particular problems with the papers. This strategy forces students to begin assessing the writing and to reread the assignments after writing the drafts. In planning our online site, we wanted to adhere clearly to our writing center's philosophies. Harris and Pemberton (1995) stated, "[p]eople who configure or plan OWLs must also weigh other options and make decisions as to which aspects of writing center theory and pedagogy are to be retained and which cannot be replicated exactly" (p. 155). By requiring that students include the assignments and individual concerns with the papers, we attempt to keep the students in charge of their writing. As Libra implied, this situation ideally occurs in face-to-face sessions: The students come to tutorials fully prepared. Too often, however, students rely on tutors for criticism, creating unbalanced interaction. Online tutoring, then, offers a potential solution.

As our most recent semester began, so began our first attempts at online tutoring. Reactions from the tutors were mixed. Although some online tutors complained about the difficulty in organizing their thoughts, in being concise and clear, and in envisioning geographically-distant students, others thought it more productive than face-to-face tutoring. Those who liked the situation felt that they could be more concise because they were tackling just one aspect chosen by the student. These tutors appreciated avoiding the rambling that goes on at a face-to-face session in trying to encapsulate a critical response. However, the main concern had been trying to make verbal language textual — to maintain a sense of informality while demonstrating standard English to a large degree.

Joanna, a three-semester tutor, said that online tutoring, for her, "opened the gate for frustration." She received an online submission from an ESL student who was concerned with her thesis, run-on sentences, sentence structure, and conclusion. The essay, for a freshman composition class, began as follows:

> Most of the juvenile delinquents happened in Americans underclass. That is, a social class having the lowest status in society. Underclass refers to the areas within a city where minority groups tend to live. They stay in that area because of social and economic pressure. In addition, unemployment, crime, drug addiction, teen pregnancy, school dropouts, and illiterates, are common in these neighborhoods. The peak times for juveniles offenses, especially of serious crimes, are in the hours immediately after school. The Department of Justice recently found that while adult violent crimes rates continue to drop, todays juvenile offenders are the fastest growing segment among violent criminals.

> The unprecedented increase in juvenile criminality is expected to result in a dramatic increase in the overall rate of violent crime as these juveniles approach majority. The reason juvenile are delinquent include watching violence on television, broken family, gang, and failure of juvenile justice system, (personal communication, September 23, 1997).

Joanna responded:

> Hi, Mai! Reading your introduction, I conclude that the main point of your paper (your thesis) is to discuss the different causes of juvenile delinquency. You do a good job of letting me know where delinquency occurs most often (America's underclass society), though be sure to make the distinction that the underclass are not "areas" in a city where minorities live, but actual "people" who live in these areas. At this point, I would like to concentrate on specific areas of your writing which need work in order to make your sentences more easily understood. The two areas that I'd like you to concentrate on are singular vs. plural, and noun possession. For example: the 5th sentence in your intro makes a list of things that are common in an underclass neighborhood. Notice the difference between singular and plural:

> * unemployment IS common ("unemployment" is singular)

> * School dropouts ARE common ("school dropouts" is plural)

> I suggest rewriting the sentence so that you are using all singular nouns or all plural nouns. Now let's look at noun possession using examples from your intro:

> * Americans underclass. Because the underclass belongs to the Americans, it is possessive. Americans' underclass.

* Juveniles offenses. The offenses belong to the juveniles. Therefore, it is the juveniles' offenses.

* todays juvenile offenders . . . means the juvenile offenders of today. Therefore, today's juvenile offenders . . .

Another example is your sentence, "the reason juvenile are delinquent . . ." You list more than one reason, so it should be plural (reasons). More than one juvenile is delinquent, so it should also be plural: The reasons juveniles are delinquent.

I believe it is a good idea for you to check through the rest of your essay to make sure your sentences use possession and plural vs. singular correctly. Thank you for submitting your essay! Please feel free to submit this again once you've checked it, or use our walk-in times to look at your paper in person. (MW 8–4) (T-Th 8–8) (Fri 8–12)

Sincerely, Joanna (personal communication, September 24, 1997)

Shortly thereafter, the student resubmitted her essay, a reaction that is not a regular occurrence in our limited online experience:

I have rectified the mistake you mentioned. Hope to receive the final correction from you. Most of the juvenile delinquents happened in Americans underclass. That is, a social class having the lowest status in society. People stay in this area due to their economic condition. In addition, unemployment, crime, drug addiction, teen pregnancy, and school dropout, is common in these neighborhoods. The peak times for juveniles offenses are in the hours immediately after school. The Department of Justice recently found that while adult violent crimes rates continue to drop, todays juvenile offenders are the fastest growing segment among violent criminals.

The unprecedented increase in juvenile crimes are expected to result in a dramatic increase in the overall rate of violent crime as these juveniles approach majority. The reasons juvenile are delinquent include watching violence on television, broken family, gang, and failure of juvenile justice system, (personal communication, September 26, 1997).

The student's revised draft indicates that she did not understand Joanna's earlier message. In a face-to-face session, Joanna could act on a student's confused look or hesitation by proceeding with another approach, saving both parties time and frustration. As Harris and Pemberton (1995) wrote, "[T]here are losses as well in this faceless, disembodied world as the lack of the personal contact may seem to dehumanize a setting that writing centers have traditionally viewed as personal and warm" (p. 155). Joanna believed that meeting with this student face to face would have been more effective. This reaction, however, was not felt by all.

Gabriel, a first-semester tutor, had a very different reaction to online tutoring:

Seated across a table, tutors try to impress upon students the importance and techniques of communicating clearly in writing. Ironically, this exchange most often occurs in dialogue rather than text. Perhaps the greatest advantage of online tutoring is that it is a dialogue concerning better writing that occurs in the form of writing. The exchange is more beneficial, as the message and the medium are self-referential, (personal communication, October 1, 1997).

Gabriel echoed a point made by Coogan (1995): "Online writing tutors . . . situate themselves not as technicians of writing . . . but as equals; writers responding to other writers" (p. 176).

A native-speaking student, also in freshman composition, submitted his paper to Gabriel with the following concerns:

Questions: 1) I am uncertain that the paragraphs flow together smoothly. In paragraph 5 on page 2, the text doesn't seem to gel well with each other. I'm noit is my topic sentence, or that I have different ideas and they need to be separated in two different paragraphs. The end of the page has a sentence thst felt awkward, but I'm not sure. 2) Is my thesis statement clearly recognizable in both the beginning, and the end of the essay? Does the thesis ffollow through the text? (personal communication, September 29, 1997).

To these concerns, Gabriel responded with the following:

I very much enjoyed reading your essay on language. I agree that there are a couple of sticky transitions, and I interjected some comments using the "***" symbol as a "flag." One place that it doesn't flow is from ex-girlfriend TO snap decisions. I can guess the link, but can you think of 1 or 2 sentences that can serve as a link, a transition? One thing to consider is: Your paper (to me, that is) seems to develop as "we speak different languages —> some people SEEM dumb —> Slang can affect how we see people." Perhaps you could try dragging section 3 to be between 1 and 2. Hence: we speak different languages —> slang affects how we see people —> Some people SEEM dumb. Maybe this simple "click and Drag" might help your paper "flow", and you might discover the transitions to more naturally "find themselves" (Or maybe not, just something to think about.)

Finally, yes, there is a consistent thesis. Your paper seems to me focused. I wonder though, if the thesis is "we speak different Englishes," which it seems the intro is hinting. It seems that your paper's consistent thesis is more complex than this, such as what the "difference" DOES.

You have a wonderful start, and I hope that you send more. I would like to see a next draft. Keep at it.

Gabriel A. (personal communication, September 30, 1997).

Engaging the Dialogue

Joanna's and Gabriel's different attitudes toward online tutoring may lie in many factors, including their students. One student is an ESL writer, and the other is a native writer. Working with grammar, as Joanna did, can be difficult, even face to face. Explaining grammar in everyday language over a computer screen can enormously challenge even the most experienced tutors. Another reason lies in the fact that Joanna is an experienced tutor who has spent several semesters tutoring face to face, gaining knowledge and skill along the way. Gabriel, on the other hand, being new, had an advantage stepping into online tutoring because he did not yet favor face-to-face tutoring. This does not mean that more experienced tutors do not bring tremendous tutoring skills to online tutoring. It does, however, offer a possible explanation for the anxieties Ginny, John, and Joanna felt that Gabriel did not.

As our online tutoring program develops, some are still bothered by the loss of face-to-face interaction. We suspect, however, that anxiety will pass with time and experience online. If the primary emphasis of tutoring writing is on the text and the writer's approach to the text, then surely online tutoring brings increased opportunity for this practice despite the change of venue. If we are to reach more students, online tutoring is a viable option to be a central element of our online tutors' work. We envision that what provokes anxiety now about online tutoring will eventually become comfortable and familiar as tutors gain experience.

Works Cited

Bohm, David. *On Dialogue*. London: Routledge & Kegan Paul, 1996.

Casal, Elvira. Group E-mail. May 12, 1998. E-list for tutors at California State University at Fresno.

Chesebro, J. W., and D. G. Bonsall. *Computer-Mediated Communication: Human Relationships in a Computerized World*. Tuscaloosa: U of Alabama P, 1989.

Coogan, David. "E-Mail Tutoring, a New Way to Do New Work." *Computers and Composition* 12 (1995): 171–81.

Harris, Muriel, and Michael Pemberton. "Online Writing Labs (OWLs): A Taxonomy of Options and Issues." *Computers and Composition* 12 (1995): 145–59.

Jordan-Henley, Jennifer, and Barry Maid. "Tutoring in Cyberspace: Student Impact and College/University Collaboration." *Computers and Composition* 12 (1995): 211–18.

Planning for Hypertexts in the Writing Center . . . Or Not

Michael A. Pemberton _____

GEORGIA SOUTHERN UNIVERSITY

As student writers become more technologically savvy and proficient at producing Web sites and other hypertext documents, writing centers will — if they have not already done so — soon begin to assist student writers with hypertext projects. In this article, which first appeared in The Writing Center Journal *in 2003, Michael A. Pemberton reviews four possible approaches writing centers might take in preparing to deliver this new*

service: (1) treating hypertext documents like any other rhetorical texts,
requiring no special training for tutors; (2) treating tutorials involving
hypertexts as rare events that call for no extensive preparations; (3) seek-
ing out and hiring tutors with expertise in hypertext media; and (4) pro-
viding special training for existing tutors. As Pemberton points out, visual
features — such as the use of color and illustrations — and a nonlinear
reading pattern are two key features that distinguish hypertexts from tra-
ditional print texts. He urges tutors and directors to learn as much as they
can about Web design but also reassures them that much of what tutors
already know about assisting students with writing will apply to the
composition and revision of new media.

It will come as no surprise, perhaps, to say that writing centers have long
been grounded in — some would say "bounded by" — the conventions of
printed text. True, writing centers, like most of the rest of the world, have been
influenced by advances in computer technology, most recently through the
explosive growth of Online Writing Labs (OWLs) and computer-mediated conferencing with students, but fundamentally, most of the interactions between
students and tutors still center on the handwritten or printed texts that are
placed on a table between them or, perhaps, shared in a word-processed file.
These texts are structured linearly and hierarchically, moving along a single
path from beginning to end, following well-known and universally taught discourse forms that have emerged from a print-based rhetorical tradition.

But times may be changing. As we enter an era when electronic publishing
and computer-mediated discourse are the norm, an era when new literary
genres and new forms of communication emerge on, seemingly, a weekly basis,
we must ask ourselves whether writing centers should continue to dwell exclusively in the linear, non-linked world of the printed page or whether they
should plan to redefine themselves — and retrain themselves — to take residence in the emerging world of multimedia, hyperlinked, digital documents.
To put it plainly, should we be preparing tutors to conference with students
about hypertexts? This is not a simple question to answer, but it is a question
that may soon demand explicit answers as our students explore and experiment with hypermedia in greater numbers in the years to come.

There are certainly compelling reasons to believe that writing centers should
learn more about digital texts and prepare themselves to help students both
navigate and create them, and more than a few writing center scholars have
urged the professional community to start their planning now. In an article on
preparing for future technologies in the writing center, Muriel Harris warns
her readers that writing center tutors will soon be conferencing with

> . . . a clientele of students who are composing texts [. . .] in multimedia pre-
> sentations, on Websites, in distance-learning projects, and so on. Computers
> as a technology interwoven in communication is a given, as is electronic com-
> munication across the curriculum. Writing centers without the technology or

staff to work with these students will find themselves no longer in sync with how writers write and with what writers need to know about writing processes as they are affected by technology. (194)

For John Trimbur, this move toward technological expertise in the writing center is inevitable and will eventually force writing centers to accommodate new rhetorical theories and practices to deal with new types of documents. "To my mind," he says, "the new digital literacies will increasingly be incorporated into writing centers not just as sources of information or delivery systems for tutoring but as productive arts in their own right, and writing center work will, if anything, become more rhetorical in paying attention to the practices and effects of design in written and visual communication" (30). As a result, writing centers may soon find themselves conferencing with students about hypertexts in progress, confronting not only unfamiliar textual landscapes but also challenging problems in document design.

Trimbur's imagined future may be approaching us more swiftly than we realize, now that the Internet and the World Wide Web have become such pervasive features of our culture and our students' academic lives. Students are not only browsing Web documents with more frequency, they are using Web sites as primary research sources in their papers and often creating such documents themselves. James Inman, in fact, asserts that "[i]n many writing classes, whether first-year composition or other courses like technical writing and business writing . . . teachers assign websites, and students look to writing centers for help, as that's where they've most often turned for peer help with writing" (II.8.3).[1]

But even if writing centers "are well suited to guide the journey into the bumpy land of learning with technology" (Cummins 206), we should ask ourselves at least three important questions as we consider what our specific role should be in this moment of transition, both at a global level (in relation to writing center theory and practice overall) and at a local level (in relation to our home institutions):

- Are writing centers generally *willing* to accommodate hypertexts?
- Do writing centers *need* to accommodate hypertexts?
- If a need exists, how should writing centers *prepare* to accommodate hypertexts?

How Have Writing Centers Viewed New Technologies?

A brief look at the ways writing centers have responded to new technologies in the past may help us answer the first of these questions and provide a useful context for answering the other two as well. Computers have been a part of writing center work for the better part of forty years now, sometimes as writing tools, sometimes as teaching devices, sometimes as resource centers, and sometimes as communications media; yet the relationship between writing centers and computer technology has been, overall, only a cordial one, with occasional fluctuations ranging from wild enthusiasm to brooding antagonism. While computers and computer software have often been praised by writing center scholars for the educational benefits they provide, they have also been seen as incipient threats — not merely to the personal, interactive pedagogies that writing centers embrace, but also to the writing center's very existence, particularly in tough budget times when administrators may view CAI programs and other technological artifacts as cheap, efficient alternatives to the labor-intensive, individualized teaching model at the heart of writing center practice.

Neal Lerner's work on the history of technology in writing centers from the 1930s to the 1970s documents the roots of this ambivalence, illustrating how new technologies, despite their potential benefits, have often been used to reshape writing center pedagogy, sometimes insidiously and frequently in ways that centers would later want to repudiate. In "Drill Pads, Teaching Machines, and Programmed Texts: Origins of Instructional Technology in Writing Centers," Lerner traces the earliest origins of a "technological model" for writing center work to social and cultural pressures that manifested in the 1930s, including the tripling of college enrollments as the children of immigrant families turned to higher education as a means of social advancement, and the concomitant cry for massive remediation as administrators had to cope with a sudden influx of students from diverse economic and cultural backgrounds with widely varying degrees of preparation (121–22). Lerner, citing Rose (1985), argues that the "efficiency movement" in education, tremendously influential at this time, responded to this crisis by producing and promoting an assortment of programmed, quasi-individualized "drill and practice technologies" that could be applied to under-prepared nontraditional students *en masse* (123). Writing labs soon became the sites where such programmed instruction and remediation took place, and the focus of this remediation work was largely restricted to grammar, mechanics, and other easily-quantifiable matters of surface structure. Through the 1950s and 1960s, this model for writing center work found an easy confluence with Skinnerian behaviorism, current-traditionalism, and an instrumental view of computer technology to produce the "Comp-Lab" model for programmed learning, a pedagogy that was prevalent in writing centers by the 1970s. As in the drill and practice writing lab of the 1930s, the "Comp-Lab" model focused on lower-order deficiencies in student writing (marked primarily by observable errors in surface structure) and "remedied" them by carefully chosen computer programs that would — with drills, exercises, practice sets, and "rewards" for right answers — gradually modify the students' deviant linguistic behaviors. This approach to writing instruction soon became a source of irritation to writing center directors as its current-traditional focus on grammar and final products conflicted strongly with the writing process model embraced by scholars and practitioners in the burgeoning field of composition studies. Writing center directors found themselves increasingly at odds with the pedagogy they were expected to support, and computers — to some extent — became avatars of a stagnant tradition rather than icons of progress and change.

Peter Carino's "Computers in the Writing Center: A Cautionary History" takes up the story where Lerner leaves off, tracing the conflicts that arose between the uses of computer technology for writing instruction and an increasingly sophisticated writing center theory that developed from the 1970s through the 1990s.[2] During this time period, says Carino, discussions of technology in writing centers primarily addressed the utility of behaviorist CAI programs like those Lerner described in the Comp-Lab model, the effect of word processors on student writing processes, and the impact computer technologies would have on the day-to-day functions of writing centers. While a fair number of these pieces offered "success stories" that stressed the benefits of computers for writing instruction, equally often writers expressed concerns about how technology would affect the mission of the center and whether or not technology might eventually dominate the center and eliminate the need for tutors altogether. "This tension between technological endorsement and technological resistance," he says, "marks writing center discourse on computers since the early 1980s" (172), and though such conflict does not, in itself, embody a master narrative for understanding the complex ways in which technology and writing center theory/practice interpenetrate one another, it is nevertheless a salient perspective from which to view and interpret what has been, historically, an uneasy relationship.

Carino's article, like Lerner's, makes several important points about technology's effects on writing center pedagogy and the corresponding positions that writing center professionals have taken in relation to those effects. Foremost among these points, perhaps, is the fact that writing centers have always maintained a healthy critical skepticism about the impact technology has had or should have on what they do. Writing centers have always wanted to be responsive to technology and the changes technology brings to the student populations they serve, but they also question whether the seductions of technology will end up diluting their core values or giving them responsibilities that they're not prepared to accept. As recently as 1995, Muriel Harris and I warned that "the lack of personal contact [in online tutorials] may seem to dehumanize a setting that writing centers have traditionally viewed as personal and warm" (156), and Nancy Grimm in that same year wrote that concerns about such dehumanization were still an "unresolved issue" (324).

The implication this history has for hypertexts, then, is that writing centers will — in principle — be willing to adjust to the demands that these new types of documents bring, but they will not do so uncritically, and they will likely remain wary. Though hypertexts, in and of themselves, may not represent the kind of depersonalizing influence (at least symbolically) that computers do, their metaphorical affiliation with a steadily encroaching technology — sometimes threatening, often unfamiliar — will probably exacerbate any hopes of easy accommodation.

What's Missing in Writing Center Discourse

Some evidence for the wariness writing center professionals feel about technology can be seen in the field's recent professional discourse about the impact of hypertexts — or rather, the near total lack of such discourse. Carino ends his historical review by noting that OWLs, LANs, MOOs and Webs have dominated the conversation in writing center discourse in recent years, but it's also worth noting that except for a smattering of writing center articles that have reflected on somewhat marginal technological issues,[3] the substance of that conversation has fallen into one of two distinct threads: discussions of online tutoring — conferencing between tutor and tutee at remote sites, mediated by computers — or the design, purpose, and function of OWLs. Rarely has there been a discussion (even in the archives of WCENTER) of the impact that the Web is having on the very nature of what constitutes a "text" or the impact that the reconstituted shape of these texts might have on writing center training, conferences, or discourse.

Though writing centers hitched their wagons to the Internet train early on, their primary research interest in this area since the early 1990s has been the collaborative possibilities enabled by email, chatrooms, listservs, and the World Wide Web. In a 1995 special issue of *Computers and Composition*, edited by Joyce Kinkead and Christine Hult, fully a dozen articles appeared about computers and writing centers, most of them reflecting on the opportunities for computer-mediated tutoring made available via the Internet. The majority of these pieces concerned themselves with one of two possible topics: (1) the mechanics of creating systems for online tutoring (Harris and Pemberton, Nelson and Wambean, Healy) or (2) the textual features of the discourse produced by tutors and students in online environments (Coogan, Wood, Chappell, Johanek and Rickly). At a time when the Internet was first making its power as an instructional delivery system felt, such research was absolutely necessary. People in the field needed to know the possibilities, and they had to be aware of the risks. Did writing centers want to develop an online presence? How should they go about doing it? What happens in online tutoring? What are the gains? What are the losses? These were the clear, important questions that writing center professionals needed answers to, and researchers regularly reported the results of their online experiences in journal publications and conference presentations.

From 1995 to the present, the substance and focus of writing center research as it relates to technology has remained largely unchanged. "How-to-build-an OWL" articles have begun to disappear in recent years as online writing labs have become the norm rather than the exception, and the sheer comprehensiveness of James Inman and Clint Gardner's recent CD-ROM, *The OWL Construction and Maintenance Guide*, may close the door on such articles for quite some time. Still, a good deal of technology-related writing center scholarship continues to focus on the textual features of dialogue produced in online collaborative exchanges between tutors and students. Sara Kimball's "Cybertext/Cyberspeech: Writing Centers and Online Magic," for example, investigates the nature of cybertext in online tutorials and discusses ways in which online identities are either constructed or obscured (see also Bell and Hubler). Recent descriptive studies of synchronous OWL conferences, the dynamics of email tutoring, and CMC interactions with distance-learning students have also employed this methodological focus in their studies of tutorial discourse (see also Monroe; Coogan; Gardner; Anderson). By no means do I wish to devalue this research or the knowledge it produces. These studies are often insightful and theoretically sophisticated, helping us to better understand the complex sociolinguistic structures inherent in the hybrid oral/textual environment of online conversation. My point here, however, is that they tend to investigate only one kind of technological "text" that writing centers are likely to generate or come in contact with.

When matters of tutor training are addressed with respect to technology, they tend to highlight how tutors can be trained to use technology effectively when working as OWL consultants, rather than how to critique HTML documents and guide students toward successful revisions. Breuch, Kastman, and Racine, for example, only encourage tutors to be sensitive to the distinctive nature of text-only environments, and offer several useful suggestions for structuring online responses and adopting appropriate tutoring roles. Similarly, three current tutoring manuals, *Tutoring Writing* (McAndrew & Reigstad), *A Tutor's Guide: Helping Writers One to One* (Rafoth), and the *Allyn and Bacon Guide to Peer Tutoring* (Gillespie and Lerner) include sections that address technology issues in writing centers, but they too focus on online tutoring alone — using email, OWLs, or synchronous chat systems to conference with students about their papers. Other sections in these texts contain advice for handling "difficult" discourse issues or conferencing sessions, but these chapters tend to focus on matters such as "what to do when a student has no draft" or "how to conference on unfamiliar subjects," rather than providing insights about how to help students whose drafts are constructed as hypermedia texts.

Do Writing Centers Need to Adjust Their Pedagogies?

If we believe that more and more writing classes will be taking Sean Williams' advice to "think out of the pro-verbal box" and allow students to write and create documents that incorporate more visual, multiliterate forms of communication, and if the Internet is spawning entirely new textual genres with their own sets of critical features, not all of which are common to print texts (Bauman), then the consequences for writing centers are clear: more students with different texts in unfamiliar genres will be making new demands on tutor expertise.

But what is the nature of these demands? What sorts of expertise will be necessary? What specific challenges do hypertexts entail, and must writing centers make significant changes in what they already do quite well — work with students, one-to-one, on papers that already span a wide range of discourse types across multiple disciplines?

Hypertexts can certainly present significant problems for writing centers, particularly with regard to the logistics of reading text itself. Hypertext documents complicate traditional rhetorical forms and can therefore subvert normal "print-based" reading strategies. Familiar notions of organization, argument, and thesis-support structures do not often translate well into Web space; comfortable understandings of format and conventions may no longer apply, and new schemas may take their place (Costanzo 13). "People write arguments in hypertext differently than they do in a more traditional format," notes Locke Carter. "When faced with the task of constructing single-author, self-contained arguments in a hypertext environment [he says] . . . authors must overcome the expectation of order" (3).[4] If what Carter says is true, then tutors would have to learn entirely new schemas for what hypertextual order entails, and at least in the short term, their ability to assess texts quickly and offer advice might be compromised. Imagine Michael Joyce coming into the writing center with a draft of his literary hypertext, *Afternoon,* a text whose opening page contains twenty possible links to other nodes or paths through the story. While many have lauded this work for breaking the shackles of conventional, linear narrative structure, a great many writing center tutors would probably find themselves disoriented and at a loss for how to give advice for revision. As Johndan Johnson-Eilola notes, a hypertext such as this "can give readers a rush of euphoria — or, for the same reasons, a rush of vertigo" (195). And though student writers may not bring hypertexts as complex or as challenging as Joyce's into the writing center, the ones they do bring in may well give tutors the same sense of vertigo, particularly if they are not trained to deal with them.

Preparing for Hypertext #1: Treat Hypertexts Like Any Other Texts

So how, then, should writing centers address hypertexts? How should they restructure their training schedules or reconfigure their theories to account for texts that elide linear patterns of organization in a digital environment? Interestingly enough, it's possible to build at least two lines of argument that maintain they shouldn't — that despite the likelihood that students will be writing hypertexts in growing numbers, there is no need for writing centers to change their pedagogies as a consequence.

The first line of argument would maintain that the problems hypertexts pose for tutors are essentially no different from the problems posed by any other texts, regardless of genre or discipline. Since there is no possibility that a tutor will be able to address all possible content or rhetorical features in a single writing center conference (or multiple conferences) anyway, then tutors should feel comfortable working with the aspects of writing they are already familiar with and not worry overmuch about those they aren't. Similar arguments have been made in writing center literature about questions of disciplinary expertise (Pemberton) and the relative benefits of having generalist or specialist tutors (Kiedaisch and Dinitz). James Inman summarizes this perspective with regard to technology when he says,

> Just as writing centers do not claim to be founts of all knowledge that is great and good about essays and other more traditional writing challenges, so we should not feel pressure to know everything about technology. Consultants' general knowledge about textuality and investment in asking questions, listening carefully, and other non-directive pedagogical approaches is all they need to help clients, I believe, no matter the nature of their visits to the writing center. (II.8.3)

It seems reasonable to claim, by extension, that despite the inflections hypertext introduces into print-based conceptions of argument and order, there will be other aspects of textual production and reception that apply across forms. Alan Rea and Doug White point out, for example, that issues of audience and purpose remain as important in Web texts as in print texts (429–30), and all tutors in the writing center, regardless of their background or level of technological expertise, are capable of directing conferences to focus on these issues. Further, tutors, like most anyone else who browses the Web, comprise a legitimate audience for hypertext documents that will appear on the Internet, and their input and responses can therefore be informative, whatever their level of technical or hypertextual knowledge.

Larry Beason's experiences teaching "future English teachers" how to critique Web pages provide some support for this position. When describing an assignment sequence that he gives to his writing students. Beason suggests that they get feedback on their hypertexts from a variety of readers, presumably including writing center tutors, because "the most common concern [he found in the drafts he reviewed] was that the page authors were indeed not taking into account the varied ways in which readers might approach a page" (33). From this perspective, then, a writing center tutor's unfamiliarity with hypertext structure and design should be no more of a concern than their lack of familiarity with economic theory or the principles of civil engineering. No one can be an expert in everything; what's important in a conference is that writers receive a thoughtful response from an authentic audience.

Preparing for Hypertext #2: Hypertexts Will Rarely Appear in Writing Centers

A second rationale for opting to ignore the complications of hypertext in tutorials is that writing centers may not, in fact, see much of it. Despite the glowing successes experienced by a relatively small number of enthusiastic computer-literate instructors and the predictions of digital visionaries, it is possible that the majority of academics will continue to assign their students linear, print-centered papers and expect students to demonstrate mastery of those forms alone. The reasons for such persistent consistency can be many and varied, ranging from simple unfamiliarity with the medium to sophisticated theoretical stances on the nature of thinking processes and academic discourse.

To a great many academics, the linear, hierarchical nature of print texts is a virtue, not a weakness. David W. Chapman makes a case for this position in his *Computers and Composition* article, "A Luddite in Cyberland, Or How to Avoid Being Snared by the Web." Though his perspective seems astonishingly provincial at times, the point he makes here is cogent and is likely shared by a great many academics in both the humanities and the sciences:

> . . . the nonlinearity of the reading experience, the widely acclaimed hypertext, undermines logical patterns of reading and thinking. The linearity of a written text is not a limitation, it is its glory. . . . No one needs to teach students to jump in random order from one "tickler" to the next. What students do need to learn is how to spend an hour or two in concentrated thought as they engage a work of complexity and depth. . . . [K]nowing how to produce a Web page is a useful skill, but there is no indication that it will improve a student's ability to write. (249–51)

Though some might well argue with this conclusion, there is no arguing the fact that the dominant discourse paradigm in academia is linear and print-based and that instructors will continue to teach that form to students, often to the exclusion of all other forms. This is not entirely a matter of clinging to tradition or resisting the need to learn something new. The controlled, linear flow of ideas through focal attention is, according to Davida Charney, one of the great strengths of print texts (243), and Clifford Lynch, the Director of the Coalition for Networked Information, believes that "some kinds of discourse — scholarly and otherwise — [may] be more effective using existing genres rooted in printed works (perhaps presented digitally as well as on paper) rather than in the new genres." For these reasons alone, most instructors in most courses could choose to rely on print text assignments for the foreseeable future.

On a more subtle yet influential level, it is also possible that some academics perceive hypertext as a threat to the educational and disciplinary goals they value and will resist it for that reason. As Stuart Moulthrop and Nancy Kaplan, two of the strongest proponents of hypertext, have observed, this threat may not be wholly imaginary. "[T]he more we experiment with hypertext in literature courses," they say, "the deeper our conviction grows that this new medium is fundamentally at odds with the aims and purposes of conventional literary education" (236). If this is true, and if it holds true for disciplines other than literary studies, then a natural response among those who are most deeply invested in a more conventional educational program would simply be to resist the incursions of hypertext whenever possible, meaning fewer hypertexts assigned or allowed, and therefore fewer students with hypertexts visiting the writing center.

But even if most instructors will not encourage hypertext papers or teach Web design in their courses, others certainly will. Technical writing classes now incorporate Web documents and design as a matter of course, and a great many information technology, journalism, and graphic design classes view Web design and hypertext as integral parts of their curricula. This being the case, writing centers may feel it is their responsibility to prepare tutors to meet these students' rhetorical needs as well as the needs of students with more traditional assignments.

Preparing for Hypertext #3: Use Specialist Tutors

If writing centers want to be proactive, to prepare for the hypertexts that students bring in — be they in small numbers (if the above writers are right) or large numbers (if the above writers are wrong) — and if they want tutors to be knowledgeable about the conventions and organizational schemas that hypertexts employ, then one way to accomplish this is to hire tutors who already have demonstrable expertise with these sorts of texts. Writing centers with a strong WAC focus often employ an analogous approach by seeking out and hiring tutors from multiple disciplines, thereby ensuring that one or more tutors will be able to respond knowledgeably to students' questions about discourse-specific rhetorical forms as well as content.

The tricky part of this solution is purely practical, however, and may be especially troublesome for writing centers in smaller schools or those with limited resources for training. Finding students who know how to create a basic Web page is easy; finding students who know — and can articulate — what makes a particular set of hypertext documents effective or ineffective *as hypertexts* may be far more difficult. Finding students who have a practical understanding of hypertextual design as well as the writing and rhetorical skills necessary to be effective tutors for conventional print texts may be nigh-on impossible. David Chapman, the self-proclaimed Luddite mentioned earlier, claims that "[r]eal expertise in document design is possessed [only] by a small vanguard of technical writing instructors, and even they are just coming to grips with the implication of Web documents" (251). If what he says is true, then any dreams of employing tutors with real expertise in hypertext may remain, as Hamlet intoned, merely "a consummation devoutly to be wished."

Nevertheless, a rich, detailed, sophisticated knowledge of hypertext structure and Web design is probably not a necessity for productive conferencing. A reasonable working knowledge of the principles of hypertext should be more than sufficient for all but the most complex and sophisticated documents, and that degree of knowledge can usually be achieved through a series of manageable, but well-focused workshops.

Preparing for Hypertext #4: Provide Specialized Training for Tutors

Workshops and training sessions on hypertext nevertheless present some problems for writing centers, partly because they represent just one more item on a continuously-expanding agenda of specialized knowledges that writing center tutors should know or learn. Already confronted with the diverse needs of ESL students, learning-disabled students, second-dialect students, nontraditional students, students from a variety of disciplines, students in first-year composition courses, graduate students, and students in professional writing classes, writing center directors may decide it's in their best interest to defer workshops on the intricacies of hypertext until the need becomes critical — or at least more critical than many of the other critical needs the writing center has to respond to. Randall Beebe and Mary Boneville recognize the pressing need for tutors to develop advanced computer literacies, to become "quite skilled in manipulating network technologies, designing Web pages, and answering computer-application questions," but they also admit that "because most tutors are overworked with face-to-face tutorials, adding another dimension to their job description hardly seems fair; many writing centers are already understaffed without the resources to provide extensive training" (47). In the face of such pressures and a relative paucity of students visiting the writing center with hypertexts, workshops on nonlinear electronic documents may quickly give way to other topics in tutor training sessions.

But if — in keeping with our general willingness to accommodate new rhetorical and digital forms — we do decide to devote at least part of our tutorial attentions to hypermedia, multimedia, and other "unconventional" electronic documents, where should we begin? What resources must we have on hand, and what training must we give our tutors — and ourselves — to meet our students' needs?

Fortunately, most tutors — as I mentioned earlier — will already have the expertise necessary to discuss hypertexts as informed, aware readers. They will know (or soon be trained in) the conventions of print texts, audience, organization, and argument, and they will also likely be skilled users of the World Wide Web, familiar with the basic conventions of linking, clicking, and scrolling. While this might not enable them to teach students about the subtleties of page design or Web site navigation strategies, their responses as users and readers of a Web page can nevertheless provide valuable guidance to hypertext authors.

Writing center directors who wish to train their tutors further in the basics of Web page design have a wealth of accessible (read: not jargony) resources available online that can be shared as training material in workshops. Among the most useful of these are the *Web Style Guide, 2nd Edition* by Patrick Lynch and Sarah Horton (http://www.webstyleguide.com), and Tammy Worcester's *Web Page Design — From Planning to Posting* (http://www.essdack.org/web design/). A great set of negative examples, guaranteed to make a dry training workshop hilarious and also raise important issues in Web site design, can be found at *Web Pages that Suck* (http://www.webpagesthatsuck.com/). The information provided on these sites and others, as well as a host of trade books aimed at computer novices (such as *The Complete Idiot's Guide to Web Page*

Design by Paul McFedries), can teach tutors how to identify and address some simple design issues — and common mistakes — that arise in student Web pages with some frequency.

Tutoring, Training, and Tough Questions

Although it would be easy to pursue this trail of possible resources further, identifying an assortment of sites and texts that could be used to teach tutors HTML and JavaScript, or how to use Microsoft FrontPage or Netscape Composer, we should stop and think carefully about how far we are really willing to go down this path in our quest to create "better" writing tutors. Ultimately, we have to ask ourselves whether it is really the writing center's responsibility to be all things to all people. There will always be more to learn. There will always be new groups making demands on our time and our resources in ways we haven't yet planned for. And there will never be enough time or enough money or enough tutors to meet all those demands all of the time. If we diversify too widely and spread ourselves too thinly in an attempt to encompass too many different literacies, we may not be able to address any set of literate practices particularly well.

The decision about whether to train tutors in the rhetoric of hypertext, then, must necessarily be inflected by local needs and resources. As James Inman notes, some writing centers offer "specialized training for consultants and the acquisition of software options like Macromedia Dreamweaver, Netscape Composer, and Microsoft FrontPage for website design" while others simply "choose not to support such website and desktop publishing assignments" (II.8.3). Each of these paths may be equally appropriate, depending on the institution, the student body, the writing center's mission, and contingencies involving time, money, and resources. The important thing for writing center directors and administrators to remember is that they should remain attuned to changes in their students' and institutions' needs and not let apprehensions about technology interfere with their efforts to learn and work with the new rhetorical forms that technology brings about.

Notes

[1] Though I don't completely agree with Inman — I suspect that a great many students still see Web design and organization as a technical rather than a rhetorical issue and do not automatically think of the writing center as a primary resource — it would only take a relatively minor change in institutional culture or student culture to alter those circumstances dramatically.

[2] Carino also argues that the conflicts over the uses of technology which arose in writing centers paralleled conflicts that took place in the larger field of composition studies, as described by Gail Hawisher, Paul Le Blanc, Charles Moran, and Cindy Selfe in *Computers and the Teaching of Writing in American Higher Education, 1979–1994: A History.*

[3] Including such topics as the need to work closely with software designers (Selfe); to ensure adequate access for students, tutors, and necessary services (Harris); and to understand

the intellectual property and plagiarism issues raised by inappropriate borrowing and linking to other texts (Haynes-Burton).

[4] This is not to say that disorder is the rule, of course. Carter goes on to describe a series of organizational and arrangement strategies that writers can use to guide readers through their hypertexts. Some of these strategies draw on traditional rhetorical schemes: using an existing argumentative structure such as a Toulmin model, or "writing prose with an eye to fundamentals of textual coherence" (8).

Works Cited

Anderson, Dana. "Interfacing Email Tutoring; Shaping an Emergent Literate Practice." *Computers and Composition 19* (2002): 71–87.

Bauman, Marcy Lassota. "The Evolution of Internet Genres." *Computers and Composition 16* (1999): 269–282.

Beason, Larry. "Preparing Future Teachers of English to Use the Web: Balancing the Technical with the Pedagogical." *Weaving a Virtual Web: Practical Approaches to New Information Technologies.* Ed. Sibylle Gruber. Urbana, IL: NCTE, 2000: 25–42.

Beebe, Randall L., and Mary J. Boneville. "The Culture of Technology in the Writing Center: Reinvigorating the Theory-Practice Debate." Inman and Sewell. 41–51.

Bell, Diana C., and Mike T. Hübler. "The Virtual Writing Center: Developing Ethos through Mailing List Discourse." *Writing Center Journal 21.2* (2001): 57–78.

Breuch, Lee-Ann, M. Kastman, and Sam Racine. "Developing Sound Tutor Training for Online Writing Centers: Creating Productive Peer Reviews." *Computers and Composition 17* (2000): 245–263.

Carino, Peter. "Computers in the Writing Center: A Cautionary History." Hobson. 171–193.

Carter, Locke. "Argument in Hypertext: Writing Strategies and the Problem of Order in a Nonsequential World." *Computers and Composition 20* (2003): 3–22.

Chapman, David W. "A Luddite in Cyberland, Or How to Avoid Being Snared by the Web." *Computers and Composition 16* (1999): 247–252.

Chappell, Virginia A. "Theorizing in Practice: Tutor Training 'Live from the VAX' Lab." *Computers and Composition 12.2* (1995): 227–235.

Charney, Davida. "The Effect of Hypertext on Processes of Reading and Writing." Selfe and Hilligoss. 238–263.

Coogan, David, "E-Mail Tutoring, a New Way to Do New Work." *Computers and Composition 12.2* (1995): 171–181

———. "Email 'Tutoring' as Collaborative Writing." *Wiring the Writing Center.* Hobson. 25–43.

Costanzo, William. "Reading, Writing, and Thinking in an Age of Electronic Literacy." Selfe and Hilligoss. 11–21.

Cummins, Gail. "Centering in the Distance: Writing Centers, Inquiry, and Technology." Inman and Sewell. 203–210.

Flanders, Vincent. Web Pages that Suck. 2003. 4 November 2003. <http://www.webpagesthatsuck.com>.

Gardner, Clinton. "Have You Visited Your Online Writing Center Today?: Learning, Writing, and Teaching Online at a Community College." Hobson. 75–84.

Gillespie, Paula, and Neal Lerner. *The Allyn and Bacon Guide to Peer Tutoring,* 2nd ed. Boston: Allyn & Bacon, 2003.

Grimm, Nancy Maloney. "Computer Centers and Writing Centers: An Argument for Ballast." *Computers and Composition 12* (1995): 323–29.

Harris, Muriel. "Making Up Tomorrow's Agenda and Shopping Lists Today: Preparing for Future Technologies in the Writing Center." Inman and Sewell. 193–202.

Harris, Muriel, and Michael Pemberton. "Online Writing Labs (OWLS): A Taxonomy of Options and Issues." *Computers and Composition* 12.2 (1995): 145–159.

Haynes-Burton, Cynthia. "Intellectual (Proper)ty in Writing Centers: Retro Texts and Positive Plagiarism," *Writing Center Perspectives*. Ed. Byron Stay, Christina Murphy, and Eric H. Hobson. Emmitsburg, MD: NWCA Press, 1995. 84–93

Healy, Dave. "From Place to Space: Perceptual and Administrative Issues in the Online Writing Center." *Computers and Composition* 12.2 (1995): 183–193.

Hobson, Eric, ed. *Wiring the Writing Center.* Logan, UT: Utah State University Press, 1998.

Inman, James A, and Clinton Gardner, eds. *The OWL Construction and Maintenance Guide.* CD-ROM. IWCA Press, 2002.

Inman, James A., and Donna Sewell, eds. *Taking Flight With OWLs: Examining Electronic Writing Center Work.* Mahwah, NJ: Erlbaum, 2000.

Johanek, Cindy, and Rebecca Rickly. "Online Tutor Training: Synchronous Conferencing in a Professional Community." *Computers and Composition* 12.2 (1995): 237–246.

Johnson-Eilola, Johndan. "Reading and Writing in Hypertext: Vertigo and Euphoria." Selfe and Hilligoss. 195–219.

Kimball, Sara. "Cybertext/Cyberspeech: Writing Centers and Online Magic." *Writing Center Journal* 18.1 (1997): 30–49.

Lerner, Neal. "Drill Pads, Teaching Machines, and Programmed Texts: Origins of Instructional Technology in Writing Centers." Hobson, 119–136.

Lynch, Clifford. "The Battle to Define the Future of the Book in the Digital World." *First Monday* 6.6 (June 2001). 9 May 2003. <http://www.firstmonday.dk/issues/issue6_6/lynch/>.

Monroe, Barbara. "The Look and Feel of the OWL Conference." *Wiring the Writing Center.* Ed. Eric H. Hobson. Logan, UT: Utah State UP, 1998. 3–24.

Moulthrop, Stuart, and Nancy Kaplan. "They Became What They Beheld: The Futility of Resistance in the Space of Electronic Writing." *Literacy and Computers: The Complications of Teaching and Learning with Technology.* Ed. Cynthia L. Selfe and Susan Hilligoss. New York: MLA, 1994. 220–237.

Nelson, Jane and Cynthia A. Wambeam. "Moving Computers into the Writing Center: The Path to Least Resistance." *Computers and Composition* 12.2 (1995): 135–143.

Pemberton, Michael. "Rethinking the WAC/Writing Center Connection." *Writing Center Journal* 15.2 (1995): 116–133.

Rea, Alan and Doug White. "The Changing Nature of Writing: Prose or Code in the Classroom." *Computers and Composition* 16 (1999): 421–436.

Rose, Mike. "The Language of Exclusion: Writing Instruction at the University." *College English* 47 (1985): 341–59.

Selfe, Dickie. "Surfing the Tsunami: Electronic Environments in the Writing Center." *Computers and Composition* 12 (1995): 311–22.

Trimbur, John. "Multiliteracies, Social Futures, and Writing Centers." *WCJ* 20.2 (2000): 29–31.

Williams, Sean D. "Part I: Thinking Out of the Pro-Verbal Box." *Computers and Composition* (2001): 21–32.

Wood, Gail F. "Making the Transition from ASL to English: Deaf Students, Computers, and the Writing Center." *Computers and Composition* 12.2 (1995): 219–226.

Protocols and Process in Online Tutoring

George Cooper, Kara Bui, and Linda Riker _____
UNIVERSITY OF MICHIGAN

In spite of potential drawbacks to online tutoring, including the loss of face-to-face interaction that is the centerpiece of most writing center interactions, George Cooper, Kara Bui, and Linda Riker argue that tutors can retain "a sense of collaboration and humanity in the online forum." They suggest that tutors begin online tutoring sessions by setting a friendly, informal tone in their introductory remarks. Doing so begins the process of building an interpersonal relationship with writers, which is one of the main challenges of online tutoring. They also advise tutors to ask questions that promote a give-and-take dialogue with student writers. Such questions can also serve an important role by tempering criticism and making clear to writers that they retain a significant role in the decision-making process. To help tutors avoid simple editing of students' papers, Cooper, Bui, and Riker recommend limiting help on grammar and mechanics to specific examples, directing students' attention to patterns of error. They also suggest tutors end online sessions with a final summation that leaves the student feeling confident, with a definite sense of where to proceed. Finally, they caution that tutors will have to remain open to creating or adapting their practices to the situations they encounter online. This essay, which first appeared in A Tutor's Guide: Helping One on One, *offers a practical introduction to online tutoring that beginning tutors will find helpful.*

Online writing centers have slowly begun to change the way some writing centers work, enabling students to submit drafts of essays or rough outlines to a writing center tutor via the campus computer network. The most advanced online operations use e-mail attachments, which transmit files directly from a word processing program but can involve compatibility problems. Other online systems rely exclusively on e-mail, which is user-friendly but not very convenient for sending formatted files. In either case, instead of having to visit the writing center, students can get help with their papers from their residence hall or their hometown, eliminating the need to make a trip to the writing center. But does online tutoring change the nature of teaching and learning that has made writing centers so successful? What are some things tutors must know about online tutoring, and how can they make it effective?

Some Background

Collaborative, face-to-face communication has become a hallmark of the work that peer tutors do in campus writing centers. In her essay "Collaboration,

Control, and the Idea of a Writing Center," Andrea Lunsford writes about collaboration and how important it is for students to take control of the tutoring situation. She describes a writing center as a place where "knowledge [is] always contextually bound . . . always constructed" and where, in Hanna Arendt's words, "for excellence, the presence of others is required."[1] In *The Practical Tutor,* Emily Meyer and Louise Smith address a similar issue in their chapter "Engaging in Dialogue." They emphasize that conversation is the precursor to development of ideas on paper. Conversation is a familiar aspect of our oral world, and it is necessary for the writer's transition into the written world. In an effort to cultivate the dialogue of conversations, some researchers emphasize the use of open-ended questions. So important is dialogue that Meyer and Smith include a section entitled "Pace and Tone of Questions," pinpointing the prominent role that dialogue assumes in their notion of good tutoring.

Online tutoring stretches and stresses the viability of these good principles. One could argue that sending a paper online to a tutor can be similar to dropping off dry cleaning — leave your paper at the center on Monday and pick it up on Tuesday with all errors marked and corrected — a practice abhorred in most writing centers. We train our tutors in collaborative learning and see ourselves as facilitators of knowledge, not dictators of it. Not surprisingly, our tutors question whether the success of face-to-face tutoring can be transferred to online tutoring. "How do we engage the student in dialogue when there is really only one of us present at a time?" they ask. "What kinds of questions should we ask to get the writer's attention?" "How can I tell whether the student understands my comments?"

Though principles of face-to-face tutoring do not transfer completely to online tutoring, we can still retain a sense of collaboration and humanity in the online forum. There are online strategies for establishing a relationship between the tutor and writer, for empowering writers to share in their own revision, and for dealing with specifics of grammar and mechanics — all done by relying on collaborative techniques and leading to a facilitated knowledge between tutor and client. As Barbara Monroe writes in "The Look and Feel of the OWL Conference," "Owl [online writing lab], then, is not just an online tutorial service, but a site where meaning and value are shared, contested and negotiated, a site that provokes and promotes new literate practices, both online and in print."[2] Embracing these principles does not solve all problems — and face-to-face tutoring has problems too — but it does result in a shared learning experience. Moreover, we have found that students using our OWL (Online Writing and Learning) service not only benefit from the feedback but even utilize the directed responses more freely, independently, and self-confidently than they sometimes do in face-to-face tutoring. In the section below, we offer some advice, based on an actual online submission and response, for how to make the benefits of online tutoring a reality.

WHAT TO DO?

Setting the Right Tone in Introductory Remarks

The writer's first encounter with an online tutor sets the tone for everything that follows. If the tutor's opening remarks are friendly and informal — as they are in the example below with its friendly greeting, contractions, and helpful explanations — the writer will read the tutor's comments as gentle and constructive.

> Hi Morton,
>
> I'm Lisa, the OWL tutor who'll be reading your paper. I've read through your questions and will make some notes within your paper about the intro, conclusion, overall structure of your paper and grammar. I'll also try to include major questions I have, as a reader, as I read, so you can get an idea of how an average reader might react. Look for my notes within the body of your paper, set off by asterisks, like this****.

But if the comments are businesslike or formal ("Morton, I read your paper and will make some comments about your introduction"), the writer may hear a harsh and scolding voice, even if the tutor intended otherwise. Written feedback works this way, and keeping the tone lighthearted and friendly is more than a nicety. It is what stands in place of a smile, eye contact, and pleasant voice.

Muriel Harris writes of the importance of this phase of the tutoring session as "Getting Acquainted Time." It is where tutors learn "students' interests and skills, information useful in helping students locate potential subjects for writing."[3] This period of time includes some social and some academic or intellectual engagements. A tutor might begin with small talk about the weather or a detail about the person's dress that sparks conversation. Such small talk is a necessary first-step in establishing trust, and the conversation soon moves toward the student's paper and what kind of help the writer is seeking. The complete process is one which Harris describes as including "getting acquainted time," "diagnostic time," "instructional time," and "evaluation time."[4]

Online Writing and Learning (OWL) environments allow for some of the same processes. Our OWL at the University of Michigan asks students who are submitting papers to include basic facts like their name, year of enrollment, and course, but it also asks students to describe the assignment and to tell what kind of help they want. This provides the same foundation of information needed in any tutoring session.

But because the writer has to type in the assignment and the nature of his request, there is more time to think about what to say, hopefully avoiding "Oh, just check the grammar," which is what students often say when they walk into the writing center and can't think quickly enough, or don't know how to ask for help in any more specific way. Some online writing centers offer students a prioritized checklist of potential problem areas (Transitions, Use of Details, Punctuation, and so on) and ask them to describe the help they seek in each particular area. In this way, it is assured that the student takes the initiative to set the agenda.

Although online comments do tend to get to the point much quicker than face-to-face tutoring, it is important to remember that the online tutor still needs to establish a relationship. By the same token, the writer must describe the assignment and its context as much as possible before the tutor can offer feedback that is genuinely helpful.

Promoting Dialogue in Diagnostic and Instructional Comments

The example below reveals the degree of dialogue that an online conference can generate with a writer.

> ****OK, so your argument is that Reich is generally incorrect in his percep-tion of the impact of foreign workers on the US economy, right? I understand your desire to include in the first paragraph every aspect and detail of his argument, but this is not necessary. In your intro you want to lay out general information about Reich's argument and then set up your thesis, which in this case opposes that argument. Later in your paper you can point by point counter his argument. Also be careful of overwhelming the reader with too many quotes in your intro. While these quotes are probably quite useful to your paper, you can sprinkle them throughout the body of the paper.****

The tutor begins with an opening question, used to summarize what she thinks is the writer's main goal. The question, indeed a rhetorical question, expects no response. Rather, it suggests an openness, a give-and-take between writer and tutor, but surely provides a foundational point of initial discussion. If the tutor gets the topic wrong, the remaining critique and turorial is under-mined. Stated as a question, however, the observation remains negotiable, a misunderstanding possibly due to the reader's interpretation rather than cued by the text. Such possibility provides the writer a common ground with the tutor, an ethos of process shared between them if not entirely a mutual under-standing of a piece of writing. The uncertainty expressed in the rhetorical nature of the question indicates the tutor's intention to proceed with an open mind. The next few sentences following the rhetorical question contribute in the way Donald Murray described as "the self proposes, the other self consid-ers"[5] or what Kenneth Bruffee refers to as a reflective thought.[6] The tutor's tone is cautionary and invites the writer to reconsider his assumptions about what a good opening approach might be.

In a typical tutoring session peer tutors read a paper aloud, stopping now and then to examine troublesome areas in the text. This puts the tutor in con-trol — and the student on the spot. But the goal for learning theorists who advocate a Socratic approach is to engage that learner, not to manipulate him. Ideally, the tutor asks questions before giving directions and engages the client's own knowledge to solve a problem. In *The Practical Tutor,* Emily Meyer and Louise Smith relate some of the background to this theorizing. They explain writing to be a dialogic process within the mind of the writer, especially the experienced writer. Through conversation, the tutor helps the writer to initiate, recognize, and cultivate the dialogic process used by experienced writers. Online tutors can also use questions to engage writers in this exercise.[7] Because the tutor is not waiting for an answer, the writer is free to act as she wishes. The door to genuine contemplation is open and the writer remains in control.

Questions can serve yet another purpose, and that is to soften criticism. Once again, in the absence of facial expression and voice modulation, the tutor must make points clearly but not coldly, as in this example:

> ****I think that you have explained your opinion well in this paragraph. My only concern for content here is, does a job as a bank teller pay the equivalent as an aerobics instructor? Or does working the line in a factory provide better benefits (i.e., health insurance)? These are things to think about when making very generalized comparisons. Generally aerobics instructors don't work full time nor do they receive health benefits. I understand what it is you're doing with this example, but I think that the comparison is unfair. Just something to think about.****

This comment occurs later in the paper and works as a probe intended to create dialogue within the writer's mind. In classic fashion, the tutor begins with a compliment before raising a criticism. The criticism is presented as a question, not rhetorical this time but genuine, and, should the writer care to consider it, one which points out a fundamental weakness in the paper; in this case, the writer has made a number of loose, poorly developed correlations. Note the tutor's comment about "when making very generalized comparisons" and how this invites the writer to again share a perspective with the tutor. Here, the tutor has established a foundation for interpretation from which the writer can, by his own will and skill, determine a path of revision. "Well, I'm not trying for very generalized comparisons," he might say. "Why would she say that I'm doing that?" "What does she mean that aerobics instructors don't work full time? That wasn't my point." And so the dialogue goes. Online tutoring cannot monitor the direction in which the dialogue unfolds or the decisions a writer makes on the basis of it — more on this later. But then, no true collaborator would wish to do that either.

Limiting and Focusing Comments on Grammar and Mechanics

Writing center tutors probably get more requests for help with grammar and mechanics than anything else. What is the best way to respond? Consider this comment from an online tutor:

> ****Two mechanics notes: 1. You want a comma between "agrees" and "explaining," just to make sure the reader doesn't read agreesexplaining, all

fast like that. The comma tells the reader to pause. 2. Did you add the word "whom" to Reich's quotation? If so, you should enclose it in [brackets]. (Do that any time you add a word to clarify the meaning of a quotation.) And, because that word represents the subject of a subordinate clause, it should be "who," not "whom."****

In responding online, the tutor has to make a special effort not to correct every matter. Anyone who has ever seen an online paper that has been meticulously corrected will immediately recognize the problem: with all the insertions of asterisks, question marks, boldface words, and underlines, the paper looks as though it has been worked over. It is ironic that painstakingly correcting every error makes a tutor feel exhausted, while the student who receives the corrected paper feels ashamed. This is not conducive to learning. Comments inserted into the body of the text and set off by asterisks or other marks ($ or % or #) can also seem like litter if they occur too often. On the other hand, e-mail attachment files make it possible to use a word processor like Microsoft Word to insert comments in textboxes or in hidden pop-up boxes and to identify edits with the Track Changes feature or by using a different font color; these look much less intrusive on the page.

Students learn in many ways. Irene Lurkis Clark's essay "Collaboration and Ethics in Writing Center Pedagogy"[8] reminds us that imitation has a long history as a prominent way of learning. Citing Lev Vygotsky, she says that human beings "can imitate a variety of actions that go well beyond the limits of their own capabilities."[9] In the example above, the tutor advises the writer about specific points of grammar and mechanics, correcting and to some degree explaining the logic behind the change. In this example the tutor takes a directive approach and, in its most extreme fashion so far, renders the tutor in the role of proofreader or editor. And yet, the tutor is striking a balance by holding corrections to a minimum (even though there were many other surface errors in this paper) and supplying them with explanation. While this may be no different than it would be when handled in a face-to-face tutoring session, the online forum can do one thing the face-to-face session cannot, and it again involves e-mail attachments. With an attachment, the tutor can insert a hotlink to a Web page that addresses the specific error in question. The writer can then just click on the link and read all about it.[10] (In a face-to-face session, the equivalent would be to tear a page from a hand-book and staple it to the writer's draft.)

Consider how another tutor responded to text-level features in the same student's paper. Notice the less directive approach regarding grammar and mechanics:

> ****Also, I would like to suggest that you go back and read your paper aloud to yourself. There are a few places where you have pluralized nouns that should be singular or tacked on an "s" to an adjective. These are relatively easy to find when you read through OUT LOUD. Silent skimming does not catch such mistakes, nor does spell check.***

Responding in this way, the tutor recommends the "read aloud" scenario used in face-to-face tutoring. (Note that although the tutor just wanted to emphasize the importance of reading aloud by using all caps, it looks like she is shouting. Our recommendation is, when responding online, AVOID ALL CAPS!) Accompanying the suggestion to read aloud is an indication of what the student might find in doing this, clueing him without telling him directly what to fix. In this way, the tutor avoids the pressure to edit a paper and instead transfers the responsibility of making simple corrections back to the student.

When students submit papers containing many errors, tutors can feel obligated to address each problem as it occurs. This process is time consuming online, pedagogically unsound, and detracts from the tutors' ability to address more global issues. Instead, tutors should locate a pattern of technical errors and use only one or two examples to demonstrate how to correct the problem. In essence, the tutor attempts to teach clients how to recognize and edit errors on their own. In the most severe cases, clients are urged to seek face-to-face help.

Creating Closure with a Final Summation

You will recognize the nature of this end comment (below). Teachers typically write such a remark at the end of a paper. In the online situation, it provides closure to the session.

> ****The overall structure of your paper is good, with ideas flowing from one another. Really what I'd like to see as a reader is more development of your ideas, especially that part at the end about education and gender equality. You can admit that it'll be a difficult transition period, but it's inevitable and in the end will be better than the current situation. I think that's the reaction I was trying to explain when you were talking about aerobics instructors. The paper looks good grammatically; do try to read it over to check for word choice (aboard/abroad) type stuff the spell check can't catch. Good luck with your revisions.****

Murphy and Sherwood say that the concluding stage "contributes to students' feelings of empowerment, providing them with the confidence they need to take the insights they have gained and apply them in new writing situations."[11] In a face-to-face conference this may be done by asking the student to write a brief evaluation note on what the conference accomplished. Online, this task is left to the tutor, but such a closing doesn't attempt to cover everything. The above comment begins by praising what is good about the paper and then reiterates a concern raised earlier about the development of ideas, and in a directive manner it briefly sketches out how the development might unfold. The client should leave this conference as he or she would a face-to-face conference, with a sense of confidence and a solid foundation from which she can proceed into the next draft.

Complicating Matters

Inevitably, the advice we offer above will be complicated by the actual tutoring sessions you will encounter. Whether our advice — or any advice — works or not can only be determined by feedback from the writers themselves, and this can be hard to come by in the online environment. Despite all the strategies tutors use to recreate a dialogue online, one element of conversation remains irrecoverable — body language. Unlike a face-to-face conference, when an OWL tutor sends a finished conference back to a client there is no way to gauge the success of the conference. Harris agrees that "nodding, smiling to show agreement, and offering other small but significant human gestures of friendliness and approval are additional means of conveying our messages" and are important for communication feedback.[12] OWL tutors cannot monitor the client's understanding or receptiveness to their suggestions without such feedback.

Occasionally the tutor has a chance to see the writer's revision. When the tutor examines changes in the revision, the tutor might make assumptions about the motivations behind each change or lack of change. For example, Morton (the writer above) sent our OWL two revisions of his Reich paper, but each version was very similar to the previous one despite requests by three different tutors for more drastic improvements in content, logic, and development. Specifically, the tutors felt that the introduction contained too many quotes, some examples were inappropriate, and his final argument only weakly supported his thesis. The tutors determined that Morton ignored their suggestions for major revisions in favor of the easier sentence-level corrections.

An interview with Morton revealed that he was a very independent writer, looking for feedback more than actual help in writing his paper. He was very concerned with clarity but was confident about what he had to say. According to Morton, one of the OWL's best assets is the opportunity to have more than one person critique the same paper. He anticipated that each tutor would have a different style and would offer different ideas — exactly what he wanted. He ignored the tutors' critiques of his introduction, however, because in class discussions his instructor praised students who used quotes. He did attempt to find better examples for his arguments but said he did not have the time or research skills to find stronger support. As for his concluding argument, Morton felt that he made sufficient changes to clarify that section of his paper. These three OWL conferences combined with his own optimistic opinion of his writing convinced Morton that he would earn an A. His instructor gave him a B–.

Morton was upset and angry. He reported that none of the criticisms his instructor made about the paper coincided with the tutors' comments. She loved his introduction, he said, but she did not feel that his arguments related to his thesis. Overall, Morton did not agree with the teacher's comments or what she felt to be good writing.

From the tutors' points of view, had Morton more carefully considered their comments he might have done better on the paper. Indeed, the fact that the teacher felt the arguments were not related to the thesis indicated to our tutors that they were on to something when they questioned the appropriateness of his reasoning and examples. Moreover, as revealed in the interview, Morton appeared to have been poised from the beginning not to make wholesale changes. His confidence "about what he had to say" may have inured him against really listening (in this case reading) closely what the tutors were telling him. But this is not unique to an online tutorial. Plenty of suggestions are not heard in face-to-face tutoring and plenty of connections are nodded to but not really made. The refusal of a suggestion is perhaps the most significant form of empowerment that a student can make. It might also be argued that online tutoring makes such empowerment even more likely to occur, accompanied as it is by an absence of social pressure.

The most salient aspect of success, if we can draw one from the conference with Morton, has to do with his wanting feedback. He wanted to share in some kind of conversation. Although he claimed that the conferences were too specific to affect his future writing and that to him, the tutors' comments were out of sync with what his teacher wanted, it is not at all clear what will actually unfold as he writes more. He asked for feedback and he got it. Like many students, Morton possessed at this moment a very pragmatic goal — to get a good grade, and that is why he went to our peer tutors. Nonetheless, each tutor had a different (and not-so-different) take on his paper, and he wanted to experience all of them, regardless of whether he chose to internalize or employ this particular advice. Each of us knows from our own experience that human beings sometimes suppress advice and remember it later in life. This, too, is a significant feature of learning; we learn when we are ready to learn, not before.

More significant than a revision to any one paper is to observe whether or not students continue to submit papers for feedback. (Despite Morton's initial disappointment with his grade, he still sends his paper to our OWL.) Even if our clients do not respond to every suggestion we deem important, they retain their independence as writers to pick and choose how they would like to revise. When clients leave conferences confident enough to take advantage of that independence, when they use the service repeatedly, whether for informal feedback or because they are committed to using the advice they are given, the OWL can maintain and even expand the valuable principles of collaborative teaching and learning.

Further Reading

Coogan, David, ed. 1999. *Electronic Writing Centers.* Stamford, CT: Ablex.

One of the most recent titles on this topic, this book takes the long view of electronic tutoring and what it means for the future of learning to write. The first chapter, Tutors and Computers in Composition Studies, invites us "to look beyond the roles that writing centers have lovingly constructed for the tutor and the writer" so that today's writing centers will continue to be a force in literacy learning in the future.

Dayton, David. 1998. "Technical Editing Online: The Quest for Transparent Technology." *Journal of Technical Writing and Communication* 28 (1): 4–37.

This article will be of interest to online tutors who work with technical papers. The author reviews discussions of online editing in the field of technical communication; he tries to explain how online editing has been shaped within the field and why many technical editors remain loyal to the traditional paper-based procedures. Explaining advantages and disadvantages of various software used in online editing, the author reports that online procedures fundamentally change traditional editing. He argues that their use and development is inevitable and ought to be approached both critically and with an open mind.

Harris, Muriel, and Michael Pemberton. 1995. "Online Writing Labs (OWLs): A Taxonomy of Options and Issues." *Computers and Composition* 12 (2): 145–59.

Though now five years old, this article still provides a good overview for understanding some of the most frequently used network technologies available for OWLs. The authors also consider the context for choosing among such a wide range of technologies. They argue that successful OWLs manage to navigate institutional and technological constraints while providing services and upholding sound pedagogical goals.

Hobson, Eric, ed. 1998. *Wiring the Writing Center.* Logan, Utah: Utah State University Press.

A helpful and informative collection of essays that shows the ingenuity and commitment of writing center colleagues as they implement technology in writing classes. Although advocating the use of online technologies in writing centers, the collection also addresses broad and daunting issues of the costs of going online, both economic and pedagogical.

Notes

[1] Andrea Lunsford, "Collaboration, Control, and the Idea of a Writing Center," *The Writing Center Journal* 12(1) (1991): 8.

[2] Barbara Monroe, "The Look and Feel of the OWL Conference," in *Wiring the Writing Center,* ed. Eric Hobson (Logan, UT: Utah State University Press, 1998), 23.

[3] Muriel Harris, *Teaching One-to-One: The Writing Conference* (Urbana, IL: National Council of Teachers of English, 1986), 41.

[4] Harris, 41–43.

[5] Donald Murray, "Teaching the Other Self: The Writer's First Reader," *College Composition and Communication* 33 (1982): 140.

[6] Kenneth Bruffee, "Collaborative Learning and the 'Conversation of Mankind,'" *College English* 46 (1978): 639.

[7] Emily Meyer and Louise Smith, *The Practical Tutor* (Oxford: Oxford University Press, 1987), 31–32.

[8] Irene Lurkis Clark, "Collaboration and Ethics in Writing Center Pedagogy" in *The St. Martin's Sourcebook for Writing Tutors,* eds. Christina Murphy and Steve Sherwood (New York: St. Martin's Press, 1995), 88.

[9] Clark, 92.

[10] The Online Writing Center at Indiana University of Pennsylvania is an example of an OWL that uses attachment technology to insert hot links into the student's online paper.

[11] Meyer and Smith, 14.

[12] Harris, 43.

Works Cited

Brooks, J. 1995. "Minimalist Marking." In *The St. Martin's Sourcebook for Writing Tutors,* eds. C. Murphy and S. Sherwood, 83–87. New York: St. Martin's Press.

Bruffee, K. 1984. "Collaborative Learning and the 'Conversation of Mankind.' " *College English* 46 (7): 635–52.

Clark, I. L. 1995. "Collaboration and Ethics in Writing Center Pedagogy." *The St. Martin's Sourcebook for Writing Tutors,* eds. C. Murphy and S. Sherwood, 88–95. New York: St. Martin's Press.

Harris, M. 1986. *Teaching One-to-One: The Writing Conference.* Urbana, IL: National Council of Teachers of English.

Lunsford, A. 1991. "Collaboration, Control, and the Idea of a Writing Center." *The Writing Center Journal* 12 (1): 3–10.

Meyer, E., and L. Smith. 1987. *The Practical Tutor.* Oxford: Oxford University Press.

Monroe, B. 1998. "The Look and Feel of the OWL Conference." In *Wiring the Writing Center,* ed. E. Hobson, 3–24. Logan, UT: Utah State University Press.

Murphy, C., and S. Sherwood. 1995. "The Tutoring Process: Exploring Paradigms and Practices." In *The St. Martin's Sourcebook for Writing Tutors,* eds. C. Murphy and S. Sherwood, 1–17. New York: St. Martin's Press.

Murray, D. 1982. "Teaching the Other Self: The Writer's First Reader." *College Composition and Communication* 33: 140–47.

III

Resources for Further Inquiry

The burgeoning interest in writing centers over the past several decades has created a wealth of informative resources for tutors. In addition to scholarly journals and books, tutors can find support for their work in professional organizations, electronic networks like WCenter, and Web sites dedicated to providing online resources for tutors.

Because writing center work has always respected the value of individual narratives and case studies, scholarship in the field often includes examples drawn from tutors' actual practice. This approach helps make writing center scholarship accessible to novice tutors, who will appreciate the conversational style of the journals, books, and electronic networks. They will also find much to identify with in the case studies and narrative examples these resources often explore.

INTERNATIONAL WRITING CENTERS ASSOCIATION (IWCA)

The primary professional organization for writing center personnel is the International Writing Centers Association (IWCA). The IWCA promotes writing center causes and provides educational materials and support services related to writing center practice. The organization sponsors the IWCA Press, which publishes books on writing center theory and practice, including its manual, the *International Writing Centers Association Handbook*.

Among its many services, the IWCA publishes a national directory of high school, community college, and college and university writing centers; sponsors a national conference; lends support to its regional organizations and conferences; gives awards for outstanding scholarship on writing centers; offers information and assistance through its committees and subcommittees on a range of writing center issues; and provides a free "starter kit" for setting up a writing center. Information on IWCA and its regional affiliates is available on the IWCA homepage at <http://writingcenters.org/about.htm>, which also provides online a useful selected writing center bibliography and the WCenter archives.

ONLINE RESOURCES

Many writing centers provide online information about tutoring and related writing concerns. One of the most comprehensive resources is the Online Writing Lab (OWL) at Purdue University. This OWL provides downloadable files on ESL instruction, grammar, spelling, punctuation, general writing concerns, documenting sources, professional writing, writing across the curriculum, PowerPoint presentations, hypertext, and use of Internet search engines.

A comprehensive guide to hundreds of writing centers online is available at the International Writing Centers Association (IWCA) homepage at <http://writingcenters.org/about.htm>.

ELECTRONIC NETWORK

WCenter is the leading electronic network for online discussions of writing center work, but new discussion venues include two blogs — PeerCentered and Friends of the Writing Center Journal — and an IWCA discussion forum.

WCenter lets writing center personnel share information, seek answers to inquiries, pose questions for further investigation, and establish a sense of community. WCenter provides an important way for writing center personnel to share the immediacy of the work and concerns. It serves as one confirming example of Jeanne Simpson's view that "the writing center movement has expanded because writing center people have learned to communicate, to form a network, to transmit information, and to exchange assistance" ("What Lies Ahead for Writing Centers: Position Statement on Professional Concerns," *The Writing Center Journal* 5.2 and 6.1 [1985]: 35–39). Subscribe to WCenter by contacting Kathleen Gillis at <kathleen.gillis@ttu.edu>.

PeerCentered is a site that encourages peer writing consultants and others to chronicle their experiences in writing centers and at writing center conferences. Bloggers and readers can find the site at <http://bessie.englab.slcc.edu/pc/>.

Friends of the Writing Center Journal, sponsored by the IWCA, allows readers and authors published in *The Writing Center Journal* to discuss issues raised by the journal's articles. The blog resides at the following web address: <http://writingcenterjournal.blogspot.com>.

The IWCA discussion forum offers another way for writing center peers and professionals to express opinions and discuss issues. The forum is accessible through the IWCA Web site or at the following address: <http://www.writingcenters.org/board>.

JOURNALS

Writing center work has two major print journals devoted exclusively to its concerns: The *Writing Lab Newsletter*, edited by Muriel Harris and Charlotte Hartlep of Purdue University, and *The Writing Center Journal*, edited by Neal Lerner of the Massachusetts Institute of Technology and Beth Boquet of Fairfield

University. Both journals are sponsored by the International Writing Centers Association (IWCA).

The *Writing Lab Newsletter* provides news on conferences and meetings as well as columns, letters, and scholarly articles on writing center practice. It regularly publishes a column on peer tutoring as well as articles by peer tutors. The newsletter is respected for its accessible style and its capacity to convey the voices of writing center personnel at work. In contrast, *The Writing Center Journal* publishes more theoretical and scholarly articles. Both journals have searchable online archives, offering full-text articles. The *Writing Lab Newsletter*'s archives reside at Purdue's Online Writing Lab homepage at <http://owl.english.purdue.edu/>. Readers can access *The Writing Center Journal*'s archives at <http://www.louisville.edu/a-s/writingcenter/wcenters/wcj.html>.

Two online journals — *Praxis: A Writing Center Journal* and *The Dangling Modifier* — also devote their issues to a discussion of writing center concerns. Sponsored by the University of Texas's Undergraduate Writing Center, *Praxis* publishes articles on a variety of topics related to consulting in or administering a writing center. *The Dangling Modifier*, a publication produced by Pennsylvania State University Writing Center in conjunction with the National Conference on Peer Tutoring in Writing, publishes brief articles on topics related to peer tutoring. Readers can find *Praxis* on the Web at <http://projects.uwc.utexas.edu/praxis/?q=> and *The Dangling Modifier* at <http://www.ulc.psu.edu/Dangling_Modifier/index.php>.

Two other journals that often include articles on writing centers and tutoring are *Composition Studies* and *Dialogue: A Journal for Writing Specialists*. In addition, the *IWCA Update*, a twice-yearly newsletter published by the International Writing Centers Association, often publishes short articles, fiction, news items, or reviews related to writing center issues.

College English, College Composition and Communication, Composition Studies, JAC: A Journal of Composition Theory, English Journal, Research in the Teaching of English, Journal of Basic Writing, and *Teaching English in the Two-Year College* have all published occasional articles on writing centers and related topics.

BOOKS

Books on writing centers, like the scholarly articles, tend to focus to varying degrees on practice, administration, or theory. The following books can serve as resources for discussions of rationales, strategies, theories, and techniques of tutoring:

Barnett, Robert W., and Jacob S. Blumner, eds. *The Allyn and Bacon Guide to Writing Center Theory and Practice.* Boston: Allyn and Bacon, 2001.

Boquet, Elizabeth H. *Noise from the Writing Center.* Logan: Utah State UP, 2002.

Briggs, Lynn Craigue, and Meg Woolbright. *Stories from the Center: Connecting Narrative and Theory in the Writing Center.* Urbana: NCTE, 2000.

Bruce, Shanti, and Ben Rafoth, eds. *ESL Writers: A Guide for Writing Center Tutors.* Portsmouth: Boynton/Cook, 2004.

Capossela, Toni-Lee. *The Harcourt Brace Guide to Peer Tutoring.* New York: Harcourt, 1998.

Childers, Pamela B. *The High School Writing Center: Establishing and Maintaining One.* Urbana: NCTE, 1989.

Childers, Pamela B., Anne Ruggles Gere, and Art Young. *Programs and Practices: Writing Across the Secondary School Curriculum.* Portsmouth: Boynton/Cook, 1994.

Clark, Irene Lurkis. *Writing in the Center: Teaching in a Writing Center.* Dubuque: Kendall/Hunt, 1985.

Coogan, David. *Electronic Writing Centers: Computing in the Field of Composition.* Westport: Greenwood, 1999.

Elmborg, James K., and Sheril Hook. *Centers for Learning: Writing Centers and Libraries in Collaboration.* Chicago: Association of College and Research Libraries, 2005.

Flynn, Thomas, and Mary King, eds. *Dynamics of the Writing Conference: Social and Cognitive Interaction.* Urbana: NCTE, 1993.

Gillespie, Paula, Alice Gillam, Lady Falls Brown, and Byron L. Stay, eds. *Writing Center Research: Extending the Conversation.* Mahwah: Erlbaum, 2002.

Gillespie, Paula, and Neal Lerner. *The Allyn and Bacon Guide to Peer Tutoring.* Boston: Allyn and Bacon, 2000.

Grimm, Nancy Maloney. *Good Intentions: Writing Center Work for Postmodern Times.* Portsmouth: Boynton/Cook, 1999.

Harris, Muriel. *Teaching One-to-One: The Writing Conference.* Urbana: NCTE, 1986.

——. *Tutoring Writing: A Sourcebook for Writing Labs.* Glenview: Scott, Foresman, 1982.

Hewett, Beth L., and Christa Ehmann. *Preparing Educators for Online Writing Instruction: Principles and Processes.* Urbana: NCTE, 2004.

Hobson, Eric H., ed. *Wiring the Writing Center.* Logan: Utah State UP, 1998.

Inman, James A., and Donna M. Sewell, eds. *Taking Flight with OWLS: Examining Electronic Writing Center Work.* Mahwah: Erlbaum, 2000.

Kinkead, Joyce A., and Jeanette G. Harris, eds. *Writing Centers in Context: Twelve Case Studies.* Urbana: NCTE, 1993.

Maxwell, Martha, ed. *When Tutor Meets Student.* Ann Arbor: U of Michigan P, 1994.

McAndrew, Donald A., and Thomas J. Reigstad. *Tutoring Writing: A Practical Guide for Conferences.* Portsmouth: Boynton/Cook, 2001.

Meyer, Emily, and Louise Z. Smith. *The Practical Tutor.* New York: Oxford UP, 1987.

Mullin, Joan, and Ray Wallace, eds. *Intersections: Theory-Practice in the Writing Center.* Urbana: NCTE, 1994.

Murphy, Christina, and Joe Law, eds. *Landmark Essays on Writing Centers.* Mahwah: Erlbaum, 1995.

Murphy, Christina, Joe Law, and Steve Sherwood, eds. *Writing Centers: An Annotated Bibliography.* Westport: Greenwood, 1996.

Murphy, Christina, and Byron L. Stay, eds. *The Writing Center Director's Resource Book.* Mahwah: Erlbaum, 2006.

Nelson, Jane, and Kathy Evertz, eds. *The Politics of Writing Centers.* Portsmouth: Boynton/Cook, 2002.

Olson, Gary A., ed. *Writing Centers: Theory and Administration.* Urbana: NCTE, 1984.

Pemberton, Michael A., and Joyce Kinkead, eds. *The Center Will Hold: Critical Perspectives on Writing Center Scholarship.* Logan: Utah State UP, 2003.

Rabow, Jerome, Tiffani Chin, and Nima Fahimian. *Tutoring Matters: Everything You Always Wanted to Know about How to Tutor.* Philadelphia: Temple UP, 1999.

Rafoth, Ben, ed. *A Tutor's Guide: Helping Writers One to One*. New York: Heinemann, 2000.

Reigstad, Thomas J., and Donald McAndrew. *Training Tutors for Writing Center Conferences*. Urbana: NCTE, 1984.

Ryan, Leigh. *The Bedford Guide for Writing Tutors*. Boston: Bedford, 1994.

Silk, Bobbie Bayless, ed. *The Writing Center Resource Manual*. Emmitsburg: NWCA Press, 1998.

Spigelman, Candace, and Laurie Grobman. *On Location: Theory and Practice in Classroom-Based Writing Tutoring*. Logan: Utah State University Press, 2005.

Stay, Byron L., Christina Murphy, and Eric H. Hobson, eds. *Writing Center Perspectives*. Emmitsburg: NWCA, 1995.

Steward, Joyce, and Mary Croft. *The Writing Laboratory: Organization, Methods, and Management*. Glenview: Scott, Foresman, 1982.

Wallace, Ray, and Jeanne Simpson, eds. The *Writing Center: New Directions*. New York: Garland, 1991.

Weiner, Harvey S., and Rose Palmer. *The Writing Lab: An Individualized Program in Writing Skills*. Beverly Hills: Glencoe, 1974.

GRAMMAR HOTLINE DIRECTORY

A *Grammar Hotline Directory* is published annually by Tidewater Community College. The directory lists e-mail, Web site, and telephone services in the United States and Canada that provide free answers to short questions about writing and grammar. To view the complete listings online or download the Directory as a PDF document, visit the *Grammar Hotline Directory* Web site at <http://www.tcc.edu/students/resources/writcent/GH/hotlinol.htm>. Or for more information, write to *Grammar Hotline Directory,* Tidewater Community College Writing Center, 1700 College Crescent, Virginia Beach, VA 23453 or phone (757) 822–7183, fax (757) 427–0327, or send e-mail to writcent@ tcc.edu.

Acknowledgments (continued)

George Cooper, Kara Bui, and Linda Riker. "Protocols and Process in Online Tutoring." *A Tutor's Guide to Helping One on One* by Bennett A. Rafoth, editor. Copyright © 2000 by Boynton/Cook Publishers, Inc., a subsidiary of Reed Elsevier, Inc., Portsmouth, NH. Reprinted with permission of the publisher.

Marilyn Cooper. "Really Useful Knowledge: A Cultural Studies Agenda for Writing Centers." *Writing Center Journal,* Volume 14, Number 2, Spring 1994. Copyright © 1994. Reprinted with permission.

Anne DiPardo. "Whispers of Coming and Going: Lessons from Fannie." *Writing Center Journal,* Volume 12, Number 2, Spring 1992. Copyright © 1992. Reprinted with permission.

Stacey Freed. "Subjectivity in the Tutorial Session: How Far Can We Go?" *Writing Center Journal,* Volume 10, Number 1, 1989. Copyright © 1989. Reprinted with permission.

Toby Fulwiler. "Provocative Revision." *Writing Center Journal,* Volume 12, Number 2, 1992. Copyright © 1992. Reprinted with permission.

Cynthia Haynes-Burton. "Thirty-something Students: Concerning Transitions in the Writing Center." *Writing Lab Newsletter,* Volume 18, Number 8, 1994. Copyright © 2003 Purdue University. All rights and Title reserved unless permission is granted by Purdue University. Material will not be reproduced in any form without express written permission.

Jay Jacoby. "The Use of Force: Medical Ethics and Center Practice." *Intersections-Theory-Practice in the Writing Center* edited by Joan A. Mullin and Ray Wallace. Copyright © 1994 by the National Council of Teachers of English. Reprinted with permission.

Andrea Lunsford. "Collaboration, Control, and the Idea of a Writing Center." *Writing Center Journal,* 1991. Copyright © 1991 by the National Council of Teachers of English. Reprinted with permission.

Joan Mullin, Neil Reid, Doug Enders, and Jason Baldridge. "Constructing Each Other: Collaborating Across Disciplines and Roles." From *Weaving Knowledge Together: Writing Centers and Collaboration,* edited by Carol Peterson Haviland, Maria Notarangelo, Lene Whitley-Putz and Thia Wolf. Copyright © 1998 International Writing. Reprinted with permission.

Sharon A. Myers. "Reassessing the "Proofreading Trap": ESL Tutoring and Writing Instruction." *Writing Center Journal,* Volume 24, Issue 1, Fall/Winter 2003. Reprinted with permission.

Julie Neff. "Learning Disabilities and the Writing Center." *Intersections: Theory-Practice in the Writing Center* edited by Joan A. Mullin and Ray Wallace. Copyright © 1994 by the National Council of Teachers of English. Reprinted with permission.

Beatrice Mendez Newman. "Centering in the Borderlands: Lessons from Hispanic Student Writers." *The Writing Center Journal,* Volume 23, Issue 2, Spring/Summer 2003. Reprinted with permission.

Stephen M. North. "The Idea of a Writing Center." *College English,* September 1984. Copyright © 1984 by the National Council of Teachers of English. Reprinted with permission.

Michael A. Pemberton. "Planning for Hypertexts in the Writing Center . . . Or Not."

Steve Sherwood. "Censoring Students, Censoring Ourselves: Constraining Conversations in the Writing Center." *Writing Center Journal,* Volume 20, Number 1, 1999. Copyright © 2001. Reprinted with permission.

Margaret Weaver. "Transcending 'Conversing': A Deaf Student in the Writing Center." *JAC: A Journal of Composition Theory,* Volume 16, Number 2, 1996. Reprinted with permission of the author.

Meg Woolbright. "The Politics of Tutoring: Feminism within the Patriarchy." *Writing Center Journal,* Volume 13, Number 1, Spring/Summer 1992. Copyright © 1992. Reprinted with permission.

ABOUT THE AUTHORS

Christina Murphy is Dean of the College of Liberal Arts and Professor of English at Marshall University in Huntington, West Virginia. She has served as the President of the National Writing Centers Association, the South Central Writing Centers Association, and the Texas Writing Centers Association. Her co-edited books on writing centers include *Landmark Essays on Writing Centers* (1995), *Writing Center Perspectives* (1995), *Writing Centers: An Annotated Bibliography* (1996), *The Theory and Criticism of Virtual Texts: An Annotated Bibliography* (2001), and *The Writing Center Director's Resource Book* (2006). She has also published chapters in *The Writing Center: New Directions* (1991), *Intersections: Theory-Practice in the Writing Center* (1994), *Writing the Wrongs: Reforming College Composition* (2000), *Writing Centers and Writing Across the Curriculum Programs: Building Interdisciplinary Partnerships* (2000), *The Politics of Writing Centers* (2001), *Assessment Strategies for the Online Teacher: From Theory to Practice* (2001), *Internationalizing Higher Education* (2001), *Identifying and Preparing Academic Leaders* (2004), *Teaching, Research, and Service in the Twenty-First Century English Department: A Delicate Balance* (2004), *Service Learning: History, Theory, and Issues* (2004), and *Spirituality in Higher Education* (2005). Her short stories have appeared in the *Greensboro Review,* the *Crescent Review, Modern Short Stories, Descant,* and *The Phoenix: A Literary Review.* Her short story "Blue Car" received Honorable Mention for a Pushcart Prize, and she has been a finalist for The Editor's Choice Award and the Jack Dwyer Fiction Prize.

Steve Sherwood is the Director of the William L. Adams Center for Writing at Texas Christian University. Currently an at-large representative to the International Writing Centers Association Executive Board, he is a past president of the South Central Writing Centers Association. His essays have appeared in *The Writing Center Journal, Journal of Teaching Writing, Dialogue, Writing Lab Newsletter, Writing Center Perspectives, Wiring the Writing Center, The Writing Center Resource Manual, English in Texas, Weber Studies, Rendezvous,* and other journals. With Christina Murphy and Joe Law, he compiled *Writing Centers: An Annotated Bibliography* (Greenwood Press, 1996), for which Murphy, Law, and Sherwood received a 1997 National Writing Centers Association distinguished scholarship award. In 2003, Sherwood's novel *Hardwater* won the George Garrett Fiction Prize, sponsored by the Texas Review Press, which published the novel in 2005.

327